Goldoni and the Venice of His Time

CARLO GOLDONI

Portrait by G. B. Piazzetta in the Correr Museum, Venice

JOSEPH SPENCER KENNARD

GOLDONI AND THE VENICE OF HIS TIME

Benjamin Blom
New York

First published 1920 by
The Macmillan Company
Reissued 1967 by
Benjamin Blom, Inc. New York 10452
Library of Congress Cat. Card No. 67-23852

PRINTED IN THE U.S.A.

CONTENTS

LIST OF ILLUSTRATIONS

CHRONOLOGICAL SUMMARY OF CARLO GOLDONI'S LIFE

Carlo Alessio Goldoni, his grandfather, dies in Venice, 1703.
Goldoni born in Venice, February 25, 1707.
Enters Jesuit college at Perugia, 1719.
Studies philosophy in Rimini, under Candini, 1720.
Runs away from Rimini with company of actors, 1721.
Lives with his family in Chioggia, and accompanies his father on his medical visits, 1721 and 1722.
Studies law with his uncle Indric, in Venice, 1722.
Admitted to the Ghislieri College in Pavia, 1723.
Expelled from college for a libellous writing, 1725.
Studies law in Modena, 1726.
Appointed clerk in the criminal chancellery of Chioggia, 1727.
Appointed to a similar position at Feltre, 1729.
Leaves Feltre (1730), and is with his father when he dies at Bagnacavallo, 1731.
Receives degree of Doctor of Law at Padua, 1732.
Mother leaves Venice for Modena, 1732.
Admitted to the Venetian bar, 1732.
Burns his tragedy *Amalasunta* at Milan, after it is refused, 1733.
Appointed secretary to the Venetian minister at Milan, 1733.
Goes with the Venetian minister to Crema when the French and Sardinians attack Milan, 1733.
Dismissed from his diplomatic position, and leaves Crema, 1734.
Imer engages him to write plays for the San Samuele Theatre at Venice, 1734.
Has love affair with an actress, who deceives him, 1735.
Goes to Genoa, and meets and marries Nicoletta Connio, with whom he returns to Venice, 1736.
Appointed Genoese consul in Venice, 1740.
From which position he resigns in 1744.
Practises law in Pisa, 1744.
Writes a play for the Medebach players who are visiting Leghorn, 1745.
Agrees to write plays for Medebach, of Sant' Angelo Theatre, Venice, 1747.
Returns to Venice, 1748.
At close of his second season at Sant' Angelo Theatre he announces that the next year he will present sixteen plays, 1750.
Contract with Medebach expires, 1753.
Signs contract with Vendramin brothers, proprietors of San Luca Theatre, Venice, 1753.
His mother dies, 1754.
Signs a second contract with Francesco Vendramin, whose brother Antonio has died, 1756.

Visits Parma and is appointed court poet with an annual pension of 3000 Parmesan lire, 1756.
Invited to write plays for the Tordinona Theatre at Rome, 1758.
Leaves Rome and, after three months in Bologna, returns to Venice, 1759.
Correspondence with the Italian Theatre in Paris, 1759.
Offered a two years' engagement at the Italian Theatre in Paris, and accepts same, 1761.
Signs a final contract with Vendramin, 1762.
With the play *Una delle ultime sere di Carnevale* says farewell to Venice and leaves for Paris, 1762.
Il Figlio d'Arlecchino perduto e ritrovato is a failure when performed at Fontainebleau, 1762.
Appointed to teach Italian to Madame Adelaide, and is given an apartment at the palace at Versailles, 1765.
Receives from the French court an annual pension of 4000 livres, 1769.
His play *Le Bourru Bienfaisant* performed at Paris is a great success, 1771.
Teaches Italian to the sister of the king, who is engaged to marry the Prince of Piedmont, 1775.
Visits Voltaire in Paris, 1778.
Settles in Paris, the Italian Theatre there is closed, 1780.
Plans a magazine, writes plays, and tries various ways of making a living, but is troubled with partial blindness and poor health, 1781–1792.
Dies in Paris at age of eighty-six, February 6, 1793.

BIBLIOGRAPHY

A Goldoni bibliography of one thousand titles would still be incomplete. In Italian alone there have been printed more than thirty editions of Goldoni's plays, besides a much larger number of "Collections" and reprints of single plays, and the number is constantly increasing. Numerous collections of his letters, and also single letters, have been printed. Very many of his plays have been translated into English and other languages. Goldoni's *Memoirs* have been translated from French into English by John Black, 2 vols., and published in London, 1814. The same, abridged, with an essay by W. D. Howells, was published in Boston, 1877. In the notes at the foot of pages 386 and 441 of the text will be found reference to more extensive bibliographies, lists of his works and correspondence, and of translations of the same.

The three following collections of Goldoni's letters include his most important correspondence:

Ciampi, Ignazio. *Lettere di Carlo Goldoni al Marchese Albergati, specialmente da Parigi.* In Il Pirata. Turin, 1862–63–64.

Spinelli, A. & A. *Lettere di Carlo Goldoni e di Girolamo Medebach al Conte Giuseppe Arconati-Visconti.* Milan, 1882.

Urbani De Gheltof, G. M. *Lettere di Carlo Goldoni*, etc. Venice, 1880.

From the many editions of Goldoni's plays the following are selected as most useful to students:

1750. Giuseppe Bettinelli. Venice.

1753–55. Paperini Successors. 10 vols. Authors' edition. Florence.

1788–95. Antonia Zatta e figli. 44 vols. Authorised edition. Venice.

1827. Complete Collection. 50 vols. (30 for the plays, 3 for the *Memoirs*, and 17 for the librettos). Prato.

1907 *et seq.* Complete collection of the works of Goldoni, brought out under the supervision of the municipality of Venice, in commemoration of the second centennial of his birth. In this the Pasquali edition has been faithfully reprinted with all the original engravings, frontispieces, etc., and this is without question the preferable edition for consultation by students of Goldoni's plays.

All books referred to in the present volume, as well as a few others which should be consulted by any serious student of Goldoni, are included in the following:

Ademollo, A. *Intorno al teatro drammatico italiano dal 1550 in poi.* Nuova Antologia, 1881. *Il Carnevale di Roma nei secoli XVII e XVIII.* Rome, 1883. *Una Famiglia di comici italiani nel secolo decimotavo.* Florence, 1885.

Algarotti, F. *Lettere inedite, Opere.* Vols. XVII and XVIII. Venice, 1794.

Ancona, A. d'. *Origini del teatro italiano.* 2 vols. Turin, 1891. *Manuale della letteratura italiana.* (With Orazio Bacci.) 6 vols. Florence, 1904–1908. *Una Macchietta Goldoniana.* In *Carlo Goldoni.* Venice, 1883.
Baccini, Giuseppe. *G. B. Fagiuoli, poeta faceto fiorentino.* Firenze, 1886.
Bartoli, Francesco. *Scenari inediti della commedia dell'arte.* Firenze, Sansoni, 1880. *Notizie istoriche de' comici italiani che fiorirono intorno all'anno MDL fino a'giorni presenti.* 2 vols. Padua, 1782.
Baschet, Armand. *Les Commédiens italiens à la cour de France sous Charles IX, Henri III, Henri IV et Louis XIII.* Paris, 1882.
Belgrano, L. T. *Il Matrimonio* and *Il Consolato di C. G.* In his *Imbreviature di Giovanni Scriba.* Genoa, 1882.
Black, John. Translation from the French of Goldoni's *Memoirs.* 2 vols. London, 1814. Same, abridged, with essay by W. D. Howells. Boston, 1877.
Borghi, Carlo. *Memorie sulla vita di Carlo Goldoni.* Modena, 1859.
Brocchi, Virgilio. *Carlo Goldoni a Venezia nel secolo XVIII.* Bologna, 1907.
Brognoligo, G. *Nel Teatro di C. G.; Il Cavaliere e la Dama; Le Femmine puntigliose; La guerra.* Naples, 1907.
Brosses, Le Président des. *Lettres familières écrites d'Italie en 1739 et 1740.* 2 vols. Fourth edition. Paris, 1885.
Campardon, E. *Les Comédiens du Roi de la Troupe Italienne pendant les deux derniers siècles.* 2 vols. Paris, 1880.
Caprin, Giulio. *La Commedia dell'arte al principio del secolo XVIII.* Rivista teatrala italiana. Naples, 1905. *C. G., la sua vita, le sue opere. Con introduzione di Guido Mazzoni.* Milan, 1907.
Carducci. *I Corifei della Canzonetta nel secolo XVI.* Vol. XVIII in Antologia di Critica Letterari Moderna.
Carrer, Luigi. *Saggi su la vita e su le opere di C. G.* 3 vols. Venice, 1824.
Casanova de Seingalt, J. *Mémoires écrites par lui-même.* Nouvelle édition collationnée sur l'édition originale de Leipsick. 8 vols. Paris, no date.
Castelnuovo, A. *Una Dama Veneziano del secolo XVIII.* Nuovo Antologia, Jan., 1882.
Chatfield-Taylor, H. C. *Goldoni.* New York, 1913.
Cian, V. *Due aneddoti, due età nella storia e nella vitc di Pisa.* Miscellanea di erudizione. Vol. I. Pisa, 1905. *L'Italianità di C. G. L'Esule sommo.* Numero unico de *Dante Alighieri.* Comitato di Senigallia, 1907.
Diderot, D. *De la poésie dramatique (1758).* Garnier. Paris, 1875.
Grimm, Le Baron de. *Correspondance littéraire,* etc. (*1753–1790*). 16 vols. Paris.
Guilbert, P. J. *Notice . . . sur Mme. Bocage.* Rouen, 1807.
Lazzari, A. *Il Padre di G.* Rivista d'Italia. Rome, 1907. *C. G. in Romagna.* Ateneo veneto. Venice, 1908.
Lee, Vernon. *Studies of the Eighteenth Century in Italy.* London, 1881. Second edition with new preface, *ibid.*, 1906.
Löhner, E. Von. *C. G. e le sue Memorie.* Frammenti. Archivio veneto. Vols. XXIII and XXIV. Venice, 1882.
Malamani, Vittorio. *Carlo Goldoni.* Nuova Rivista, Nos. 50–3. Turin 1882. *Nuovi appunti e curiosità goldoniane.* Venice, 1887. *Il Settecento a Venezia.* Turin, 1891–92.

Mantovani, Dino. *C. G. e il teatro di San Luca a Venezia, Carteggio inedito (1755–65).* Milano, 1884.
Marchesi, G. B. *I Romanze dell'abate Chiari.* Bergamo, 1900.
Masi, Ernesto. *La Vita e le opere di C. G.* Bologna, 1880. *La Vita, i tempi, gli amici di Francesco Albergati.* Bologna, 1878.
Modena a Carlo Goldoni nel secondo centenario della sua nascita. Publicazione a cura del Municipio e della cassa di risparmio. Modena, 1907.
Molière. Cf. M. A. D. Regnier's collection, *Les Grands Écrivains de la France, "Molière."*
Molmenti, P. G. *C. G. Studio critico-biografico.* Second edition. Venice, 1880. *La Storia di Venezia nella vita privata dalle origini alla caduta della republica.* Fifth edition, profusely illustrated. Vol. I, *La Grandezza;* Vol. II, *Lo Splendore;* Vol. III, *Il Decadimento.* Bergamo, 1910.
Muratori. *Annali d'Italia.* Vol. VII. Venice, 1848.
Musatti, Cesare. *Goldoni in scena.* Venice, 1893. *Spunti di dialetto veneziano nei "Rusteghi" di C. G.* Venice, 1910.
Neri, Achille. *Carlo Goldoni.* Pavia, 1907. *Bibliografa goldoniana.* Giorn. degli eruditi e curiosi. Vol. III. Padua, 1883.
Ortolani, Giuseppe. *Della Vita e dell'arte di C. G.* Venice, 1907.
Parfaict, Frères. *Histoire de l'ancien théâtre italien depuis son origine en France jusqu'à sa supression en l'année 1697. Suivie des extraits ou canevas des meilleurs pièces italiennes qui n'ont jamais été imprimées.* Paris, 1767.
Rabany, Charles. *C. G. Le théâtre et la vie en Italie au XVIIIe siècle.* Paris, 1896.
Rasi, Luigi. *I Comici italiani, Biografia, Bibliografia, Iconografia.* Florence, Vol. I, 1897; Vol. II, 1905.
Raynaud, Maurice. *Les Médicins du temps de Molière.* Paris, 1862.
Regnier, A. D. *Les Grands Écrivains de la France, "Molière."*
Riccoboni, L. *Histoire de l'ancien théâtre italien,* etc. 2 vols. Paris, 1730–31.
Saint-Didier. *L'Italie vue par les Français.* Librairie des Annales. Paris, 1915.
Saint-Evremond. *De la Comédie Italienne.* Paris, 1777.
Saintsbury, George. *Short History of English Literature.* London, 1908.
Sanctis, Francesco di. *Storia della letteratura italiana.*
Scala, Flaminio. *Il Teatro delle favole rappresentative,* etc. Venice, 1611. Collection of 50 scenarios.
Sommi-Picenardi, G. *Un rivale del Goldoni,* etc. Milan, 1902.
Spinelli, A. *Goldoni a Modena.* Ermanno von Löhner edition. A. G. Spinelli. Modena, 1893. *Bibliografia goldoniana,* etc. Milan, 1884.
Stendhal. *La vie de Metastasio.*
Tammaso, Niccolò. *Storia civile della Letteraria.* Turin, 1872.
Tipaldo, G. di. *Biografia degli Italiani illustri.* Venice, 1837.
Toldo, P. *Se il Diderot abbia imitato il Goldoni.* Giorn. stor., etc. Vol. XXVI. 1895.
Vaumorière, de. *Lettres sur toutes sortes de sujets.* Paris, 1714.

[For reference to lists of Goldoni's plays see notes at foot of pages 386 and 441.]

GOLDONI'S PLAYS

In all Goldoni composed nearly three hundred plays, interludes, books for operas, cantatas, and miscellanea; besides many "compliments," mainly in verse, for his patrons.

Many of the plays so catalogued as separate plays are in fact duplicates, being played under one title in Paris and being sent to Vendramin with another title, for performance in Venice. Goldoni's spelling of the titles of his plays in his letters, his memoirs, and the published plays is not uniform, and this variation has at times been followed in this book.

In the present list are included all the plays mentioned by Goldoni in his *Memoirs* as well as such others as it seemed desirable to record. Unless otherwise noted, all these plays are comedies. In some cases the dates are approximate, as Goldoni is himself frequently inaccurate.

Adulatore, L', 1750, three masks.

Amalasunta, tragedy, burned.

Amante de sè stesso, L', *see* L'Egoista.

Amante militare, L', 1751, three masks.

Amanti in locanda, *see* La Locandiera.

Amor paterno, L', 1763 (L'Amore paterno), two masks, for both Paris and Venice.

Amori di Arlecchino e di Camilla, Gli, *see* Amori di Zelinda e Lindoro, Gli.

Amori di Zelinda e Lindoro, Gli, 1764 (Gli amore di Arlecchino e di Camilla, 1763), improvised comedy.

Amore paterno, *see* Amor paterno.

Apatista, L', 1758, verse, five acts.

Avare fastueux, L', 1776, prose in French, performed at Fontainebleau, a failure.

Avaro, L', 1756, one act.
Avaro geloso, L', 1753 (Il geloso avaro), Goldoni's first play at Sant' Angelo Theatre, two masks.
Avventure della villeggiatura, Le, 1761.
Avventuriere onorato, L', 1751.
Avvocato veneziano, L', 1750, one mask.

Banca Rotta, La, 1741 (Il Mercante Fallito; La Bancarotta), four masks.
Baruffe Chiozzote, Le, 1761.
Belisario, 1734, tragedy (Belisarius).
Bella Selvaggia, La, 1758, in verse.
Birba, La, 1735, interlude, three acts.
Bisticci domestici, I, 1752 (I Puntigli domestici), four masks.
Bona mugier, La, *see* La Buona Moglie.
Bottega del caffè, La, *see* Il Caffè.
Bourru bienfaisant, 1771 (Il burbero beneficio), prose in French, performed at Comédie Française, 1771.
Bugiardo, Il, 1750, four masks.
Buona famiglia, La, 1755.
Buona figlia, La, 1754 (?) (Buona figliuola), one of three works composed by order of the Duke of Parma.
Buona Madre, La, 1759.
Buona Moglie, La, 1749 (La Bona mugier), three masks.
Buono e cattivo genio, Il, 1768, performed in Venice but not in Paris.
Burbero beneficio, Il, *see* Bourru bienfaisant.

Caffè, Il, 1750 (La bottega del caffè; Il Maldicente alla bottega del caffè).
Cameriera brillante, La, 1753, three masks.
Campiello, Il, 1756, in free verse.
Casa nuova, La, 1760 (La casa nova).
Cavalier giocondo, Il, society comedy in verse.
Cavaliere di buon gusto, Il, 1750 (L'Uomo di gusto), four masks.

Cavaliere di spirito, 1757 (L'Uomo di spirito), verse, five acts.
Cavaliere e la Dama o i Cicisbei, Il, 1749, three masks.
Cento e quattro accidenti in una notte, *see* La Notte critica.
Contrattempo, Il, *see* L'Imprudente.
Convitato nuovo, Il, 1736 (Don Giovanni tenorio), blank verse, five acts.
Cortesan vecchio, Il, 1754, *see* Il Vecchio bizzarro.
Cortesan venezian, Il, subtitle of L'Uomo di mondo.
Curioso accidente, Un, 1757 (?).

Dalmatina, La, 1758, tragi-comedy, in verse, five acts.
Dama prudente, La, *see* La Moglie prudente.
Dama sola, La, 1757 (La Donna sola), verse, five acts.
Don Giovanni tenorio, *see* Il Convitato nuovo.
Donna bizzarra, La, *see* La Moglie capricciosa.
Donna di garbo, La, 1743, two masks.
Donna di governo, La, 1758, five acts.
Donna di maneggio, La, 1757.
Donna di spirito, La, 1757.
Donna di testa debole, La (L'Uomo sincero), two masks.
Donna forte, La, 1759 (La Sposa fidele), verse, five acts.
Donna prudente, La, *see* La Moglie prudente.
Donna sola, La, *see* La Dama sola.
Donna stravagante, La, 1756, verse.
Donna vendicativa, La, 1753, one mask.
Donna volubile, La, 1751, three masks.
Donne curiose, Le, 1753 (the last of his contract with Medebach), three masks.
Donne di casa soa, Le, 1755, five acts.
Donne gelose, Le, 1752, one mask.
Donne puntigliose, Le, 1750 (Le Femmine puntigliose; I Puntigli delle donne), three masks.
Due gemelli veneziani, I, 1748, three masks.
Due pantaloni, I, *see* Mercanti.

Egoista, L', 1756 (L'Amante de sè stesso), comedy in verse, five acts.

Enrico re di Sicilia, 1737 (Henry III of Sicily), tragedy.

Erede fortunata, L', 1750, one mask.

Famiglia dell'antiquario, La, 1750 (La Suocera e la Nuora), four masks.

Femmine puntigliose, Le, *see* Le Donne puntigliose.

Festino, Il, 1754, verse, five acts, one of three works composed by order of the Duke of Parma.

Feudatorio, Il, 1752.

Figlia obbediente, La, 1752, three masks.

Figlio d'Arlecchino, perduto e ritrovato, Il, 1746 (?), improvised comedy.

Filosofo inglese, Il, 1754, verse, five acts.

Finta malata, La, 1751 (Finta ammalata, Lo Speciale o sia la Finta ammalata), one mask.

Frappatore, Il, *see* Tonino bella-grazia.

Gelosia di'Arlecchino, La, *see* La gelosia di Lindoro.

Gelosia di Lindoro, La, 1764 (La Gelosia di'Arlecchino, Paris, 1763), improvised comedy.

Geloso avaro, Il, *see* L'Avaro geloso.

Genio buono e il genio cattivo, Il, 1768, two masks, five acts.

Giuocatore, Il, 1750, three masks.

Gondoliere veneziano, Il, 1733, Milan, musical interlude, for the "Anonymous," Goldoni's first comedy performed in public.

Griselda, 1735, tragedy, three acts.

Guerra, La, 1761.

Impostore, L', 1754, four masks.

Impressario di Smirne, L', 1757 (Impressario delle Smirne).

Imprudente, L', 1753 (Il Contrattempo), two masks.

Incognita, L', 1751 (L'Incognita persequitata), three masks.

Incognita persequitata, L', *see* L'Incognita.

Innamorati, Gli, 1759 (Gl'Innamorati).
Inquietudini di Camilla, Le, 1763 (Le Inquietudini di Zelinda), improvised comedy.
Ircana in Ispahan, 1756, tragi-comedy, verse, five acts.
Ircana in Julfa, 1755, tragi-comedy, verse.

Locandiera, La, 1753 (Gli Amanti in locanda), comedy in three acts, without masks.
L'Uomo Prudente, *see* Uomo Prudente.

Madre amorosa, La, 1754, three masks.
Malcontenti, I, 1755.
Maldicente alla bottega del caffè, *see* Il Caffè.
Massare, Le, 1655 (Le Massere), verse, five acts.
Massere, Le, *see* Le Massare.
Matrimonio per concorso, Il, 1763.
Medico olandese, Il, 1756, five acts.
Mercante fallito, Il, *see* La Banca Rotta.
Mercanti, I, 1752 (I Due pantaloni).
Moglie amorosa, La, *see* La Moglie di buon senso.
Moglie capricciosa, La, 1758 (La donna bizzarra), verse, five acts.
Moglie di buon senso, La, 1752 (La Moglie saggia; La Moglie amorosa), three masks.
Moglie prudente, La, 1751 (La Donna prudente), 1754.
Moglie saggia, La, *see* La Moglie di buon senso.
Molière (Il Molière), 1751.
Momolo cortesan, *see* L'Uomo di mondo.
Momolo sulla Brenta, *see* Il Prodigo.
Morbinose, Le, 1759, in verse, five acts.
Morbinosi, I, 1758, in verse, five acts.

Notte critica, La, 1740 (Cento e quattro accidenti in una notte), improvised comedy.

Padre di famiglia, Il, 1749, three masks.
Padre per amore, Il, 1757, verse, five acts.
Padre rivale del figlio, Il, *see* Il Teatro Comico.
Pamela, 1750 (Pamela nubile; Pamela putta).
Pamela maritata, 1759, sequel to Pamela nubile.
Pamela nubile, *see* Pamela.
Pamela putta, *see* Pamela.
Peruviana, La, 1754, verse, five acts.
Pettegolezzi, I, 1751 (I Pettegolezzi della donne), two masks.
Pettegolezzi della donne, I, *see* Pettegolezzi.
Poeta fanatico, Il, 1750 (I Poeti), verse and prose, two masks.
Poeti, I, *see* Il Poeta fanatico.
Prodigo, Il, 1739 (Momolo sulla Brenta), three masks.
Puntigli delle donne, I, *see* Le Donne puntigliose.
Puntigli domestici, I, *see* I Bisticci domestici.
Pupilla, La, 1734, interlude.
Pupilla, La, 1757, verse, five acts.
Putta onorata, La, 1749, three masks.

Raggiratore, Il, 1756.
Ricco insidiato, Il, 1758, verse, five acts.
Rinaldo di Montalbano, 1736, tragi-comedy.
Ritorno dalla villeggiatura, Il, 1761.
Rosmonda, 1735, tragedy.
Rusteghi, I, 1760.

Scozzese, La, 1761, five acts.
Serva amorosa, La, 1752, three masks.
Serva Riconoscente, La, *see* L'Amore paterno.
Servatore di due padroni, Il, *see* Servo di due padroni.
Servo di due padroni, 1745 (Il servatore di due padroni), four masks.
Sior Todero Brontolon, *see* Todaro.
Smanie della villeggiatura, Le, 1761.
Speciale o sia la Finta ammalata, Lo, *see* La Finta malata.

Spirito di contradizione, Lo, 1758, verse, five acts.
Sposa fidele, La, *see* La Donna forte.
Sposa persiana, La, 1753, tragi-comedy, five acts.
Sposa sagace, La, 1758, in verse, five acts.
Suocera e la Nuora, La, *see* La Famiglia dell'antiquario.

Tasso, Torquato, Il, *see* Il Torquato Tasso.
Teatro Comico, Il, 1750 (Il Padre rivale del figlio), four masks.
Terenzio, 1754 (Il Terenzio), verse, five acts.
Todaro, 1761 (Sior Todero Brontolon; Il Vecchio fastidioso).
Tonino bella-grazia, 1748 (Il Frappatore), two masks.
Torquato Tasso, 1755 (Il Torquato Tasso), verse, five acts.
Trentadue disgrazie d'Arlecchino, Le, 1740, improvised comedy.
Tutore, Il, 1753, three masks.

Una dell'ultime sere di Carnevale, 1762, last comedy given in Venice before Goldoni's departure for Paris.
Uomo di gusto, L', *see* Il Cavaliere di buon gusto.
Uomo di mondo, L', 1738 (Momolo cortesan), three masks.
Uomo di spirito, L', *see* Il Cavaliere di spirito.
Uomo prudente, L', 1748, three masks, written in Pisa.

Vecchio bizzarro, Il, 1754 (Il Cortesan vecchio), three masks.
Vecchio fastidioso, Il, *see* Todaro.
Vedova scaltra, La, 1748, three masks.
Vedova di spirito, La, *see* La Vedova spiritosa.
Vedova spiritosa, La, 1757 (La Vedova di spirito), verse, five acts, afterwards in prose, three acts.
Ventaglio, Il, 1763, the play of Goldoni's most frequently performed in English.
Vero Amico, Il, 1750.
Viaggiatori ridicoli, I, work composed by order of the Duke of Parma.
Villeggiatura, La, 1755.

Goldoni and the Venice of His Time

CHAPTER I

Italian comedy before Goldoni — Italian comedy was result of intentional imitation — was a continuation of Roman comedy — religious drama — "Classical comedy" a hybrid contradiction — Ariosto first Italian writer of Classical comedy — Machiavelli's *Mandragola* a masterpiece — it is deeper than a satire, presents a social thesis — Aretino's plays are light comedy — Florentine writers who influenced Goldoni — Florentine Academy — Grazzini, Gelli, and Cecchi — the popular comedy, or *La commedia dell'arte* — Beolco, *il Ruzzante*, an initiator of improvised comedy — dialect in popular comedy — century of Arcadia produced few good comedies — Andreini as author-actor-manager — Neapolitan comedy an imitation of Spanish — Florentine popular comedy — seventeenth century supreme period of *commedia dell'arte* — vulgarity characterised improvised comedy — Goldoni's poor judgment of other writers — Fagiuoli, Gigli, Nelli depict Florentine life — other contemporaries of Goldoni are unimportant.

THE importance of Goldoni's reform of the Italian comedy can be computed only by comparing it with what the Italian comedy had achieved before his time and by considering what others had previously tried to accomplish on similar lines and with like purpose. Goldoni is, as he claimed to be, a reformer and an innovator. Few men originate anything, but many share in the never-ending evolution by continuing the task of their precursors. Goldoni did this.

When Goldoni undertook to reform the Italian comedy, he imprudently asserted "*de bonnes comédies il n'y en avoit point,*" but in fact his greatest difficulty was to select from much accumulated material those elements from which might be created that complex, puzzling, interesting thing — a comedy; to combine simple form, direct purpose, appropriate means in the measure required at his time and in Italy. That some of his works have sufficiently fulfilled his program as still to command a world-wide audience is the result of his genius rather than of his avowed purpose of reform.

To appreciate this purpose, and to measure this achievement, something must be said of Goldoni's precursors — not a complete review of the early Italian comedy, but just a glimpse at the history and progress of this particular branch of literature. No attempt will be made to analyse his tragedies, though Goldoni wrote several, or that species of drama which developed into the modern opera; because Goldoni is only great in the older and nobler form of literary composition, the comedy.

The court circles of Rome, Venice, Ferrara, and Naples were neither less refined nor less self-conscious than those of Versailles and Whitehall, and it would seem natural that they would be equally prompt to mirror their own vices, foibles, manners, and customs on the stage. Yet the Italian comedy sprang late into life, and was mainly a product of imitation — imitation avowed, and stated as a fundamental principle by the writers of classical plays; imitation also, and almost as faithfully practised by the authors of popular plays. It was indeed a continuation rather than an imitation of the different sorts of plays composed and performed by the Romans, which were certainly performed, in Italy, even during the darkest Middle Ages.

The Italian gift of acting, mimicking, improvising, singing, must have found expression, in some form. There must have been a continuation, through the centuries, of the different forms of Latin comedy.

Fabulæ, Protestatæ, Togatæ, Tabernariæ, Atellamæ, Planipedes, and other sorts of mimes and pantomimes may have been acted in Mediæval Italy as frequently as the various sorts of religious performance, favoured by the clergy, or as often as the improvisation of long tales under the name of *gliommeri*; or the playful jousts of extempore *contrasti*. Such performances are still popular in Italy.

What this tendency and gift might have produced if allowed to develop in harmony with the gradual evolution of the people, we cannot know, as there is no certainty what more regular form of art might have developed out of the religious ceremonies and representations, if they had continued their regular performances under the guidance of the Church.[1] There is no telling, because the Renaissance movement came sweeping over Italy, destroying some things, transforming many others. In so far as it was a revival of antiquity the Renaissance widened the abyss

[1] It is only in Umbria, the land of *flagellanti* and *laudi*, that religious drama developed into importance, and it is there that a certain sort of

between literature and life, — an abyss fatal to comedy. Other literary forms may stand aloof from everyday actual life, but in comedy the elements of composition and also the means of performance must be directly borrowed from life. Both the actors and the audience are part of that society which is represented, part of that imaginary world evoked on the stage. Yet the spirit of the Renaissance so infatuated Italian minds that comedy was reshaped on that single principle, imitation — imitation of the Latin comedy, which in its turn was imitation of the Greek comedy.

Renaissance thus created this hybrid contradiction in terms, a classical comedy. Comedy is essentially occasional, contingent, dependent on the changing circumstances of time and surroundings; yet this absurdity had its short-lived days of glory, which could never outlive the peculiar circumstances which gave it birth. Only authors steeped in classic tradition, only princely patrons infatuated with admiration for antiquity, only the over-refined scholars and courtiers of the

pageantry is even now performed on different annual feasts. In Florence such performances, though originally meant to be religious, soon assumed a worldly character. G. Caprin, in his *Life of Goldoni*, thus resumes the situation: "The religious drama was at its turning point, just taking a regular form when it found the way foreclosed by the classical conception of literature at the time of the Renaissance supported by the favour of scholars, and an æsthetic directly derived from antiquity. A conciliation was attempted, and promised success when Poliziano gave his *Orfeo*, a genuine expression of pagan ideal blending with the construction of a religious drama. The combination was not continued then, nor ever afterward. Religious representations similar to those which were performed during the Middle Ages are still performed in villages."

Italian courts, could have found pleasure in the performance first of Latin plays and then in translations of them. Yet these enlightened patrons vied in the splendour and magnificence of the embellishments with which they supplemented these performances, — halls whose decoration was directed by Baldassare Peruzzi, Bernini, and even Raphael; music and gorgeous allegorical ballets; authors that were famous in the republic of letters.

Ludovico Ariosto[1] stands first on the list of Italian writers of classical comedies. His *Cassaria* and his *Suppositi* opened the lists. His own voice dictated the precepts that were to govern the stage for more than a century. The letter of his contemporary, Baldassare da Castiglione, the author of *Il Cortegiano*, describes those first representations at the court of Ferrara. What wonders were achieved when magnificence and erudition combined to produce courtly spectacles. The author himself, when a second versified perform-

[1] Ludovico Ariosto, son to Niccolò, was born in 1474. He entered the service of Cardinal Ippolito d'Este, bishop of Ferrara, in 1503. He rendered many important diplomatic and other services to his patron, besides praising d'Este in his immortal poem; but he was not adequately rewarded. He declined attending the cardinal in Hungary, and was dismissed. Alfonso d'Este then employed him in many ways and finally made him governor of Garfagnana. Toward 1526 Ariosto moved to his own house, which he adorned with the well-known verse, "*Parva sed apta mihi.*" There he peacefully ended his active life, comforted by the constant devotion of the woman he loved, Alessandra Benucci, the widow of Tito Strozzi.

Of all Ariosto's writings we mention only his plays: *La Cassaria*, performed in 1508; *I Suppositi*, 1509, first at the Court of Ferrara and soon afterwards in Rome before Pope Leone X in a theatre decorated by Raffaello; *Il Negromante*, dated 1520; *La Lena*, 1528. The play *Gli Studenti* he left unfinished.

ance of his play was enacted, stepped out of the curtain to explain in a prologue the intents and purposes that directed him. He boasts of having imitated his Latin models as closely as he could; he states that one must not merely borrow the subject from classic models and imitate the classic style of writing but also follow submissively the antique pattern. Customs, manners, characters, the construction of the play, everything must be imitated from the Latins, "just as these had imitated their Greek precursors."

But Ariosto, the most imaginative of Italian poets, could not strictly apply this strange conception of art. Even he introduced vital elements of contemporary actuality into his classical imitations. Though he imitated Plautus and Terence, though his stage characters and incidents were approved by his masters, he could not help introducing some satire, some supplementary colour, that were his very own. Thus even while Ariosto adopts the plot entirely turning on the intrigues of the lesser characters, even while he submits to the limitation of a single scene for all the acts — and that one a street, — so as to contrive separate entrances and exits through different house doors for each personage, even while he adopts the usual dénouement by the recognition or unexpected return of one person that was either supposed long dead or concealed under a different name, yet he introduces such traits of satire as this one, aimed at overbearing men in office.

(*Cassaria*, act iv, sc. 2) "If we were to go now and see the Bassa, we would lose our pains; we would find him eager for his supper; or playing at cards or dice; unless, tired with his day's work, he wished to enjoy his rest. Do I not know the ways of those in command? When they are most alone and most idle, they pretend that they are most busy; they set a servant at their door with orders to admit none but gamblers, harlots, ruffians of all sorts, and to keep off all honest people and worthy citizens."

Thus satire finds its way into the dialogue, and portraits are delineated in caricatural lines, under the antique pattern. For instance the play of *Negromante* (sorcerer) is evidently designed to represent the pedantic astrologer speculating on the credulity and superstitions of Ariosto's time "just as all the Great." Ariosto's other novelty is the metrical form. For Ariosto after writing his first plays in prose afterward translated them into poetry, and he versified his later ones. The special form of metre adopted is a delight to the ear with its easy flow and brisk harmony, fit for recitation.

Ariosto's contemporary and imitator was Bernardo Dovizi,[1] Cardinal Bibbiena. His *Calandria* has the

[1] Bernardo Dovizi was born in Bibbiena, in the year 1470. He sided with the Medici and was attached to Giovanni, son of Lorenzo, whom he followed into exile, under the pontificate of Giulio II. He afterward succeeded in making his patron Pope under the name of Leone X. On several occasions he was papal legate and was made cardinal of Bibbiena and Secretary of State. His portrait painted by Raffaello is almost as well known as the Pope's. Baldassare da Castiglione introduces him in his *Cortegiano* (see

faults and few of the beauties of Ariosto's plays. It is considered one of the most licentious plays ever written. Yet it was performed at the Vatican before a splendid audience of princes, prelates, and Pope Leo X himself. The ribald equivocations, the shocking jokes which offend the delicacy of modern critics, were enjoyed by these scholarly cardinals. They keenly appreciated the imitation of Plautus' *Casina* and a repetition of their favourite *Menæchmi*, made more piquant by the difference of sex between the twins, and for the same reason, as in Shakespeare's similar imbroglios, the feminine rôles being performed by boys.

Fortunately for Italian comedy, even in this initial stage of its existence, a masterpiece was produced to remain as a model for future ages. Voltaire proclaimed Machiavelli's *Mandragola* worth "all the plays of Aristophanes." Although Goldoni speaks rather disparagingly of this play, he certainly learned from it. Comparison between Machiavelli [1] and Goldoni is not

Il Cortegiano de B.D.C. riveduto da Giuseppe Rigutini, Firenze, Barbera, 1889) as the paragon of good manners and courtesy. He died in Rome, 1519.

His letter to Lodovico Canossa describes the representation of the *Calandria* at the court of Urbino (quoted by D'Ancona and Bacci, *Manuale della letteratura italiana, op. cit.*, vol. ii, page 391 and following).

[1] Niccolò Machiavelli (1469–1527), born in Florence, was the son of Bartolommea de Nelli and of Bernardo Machiavelli, a lawyer. Little is known about his early education. His earliest writing is dated 1497. The following year he was secretary to the second *cancelleria* of the Florentine Republic and soon afterward secretary to the *Dieci della Pace e Liberta.* He retained this place until 1512, when the Medici were reinstated in Florence and he was exiled. Charged with complicity in the Boscoli and Capponi plot, 1513, he was imprisoned and tortured. He then retired to a little place in the country near San Casciano. There he wrote his *Mandragola.*

possible. It is only in this comedy of Machiavelli's, the pastime of an idle hour in his busy life, his diversion in a time of exile and disappointment, that they chance to meet on the same field.

When a thinker who has probed the depths of human conscience, when a statesman who seems to have investigated all the problems of his age, and foretold many problems of future ages, undertook to write so simple a thing as a comedy, he was sure to carry some of his deeper insight and clearer observation in this work.

In the narrow mould which Ariosto had fixed, in the small compass that was then allowed to comedy, Machiavelli has drawn a number of living characters. He has painted an amazing picture of the vices that disgraced his times, and of the ignorance and superstitions he hated.

Like Goldoni, he only introduces indispensable innovations, but he retains such external forms and restrictions as do not interfere with the real significance of his work. Neither does he multiply his characters, nor does he change those traits which suit his purpose yet respect the established custom. There is no shifting of scenes, the plot is simple, there are the usual personages. A foolish husband, an impudent lover, a

He recovered favour with the Medici. For Cardinal Giulio — afterward Pope Clemente VII — he wrote the *Annals of Florence*. At the fall of his patrons he was denied the place of secretary which he claimed. He died in poverty, 1527, and was buried in Santa Croce.

We do not attempt to mention his activity as a statesman and a writer of the most famous book on statesmanship.

bigoted old woman, and a prudent young one, an intrigant, and a friar: from this receipt he mixes and then unravels the simplest of intrigues. But all these classical, cold, dry elements throb with life by the imponderable spark that marks the masterpieces of genius. Truth shines through all that is conventional, and a far-reaching moral lesson under the licentiousness which custom then tolerated and, lacking which, the lesson would probably never have found listeners.

The plot is familiar, Callimaco, a student in Paris, has heard the praise of Madonna Lucrezia, Maestro Nicia's wife, and he comes ranting with that sort of passionate desire, which was so often mistaken in the Middle Ages for love, saying that if his desire cannot be gratified he will "do something terrible," stab himself on the lady's doorstep, or drown in the Arno, for a woman he has never yet seen. Ligurio, the fawning intrigant, like the slave of the antique plays, serves his young master and deceives the old one. Ligurio's shrewdness, hypocrisy, his glib tongue, his proper manners, make him a cinquecento Florentine, well qualified to persuade the pedantic sot Nicia. Friar Timoteo is a party to the intrigue, and between the three, with the unconscious connivance of Lucrezia's mother, they persuade Nicia that if he wishes to have children he must induce Lucrezia to drink of a certain beverage concocted out of the juice of the mandragola (mandrake), for his special benefit, by the learned physician, Callimaco of course. This sort of thing was just what any Florentine of his time might have believed, or made his fellow believe. Machiavelli added to the popular superstition a more amusing trait. Nicia is told that the portentous effect of the beverage will make it mortally dangerous to — to — let us say kiss, Madonna Lucrezia immediately after she has taken it. Someone has to do the — the — kissing and be offered as a victim. A street boy may thus be sacrificed in order to secure the posterity of a most honourable citizen. Indeed, explains Callimaco, who expects to play under an appropriate disguise the part of the street boy, indeed the greatest princes and even the King of France have resorted to this artifice so that their family should not end with their own lives.

Nicia is easily persuaded, because his foolish pate is crammed with abstruse reading, and his confidence in his own wisdom is swelled in proportion. "*Un sot savant est plus sot qu'un sot ignorant*," truly says Molière.

The difficulty is to convince Lucrezia, who is genuinely pure and not a bit foolish. Indeed this character of a real woman is one of the best innovations in Machiavelli's play. She is wearied and worried by her mother's and her confessor's arguments; torn between the scruples of her natural honesty and instinctive common sense, and the religious principles instilled by education and example. Her common sense is not proof against the sophisms of Friar Timoteo; her filial respect compels obedience to what her mother tells her to be her duty. Indeed laughter at the comical plot and witty repartee dies out as the dire consequences of such a tormenting struggle is better understood. What moral misery was thus prepared for innocent hearts!

The friar's character is completely and studiously delineated. How he argues to persuade the woman that "this thing which she is asked to do is no capital sin, but just as bad as eating meat on a Wednesday; it can be laved by a sprinkling of holy water." His ready tongue supplies the clever sophisms which she cannot answer. "Why does she trouble about the means; the aim is everything. Is not her aim to fill a seat in Paradise?" And so on, until he, Timoteo, changes his tactics and uses the deceitful art of unctuous tenderness: "Go, my daughter, and I will in the meantime say the orison to Archangel Raphael, that he may watch over thee." Let her make haste, since night is drawing near.

These were indeed deadly thrusts aimed at the whole priestly brotherhood, nothing like the attenuated strokes and noisy, but harmless, flourish which the creator of Frère Jean des Entommeures aimed at his brethren.

Yet is Machiavelli's play something even deeper than a satire of his times, and of the peculiar vice of religious hypocrisy; there is a social thesis, which anyone may discover if he but reads, and this thesis will also be found in Goldoni. The great statesman and the modest playwright meet in this simple conception of social progress. Since the cause of much evildoing is due to the relaxation of family ties, the best means to oppose the decadence of society is to expose and condemn all that tends to relax these ties. The best ideal is the family group made whole and strong again. Let the perverting friar be held up to the pillory of ridicule; let the infatuated, bigoted mother be shown in her real colours, the slave of an unscrupulous clergy; let the husband be denounced for his failure to fill his rôle of guide and protector.

Machiavelli developed this thesis, made it even more clear in another play, *la Clizia*, and further explained it in a song that was added, as an interlude, for both the comedies, and in which the purity of simple life is sung in accents of real poetry, though the metrical form is not equal to his marvellous prose style.

Narrower views and less noble aspirations are found in Aretino's plays.[1] His plays were only his pass time;

[1] Pietro Aretino, so called from his birthplace, Arezzo, was the illegitimate son of a cobbler. He studied painting and letters in Perugia. He obtained favour and notoriety from having been wounded in a quarrel. Giovanni della Bande Nere was his friend, and Aretino gave him a devoted attachment in return.

Aretino lived and throve "on the sweat of his pen." For him and others who could write on almost any topic with equal fluency and inflated eloquence the term of *poligrafo* was invented. Pietro Aretino is the first journalist — in the worst meaning of the word. He fawned and flattered, bit and threatened. His pen was always busy for the highest bidder. He served François I before siding with Charles V. He corresponded with almost every important personage of his time, discovering some most amiable qualities to redeem his many faults. Grasping for money and favour, he is also generous in giving to the women he loves and the daughters they bore him. He encouraged art and artists, his taste was good, although he often writes in the over-ornate style which announces *il secento*.

Besides many other writings Aretino composed *Orazia*, a tragedy which Pierre Corneille imitated in his *Horace*, and five other plays. He died in 1556.

his life's work was court intrigue and advancing his fortune. And because these plays were merely composed to amuse his hearers, they are important to our study; they give us a first sample of that light comedy which the Renaissance men liked to hear, and which Goldoni has imitated.

Cardinal Bibbiena is another author whose comedy owes little to its slight plot, yet provides matter of amusement to the audience by presenting a number of unfinished sketches, which being but loosely bound to the general plot have no real significance. His style has the originality of the man himself. It is emphatic and swollen with adornment, figures, and bombast peculiar to the writer, who used his pen as a double-edged sword, to prick or to stab.

Bibbiena's viewpoint of life is realistic and contemptuous of the lower classes that he selects to picture, and paints very black. With him the intrigues and the characters are of the basest.

Like him, a court poet and a courtier, was Lorenzino de' Medici,[1] conspicuous in the history of his country for his murder of Alessandro de' Medici, his cousin and boon companion of debauch. His *Aridosia*, one

[1] Lorenzo, son of Pier Francesco de' Medici, better known as Lorenzino — the Lorenzaccio of Alfred de Musset's play — was born in 1514 and brought up by his mother, née Soderini. He murdered his cousin Alessandro in January, 1537. This crime has been variously viewed. For some Lorenzo is a hero who delivered his country from a tyrant; others think him an ambitious fool. Sem Benelli's play, *la Maschera de Bruto*, presents the interesting enigma, without attempting to solve its mystery. The last act gives an accurate and striking representation of Lorenzo's death in Venice, 1540, by the daggers of Cosimo de' Medici's followers.

of the many imitations of the Aulularia, attributed to Plautus, may have provided a model to Goldoni's *Avaro*. But the character was so often used by writers of prose fiction and of plays that there is no telling how much Goldoni is a debtor of Lorenzino. Indeed the miserly old man and the foolish pedant were the two favourite laughingstocks of the age. Goldoni dropped almost entirely the pedant, and this is why we omit Giordano Bruno's comedy *Il Candelaio*. And many others are omitted either because they are little known to fame, or because of their slight influence on Goldoni.

A more complete study of the comic theatre during this, otherwise, glorious century would reveal its poverty of invention and its subservience to classicism, keeping the regular comedy within very narrow bounds and facilitating the composition of works that only reproduced familiar models, and did not attempt anything like novelty.

The splendour which presided at the staging of ballets and interludes, the imagination which brightened allegorical spectacles, affording opportunity to all sorts of decorators, musicians, and artists, left the comedy untouched in the poverty of its single scene, in the representation of none but humble folks. The wonder is that, thus shackled, the Italian comedy prospered and that so many able writers composed new plays, or adapted old ones.

We shall attempt to trace the transformation of the classical comedy as it was understood and practised by the wealthy and educated class of citizens in Venice and in Florence. Other Italian centres produced many interesting works; but they were unknown to Goldoni, and, moreover, they did not greatly influence the traditions that combined to form his genius, the double tradition of classical and improvised comedy.

When Goldoni penned that imprudent sentence, "*de bonnes comédies, il n'y en avoit pas,*" he either confessed an unpardonable ignorance or denied the source of his own inspiration.

How could he say that there were no good comedies, when in the archives of the craft, in the memory of actors and theatregoers, the Florentine plays of the cinquecento must have been preserved, at least in incomplete form, if not in their entire text? These were not composed for the great in power and wealth; but for the great in learning and wit. They were conceived by writers of the great middle class, which for this reason they could understand and faithfully represent; they were classical in a certain measure, because those who wrote them, and many of those who listened, were steeped in the knowledge of fine letters, but still they were comedies of the bourgeoisie.

Three writers may be selected: Francesco d'Ambra,[1] Giovan Maria Cecchi, and Giambattista Gelli. They have traits in common with Goldoni just as their time had traits common to the seventeenth and eighteenth

[1] Francesco d'Ambra, contemporary, friend, and fellow *Umido*, wrote several plays in verse, remarkable for a superfluity of intrigue, mistakes, and errors. His Italian, however, is elegant.

century Venice. They enjoyed, as Goldoni did not enjoy, the advantage of companionship and mutual encouragement.

L'Accademia degli Umidi (the damp), which, later, became the Florentine Academy, was then delightfully free from pedantic presumption. It was like a club, where people expected to find superior amusement. Let every man of good company and wit pay homage to the promoter Giovanni Mazzuoli, detto lo Stradino (or lo Strascino) who led the way that so many have followed. Francesco d'Ambra composed, and probably shared in the performance of, unpresuming plays that were given at this Accademia. He imitated the Latin classics, but he padded his imitations with many jokes and accumulated incidents, borrowing from several old plays to make up a single new one.

Grazzini,[1] the most illustrious of the *Umidi*, under his name of "Lasca" in homage to the name of the club, is the author of many world-famous *novelle.*

[1] Anton Francesco Grazzini — il Lasca — is a fine representative of the Florentine citizen. He championed Italian letters versus Latin and Greek literature. He endeavoured to persuade his fellow-citizens that Dante and Petrarca were greater than Homer and Virgil. He admired and imitated Francesco Berni's *rime bernesche.* In November, 1540, with some boon companions he founded the Accademia degli Umidi, at first as a modest club for the purpose of pleasant meetings in the house of Giovanni Mazzuoli, one of the members. Things went on well for some time; about 1547 the easy-going club turned into a ponderous academy entitled Accademia Florentina. Then Lasca turned the arrows of his ready wit against its affectations, purism, and airs of authority.

Lasca wrote many small plays. These plays, printed much later, are inferior to Lasca's *novelle,* his greatest title to fame being the elegance and purity of his Italian.

He was also a man of sound critical taste, which he showed both in practice and in delivering such good advice as this: "Since nowadays people that were thought dead do not suddenly reappear, since no one now goes to market selling or purchasing slaves and no one dares publicly to bargain and barter for pretty young women as the Roman panders did, it is time we should not represent Roman manners and ways but our own."

Such teachings he delivered, as the fashion then was, in the prologues of his plays, prologues that then did duty for much that now goes into critical essays and reviews directing public opinion and promoting profitable discussion. Did not Goldoni attempt to do the same two centuries later? Grazzini, who knew no Greek and only as much Latin as was required for exerting his profession of *farmacista*, did not entirely reject the classical model; he borrowed from ancient plays and from classical reminiscences, but he opened a new path by setting largely on the stage the materials of his own and of other writers' *novelle*. He mixed up the Decameron and Plautus in true Italian spirit to bind up the past with the present, passing on to the coming ages the inheritance of older centuries.

Giambattista Gelli,[1] with even greater talent for

[1] Giambattista Gelli, 1498–1563, was a scholar and a philosopher. Such qualities were sufficiently appreciated then to open for him even the doors of the celebrated "Orti Oricellari." His greatest ambition was realised when he was appointed to "read Dante." His *La Circe* and *I Capricci del Bottaiol* sum the ideas of his time, borrowing largely from the ancients yet adding that originality which is the character of humanism.

His play *la Sporta* is in some parts so good that it was believed Gelli had

the comic art, and with much erudition, pursued the same system. Though he was so learned that he could continue — after Boccaccio — to explain the *Divina Commedia* and although he could pen a series of much admired philosophical dialogues, Gelli always followed his trade of shoemaker.

He too remained faithful to classical tradition, as is shown in his *Sporta* (small basket) by the choice of the principal character, *Ghirigoro*, the typical miser, and by some incidents of the plot; but that he could walk with his own legs he showed by the management and construction of many episodes. Molière and Goldoni both are indebted to this Florentine cobbler who produced one more picture of dissolute old age baffled and exposed by youth. It would be interesting, if it were relevant, to discover how much of this Italian comedy was imported into England. The borrowing from the Italian tales by Ben Jonson, Marlowe, and Shakespeare has been often investigated; how much they directly pilfered from Italian plays is less known.

We come nearer to Goldoni and his reform when we exhume from the dusty past that second branch of comedy which, starting into life almost at the same date and almost in the same places as the classical comedy, developed on parallel lines the popular comedy, or to give it its Italian name, *La commedia*

discovered fragments of a play on this subject by Machiavelli. Another play *l'Errore* lacks originality. About his *Ghirigoro*, the miser, something more will be said when comparing it to Goldoni's.

dell'arte. Because it is so perfectly appropriate to the spirit and the ability of Italians, it is almost certain that it existed in some form even in the dark ages. Just as the French *Fatrassies sotties* and other forms of "farces" were probably performed as often as the "Mystères and Miracles" and other religious representations, it is also most probable that the two sorts of spectacles were at times certainly intermingled, and they were performed alternately, by the same players, and only in the sixteenth century was the distinction clearly recognised. And even that distinction was then rather formal than essential, since the line was only drawn later and not exactly where the contemporaries of Ariosto and the first *commedianti dell'arte* would have drawn it.

All over Italy and especially in Naples, actors, professional or amateur, some of the latter amongst the highest born and the most powerful, performed or improvised *frottole*, pantomimes, and similar spectacles.

We disregard the Neapolitan theatre since Goldoni ignored it, or only knew it through the traditions *dell'arte.* In Florence, the most enlightened Italian city, the distinction was sooner realised and found its clearest definition. Giovan Maria Cecchi,[1] the author

[1] Giovan Maria Cecchi, 1518–1587, boasted that he had never lost sight of his dear "campanile." A genuine Florentine, he was a notary with a taste for intellectual pleasure, without aspiring to the name of *Letterato.* His plays, twenty-one in number, are more classical than Lasca's, yet they never lose touch with every-day life, and often reproduce plots and characters from the popular *novelle.* His most admired play, *l'Assiuolo,* is sometimes compared to Machiavelli's *Mandragola,* though it lacks the depth and meaning

of several plays, some of which almost wholly answer to his independent program, says in doggerel verse: "The *farsa* is a new thing, which stands between the tragedy and the comedy, avoiding thus the difficulties of both. Since it admits both great men and princes — which the comedy cannot do — and since, like an inn or a hospital, it shelters people of all sorts: villains and country louts — which the tragedy is not allowed to do — it can range over all sort of subjects: merry or sad, worldly or religious, polite or vulgar. It can locate its scene in any place, the village common or the church door; and when a day is not sufficient it can expand to three or four."

This declaration of the freedom of the comedy from cramping rules of construction takes added importance from being issued in Florence by one who was a scholar, in the presence of the *Signoria*, whose patronage extended to every form of art.

About the same time almost the same ideas were expressed in Venice, 1588, by Jason de Noves, who pompously explained how comedy was required to be the reproduction by *imitation* of a complete action, of adequate importance. The characters introduced should belong to the middle class. The story was to begin sadly and terminate happily. Similar regulations were often repeated with the characteristic injunction that comedy should be "proper," that is to say, should be so arranged as to offer a moralising teaching.

of its model. Cecchi is an interesting guide to the ways and manners of his time and city, his gallery of personages being very extensive.

From the very first the intention was to adopt the ancient motto *castigat ridendo*, but there was endless divergence in the practice. It was the accepted idea that three or more acts of triumphant wickedness were amply compensated by a few last scenes of repentance or punishment.

Pierre Larivey, the Frenchified Italian who translated and popularised many Italian plays in France, thus sums up the ideas of his models: "Comedy being the mirror of our life, the old may learn in it how to avoid doing things that are ridiculous in the aged; the young must learn in it how to behave themselves in lovemaking; the ladies how to keep their modesty; the parents how to regulate their family affairs. If other pleasures are only meant for the young, this one is good for teaching, amusing, directing the old, the young, and everyone."

A Venetian author of *Il Giusto Solegno* added with more realistic intent "that it was good for servants to see how the mischief they make is punished, and the maids are well warned, by example, of the horrid diseases they run the risk of taking when they misbehave themselves."

With these honourable purposes in view, one finds among the first actors, or authors, of improvised comedy most devout and God-fearing people. One of the first whose name is known, and whose works have been recorded, is Angelo Beolco, the impersonator of a bucolic, rustic character *il Ruzzante* and consequently known as *il Ruzzante*. He has been traced back to

Venice, and more exactly to the palaces of the Foscari in the year 1520, performing a play of his invention *a la villanella* with the collaboration of a company of players, all, like him, coming from Padova. He was applauded, he was called back to Venice in the following years, and at last he was permitted to perform his "Pastoral" at the very same court of Ferrara that had so lately seen the first blossoming of classical comedy. Here was a pathetic plot enwreathed in many funny episodes, and here was also one of the most characteristic traits of the improvised comedy, the use of dialect.

Even here some distant echo of Plautus's *Rudens* or *Asinaria* reminds us that we are still in the age of revived humanism. The elements of realism, however, are predominant. The personages speak their own native parlance, and they express in undisguised roughness and vulgarity their rustic feelings. Thus "Fiore," the heroine of *la Fiorina*, is not the simpering damsel of classical plays, but the country girl who, courted by two swains, shows preference for one of them; but when the other succeeds in carrying her away she neither mopes nor reproaches, but accepts the situation and settles down as a good wife with the husband who has conquered her.

Beolco was not only the manager and author, but also one of the actors of this first among the *compagnia dell'arte:* he impersonated the character of a countryman almost as boisterous as the "capitan Matamore," as sly as "Arlecchino," and with some traits of simple-minded "Brighella." He was specially qualified to represent country folk as he lived a part of every year on the lands he owned near Padova. Some of his plays have been preserved and those *Dialoghi in Lingua Rustica* which have been lately analysed afford matter for interesting study.

In order to sympathise with and understand the Italian people and their literature we must realise how important is this question of dialects. It is the index of the infinite diversity of race, temper, degree of civilisation, manners, and customs that is the charm — as it has been the weakness — of the whole nation. No literary representation of the people should ignore these differences; no writer can reproduce the graphic expression of feelings and thoughts, unless he translates them in the style appropriate to the part of the country he has in mind to interpret. This rule holds good even to this day; after almost a century of political union, after five centuries of literary communion. It is valid for every sort of fiction; but particularly for the comedy. Hence the great success lately obtained by the Venetian, Sicilian, and Roman dialect actors is not due to a mere fad, to a passing mode; it is the natural and logical consequence of a condition of things which, though now largely removed, has left its effect and which, especially for the scenic art, must be taken in consideration.

From this early awakening of a popular form of comedy spoken in the local vernacular the different dialects inevitably forced their entrance into the written plays, as well as into those that were improvised by the actor. Even when the authors did not, as they often did, characterise with this distinctive trait their personages, the actors impersonating them were likely to add those traits of manners, those peculiar sayings, proverbs, or idioms which came glibly to their lips, because they were those that best expressed their own ideas and most appealed to their audiences. The actor thus blended his own personality with the rôle he played and between them they gave a complete type that was soon perfected by the additions and improvements of other actors, taking up the personage and continuing the tradition.

The contemporary appearance of dialects, and of popular fixed types — some of them wearing a mask and others not — representatives of different cities or provinces, emphasises this character of regionalism which is the most accentuated trait of the Italian comedy.

This analysis will only attempt to trace back to their probable origin the characters and masks of Goldoni's plays, and not the many others which he has discarded. In the endeavour to catch the very first glimpse of the comedy as a picture of real life, we simply point out that the first direct imitation of life admitted the regional differences of character and language. Not only Beolco and his disciples, but all succeeding writers who wanted to be popular used dialects. Indeed those who wrote "Italian," in the Florentine manner of speaking, used a language that was the dialect of a certain part of Tuscany. There is a difference of style and of accent between the country folk and the citizens; the characters that represented Sienese or Lucchese people did not speak just the same Tuscan as those of Florence.

Such nice distinctions show how the classical comedy was turning into the popular comedy; how instead of borrowing all their materials, copying their dialogues, and imitating their plots from the ancient Latins, the playwrights were beginning to look about them for models; how they were urged on and directed by their interpreters, and finally how the two professions became so mixed together that it is difficult to decide which was the more important.

Angelo Beolco directed as a manager and acted in the plays he composed. He could also deliver a speech, as he did twice in Padua when he was asked to welcome the cardinals Cornaro on their elevation to the Holy See. His speech was divided into the five parts required by the rules of eloquence, each of the several points demanding some practical and necessary relief from some form of opposition. All these traits will be found reproduced in Goldoni, Ruzzante's worthy heir.

Andrea Calmo, 1510–1571, with more education than Beolco, acquired a freer speech and a more definite consciousness of his aim. He disregards classical models and bravely tells the audience — in a prologue to his *Santuzza* — that if they do not approve of his method they are welcome to rise and depart. But he will not condescend to repeat the usually banal improbabilities, neither the sudden return of long-dead personages nor the recovery of children lost and stolen, because he means to represent the times as they are, and not the stupidities which were popular in past ages.

Such examples influenced public opinion and even those pedantic writers who might have drifted back into classicism. Thus Lorenzo il Magnifico wrote in vernacular Florentine his *Nencia da Barberino*, thus Francesco Berni composed his *Catrina*, and Giordano Bruno his *Candelaio* in a style that resembled the popular comedy, even while the deeper thoughts of the writer were expressed under the simplicity of the dialogue. Nor was the glory of the Italian comedy and comedians, during this sixteenth century, confined to their own country. The French court first learned to admire them when Catherine de' Medici called the *compagnia dei Gelosi* to adorn the festivities celebrating the union of the Medicis with the reigning house of France; but the French poets and writers had expressed already or were soon to express their admiration for the witty, graceful artists who, according to Du Bellay's well-known sonnet, could charm and amuse.

The seventeenth century is considered a time of decadence in Italian letters and arts. Certes it was a century of luxury and hypocrisy, of foreign oppression and degradation, which was made worse by the religious persecution following the Council of Trent. Yet it was also the century in which Galileo Galilei initiated the revival of science, and a new impulse was given to plastic arts by Bernini.

The century of English euphuism, of Spanish

Gongorism, of French *style précieux*, of Italian "Arcadia" was not fruitful of good comedies. The tendencies of the time inclined away from extravagant conventionalism and toward pastoral poems and plays. Classical comedy lost favour. With the possible exception of the Neapolitans, Giambattista Porta and Francesco d'Isa, there is no name of the first rank. More interesting as a precursor of Goldoni is Giambattista Andreini, author of that religious poem *Adamo*, which Milton must have had in mind when he wrote his *Paradise Lost.*

Giambattista Andreini, though not the earliest, is one of the most complete specimens of the author-actor-manager man of letters that Goldoni, to a degree, impersonated in himself. The son of two famous players, Francesco Andreini famous in France and Italy as the "*Capitan Spaventa di Vall' inferno*" and the exquisite Isabella in whose honour so much ink dripped from the pens of poets, in whose honour a medal was coined, Giambattista inherited talent for the stage, and was also carefully educated. His career as an actor is registered in the annals of his time; his serious writings are merely used as landmarks for the learned who deal in comparisons; his comedies are forgotten, else they would be condemned as the most licentious that were ever acted.

Yet in his lifetime they were enjoyed by the same persons who admired the piety and spiritual elevation of his religious poems. The contrast, then, between the two entirely different styles was not offensive, indeed was not surprising. The pen which traced the choiring songs of angels bearing heavenward the purified soul of *Maddalena* also wrote the lascivious and prurient pleasantries which the author himself spoke on the stage or taught his comrades to speak. Which was the real Giambattista? Probably both, so strange and complex a thing is a human personality.

Goldoni mentions Andreini's comedy *I due Lelli simili*, one more repetition of the Menæchmi, that were seldom left out of sight. But he certainly knew many more of Giambattista's works either in their original text or in the adaptations which the comedians gave of them. Another name mentioned by Goldoni is Cicognini, probably the elder, who left but few works, and those of contested authorship. Cicognini, or whoever wrote those disputed comedies, imitated the Spanish plays.

On Spanish imitation, and on the caricature of Spaniards, the Italian comedy grew and prospered in Naples. It is interesting to notice how some of the ancient characters were reshaped and transformed. The *Miles Gloriosus* for instance turns into the *Capitan*, the *Matamore*, and the many other impersonations of bombastic heroism and poltroonery. This character, one of the favourites with cosmopolitan audiences, can be traced in its many ramifications, just as the *spagnolised* comedy may be seen spreading from Naples to France and England; but the little that Goldoni did borrow he transformed, because neither his own genius nor the Venetian conditions in any way resembled the spirit of the Neapolitan Spanish comedy.

Of greater importance is the Florentine. There the conditions of life and manners favoured the development of popular comedy, both in its almost literary form of written dialogues and in its more original form of improvisation. The written comedies which have survived are, however, in the style of the improvised ones — slovenly in style, loose in plot, and characterised by the use and the abuse of dialects.

Michelangelo Buonarroti — il Giovine — nephew to the great sculptor, produced a medley under the name of *Fiera*, in which long and cumbersome picture crowd the masks, types, costumes, and disguises then popular in Florence and which the immortal drawings of Callot have fixed on paper. Five days — or five plays — each one divided into five acts, Buonarroti composed in order to give a place to all the persons he wanted to strut on the stage just to say a word, play a prank, and give way for others.

If one could by an effort of imagination, or by the patient study of texts and engravings, reconstrue this medley, one would have an idea of that ample material carried far and wide by the *commedianti dell' arte*,[1] which Goldoni was to reshape into artistic form.

[1] The *commedia dell'arte* has many different origins. It would be interesting to trace it back to the *pastorale* and to the *bucoliche* ridiculing the manners of country people and the sentimentality of heroic poems. This hybrid was taken up by the Sienese *Accademia de Rozzi*, wherein it took a sort of literary regularity. This academy was founded in 1531 with the intent of providing amusement for holidays. The members met to read

Also if one could read in its original text the comedy of Virgilio Verucci, one would have an idea of the number of dialects admitted on the stage. If not quite the five hundred collected in one volume, reproducing one of Boccaccio's short tales, the Italian dialects used by Virgilio Verucci in one play amounted to ten, and in other plays varied from four or five to six. Goldoni adopted but a small part of this superabundant material.

If the seventeenth century lacked regular comedies, it saw the greatest glories of the *commedia dell'arte*. How this peculiar art or profession was exerted deserves mention. Even before Beolco and Calmo, it had been the privilege or the ability of some one actor to take the lead of a small troupe of players and with them to wander from city to city performing all varieties of plays, in all sorts of manners, according to the circumstances, their capacities, and the opportunities offered. The best of these troupes soon found their way to France, where they prospered.

The company was generally composed of ten persons,

poets and to perform plays. From this popular pastoral two different sorts of compositions branched out: the poem, such as Tasso's *Aminta* and the comedy, which blended into the *commedia dell'arte* and thus lost its character. The first *commediante dell'arte* recorded is Francesco Cherea, a protégé of Leone X, but very little is known about him and his performances. There were *commedianti dell'arte* in Mantova in 1566.

For all the *commedianti* see the *Dizionario dei Comici Italiani* di Luigi Rasi, an accurate study which includes the many older works on the subject. For the origins of Italian comedy see Alessandro d'Ancona, *Origini del Teatro Italiano*, Loescher. For collection of canvases, besides the often mentioned works of Alessandro d'Ancona, see Adolfo Bartoli, *Scenari inediti della commedia dell'arte*, Firenze, Sansoni, 1880; also Benedetto Croce, *Una nuova raccolta di scenari* in Giornale Storico xxix.

just as the troupe Medebac was in Goldoni's own time. Ten characters were considered sufficient for the representation of life. These ten characters are well known. Of course they extended to more, as the same actor would at times take a rôle that was akin to his own. There were the characters *sérieux*, as Goldoni calls them, and those burlesque. The mask was not always the badge of greater vulgarity. Two old men, Pantalone and il Dottore; two young men, Lelio and Leandro; two Zannis (servants), Arlecchino and Brighella; three women, the duegna, the amorosa, and the servetta, a capitano or some other additional character made up the number.

Each actor was so completely identified with his rôle that he was known by its name. Such an identification was the cause of a greater ability in playing it, and of a more dangerous tendency to adapt it to one's own character. Thus if we were to trace back the transformation of each one of these types, we should have to find out, not how any particular author at any distinct moment had imagined it, but how, as it passed from one to another player, the figure, the clothing, the mode of address, the general outline, and the supplementary traits were modified. At the first appearance of a character, or the branching out of a new diversity from an old one, we generally find a famous actor, an artist that gave the intonation and fixed some of the elementary traits. Thus in France, Ganassa created the type of Ganache. Thus Tabarin and Scaramouche are characters which originated in the Italian actors whose names have thus found immortality.

In Italy some typical cases might be quoted: thus for instance Salvator Rosa,[1] being displeased with his countrymen's lukewarm approval of his pictures, resorted to the trick of disguising as Coviello and selling horoscopes, telling fortunes, playing an infinite number of *lazzi* in the crowded streets of Naples. Such was the success of this Coviello that the artist himself developed it into two personages, "Coviello Formica and Coviello Patacca," which, both, have remained in the repertory of Neapolitan masks. The four masks and the other characters adopted by Goldoni will be fully discussed in the analysis of Goldoni plays.

Although the *commedia dell'arte* started on the plan of a larger independence, it soon fell into a narrow channel, and was confined by rules even more cramping than the classic models. During this entire century, though prosperity and favour attended the profession, there was little real progress. Though some of the comedians possessed ability and some talent, they lacked invention. Their practice was almost uniform from one company to another.

[1] Salvator Rosa, 1616–1673, is so much better known for his painting that his other talents are forgotten. The history of his life reads like a novel, with its episodes of bloody quarrelling, and plottings in Rome and in his native Naples. As an amateur actor and the creator of that peculiar character of the blustering *capitano* he was most successful, his own sunny disposition, his rebellious spirit, and his artistic taste giving to such amusement a larger sense. As much might be said of the several creations of Bernin. See Jacques Calot, *La Fiera dell'Impruneta* and *I Balli de Stessania*, for the largest collection of Italian customs ever drawn.

An outline of plot, either composed by one of them, or selected out of the stock of such documents as the troupe possessed or from a classic play, was nailed on to a poster behind the scenes and first *spiegato*, that is, explained and developed by the chief actor or director, in order to fix the distribution of parts, the length and importance of episodes, the general outline, and the proportions of the play. It is easy to imagine the amount of discussion and quarrelling at such rehearsals. One can picture the unwillingness of the lazy player to undertake his share of the work, and the boisterous claims of the ambitious star who wanted to do more than his share and outshine his comrades.

When the general line was thus settled, each player turned to his own private stock of material, in order to prepare for improvisation. Each one possessed a *zibaldone*, a sort of memorandum book containing the long-winded speeches, or the short sallies, that suited his habitual character, strange collections of sayings, proverbs, snatches of song, quotations from all sorts of books, that were handed down from one actor to another, always amplified with newly collected material. Some of the tricks of the so-called *lazzi* were learned by imitation and repetition. These were perhaps the best index of the degree of vulgarity and ribaldry that was tolerated and applauded by the audience. The actor who catered for plaudits, and was trained to translate his audience's wishes, drifted into coarseness and worse, because the people who filled the house or circled round the raised boards demanded such seasoning.[1] This absolute dependence of the improvised comedy on the favour of the public resulted in much vulgar gesture and gross speech; but during the palmy days of the late sixteenth and early seventeenth centuries it had urged the actors to perfect their art, and to keep faithful to reality.

The number of plots that were used is not known, almost every Italian collection possessing a different selection. Different at least in titles, it very often happened that the same plot with very few changes appeared under several titles. Then also a play well known in its original classical text was cut down to a sketch, or a play developed out of a sketch. Goldoni himself sometimes resorted to such arrangements. And if he, the reformer, could not avoid this practice, one may imagine how it was unscrupulously applied by others before him.

One of the most interesting of these collections and one of the oldest was published by Flaminio Scala under the title of *Teatro delle Favole Rappresentative* (fifty canvases) as far back as 1611, this Scala being then in Paris with his company of players. Another noteworthy collection is due to the care of Adolfo Bartoli, who gives only twenty-four plots but much information as to the players. Carlo Gozzi

[1] A. Ademollo, *Intorno al teatro drammatico italiano dal 1550 in poi*, Nuova Antologia, Marzo, 1881, says that in Venice the noblemen crowding the house incited the actors to the most ribald jokes and speeches, even when they were in company of their wives and daughters.

The Venetian laws were severe against these exhibitions; decrees were issued against the immorality of plays, apparently with little effect.

speaks of no less than three hundred of these plots, but his authority is doubtful.

Lelio Riccoboni must be mentioned both for that which he endeavoured to accomplish and for that which he has written about the Italian comedy. His *Histoire du Théâtre Italien* gives a definition of the *lazzi*. The word means a knot and has the same origin as the Spanish *lasso*. We call *lazzi* the byplay which Arlecchino or the other masks perform during a scene, which they interrupt by feigned terrors or other pranks having nothing to do with the matter in hand, to which one is always obliged to return. These tricks, invented freely by Italian actors, are called *lazzi*.

No one better than poor Riccoboni — the Lelio who vainly tried to direct public taste toward regular comedy — knew how these practical jokes lowered Italian comedy in the esteem of critics; yet none better learned, at his own cost, how they were acclaimed by the paying public. Like Goldoni, Riccoboni expected Paris to appreciate his reforming purposes, and like Goldoni, he found that bad taste and an accredited tradition of looseness weighing on the Italian comedy were against him. Like Goldoni, he learned that the art which almost entirely relied on communion with the audience could not develop its best qualities in a foreign land.

Goldoni knew little and cared less about his contemporaries, the playwrights of early 1700. The few appreciations in his *Memoirs* — and the blundering opinions he records about later French plays — show that Goldoni was unable to judge of the relative merit of other writers. Yet something was achieved, something attempted in his neighbourhood which was worth notice. In Florence were Fagiuoli, Nelli, and Gigli. A court poet, a skilled courtier, was Fagiuoli,[1] yet with an uncommon turn for satire and sarcasm. Indeed there was not a *bon mot*, not an amusing anecdote, not a spirited repartee, that tradition did not attribute to him for more than a century after his death.

How this reputation for professional wit could outlive the performance of his plays is strange. He rehearsed the worn plots showing the familiar characters of the ancient play — the old man and his senile infatuation, the noisy, swaggering captain, the familiar foolish lovers. Instead of employing the masks he introduced Florentine servants and other low people; he made them talk their nonsense in the highly flavoured Florentine dialect, and thus earned the title of originality. Just one of his characters, *Vanesio* in the *Sigisbeo Sconsolato*, deserves mention as a first sketch of the *Cavalier servente*, a mere daub that, however, suggests none of the delicate etching and amusing caricature Goldoni made of the personage.

Jacopo Nelli[2] might have been utterly forgotten but for the success his little opera *la Serva Padrona* obtained in virtue of Pergolese's music. His many

[1] Giovanni Battista Fagiuoli, 1660–1742, has written nothing half so amusing as the jokes that were attributed to him, — Giuseppe Baccini, *G. B. Fagiuoli, poeta faceto fiorentino*, Firenze, 1886.

[2] Jacopo Nelli, 1676–1770, a satirist and a playwright of slight importance. He wrote for drawing-rooms and academies, indulged in personal satire and caricature in his *capitoli* and the plays he composed for amateurs and school boys.

other plays represent the dissolute, flimsy Florentine society of his time, with just one note that is almost original — the caricature of henpecked husbands and hectoring wives. Women characters in the older plays were seldom ridiculed; they were either pathetic or pert, victims of plots or objects of worship, but as a rule dimly delineated on the worn-out pattern of classic repertory. Now with the decline of social life, with the decadence of every manly activity which is the characteristic trait of this unfortunate period, woman received a social importance and an authority which she did not owe to any development of her own qualities, but to the lowering of the other sex.

Fagiuoli has a character of a hypocritical prude, which, though drawn with slight talent, is interesting as a symptom of the coming time. Nelli's plays are even in their titles indicative of a tendency (*Serva Padrona, la Moglie in Calzoni*).

With greater talent, and more conscious aim, Gerolamo Gigli [1] entered the lists of comic playwriting.

[1] Gerolamo Gigli, born in Siena, 1660, died in Rome, 1722, fearlessly exposed one of the evils that Goldoni did not discuss—the convent as a perpetual threat for disobedient girls. *Il Don Pilone*, act iii, sc. 13, is entirely of his invention, an addition to the stage which even Molière could not surpass.

"Marianna. If a girl has to be shut up for her entire life, let her at least first enjoy some pleasure for three or four months. Let her see something of the world, and share in some of its amusements.

Valerio. If you want me to sleep quiet to-night, you must go into the convent at once.

Mar. I see, that you may rest quiet to-night, I will have to live in torment all my life."

Then both her brother and Valerio plead with her and sing the praise of

In a city and a time wholly ruled by clerical hypocrisy, this scholar challenged the Jesuit rulers, and ridiculed their influence.

Gerolamo Gigli was one of the unfortunate people who cannot endure that which they esteem wrong. In more heroic times he might have been a glorious champion, or a lamented martyr for the sake of some bright ideal; in Tuscany and in the seventeenth century he was only a quarrelsome linguistic, an intemperate pamphleteer, an imprudent playwright, who paid for all his attempts at rebellion. He quarrelled with the Florentine Accademia della Crusca, because he wrote a very learned and witty *Vocabulario Cateriniano* and other tracts to show that his native dialect of Siena should be preferred to the Florentine. His book was burnt on the public Piazza for such heretical opinions. He indeed ran the risk of being burnt himself or at least spoiled of all his goods for the two plays he dared to write and to perform.

The first one, *Il Don Pilone*, is a translation of *Tartuffe*, with some additions in the form of interludes and ballets, and made more pointedly offensive by the author himself appearing in the principal character so trimmed and painted as to look like a portrait of a well-known and much-disliked Jesuit. The second play is the *Sorellina di Don Pilone* in which Goldoni won a little sprig of laurel when he performed in his

that convent. "The rule is not very strict. . . . The convent is very wealthy. . . . Among other advantages the nuns are never made to fast. . . . And they can go out and please themselves twice a month."

beardless age the part of the pseudo-sister to Don Pilone.

If by his first play he won the terrible enmity of the clerical, by the second one he kindled the wrath of his own middle-aged wife, whose avarice and bigotry he had but too faithfully exhibited. Nor does he spare himself, for the plot is but an anecdote of his own conjugal life where he does not appear to great advantage. With all this it is little wonder if Gerolamo Gigli was deprived of his *catedra* at the Sienese University, spoiled of his wealth, and driven out of the state by offended foes and vindictive dignitaries. It is significant that he found shelter and rest in Rome after doing public penance in Florence.

Gigli's plays are worth studying for their own sake, and also as showing one of the principal traits — which Goldoni more fully developed. Gigli is not satisfied with the clear, neat outline; he adds little touches that sometimes blur, sometimes perfect the drawing. Compare his translation of Molière's play with the original and note the differences. Where the French poet gives but one masterful dash, Gigli lingers in tiny arabesques. For instance, the first appearance of Tartufe with that single masterful trait, his turning toward the scene to tell his servant, "*Laurent, serrez ma hère avec ma discipline,*" . . . which becomes in Gigli's play, — "Piloncino, mind thou dost carefully wash the blood from my horsehair shirt, and remember thou must add two nail points to my discipline. Take good care, if the maid come in to tidy the bed, thou must not raise thy eyes. Conceal the kneeling chair behind my bed. If anyone come for me thou mayst tell them that I went to the prisons *delle Stinche* with alms for the poor prisoners, and that I afterward will go to take a piece of cloth to that shameless hussy, that she may lengthen her petticoat." This minute exactness, which Thackeray and some other English writers of fiction carried to perfection, is adequate for stage effect. Goldoni used it, but not always with success.

Other contemporaries of Goldoni are hardly worth mentioning either for their own sake or for the influence they may have exerted on him. Luisa Bergalli's attempt at a realistic play *Il Poeta* may have shown Goldoni the danger of two minute and depressing pictures of poverty. Scipione Maffei's *Ceremonie* taught him, as he says, a good lesson of moderation in the way of reform.

The lavish praise which Goldoni gives to Scipione Maffei seems to contradict our assertion. To read certain prefaces, letters, and passages in the *Memoirs*, it seems that Maffei, justly famous for his tragedy *Merope*, is also a precursor, a star of magnitude in the field of comedy. In fact his two plays *Le Ceremonie* and *il Raguet* are now forgotten.

About Chiari and Carlo Gozzi more is said in Goldoni's life and in the analysis of plays. Their influence was harmful: Chiari's, because his intense competition goaded Goldoni to distracting efforts; Carlo Gozzi's because, with more talent, he tended to waylay Italian comedy out of its course. His anticipated romanticism, his unruly imagination, were so utterly unlike Goldoni's well-balanced mind that they could never understand one another. Their lines diverged from the first. While Gozzi conquered immediate approval abroad and found in Goethe an admirer, and the imported school of Italian romanticism celebrate him as precursor, Goldoni's more durable glory was to gather the threads of the past, both the golden thread of classical comedy and the homespun of improvised plays, so as to mix them and prepare the woof for modern comedy. A woof so finely built, so well fitted for its purpose that it still holds and promises to hold good not only in serious comedy of customs and characters, such as they are understood actually, and apart from the elements of foreign importation, but it is the basis of a splendid revival of regional comedy, a revival which the social and political conditions of the nation happily encourage, a revival which is in the spirit of Goldoni's plan; taking in full consideration the variations to be found in different parts of Italy without losing contact with the glorious traditions of the past.

It is dangerous to prophesy in such uncertain and threatening times; still, if anything can be discernible, it is that Italian comedy will, on recovering with the whole world from the actual malady, return to the way pointed out by Goldoni — the way that comes from the past and goes toward a brighter future.

CHAPTER II

FIRST PART OF GOLDONI'S LIFE, 1707–1732

Material from which to construct a history of Goldoni's life and works — reasons why his autobiography is not sincere — Goldoni had nothing to conceal — is a typical Venetian citizen of his time — importance of the middle class in Venice — the Venetian merchant petted and protected — Venetian amusements shared by all the people — Venice well governed and orderly — Venetian religion a ceremonial and without faith — Goldoni family citizens of Modena — Carlo Alessio, Goldoni's grandfather, settles in Venice — his hospitality and extravagance — Goldoni born in Venice in 1707 — his father Giulio, a physician, mother of good family — Goldoni's estimate of his father and mother — Giampaolo, his brother, born in 1712 — Carlo mother's pet — happy home life — at eleven he composes his first comedy — obedience and "manners" Italian ideal of education — schools were clerical — Carlo goes to school in Perugia — acts female rôle in Gigli's play, *Sorellina di Don Pilone* — his family leaves Perugia for Chioggia 1720 — he leaves Rimini for Chioggia with theatrical troupe — enters Ghisleri College at Pavia 1722 — is expelled — his travels — his relations with women inside and outside theatre — immorality of Venetian convents — Goldoni studies law at Modena — enters Chancellery of Chioggia — father dies — admitted to Venetian Bar 1732 — is not successful as lawyer.

IN the two volumes of his *Memoirs*, in the prefaces to his plays, in many short poems, and in a few letters, Goldoni has provided much material from which to construct a history of his life and works. This fragmentary material, however, affords only a reticent portrayal of his character. Why did a man of Goldoni's expansive nature, having nothing to conceal, no reason to screen or disguise himself, leave an incomplete account of his life and a purposely blurred and distorted picture of the events and persons that were a part of it? A general and a personal reason account for this inaccuracy.

Goldoni belonged to a society that worshipped decorum, that blindly obeyed the code of politeness, that abolished the last remnant of sincerity, and that stifled all self-revelation and real feeling. A typical Venetian of his time, he reverenced propriety; he could not, even if he tried, frankly reveal his whole mind, either about himself or about others. Violent expostulation, a display of his real feelings, would have seemed to him undignified.

Also, he was a playwright, which means that he had learned the art of making up a personage, and had caught the knack of presenting it under the best light in the best pose. He knew what stage optics require — shortening of lines, contrast of colours — to set a personage in appropriate relief. He knew how a player should paint his face, what brilliant clothes he should wear, how he should exaggerate his gesture and force his voice, how omit details and emphasise his intonation, so as to produce the desired effect on the audience. The multiple demands of the footlights have no better interpreter than Goldoni.

When he writes about himself he instinctively applies the technique of his art. Seeing himself on the world stage as an actor, he says only that which fits with the general outline and colouring of the personage, such as it is in his mind, such as he wants people to see it. And because he is very clever, because he has mastered all the secrets of his profession, he succeeds in his performance. His autobiography is not a portrait, then, but an interpretation. He sees himself under an artificial aspect, and he paints himself according to a special method which may be called truth, adapted to suit a fixed plan. The portrait has lost in absolute sincerity, but it has gained in power and relief. The elements composing it are all true to life; it is the artistic arrangement, the general outline, the disposition of lights and shades, the choice of attitude, that give it a special character.

Not that Goldoni ever aimed at exalting his own personality. He is delightfully free from petty ambition. Unlike every other writer of *Memoirs* of his time, he neither attacks other people nor defends himself. He merely puts himself upon the stage in the same manner and with the same technique which he used for depicting so many others.

This instinctive preoccupation appears not only in the *Prefaces* and the *Memoirs*, but even in the *Letters* that were never meant for publication. The *Prefaces* were written *currenti calamo*, in order to supply some explanation to the volume containing plays already performed. He afterward used them as memoranda for the painful compilation of the two volumes, in French, of his *Memoirs*, published by subscription in his old age. No wonder, then, if the anecdotical material when compared with reality appears inaccurate, and evidently coloured to suit his readers, and to supply padding for his book. There is the same mental attitude, the same unconscious pose in the letters he wrote to his friends and patrons.

The character of himself which Goldoni has thus composed is singularly attractive. It beams with smiles, glows with spontaneous carelessness; it possesses the charm of persisting youth and unruffled cheerfulness which has won the sympathy of readers for almost two centuries.

Yet the genuine Goldoni, when stripped of the thin veil of semi-confessions and more or less inaccurate anecdotes, appears even more lovable and more honourable, in its prosaic simplicity. His gain in human reality exceeds his loss in artificial grace; though less debonaire he is more manly. His individuality acquires greater consistency, yet he remains the representative of a class and of an epoch. He is the typical Venetian citizen in the first half of the eighteenth century.

A simple bourgeois he is by birth, and a bourgeois he remains through all the vicissitudes of his life, in close communion with the middle class of which he writes with loving comprehension. Notwithstanding many travels and a long exile, he remains at heart and in spirit Venetian.

An ignored world, this Venetian middle class. A little world which foreign travellers disdained, which contemporary Italians disregarded, but which modern critics eagerly investigate, searching for the origin of that, otherwise, unaccountable revival of the nation and its civilisation.

The splendour and the magnificence of Venice were solidly grounded on the extensive trade of a great body of merchants, pioneers of commerce abroad, purveyors of costly goods at home. The autocratic rule of the State as well as traditional reverence for the patrician caste, confined the middle class within the rank long since assigned to them, even while none of their activities, their spirited enterprises, lacked encouragement. No European nation has more forcibly conserved the class distinction, none has more constantly upheld an aristocratic government; yet in no other European nation were relations between the different classes more cordial or the sense of social solidarity more pronounced.

Only superficial or prejudiced foreign visitors, misunderstanding the magniloquent spagnolism of certain complimentary formulas, have interpreted as servility that which was only an exaggeration of politeness, an inveterate inclination to ceremonious rites.

For centuries, the Venetian merchant, giving support, providing wealth for the State, had acquired consciousness of his own power and importance; it was not certainly in the eighteenth century, when the oldest and largest patrician estates were threatened with ruin, when the Senate made money by offering for sale titles and honours, till then reserved to birth and rank, it was not then, certainly, that the merchant would surrender any of his well-earned pride. The pioneers who carried the winged lion of Saint Mark to the distant shores of the Adriatic, to the farther coasts of the East, begot generations of proud descendants whom the Senate honoured and, in the first twilight of decadence, even cajoled and flattered in many ways. Almost every week saw some new decree issued for the protection of trade, for the defence of Venetian rights of commerce, for the safety of ships, or the increase of customs taxes, in the vain hope of averting foreign competition and political decline; but also with the immediate purpose of pleasing the commercial class.

The senatorial government, in its dotage, was anxious to bestow a maximum of order, comfort, and support on its subjects. Every branch of public service, education, assistance, justice, amusement was masterfully ordained in Venice; yet the rulers were constantly reforming, perfecting things.

Pompeo Molmenti's erudite and patient reconstruction of *Venetian Life and Customs* provides exhaustive information on the matter. The number and the accuracy of regulations, the frequent correction and revision of decrees, testify to the good will of that government which romanticism has painted so ominously black. If wisdom and good government could save a nation from the decadence and oppression to which geographical conditions and foreign competition fatally doomed her, Venice would have prospered under the government of an illuminated patriciate, for the greater benefit of the whole people.

Impending ruin could not be averted by the foresight of any Council. It was not possible for the

Venetian Senate to save the commonwealth. Unable to grapple with the distant causes of decay the Venetian Senate fought against the symptoms of the incurable disease. Nor did they perceive the hidden danger of dissolution then threatening almost every European government. Their policy was to ensure public peace by granting privileges, by encouraging every class and especially the industrious middle class.

Thus protected and petted the Venetian merchant, as blind as his rulers, basked in the sunlight of favour, and rejoiced in the many advantages offered by a rule so paternal yet so indulgent. Trade, indeed, was slackening; but banking was increasingly remunerative, while magistrates condoned usury, that last resource of an aristocracy in distress which upheld many a patrician house.

The Church, the Law, the Civil Service offered brilliant opportunities which universal favouritism encouraged, promising success to all who knew how to push their way. Schools of commerce and navigation, public lectures on almost every branch of learning, lent a false appearance of modernity and enlightened responsibility to the government. In fact it was not so. It was simply the continuance of ancient and adequate laws; it was the nation's evolution, as yet untrammelled by foreign interference; it was the normal growth of all the civic virtues fostered by peace and prosperity; it was the development of a sense of solidarity promoted by a good government careful of every class of citizens.

There were other capitals in Europe which rivalled Venice in magnificence, but no other city in the world equalled it in gaiety. In other cities pleasure was the privilege of a few; in Whitehall or at Versailles the courtiers alone enjoyed the prerogative of gaiety and dissipation; in Venice all the people were included in the perpetual round of public festivities. Everyone could claim a place in the sunshine of State ceremonies, everyone could hold a rôle in the grand pageantry, and everyone contributing to the general effect partook both of the actor's and of the spectator's enjoyment.

It was an endless chain which linked, into a consistent whole, this multifarious crowd. The patrician in his scarlet robe who filled the principal place was, in the eyes of many, a reliable protector, or patron under whose wing they expected to find a refuge, in case of need, with whose help they hoped to make their way in the career of public employment. It was a perpetual exchange between the merchants and their noble-born patrons. The former needed protection, the latter needed votes for election to public offices, and ready money to support the splendour of their position. On public occasions, in the days of pomp and pleasure, they spontaneously joined in perfect concord.

Visitors who at that time noted the undisturbed order presiding over crowded meetings, "not more than three officers being on duty"; the unanimity of feelings that "transformed the assembled crowd into one family," did not realise that the fundamental cause of this cordiality was the bond of reciprocal assistance and equality in the pursuit of pleasure — the only equality which, at the time, was claimed by the people.

In Venice, the middle class enjoyed, if possible, a larger share of amusements than the nobility. If the patricians held the first places in public solemnities, they were merely spectators in a larger number of festivities, celebrated by the humbler classes of citizens — regattas and fairs, processions and dances.

If a few doors were closed to the plebeian in his own garb, even those opened wide before him when he wore a mask and a tabarro.[1] As good coffee was sipped in popular *bottaghe*, as good wine was drunk in the *malvasie*, as good jokes cracked, as hearty fun enjoyed, in the *campiello* as in the *palazzi*. Venice was bountifully provided with luxuries unknown to other cities, — easy communications, well-lit streets, hygienic conditions, and police regulations which gave to this Mecca of pleasure-seekers a security and a charm recognised by all visitors. The special charm of Venetian life was its habitual mirth. Such a happy disposition of the mind was both cause and effect of the customs. Venetians were cheerful because they were well governed; and their government was good because the national temper was so happily inclined. All contemporaries, every document, every tradition, and Goldoni, most distinctly confirm this fact.

An atmosphere of peace and serenity pervaded the

[1] Tabarro, cloak, domino.

quiet corner of tormented Europe where Goldoni was born. People lived there in the contentment due to equipoise between aspirations and possibilities. That was the unique and fugitive moment in which a nation's ideals fitted exactly with the material conditions of life. It can never come but once in the life of a nation, and the Venetians were then enjoying it. They ensured their peace of mind by obeying blindly, and never indulging in speculations.

A narrow and strict code of morals, stringent regulations for all social and family relations, rules of propriety established on the rock of tradition, refinement of manners, elaborated through centuries of politeness and courtesy, all combined to form this atmosphere of quiet which the Church carefully forbore to trouble by any uncalled-for rigor.

In Venice the Church vied in leniency with public opinion, moulding her code of laws on the same pattern of numerous, precise rules for ceremonial worship and almost unlimited indulgence in regard to faith. Just as social life ran smoothly along the lines of many petty duties and exact rules of etiquette, leading strings for timid worldlings, so the religious life of Venetians was ruled by an infinity of external practices, adapted to every private or public occasion, forming a comfortably padded pillow for timorous consciences and piously inclined souls.

For the average middle-class man or woman who blindly followed both the rules of worldly etiquette, sanctified by tradition, and the religious observance, dictated by complacent clergy, what greater source of satisfaction, what greater promoter of quiet, than this persuasion of duty accomplished in the total absence of disquieting doubts?

Conscience, cradled in a bed of formalism, ignored the torment of questioning articles of faith; ignored the sting of controversy, the bitterness of doubt; moreover, in every occurrence, in family or business relations, in social meetings as in private transactions, a formulary of polite prescriptions was always there, handed down by generations of honoured forefathers, ripened into perfection by uninterrupted appliance.

The people who accepted these two guides, and obeyed the minutely detailed unvarying rules of civil and religious conduct, without ever trying to brush aside their ordinances of etiquette and custom that involved their whole life, were, in a measure, a nation of overgrown children. Some of the puerile grace of childhood outlived in the sweetness of manner, in the soft, lisping dialect, in the constant mirth, which characterised the Venetian middle class in early 1700, when Carlo Goldoni's birth enriched it with the addition of a new member.

The patronymic name being spelled Guldoni in some ancient registers, has suggested an improbable, distant Teutonic origin, but not the slightest alien ethnical trait can be found in Goldoni's figure or face; not the faintest shade of foreign character can be discovered in his psychology; he incarnated a purely Venetian spirit in a typically Italian body.

The Goldoni family was settled in Modena, enjoying an official and comfortable position, when our author's grandfather, Carlo Alessio (or Alessandro) decided to transfer himself to Venice, attracted there by an instinctive affinity. No man born and bred in the *laguna* was ever more Venetian in temper, taste, spirit, and character than this Modenese.

The bigotry, the deadly seriousness of his native Modena jarred with Carlo Alessio's sunny nature and extravagant tendencies. Venice offered a more fitting theatre for his aptitudes, more congenial conditions for the expansion of his natural gifts. His ambition, guided by tact, served by grace of manner and *savoir vivre*, his sociable and artistic inclinations, carried him through a prosperous career of public charges, and landed him safe in a second marriage and useful connections, so that he was able to lead a life of brilliancy and pleasure until his persistent good luck brought him to a timely death at the moment when the effects of his extravagance threatened his position.

His office in the court of "Dei Savi del Commercio"[1] was no sinecure. To this special court of justice resorted all doubtful cases between foreign merchants. A delicate and most important jurisdiction, in the international mart which Venice then was. The Greek, the Turk, the Oriental, the Jew, all relied on obtaining fair judgment from the people whose rallying cry was "*Pane in Piazza, Giustizia a Palazzo*" (Bread in the market and justice in the palace).

[1] Five Commercial Sages, originally instituted to supervise commerce.

It must be inferred that Carlo Alessio Goldoni honourably fulfilled the duties of his office, since he remained in charge until his death, yet, according to his grandson's narrative, he found sufficient leisure for squandering his money, living according to the standard of the times, when the pursuit of pleasure was the supreme ideal of Venetians.

Carlo Alessio's notion of hospitality included a large house and dinner parties, in his city dwelling in *Cà Cent anni* as well as in his villa on the banks of the Sile. To keep up appearances, to remain on parade, to uphold one's rank and decorum, such was the supreme ambition of every Venetian. However large or small the world, the set, the coterie he belonged to, the object was the same, and, for its sake, Venetians endured everything. They curtailed even necessary expenses, restrained their natural inclinations, checked their passions and desires, disciplined themselves by a self-denial that, turned to a higher purpose, would have been heroism. Vanity did duty for sterner qualities and smothered more dangerous vices.

Foreigners, like the semi-anonymous author of *l'Espion Chinois*, noted this mania without suspecting that some proportion of good was mixed with the evil effects of vanity. A constant preoccupation about other people's opinion, an unflagging desire of approval, are not always incentives to wrong-doing; occasionally they prevent or restrain it.

Goldoni, himself inclined to this social tendency, dwells with complacency on these acts of his grandfather. "He was a fine gentleman, but he lacked economy. He was fond of pleasure and adopted the manners of Venice." He further tells how the villa on the Sile was always crowded by visitors "from every part of the country"; how the greater lords of the neighbourhood were jealous of the splendid entertainments given at this princely villa, and how they endeavoured to drive Carlo Alessio out of the place, and how he managed to undermine their plans, by obtaining further grants and further authority from the Duke of Carrara, his patron and landlord.

Goldoni carefully mentions that his grandfather used to have theatrical performances by "the best artists of the time." He further adds that he was born during this time of gaiety and extravagance, hence that he was bound to be inclined toward gaiety and extravagance. "Could I help liking the theatre? Could I help being gay?"

The picture is pretty. As a preface to a first volume of plays it was an amusing scene; in his *Memoirs* he makes it an interesting first chapter, but — it is only a fib, a first lapse into that preconceived plan which the writer means to keep up all through his *Memoirs*. He strikes, even from the first pages, the note of gaiety and carelessness and the predestination to the theatre which he persuades himself, and would persuade his readers, to have been there from the first.

Carlo Goldoni was not born in the splendid dwelling of his spendthrift grandfather; he came into this world four years after this jolly ancestor had left it.

The official death certificate of Carlo Alessio dated 1703, the baptismal certificate of Carlo dated 1707, destroy the pretty scaffolding, and betray the hereditary megalomania transmitted from grandfather to grandson. Did Goldoni mistake for early reminiscences that which he heard from family stories, or did he embellish his narrative with purely literary intent?

Anyhow, the death of Carlo Alessio did mark a change in the tide of family affairs. Under the patriarchal system which ruled Venetian families the sudden disappearance of the chief generally heralded much unexpected havoc. Carlo Alessio had sadly neglected to provide for his son Giulio's future career, the boy's upbringing having been entirely entrusted to a stepmother. His education consisted of the usual smattering of classics that led to nothing in particular. Giulio Goldoni was poorly prepared to fight life's battle. His father, exerting the authority of the paterfamilias, disposed of his son; or, according to the adopted term, *gli diede uno stato* (*lui donna un état*) by choosing a wife for him.

Margherita Salvioni possessed the virtues and merits which would please a father-in-law. It is not evident that she possessed the charms that would ensure the love and the fidelity of a young husband; to Carlo Alessio that was a superfluity. Margherita Salvioni came of a good family, distantly related to the Goldonis she brought a comfortable dot, secured influential connections, was pious, modest, and thrifty. What more could a father-in-law require?

The very youthful bridegroom — Giulio was twenty at his father's death — was probably not asked for his opinion, else he might have objected to a wife who was seven years his senior, who was lame, and who, instead of sharing his own sociable disposition, preferred church-going, convent-visiting, and clerical friends.

Giulio did not succeed his father in the office of notary or secretary at the Council of Commerce. "A Greek more clever got the place," says Goldoni. "My father did not like to dwell on painful thoughts; he decided to start on a trip to Rome as a diversion." Here Goldoni alters facts and wrongs his father. Giulio Goldoni did not leave immediately for Rome. He first went to Modena, and did his utmost to realise the remainder of his patrimonial estate and settle other financial matters. Then when he found it necessary to make his own destiny he went to Rome, and started on a course of medical studies. When Goldoni writes, "My father left home for a few months and remained away four years," he throws discredit on that which was a wise and manly resolution.

These must have been four years of hard study, since Giulio Goldoni obtained his medical doctorate and won the esteem of famous Doctor Lancisi, the physician of Pope Clement XI, who favoured him with his patronage. Inasmuch as, like many another Venetian husband, Doctor Goldoni might, without offending public opinion, have lived quietly at home on his wife's income, but preferred instead the manlier and more difficult way of earning his own living by pursuing a course that was neither smooth nor common, his son might have introduced Doctor Giulio with an interpretation of his departure better responding to its aims and motives.

"My father was, perhaps, a good doctor; he certainly was a very amiable man of the world. To the pleasant ways of his countrymen he joined the refinement of the polite circles wherein he always moved."

If he did not always cure his patients of their real illness, he never failed to cure them of imaginary ones. Doctor Giulio wisely forbore to undertake difficult cases; he was neither quack nor humbug. He possessed tact and great power of pleasing. Neither parasite nor toady, a gifted conversationalist, he conciliated favour without being a dependent. No gambler but a fair player, useful for organising the customary card tables, but even more indispensable for the staging of theatricals, he possessed that common sense and understanding of things and men which smoothed his own way and helped him to direct wisely his son's affairs.

It was clever of him to move from one city to another when he realised that the first bloom of his fame was fading. Whenever a colleague attacked him, whenever a powerful patron showed signs of weariness, Doctor Giulio lifted his tent, and in some new environment again began the cycle — a warm welcome at some great man's house, a pleasant season of professional and social work, then another timely departure.

What capacity Giulio Goldoni might have developed for the education of his son was lessened by these frequent absences. Then Doctor Goldoni lacked the prestige, the self-assertion which strengthened the authority of his own father, who was sure he was always right and permitted neither opposition nor contradiction; while Giulio was in advance of his time, allowing his wife or his son to discuss his commands. On the whole he proved a good father, according to unambitious standards. He promoted his son's interests, got him out of scrapes, obtained for him the patronage of powerful men, delivered appropriate lectures about the ways of the world and the peril of imprudence, and he also set him an example of self-respect, of honesty, and of amiability.

Goldoni has better loved and better understood his mother. "My mother gave me birth almost without suffering, and always loved me the better for that." A somewhat puerile explanation to account for a life-long affinity of temperament, a communion of souls.

Behind the veil of tenderness which haloes Goldoni's picture of his mother, Margherita Salvioni appears fairly representative of her time and of her class. She was the submissive stay-at-home wife who ignored her husband's wanderings, forbore from recriminating, and was ever willing to assist in rebuilding the family nest, in order to welcome back its prodigal master. Rather pretty, though her complexion was dark, graceful in spite of her lameness, she possessed the tact and common sense, the easy flow of talk, the prompt repartee typical of Venetian women. Without ever asserting herself, she managed to have her way in most things.

The same narrow piety which encouraged the visits of clerical friends, and devoted her leisure hours to visiting the convent *parlatorios*, also prejudiced her against her second son Giampaolo for his refusal to take holy orders.

Giampaolo, the undesired offspring of hard times, the latecomer whose boisterous nature jarred with her own prudish notions, contrasted with Carlino's pretty manners, with his father's refinement, was first sent out to nurse in the country; afterward to a school of friars, as a preparation for monastic life. Giampaolo developed a rebel disposition, a spirit of adventure that found, later, its vent in a military career, and caused much trouble to himself and to his family.

That tenderness and care which she stinted to her second son, Margherita Goldoni lavished on her first born, on her Carlino. She was proud of his precocious wit, and rejoiced in his gentle disposition which welcomed her fondling and petting. On her husband's departure, Signora Goldoni kept house with her maiden sister on their small joint incomes. "She had only me to care for; she wished to bring me up under her eyes. I was a quiet, good-tempered boy; when only four years old I could write and read. I learned my catechism by heart, and I was given a tutor."

Thus while Giampaolo in exile grew up a stranger to his own mother, Carlino, "*le bijou de la famille*," was brought up in his mother's lap, nestled in more comfort and tenderness than ever he could have enjoyed in the crowded, sumptuous villa or city palace of more prosperous days.

To this great and rare boon of a happy childhood, Goldoni owes the great and rare privilege of a sunny nature, of that moral and physical health, that perfect balance of mind and body, ripening in self-confidence and cheerful courage. Home life was delightfully quiet and pleasant between the two ladies, who stinted their own expenses in order to provide largely for the little darling's education. A quiet but not a lonely home. Signora Goldoni being a thorough Venetian admitted many friends to her *conversazioni*. Of course the child was made much of by visitors, who wished to please the mistress of the house; of course Venetian politeness praised his progress.

Goldoni dwells on this first childish success; he inaccurately records a comedy composed by him, at some uncertain date, but not, certainly, at the unripe age of eight as he says. More probably at eleven, the age suggested by his biographers.

He makes a pretty picture of the admiring group centring round his own childish person; a nurse being the first confidant, his aunt laughing, his tutor wisely pronouncing that the composition showed more wit than the age of the writer justified. Then in comes a godfather, "richer in money than in learning," who pretends that he cannot be persuaded of the boy's authorship; whereupon the tutor grows angry and the quarrel is warming up when a third personage — he is an abbot — comes in and settles the question. An areopagus of three, a magistrate, a tutor, and an abbot, disputing over the first paper Goldoni darkened with penmanship, his mother sitting with a smile of exultation and listening to the discussion. Is it not a pretty picture of Venetian customs? It was a happy idea to use this subject for the engraving prefacing the first volume of plays. We hope it was true. Such a system of education threatened to turn the boy into that absurdity, a youthful prodigy, when his father sent for him.

Nothing is more significant of a nation's degree of civilisation than its ideal of education. In 1700, in the Italy morselled into many States, still more divided by different traditions, tendencies, customs, and even languages, a few common traits remained as tokens of past unity, as links for future reunion. Among the strongest and most persistent of these links was the ideal of education, the plan of studies. From childhood to the tardy emancipation of youth, from the grammar school to the university degree, the line was unbroken.

The keystone of this system was obedience. His parents first, his teachers afterward, his confessor always, were expected to guide the boy's every step. This was not an abstract theory, but a fairly working social and familiar system. The child was to imitate the example of the other members of the family in their allegiance to the chief of the household. Naturally, especially in Venice, this allegiance was often infringed in practice, but appearances were safe, at least as far as the child could see them.

Children were kept out of the way, not for lack of love, but because there was little time for the privacy of home life. Habits of inveterate dissimulation, of exaggerated politeness, tinged with a mannerism that checked the free expansion of a child's spirits, kept him in great respect of his elders. The dogma of familial hierarchy was still inflexible, for the child.

Beyond this lesson of obedience the child was taught "manners," how to behave himself, how to speak and move about with elegance and grace according to the infinite rules of deportment. The lesson began at home where, in every word, gesture, and look, he saw the same desire of pleasing, the same constant endeavour to avoid disagreements and make everything smooth for one's self and for others. This standard of gentility was adopted by every class of citizens. All professed, and taught to the growing generations, the supreme virtue of old-fashioned *gentilezza*, untranslatable word or untranslatable idea, comprising much more than mere politeness and elegance, of a politeness that stretches even to the unspoken feeling; of modesty which applies to every word and look; a tact for smoothing angles, for restraining impertinence and malice; a determination never to annoy one's fellow-creatures, and to amuse them, whenever opportunity offered.

Children were taught to practise this *gentilezza* long

before they could realise its general purport or resent its limitations. In consideration of other people's feelings, they were drilled to disguise every annoyance under a smile; they were instructed to speak no word, to make no movement, but those which could give pleasure to onlookers. Such an education paved the way to very agreeable social intercourse.

To Carlino Goldoni these teachings were imparted with the added sweetness of some extra petting, and much maternal devotion.

Like other Venetian ladies — perhaps even more than others — Signora Goldoni visited at the grates of convents. When Carlino attended her in this round of visits, he enjoyed an early opportunity for perfecting his manners, in these substitutes, and rivals, of drawing-rooms, amid the crowd of visitors, the prattle of pretty girls, whilst sweet-meats were handed round and music was performed. There he was taught the elegance of manners, the refinement of conversational wit, which enabled him, later, to visit at the grandest houses, to attend princely and royal courts, and always appear perfectly at ease.

So far and not farther, did the rôle of parents go in the education of their offspring. In aristocratic families, boys were entrusted to a tutor, generally an abbot, whose task it was to prepare them for school, by teaching them the first rudiments of Latin, whose situation in the household was something between the *cavalier servente* and the lackey.

Goldoni, like most boys of his social standing, was

provided with tutors who taught him arithmetic, catechism, and Latin. Sooner or later every boy went to school, clerical schools generally, the Church having almost monopolised the so-called "humanities," and controlling the universities. Under their direction, the classical curriculum narrowed to little more than the trivium and quadrivium of earlier ages, but, on the other hand, it gained in consistency and unity. Centuries of civilisation, of unbroken peace, of religious formalism, of but half-concealed scepticism and dissipation created a special atmosphere in the Venetian society; centuries of classical training and undiscussed empirism created the moral and intellectual atmosphere of the Venetian schools, as indeed of most Italian schools.

The strength of their system was chiefly due to its narrowness, to its exclusiveness, which smothered all contradiction. Moreover there was no break of continuity of the several stages of education. From the first stammering of Latin verbs to the ceremonious granting of university degrees, all was directed by the same spirit. What value such a course of studies had in the development of intellect, in the formation of character, it is not necessary to consider in Goldoni's case, since his schooling was intermittent and he was such an indifferent pupil.

It is worth noting, in the much divided Italy of his time, that he could pass from one city to another, from one school to another, without any perplexing break, without finding any sudden change of direction.

When he was eight years old, according to his *Memoirs*, or eleven, according to late biographers, Carlino was sent to school. He tells us that the play composed by him and sent to his father suggested to Doctor Giulio this extraordinary reflection: "Reckoning on arithmetical principles, he said that if nine years gave four carats of wit, eighteen years must give twelve, and so on in arithmetical progression, until a fine degree of perfection." It is more likely that Doctor Goldoni being then in Perugia the medical adviser, or favoured protégé, of the Baglionis and the Antinoris — two of the greatest families of the city — he wanted his son to have a share in the advantages of his situation, and to get some better schooling than he could get at home. Carlino left home gaily, voyaged pleasantly to Rimini, then journeyed to Perugia, and finally entered the school directed by Dominican friars.

His first year at school was such as might be expected from a boy brought up by women and over-indulgent teachers. The youthful prodigy who boasted about the play he had written was chagrined that his comrades did their Latin exercises much better. Introduced as a pupil ripe for the higher form, he hardly managed to keep in the lower form. Instead of admiring him, as his teachers at home used to do, his comrades laughed at him. The school register for this year confirms this unlucky start, and also gives further evidence of Goldoni's method of adapting truth, when he tells his own history. These records show that, at the end of the year, Goldoni was not promoted to the higher form, but that, with three other boys out of threescore, he was kept in the lower form.

Yet in a preface first, and afterward in his *Memoirs*, he tells this pretty story, which is consistent with Goldoni's character. In the *Memoirs* he writes: "The end of the year was fast coming; we expected the Latin exercise which is called 'of promotion,' as it decides the passage to the upper form or retention in the lower form. I foresaw that the latter misfortune was likely to befall me. The day comes, the Regent dictates, the pupils write; everyone does his very best. I summon all my forces, I set before my mind's eye my ambition, my honour, my parents' wishes. I notice that my comrades are slyly eyeing me and laughing, *facit indignati versum.* I am pricked by shame and wrath; I read the theme, I feel my head cooling, my hand is steady, my memory in full activity. I am the first to finish the translation and to seal my paper. I give it to the Regent and depart well satisfied with myself."

The translation was all right, and the author of it complimented and promoted. But it all happened one year later. Goldoni accomplished the feat which, at every future crisis of his career, he is able to repeat. At every decisive moment, whenever his pride or his ambition is roused, his sense of obligation is stirred or his anger kindled, Goldoni thus responds. Under the lash of his will he accomplished greater things on other occasions. It is typical of him that he does not anticipate the crisis, nor realise the importance of the effort; he merely rejoices at its accomplishment.

In Goldoni's time holidays were long and frequent. Doctor Giulio made the most of them, in order to provide his son with short excursions, entertainments, which fill many pages of his *Memoirs*, after providing many pages of prefaces for his editors — with pretty anecdotes of doubtful authenticity, but undoubted attraction. These anecdotes are valuable for the information they furnish about the manners and customs of the time, but are not reliable information about the boy's doings.

As a reward for some promotion at school, Doctor Goldoni treated his son to that amusement *par excellence* of his time and nation — amateur theatricals. A powerful patron of his wanted coaxing, and Doctor Giulio, turning into a stage manager, set up the performance of Gerolamo Gigli's *Sorellina di don Pilone.*

His contempt of bigotry was evidenced in the choice of this play, the most daring attack then made against clericalism. It is most characteristic of the inefficiency of the Church's regulations that while, in Perugia, women were not allowed to act in the theatre, yet this anticlerical comedy was permitted, under the protection of the Baglioni escutcheon. Carlino was then a handsome boy and remained so until marred by the smallpox. In the female rôle of *la Sorellina*, he won a success not entirely due, as he claims, to his acting. He was also applauded when he delivered a prologue in verse probably written by Baglioni's aristocratic pen, so stuffed with the hyperboles and antitheses then popular that the remembrance of it amused him ever after.

On this occasion his father declared that he did not lack understanding, but would never be a good actor.

Margherita Goldoni, for her son's sake, endured the rough weather of Perugia, so different from the mild Venetian climate, and the uncouth manners of the Perugians, so different from her Venetian friends. "She suffered and grew so ill that we feared for her life; but still she overcame pain and danger, as long as she thought that it was good for me to stay in this city and finish my studies." When Carlino finished his course, and as at the same time the Baglioni-Antinori patronage declined, the whole family left Perugia.

The original plan was to leave Carlino in Rimini, in care of Dominican teachers, for his class of "philosophy," while his parents returned to Venice. But when the ship stopped at Chiozza, and the doctor discovered there some useful and willing patrons, they landed and settled there for some years. Doctor Giulio started a fair practice in the island, then far more prosperous than it is now.

Goldoni was seldom happy away from Venice. He was decidedly unhappy in dull Rimini, where his first experience was an attack of smallpox severe enough to disfigure his face for life. Goldoni's stay in Rimini was brief. His good luck provided him with a double incentive to leave, first a teacher more than usually dull, who could not conquer Goldoni's distaste for abstract logic and pedantic philosophy; then, as an additional motive for leaving, the pleasant temptation of a whole bevy of actresses.

Rimini being only indirectly under the rule of Rome, women were allowed to appear on the stage; the Riminise were spared the unpleasant spectacle of closely shaven men impersonating feminine characters. When Goldoni went behind the scenes at the theatre, he was welcomed by the actresses who, as it happened, were all Venetians and bound, after a short stay in Rimini, for Chioggia.

It was the opening of a new world to Goldoni, his first introduction to a class of people, to a manner of life, which answered so exactly to his own disposition that in spite of his disenchantment it always appealed to him. And how prettily he tells of his experience. His landing at Chioggia is almost as amusing as the trip on board the boat. His mother's welcome was what he expected, but his father, Doctor Giulio, who now saw all his plans for his son imperilled by a bit of imprudence, was disappointed. Goldoni charmingly describes the interview between father and son.

Despite the gaiety of the picture, it is evident that the Goldonis were displeased with their boy. By the favour of a patrician namesake, Marquis Goldoni Vidoni Aymi, then Governor of Pavia, Doctor Giulio next obtained his son's admission to the very exclusive Papal College of Ghisleri, a high favour coveted by young men of good families, as an excellent opening into an official career.

According to the Italian university plan, a young man could, while staying at the Collegio Ghisleri, attend any course of lessons he preferred. Goldoni intended to become a doctor of medicine. As a preparation for these studies, as a punishment for his escapade, or perhaps in hopes to keep him out of mischief, Doctor Giulio decided that he should begin a sort of medical apprenticeship. It was a singular idea. Carlino was to accompany his father on the daily round of visits, in order to learn the manners and language of a doctor, with a view to facilitating his knowledge of technical terms. This premature exposure to dangers and temptations beyond his age nearly resulted in disagreeable consequences, fortunately averted through the vigilance of his mother, who discovered the perilous intrigue prepared by a disreputable mother and daughter.

Goldoni showed no disposition for the career of a physician. His sympathetic nature could not endure the spectacle of either bodily or mental suffering.

The comedians had gone; Chioggia (Chiozza) offered no amusements. His attendance on his father's calls was irksome, he lost his habitual high spirits; that was more than enough to secure his mother's help, and to obtain from easy-going Doctor Giulio a radical change of plan. Without giving up his place at Ghislieri College, Carlino was inscribed for the study of law, so as to become an *avvocato*. In the meanwhile he would stay in Venice in a sort of apprenticeship. Signora Goldoni remembered that her uncle, Parlo Indric, was a lawyer. Thus Carlino spent a few hours daily in the "studio" of a Procuratore, and many more hours in discovering Venice.

Venice, the city of his heart, the abode of pleasure, the centre of intellectual life, answered to his deepest desires. Long, weary years later, as he describes these first impressions of Venice, *La Serenissima*, his awkward French becomes eloquent through retrospective emotion. It was love at first sight, and a lifelong passion. He never quitted Venice without a pang, he always returned to her with the exultation of a lover returning to his mistress. In later years this affection for Venice often reveals itself in unguarded moments.

Goldoni at college affords an amusing insight into contemporary student life. He was transformed into a little abbot — tonsure, little collar, certificates, and permissions by clerical authorities, which did not bind the students to the Church, but was enforced by the articles of the college, founded by Pope Ghisleri. This priestly garb was little more than a masquerade. Its adoption shows the persistence of formalism, and religious indifference.

On finding that Carlino was younger than the age of admittance, his father accomplished a miracle; Carlino went to bed only sixteen years old and he rose next morning full eighteen. Luxury and no restraint were the college customs. Students came and went almost as they pleased, provided they went out and returned in pairs. They parted company at the first street turning and went their ways, sometimes to the halls of learning, more often to fashionable resorts and social gatherings, and frequently to gambling houses and other undesirable places. When they came in too late at night, or singly, they paid hush money to a porter, who made more than a minister of state's salary out of these illegitimate profits.

College regulations also protected the students. The costly and gorgeous *sovrana* (cloak) worn by them, the *stola* fixed on their left shoulder and bearing in gold embroidery the keys of Saint Peter, which was the Ghisleri escutcheon, enforced respect for the spruce abbots who took advantage of their privileged position and behaved "like officers in a garrison." They visited the very best and the very worst resorts; they flirted, gambled, and fought duels; but they also cultivated the arts of a gentlemanly education. They practised fencing, music, painting, as well as games of cards and dice.

Goldoni's amiable manners received here a polish, even while license and bad example got him into some scrapes. First he was entrapped into a disgraceful expedition. On being discovered he committed the unpardonable mistake of betraying the names of his accomplices, thus ensuring for himself enemies. These decoyed him into a compromising situation which resulted in his banishment from college, which is thus recorded in the archives of the establishment, at the date 1726: "*Propter satiricam poesim fuit evictus.*" He now relinquished his legal studies, but resumed them, first in Udine, under the celebrated Morelli, then again in Modena, and finally in Padua, where he secured his degree.

Goldoni travelled much. In 1726 travelling was not the monotonous affair it has since become, but required exertion and courage, because of banditti and the many other dangers of the road. Post chaise and stage coaches were liable to get overturned or to stop at inconvenient places, inns were crowded or scantily stocked with food. The traveller who could make himself useful and agreeable to his companions, who was cheerful and good-tempered, could find much pleasure in a journey, and Goldoni not only possessed all these requisites, but also knew how charmingly to describe his adventures and perhaps sometimes to invent them.

Whenever Goldoni was asked to write a preface or a poem, he fetched from his memory or his imagination some anecdote, he turned it into a pleasant little picture, a lively scene wherein he managed to play a rôle, and, since he was not on oath and harmed no one, he spoke just that proportion of truth which his sense of art required. These spontaneous pictures are charming sketches. If they are not absolutely true, they are perhaps even more interesting as imaginative creations and elaborations.

His first leaving home, his first ride along the hilly roads from Rimini to Perugia, his first experience with a horse, was a startling experience for any Venetian boy, who could have seen little more than the bronze horses of St. Mark. A trip in *burchiello*, the long flat boat enthusiastically described by Président des Brosses, makes a pretty picture of customs. He describes the luxurious and comfortable barge with its carved wood furniture, its padded couches, its many windows and sculptures, and the delightful company. As the barge containing, besides our Goldoni, the Venetian ambassador's secretary and other persons of his household, glides along the Po, it is a perpetual round of concerts, dances, suppers that marks its passage. Everyone on board plays on some instrument or sings; and Goldoni's, the young poet's, share is to chronicle all these adventures day by day in rhyme.

He gives scant information about the places he visits, he has no eye, no sympathy, for that which is not Venetian. His account of a trip in Carinzia and in Friuli, as in later times his descriptions of Paris, is superficial. Outside of his Venetian world, he even loses his facility for reading a character, and interpreting ways and manners, but that which appeals to him he describes delightfully. Naturally during these trips he has many love affairs, which he tells with a reticence that bears evidence to his good taste, besides discovering his consideration for the only woman he ever really loved — his wife, who was his secretary and amanuensis in writing his *Memoirs*.

In his relations with women Goldoni is of his time and of his class. Fine letters and arts and social life made a throne for woman, and paid her homage. She was the incensed idol, extolled in verse and prose, saluted with compliment and flattery, her power was exerted in intrigues, and her occult influence felt in public as in private affairs; yet woman was denied the simplest and most natural of rights. The right of fair play was reserved to the stronger and ruder sex. To abuse her innocence or to make dishonourable profit out of her weakness was a petty sin that did not discredit a man.

Goldoni, always a devoted son and a kind husband, a model of honesty in his dealings with men, is, according to his own account, not above suspicion of levity in his behaviour with women. If the stories he tells about himself are not exactly true, they are consistent with what he thought to be becoming and creditable. His flirtations with actresses are of little consequence. Goldoni was at first a toy in their pretty hands, and when he became an important person, the man who could give a rôle, he in turn toyed with their petty vanities and rivalries.

His adventures outside the theatre are more characteristic. One of the most typical is to be found in the first part of his *Memoirs*. He was staying in Udine — reading for the law — when he noticed a pretty girl; he followed her to church, obtained the favour of some sly glances, and was further encouraged by the offer of the young lady's maid to carry messages and presents. He wrote love letters, he sent presents, at night he sighed under a closed window and was rewarded by a glimpse of a little head half concealed in a cap, and a merry laugh, half smothered by the closing of a casement. His pride in his conquest is, however, soon crushed; he discovers that the chambermaid, and not the lady, has got both presents and love letters. Goldoni has excuse for being angry, but his manner of revenge is not creditable.

Goldoni's excuse for thus using the women of his time is that they were usually worthy of little regard. Without adopting a Casanova's standard of feminine virtue, in Venice, and especially in Venetian convents, one must recognise that those women who, since they had adopted the religious vows of seclusion and chastity and had solemnly promised to direct and protect young girls, should have set an example of modesty, nevertheless lacked even common honesty. Président des Brosses talks much about their musical skill and their pretty costume. Goldoni supplies an anecdote that is a revelation of the influence of nuns.

In Chioggia (Chiozza) he frequently visited a convent in which the *parlatorio* was probably one of the most lively resorts of the town. Goldoni saw there a young *pensionnaire* and fell in love. The Mother Abbess smiled on this courtship; she promised to manage things for the best. A little while later Goldoni perceives a change, the young lady cannot be seen. He complains to the "Mother," likely the real mother, and he gets the most extraordinary answer. The world-wise abbess says that the guardian has decided himself to marry the young lady; but "as a young wife is likely to shorten the days of an aged husband you will soon have a rich widow who has only been a wife in name — trust me to keep watch over her, I give you my word of honour." Never was "word of honour" more extraordinary. It is terribly significant, the more so as Goldoni is not an anti-clerical.

Never in his plays, rarely in the *Memoirs*, does he describe clericals. The friar he met on board the boat that brought him home, after his eviction from the Collegio Ghisleri, is one of the few. If loyalty to his own training by clericals had not prevented him, he could have described much and most interestingly. Possibly fear of the censor restrained him.

There is only one episode in his life in which a religious terror played an important part. It betrays a strange spiritual condition. His father had sent him to Modena, to pursue those endless studies, also with the intent of recovering certain rights of Modenese citizenship which the Goldonis never entirely relinquished. Goldoni was apprenticed to a lawyer, *il notaio* Zavarisi, who assisted him in the reëstablishment of his family in Modena in their ancient position.

A recent edict, issued by the Duke of Modena, raised the tax which absentees were made to pay. Goldoni by taking his abode in Modena could have obtained exemption from this tax. Strangely enough, Doctor Goldoni, though a thorough Venetian, was also a citizen of Modena, and managed to retain a double citizenship, almost a double nationality, so that his son might have the choice. Goldoni, like his father, always paid the Modenese tax on absentees and rendered some sort of verbal homage to the Duke of Modena; but to stay in that dull and bigoted city was beyond even the power of his filial obedience. Yet he went there and entered the legal office of his relative and friend, Zavarisi. But he also got into a nest of bigots. Bastia, the captain of the boat that carried him to Modena, ordered all on board to say their beads before going to bed, and to sing litanies every day. In Modena Goldoni lodged with this Bastia, and was persuaded to join in the psalm-singing and church-going, and seemed for a time under deep religious impression, when a shocking event drove him out of Modena.

On the public Piazza, surrounded by all the impressive array of such terrible spectacles, he saw a man [1] in the pillory cross-examined and tortured by a priest and his acolytes. The degradation, the humiliation, and the pain endured by the man, who was only guilty of indiscreet speech, so shocked Goldoni that he fled in terror. He could neither think nor talk of anything else. He trembled for his own salvation, fell into morbid depression, and spoke of entering a convent, to expiate his sins and to avoid temptation.

Prudent Doctor Giulio, far from opposing this religious frenzy, promised to consider the matter, and invited his son to Venice, in order that the religious authorities there might be informed of his plans. The

[1] Von Lohner supposes this man to have been Gio. Battista Vicini the poet.

wind that blew on the shores of Venice, on the sunny Piazzetta, on the Campiello, soon blew away Goldoni's vocation for the cloister, and even that thin veneer of mysticism adopted by contagion in Modena.

He was twenty in 1727, and as a return to Modena was out of the question, Doctor Giulio resolved that it was time for his son to secure "an honourable and remunerative place that should cost nothing." Through his influence, Goldoni was appointed "*Aggiunto del Coadgiutore, dipendente dalla Cancelleria Criminale.*" It was the lowest place in the magistracy, but a pleasant situation. Board and lodging at the governor's house, besides dinner parties, concerts, and plays were included, but no salary was attached to the position.

Goldoni records with pride how he toiled at his desk, how zealously he fulfilled his official duties. His business being to examine the suspected culprits, he fully realised that it is the examiner's duty to reconcile the demands of justice with the pity due to the offender, but he says not one word of how in order to accomplish this examination he was forced to apply torture. But the engraving which adorns the first page of the volume shows Goldoni at his desk, and in front of him a man whose hands are tied behind his back to the rope that hangs from the ceiling. In the background the assistant is seen standing by the torture wheel. In a private letter Goldoni confesses that "at first it was painful to interrogate a man just released from the rope"; but in time he grew accustomed to the thing. When Goldoni's immediate superior, the chancellor, was transferred to Feltre he offered to take Goldoni with him as *Coadgiutore*. More work and more responsibility, but also more honour.

In contrast with the dark pictures of Venetian justice, so often presented, one should read Goldoni's account of his expedition to a village where some crime was to be investigated. A party of twelve persons walking gaily along shaded roads and flowered paths, in the low, fruitful country, stopping at hospitable convents or village inns, drinking milk at cosy farms, singing blithely as they marched through village streets, and rehearsing comedies and even tragedies wherever they could raise anything like a stage.

Goldoni's career was once more arrested by circumstances beyond his control. His father, Doctor Giulio, seemed to have settled permanently in the quiet little city of Bagnocavallo, when he suddenly fell ill, and died peacefully in the arms of his wife and son. Goldoni dried his own and his mother's tears, and accompanied her back to Venice. During the journey, Signora Goldoni entreated him to give up his actual career, complete his legal studies, and obtain the title of *avvocato* in Venice. The magic title of Venetian lawyer answered to the ambition of middle-class parents, it bridged the distance between them and aristocracy, it also promised financial advantages.

The promising magistrate was once more transformed into a student preparing for his final examination in the Venetian university of Padua. Things were so cleverly managed that the usual long course of study was shortened into a few months' coaching. The chapters describing his preparation and his passage through his examination form a series of Goldonian sketches unparalleled in his plays. A great deal of amusement and even more sound information may be got from this truthful picture.

It contains several portraits. First Signor Radi, a teacher who coached the pupils supposed to be studying in Padua, where they put in an appearance, four times a year, just to obtain the required certificates. Though he had plenty of pupils Signor Radi's irresistible propensity for gambling kept him in perpetual poverty, his own pupils winning from him at cards the price of their lessons. Indeed on the very eve of his examination, Goldoni was persuaded to spend most of the day and the whole night gambling. When called to put on the robe and cap, Goldoni rose from his cards and proceeded straight to the hall, where the areopagus of professors sat in judgment.

In order to gain admittance to the bar, Goldoni should have practised two years in the office of a barrister, yet as early as March, 1732, Goldoni was presented at the *Palazzo*. This presentation is a landmark in his life, the crowning of his youthful ambition, the conquest of a title he held in the greatest honour. As he fulfilled the rites of the ceremonial, standing between two colleagues at the foot of the Giants' Stair, bowing so low and so often that his ample wig was tossed about like a lion's mane, we may be sure that in his elation he had forgotten the theatre.

Immediately after this solemn introduction to his new dignity he was offered the opportunity of seeing quite the opposite aspect of his profession. A woman, all dimples and smiles, with flashing jewellery and in gay dress, approached him one day, and after complimenting him on his appearance offered her influence to facilitate his first steps. She was born and bred in the palace, she said, her father having made his living by listening at doors, and carrying the first news of the magistrate's decision to the parties. She followed the same practice; and, knowing everyone and known by everybody, she could bring customers to lawyers who wanted them. Goldoni smiled, and dismissed the woman.

Of the many qualities required for the successful barrister he possessed the two rarest and most difficult to attain, charm and entire honesty. For the less brilliant part of an *avvocato's* work, the preparation of briefs, he was also gifted, as he showed a few years later in Pisa. Yet his début in Venice was not successful. Few persons found their way to his office, and those who came did not pay him for his advice. Far from providing for his mother, he was supported by her, getting into debt. He tells a vague story of an intrigue and broken marriage, which reads like a scenario for improvised comedy; he gives several reasons to account for his sudden departure, and slips, as lightly as he can, over the only true one, which is also the most honourable.

CHAPTER III

LIFE OF GOLDONI, 1732 TO 1747

Goldoni leaves Venice 1732 — his extravagant habits — becomes a playwright and goes to Milan — burns *Amalasunta* after its refusal 1733 — enters Venetian diplomatic service in Milan — sees battle between Sards and Austrians — intrigue with an adventuress — influence of the charlatan Bonafede Vitali on Goldoni — Casali orders a play — Goldoni meets the Imer troupe in Verona — his play *Belisario* is accepted and he is engaged as playwright for Grimani's theatre in Venice 1734 — in love with actress "la Passalaqua" — meets and marries Nicoletta Connio of Genoa — attack of smallpox on honeymoon — his comedians are his models as well as his interpreters — from them he learned much — becomes Genoese Consul in Venice 1740 — consulship comes to sudden end 1743 — Goldoni's wanderings over Italy — visits Florence — begins practice of law in Pisa — praises Perfetti's extempore poetry 1744 — admitted to Pisan colony of Arcadia — engages to write a play for actor Darbes — meets Medebach troupe.

It was a fateful moment for Goldoni when by one decision he relinquished his career as a lawyer and also left Venice. And in spite of his affectation of indifference in his account of this decisive moment he was conscious of its gravity, yet courageous and hopeful for the future. There is no hint of the bitter disappointment which was to follow. Evidently he would not have left Venice, his mother, and his position at the bar if the prospect in Milan had not been attractive.

Goldoni disguises his real motive because he shares,

with the writers of his time, the foolish idea that the poet is disgracing himself and his art when he wishes to make his living out of his work. He will not confess that he conceived the idea of writing a tragedy, and of having it performed in Milan, the moment when it was suggested to him. Zeno,[1] Metastasio,[2] and other poets had made money in Vienna, and now even

[1] Apostolo Zeno, 1668–1730, has an honourable place among historians and scholars. He was a precursor of Muratori, pioneer investigator and interpretator of documents; he was also a *collectionneur*. To Goldoni he most opportunely gave that which Goldoni calls "*des corrections muettes*." The anecdote is to be found in *Mem.* i, ch. xli. Goldoni wrote a lyrical tragedy bearing the title "Gustavo Wasa" and carried it to Zeno "lately returned from Vienna," where "Metastasio remained as his successor." "I found this worthy scholar (Zeno) in his studio; he welcomed me politely, listened to the reading of my play without uttering a word. . . After finishing I asked his opinion. 'It is good,' said he, 'for the fair of la Senza.'" Goldoni understood that the manuscript was pronounced only good for popular festivities. Zeno wrote about sixty dramas and twenty oratorios, all now forgotten, though they exerted a powerful influence on the evolution of the Italian theatre. He founded the "Giornale de Letterati d'Italia," which lasted from 1710 to 1718.

[2] Pietro Metastasio, 1698–1782: His great fame influenced Goldoni's career. Like Goldoni he was born in the *petite bourgeoisie*, like Goldoni he read for the law and held office, and was admitted into Arcadia. "Artino Corasio": His fame was European until fashion turned and ridiculed his sentimental compositions; but now the pathos and metrical form of his lyrical dramas, the sweet cadence of his shorter poems, are again admired. (See Vernon Lee's, E. Masi's, and O. Tommasini's studies.)

Goldoni says in his *Memoirs*, part i, chap. xxi, "The operas of Metastasio were then performed everywhere, even without any music"; and in another chapter (xli) he extravagantly praises his work. To Metastasio Goldoni reverently dedicated his play, obtaining in return this handsome acknowledgment: ". . . your friendship is such a gift that it is accepted with joy at whatever title it is offered." For an analysis of Metastasio's works see Stendhal, *La Vie de Metastasio*. Carducci has also praised Metastasio. *I Corifei della Canzonetta nel Secolo XVI*, vol. xviii, in *Antologia di Critica Letterari Moderna*.

Pariati [1] and other writers, whom posterity has forgotten, were achieving fame and fortune by producing *dramma lirico* and *dramma musicale.* Goldoni felt that he could do at least as well, and he needed the money.

All his mother's tenderness could not disguise that he was draining her scanty income; all his affection for her could not restrain him from extravagant habits and gambling. He resolved to turn a new leaf. His decision did him credit. Yet in his *Memoirs* he disguises both the earnestness of his purpose and the reasons for it. To account for his departure he tells a probably fictitious little story of a foolish love entanglement, a breach of promise.

To obtain his mother's consent he may have given some such reason; and with her, "*toutes mes raisons étoient bonnes.*" [2] Signora Goldoni was not only a fond mother, she was a Venetian bourgeoise, hence ready to recognise the right of the man in the family to have his

[1] Pietro Pariati, a native of Reggio, driven from his native city by the persecution of Rinaldo d'Este, came to Venice in 1699, thence to Vienna, where he was the only court poet until Zeno joined him.

[2] *Mem.*, part i, chap. xxvi: "I lacked the means for settling and keeping house. . . . I explained matters to my mother; she realised with overflowing eyes that some energetic measure was required to save me from ruin (allusion to an almost incredible story of entanglement). She mortgaged her estate in order to pay my debts in Venice. I transferred to her my estate in Modena for her wants and I resolved to leave. . . . After my most flattering début at the Palace (of Justice) in the midst of my success at the bar, I leave my country, my relatives, my paramours, my expectations, my position; I leave and only stop at Padua. The first step was over, the others cost me nothing, thanks to my happy disposition, with the exception of my mother I forgot everything."

will. After obeying her father-in-law, she submitted to her husband, and now she accepted the rule of her eldest son. Goldoni was ready to answer every objection. He allowed her to pay off some small debts, and he stopped any possible remonstrance by telling her how he had, previously, for her sake, given up his position at Feltre, and by promising her an ample share of the profit he was sure to make.

Goldoni was elated with great expectations and ambitions, which took form and direction during the weary hours when waiting for the clients who did not come. During the pleasant hours spent in the Venetian coffee houses, round the tables of *tresset*, where the news of the world and theatrical gossip were current, he could feel the pressure of growing debts and of his mother's anxiety, all tending to show the empty value of the proud title *avvocato*. He will not live at his mother's expense, yet as long as he stays in Venice he must gamble and spend more than he can afford.

While he was in Collegio Ghisleri and during his apprenticeship at the Chancellery, Goldoni fell into habits of extravagance which in Venice it was especially difficult to reform. It was easier to sever all past associations and tear himself away. Afterwards he says and perhaps believes that his dramatic vocation was always imperative, but the fact is he turned to playwriting at the moment when his prospects were darkest and playwriting was yielding glory and gold for others.

Venice was a hive of literary gossip. In the *ridotto*, the book shops, and the *botteghe* Goldoni heard much talk about the latest theatrical performances. He was certain that he could accomplish what so many others were doing. He ignored difficulties; his superficial stage technique was to him no obstacle. He writes facile rhymes, he can stage amateur performances and arrange the play to the taste of the audience, he has been behind the scenes, and chatted with actors and made love to a *servetta* and perhaps a *primadonna*, he is always welcome; why should he not write plays? Besides, he carries with him the manuscript of a tragedy — or drama — that, if turned into an opera, he is sure to sell to some Milanese theatre manager.

The choice of Milan for a début was ambitious, but not unwise. The city was munificent, an important centre of business, its theatregoers less fastidious than Venetians; furthermore Goldoni was provided with credentials. The Venetian Resident Minister was on his list, and there were others, a superintendent of the theatres, a celebrated ballet dancer, and of course churchmen. Goldoni took all precautions.

So off he went,[1] but not straight to Milan. There were visits to pay along the road, more letters of introduction to obtain, and more approval of his tragedy, the manuscript being always at hand for a reading, if only a listener could be discovered. With

[1] For date of departure see preface to vol. x, Pasquali Edition. "After eight months of my reception," May 20, 1732. Hence toward the end of the same year.

Parmenione Trissino[1] the stay was long enough to admit of some discouraging criticism, which Goldoni perhaps interpreted as the effect of jealousy, Trissino being better known for his illustrious name than for his own literary productions.

Goldoni did not succeed at first, probably his work was not such as the ruling taste then required. He lacked the practical knowledge, the technique which he afterward acquired. Hence his disappointment at failure was bitter. With much humour and less of his habitual benevolence, Goldoni describes the reading of his tragedy.

Caffariello, the celebrated soprano, stands up and modulates in his silvery voice the title *Amalasunta*, and pronounces it long and unmusical, whilst another "soprano," a wizened little monkey, sings out "*de sa voix de chat*" that the *dramatis personæ* are too many. Signora Grossatesta, the mistress of the house, Count Prata, the most influential and the only learned person in the room, both try to obtain silence, and the reader begins. He is ill at ease, he feels the hostility of his hearers and loses heart. Somehow he gets to the end and is saluted by a shower of adverse criticisms. Count Prata speaks as a theatre manager and warns Goldoni that each one of the principal rôles must be given an appropriate number of airs, a just proportion of duets, that the secondary rôles must be restricted in their opportunities, the *arie di bravura* must come close after the pathetic *andante*, and so on.

[1] See note on Parmenione Trissino.

All the petty devices and contrivances which then fettered the steps of the opera are mentioned.

Goldoni, crushed by the failure of his cherished plan, maddened by the buzzing of such nonsense, rushed in despair to his own room and flung the manuscript into the fire. He had left Venice without thought of return; he could not now fall back on his mother, nor could he remain in Milan without funds. He sat staring into the blaze which his manuscript lighted, the prospect was as gloomy as possible; yet when nothing remained but a little heap of ashes he thought out a plan.

With morning came courage and, a true Venetian, he turned for help to his countryman. Senator Bartolini, the Venetian Resident, appreciated pluck, and knew a good story when told him. He laughed at Goldoni's mishap, enjoyed his unaffected ways, perceived his sterling qualities, and immediately offered him the place of private secretary, which was little more than an usher, a sort of confidential attendant. But as this provided Goldoni with board and lodging, also with small wages, he was perforce satisfied.

It is difficult to determine from Goldoni's account the character of his diplomatic service in this Venetian Embassy. The contemporary presence in Milan of two representatives of the *Serenissima*, with slight difference in their title, each directed to keep the Senate informed of the doings of the other, besides keeping in touch with the Milanese State, explains how Senator Bartolini found it useful to have two private secretaries,[1] the official one and the non-official, Goldoni.

Goldoni's incomplete account of events is unsatisfactory. His dates are wrong; his records of the movements of troops, sieges, or other incidents of the war then in progress are inaccurate. Goldoni was not interested in his work, except in so far as it afforded him a living. Even when promoted to a more responsible position, his heart was not in his task. He had no gift for diplomacy and was not interested in the succession of wars that left Venice untouched; like most Italians of his times he was only a spectator in the fight.

He witnessed a battle,[2] either in 1733 or in 1734, between the Sards and the Austrians near Parma; his curiosity took him to the city walls and he objects to the smoke which clouded the "rare spectacle he would otherwise have enjoyed"! Goldoni's slight French

[1] The *Memoirs* record: "This Minister was not the only one in charge. Another man was sent from Venice at the same time, in the same city, a Senator bearing the title of Provveditore Straordinario; both vying in efforts for getting information and for sending to the Senate the surest and latest news (*Mem.*, part i, chap. xxi). The Minister took advantage of this opportunity for dismissing his Secretary whom he disliked and entrusting me with this commission . . . (*Memoirs*, part i, chap. xxxi). We got every day some ten or twelve letters and sometimes even twenty. . . . It was my duty to read them, to make extracts, and out of them to compose an official despatch, grounded on the intelligence that seemed most reliable. . . ."

Goldoni records with satisfaction that in these occupations he acquired much knowledge "diplomatic and political," knowledge which he found most useful later for his consulship.

[2] The war alluded to was fought by Carlo Emanuele of Sardinia (the title then of the House of Savoy, allied to Louis XIV of France) against Emperor Charles VI. See Muratori, *Annali d'Italia*, vii, page 379. Venice, 1848.

hardly excuses here the verb *jouir*. He languidly describes the battlefield, as he visited it on the day after the combat. He is disgusted with the heap of naked bodies, and there are limbs and skulls scattered about; but he complacently records how tons of lime were scattered over this offensive display to prevent infection.

He describes with more warmth his mission "*en qualité d'espion honorable*," which seems to mean a sort of attaché, to the camp of the Allies, and was invited to partake in the pleasures of an armistice. These half-hearted occupations were not sufficient to occupy Goldoni's restlessness. He was sure to get into scrapes, when he searched for congenial diversions. Dissipation in Milan was more dangerous than in Venice, and Goldoni's footing less secure. Cards were the principal danger.[1] This was not the sort of play practised in Venetian drawing-rooms, in the intervals of conversation, but real gambling, in very mixed company. Goldoni was incurable, though more than once decoyed and cheated.

He also narrates in his *Memoirs* [2] an intrigue with an

[1] For card playing in Venice, see analysis of *Il Giuocatore*. Several anecdotes in the *Memoirs* make amusing pictures of customs, yet they should be accepted with caution. Goldoni first told them to amuse his readers in various prefaces, then selected them to pad his volumes of *Memoirs*. See for instance part i, chap. xxi, a narrative of journey from Feltre to Bagnacavallo (page 128, original text).

[2] The story of this entanglement with "a young and pretty Venetian" fills many pages of the *Memoirs*, chaps. xxx, xxxiii, xxxiv, but seems not to have deeply affected Goldoni's heart, though possibly the signora is in some degree responsible for his dismissal. Any other such incident might have caused the same result. Goldoni wanted only an excuse.

adventuress, attended by a most disreputable uncle or protector, which cost him trouble and money, and was finally the cause of his release from his diplomatic bondage. His story, unsupported by documentary evidence, reads like an invention to explain his departure from Milan, which many other causes must have prepared. He relates that, Senator Bartolini having ordered him to copy an important secret diplomatic document, he made his copy, locked it in his desk, and went out to supper with his lady-love and a party of gay companions. He remained at the card table, or otherwise, all night, and on returning home in the morning he found that the angry and suspicious Senator had been sending repeatedly to his rooms, asking for the secret document and the copy. Goldoni was reprimanded, lost his temper, was threatened with punishment, and fled for refuge to the archbishop's palace. Bartolini recognised that his secretary was guilty of nothing worse than dissipation; Goldoni was satisfied, but he insisted on leaving.[1]

[1] "On coming home, I met one of the Resident's servants. They had been asking for me everywhere. The Resident had been up since five in the morning, having sent for me. He had been told that I had been out all night. He was very angry. I run to my room, take both the folios, and bring them to the Minister. He receives me ungraciously. He even suspects me of having shown the King of Sardinia's Manifesto to the Provveditore Straordinario of the Venetian Republic. This charge offends me, and grieves me. I lose my temper — a most unusual weakness in me. The Minister threatens to have me apprehended. I hurry out of the place. I go straight to seek asylum with the Bishop of the city. The Bishop takes my part, and offers to make my peace with the Resident. I thank him, but I had made up my mind. I only wanted to be justified and to depart" (*Memoirs*, I, chap. xxxii).

Investigations made by Goldonians fail to identify the secret document, cause of this incident. Probably Goldoni invented this anecdote, as a picturesque conclusion of his diplomatic experience, rather than confess his determination to try once more his fortune as a playwright.

Even in the first months of his stay in Milan, Goldoni met a person that was to exert much influence on his evolution. Bonafede Vitali [1] was a representative of old times, yet was he also a precursor of the new order; he links up past traditions with modern methods of advertisement. He was a scholar and had obtained degrees and diplomas from Canterbury, Palermo, and Catania universities. An able physician, he had cured Marshal Schomberg and other great men and had conquered a violent epidemic in Parma. A traveller, too, who had visited almost every country of Europe, and spoke almost every European language. Just then, Bonafede Vitali was exerting in Milan, with great profit and honour, the difficult profession of a charlatan. Famous under the name of l'Anonimo, he attracted immense crowds round the raised platform where he stood, attended by several masked assistants, and was ready to answer any question that was put to him on any subject, ready to sell pills and

[1] "His name was Bonafede Vitali, from the city of Parma; he went under the name of the Anonym. He belonged to a good family" (*Memoirs*, part i, chap. xxix). For B. Vit. see in "Numero Unico, Carlo Goldoni" a paper by A. D'Ancona, "Una Macchietta Goldoniana" (Venice, 1883), also "Biografia degli Italiani illustri di E. di Tipaldo, Venezia," 1837, pp. 292–299.

liniments for any disease. Men of learning and reputation did not disdain to probe his cyclopedian knowledge or to enlarge their own. Goldoni asserts that to every paper sent up to him Vitali gave an answer and as often as not disserted at length on the topic started, whether in literature, science, history, or mathematics.

This man, whom Goldoni admired for his learning, was also stage manager and director of an itinerant troupe of comedians. Imitating a time-honoured practice, Bonafede Vitali advertised the sale of his drugs by having the four masks of the "*commedia dell'arte*" on parade with him on the platform, assisting him in handing down boxes and phials, and catching the *soldi* thrown into the same kerchiefs. The *lazzi* and pranks of the masks filled the intervals of his learned speeches and attracted a crowd of spectators and customers. In the evening, the same comedians performed short plays by the light "of white wax candles." The luxury of white wax added a finishing touch to the prestige of the spectacle.

This was indeed a revival of the oldest forms of comedy, a return to methods that were fundamental; it brought artists into close contact with their audience, which was not merely a reminiscence of the past but an indication for the future.

Did Goldoni realise all that Bonafede Vitali's system represented? Not entirely, and not clearly, though he certainly learned something. He saw with his own eyes the good effects of an able and illuminated direction inspiring the actors to higher efforts; he realised also that comedy, though different, was not inferior to tragedy, and he may have felt encouraged to pursue a course that Bonafede Vitali did not disdain. Goldoni, being so attracted by his new friend, offered to assist him in securing the theatre for a season. He was rewarded with a front box at the spectacle and also with the favour of free admittance behind the scenes.

Vitali asked him to write a short intermezzo, which was performed with some success in this year 1733. The comedians with whom Goldoni mixed were among the best of the time; Casali played the rôle of *amoroso*, Rubini was the *Pantalone*. They encouraged him with several proposals, and Casali asked for a tragi-comedy, and offered to pay for it.[1]

On leaving Milan, Goldoni, after some wandering, finally alighted in the Arena of Verona,[2] just when Casali was stepping out from the curtain to deliver a speech to the audience. Was it a providential ac-

[1] For Casali, Rubini, and indeed for every actor mentioned see Luigi Rasi, *op. cit.* In preface to vol. xiii of Pasquali's edition, Goldoni says that Casali "was an honourable gentleman, endowed with great cleverness and professional ability, a fine figure and face, a pleasant voice and beautiful pronunciation."

[2] Goldini in his *Memoirs* (see part i, chap. xxxiv) mentions that the ancient Arena, "a Roman monument, whether of the Trajan or Domitian times one cannot tell," was still so well preserved that it was used as a theatre just as it was "in the first time of its building." This statement is not accurate. The arena was reduced to smaller proportions and more practical use by the erection in its midst of a raised platform, wooden wings, etc. An engraving of this Veronese theatre may be seen in the reproduction of vol. xii of Pasquali's edition, or in the splendid new edition of Venice. A description of such arrangements is in the well-informed volumes of L. Rasi, "I Comici Italiani," *op. cit.*, I, 590.

cident, as the *Memoirs* relate? Or was it the result of some previous arrangement, this meeting with Casali, and Goldoni's introduction to the whole troupe, then under the direction of Imer,[1] and in the pay of His Excellency Grimani? [2]

His description of the scene should be read in full. Of course he had the manuscript of a tragi-comedy in his pocket, the *Belisario* Casali had suggested. Of course, he was willing to read it, and his host was eager to hear it. Casali seized the manuscript and claimed it as his property. Imer was almost as eager to make another offer, and Goldoni was even more eager to be engaged.

This *Belisario* holds a small place in the history of

[1] Imer, see *Memoirs*, part i, chap. xxiv. Goldoni represents Imer as an artist who could conquer nature. He was successful both as a manager of this Grimani troupe and as actor and singer. "With his short, thick neck, his small eyes and turned-up nose, he was ridiculous in serious parts . . . ." Imer "knowing no music could sing well enough; he learned his part by heart, caught the intonation and time, and made up for his lack of knowledge and of voice by his ability in counterfeiting, by the funny style of his dress and his impersonation of characters" (Preface to vol. xiii, ed. Pasquali).

[2] One Grimani Gian Pietro was Doge of Venice from 1741 to 1751, viz., the decisive moment when Venice by adopting the policy of neutrality lost the chance of asserting her rights in the wars of succession of Austria after the death of Maria Theresa.

Goldoni's Grimani was Michele, a patrician and a Senator, the owner of two theatres, San Moise and San Giovanni Grisostomo. Goldoni says in his *Memoirs*, part i, chap. xxxiv: "Sr. Grimani was the most polite man of the world; he had none of that haughtiness which wrongs the great and humbles the poor. By birth illustrious, by his talents esteemed, he only wanted to be loved; his kindness captivated every heart." It was said that Goldoni represented him in *Il Prodigo* under the character of easy-going, imprudent *Momolo*.

Goldoni's plays, but in the evolution of his personality this admittance within the circle of professionals, this first engagement as an author are decisive. Goldoni has finally found the profession which satisfies his dearest wishes; he can reconcile his desire of financial independence with his thirst for amusement. He mixes with people he likes, and who like him.

His Excellency Grimani, the owner of the San Samuele theatre, was not an exacting employer. Goldoni says that he was delightfully free from the supercilious hauteur "which lowers the great and humiliates the humble"; he further immortalizes the kindness of this debonaire (*Il Prodigo*) patrician by taking him as a model for his *Momolo sulla Brenta.* How gladly Goldoni followed the actors to Venice! How gladly he began work for them! He accepts any job that is offered, even the cobbling of other author's plays. He makes a funny little anecdote out of his collaboration with a red-haired abbot, the musician Vivaldi, and their rearrangement of an opera by Pariati and Zeno.

He proudly records that at this moment he was writing tragedy, comedy, and opera. He is in Venice; though he does not live under the same roof, he sees his mother frequently. If there had been some misunderstanding or disappointment when he left Venice for Milan, it was fully explained, and Goldoni conquered once more that place in the family which a real Venetian bourgeois held dearer than public office. Relatives such as the highly honourable Paolo Indric were probably shocked at Goldoni's sudden exit from Venice, and more offended when they heard of his engagement with the comedians. Signora Goldoni did not want her darling son to remain under a cloud, so she arranged a little dinner party for his home-coming; a gathering of all the wiseacres and prosperous members of their family. Then it was Goldoni's turn to win back their favour by the amusing tales of his adventures. He confesses that he added to and transformed the stories he had already told to his mother, so that the dear lady, with tears of joy and pride, will ask the hero for explanation; she laughs, she weeps, she exclaims: "You little rogue, this thing you never told me!" More than enough to conquer the diffidence of relatives, who smiled on the prodigal son and his mother.[1]

Also he enjoys his life with the comedians. Actresses exert on him an attraction which is not altogether sensual. Even his fragmentary account reveals that his artistic sense is so closely inwrought with his affections that he can hardly tell whether he is in love with the woman, or with the interpreter of his creation. Goldoni is no slave of passion, though he enjoys the fluttering of Cupid's wings. He is fast cooling down

[1] For this influence of relatives over Goldoni's career, and indeed over that of every other man in Venice, in the eighteenth century, see the whole of Goldoni's works and pictures of customs; in Gaspare Gozzi's essays, in Nievo's novel, in every document of the time.

For Goldoni's family see the notes by Ehrman von Löhner: Modena, etc., *op. cit.*, also an essay by Lazzari in "Rivista d'Italia," Roma, Feb., 1907: "Il Padre di Goldoni." Also "Fogli Sparsi del Goldoni" by A. G. Spinelli.

into an amiable man who has a kind word for everybody, a pretty compliment for every woman, who winks at petty contrivances, and listens to confidences, but longs for a quiet marriage and a peaceful home.

He was ripe for marriage, his only fear being to fall the prey of one unworthy to be his mother's companion. He does not conceive marrying as a personal affair, that was not the standard of his time; he thinks of marrying, in order to settle down in happy and respectable obscurity. He is ripe for this crisis because he has fortunately escaped several dangers. The stories he told his mother on first coming home were not so improper that they could not be printed, with a few omissions and corrections. His sentimental apprenticeship was over; he could look back with amusement on passed perils.

In Feltre, when he was there in the quality of a magistrate with the prospect of advancement and the halo of social glory, Goldoni had loved a young lady of good family. He noticed, however, that the little thing was fragile. He learned that her sister had faded away after her first baby, and he feared a sickly wife. Then the girl, "whom I loved with all my heart," had disliked the theatre; worse still, she was jealous, and wept when Goldoni played his rôle and received the compli-

[1] Some of Goldoni's biographers have recorded all the love passages he relates in his *Memoirs*. Believing that they were mostly invented or exaggerated, we omit them from this interpretation of his character and life. They are amusing pictures, complementary scenes of comedy, and as such we give a few of them elsewhere.

ments due to his management of amateur performance. A few tears, a parting sigh, a tender reminiscence, and then away toward other experiences.

In Milan an adventuress could still beguile him into forgetting or neglecting his duty. Henceforth he allows no woman to interfere with his work. Rather he manages to find practical advantage in his love affairs. He is fond of actresses, and he has such necessity of pleasing them that he falls in love with several among them. Generally with the younger one who takes the part of the *servetta*.

His attachment to Madame Ferramont is typical. Goldoni wrote several rôles for the lady, and thus excited the jealousy of the other actresses; then the poor woman suddenly dies in childbirth. Goldoni is much affected, but finds unexpected comfort in mingling his tears with those of the lady's husband. The same situation is repeated, later, after the death of another actress, Signora Baccherini, but then be it noted it is Goldoni's wife who sympathises with and comforts her husband in his bereavement.

The only actress who for a time mastered his senses and his imagination is "la Passalacqua,"[1] whom he

[1] La Passalacqua — Elisabetta Moreri d'Affisio. Bartoli in his "Notizie istoriche de Comici Italiani," *op. cit.*, i, 1–2, says that she could sing in Operas and in Intermezzi; that she could perform the favourite dance "della Bandiera" and also fence with wonderful skill. Goldoni says that in the troupe she was entrusted with parts as a singer and with others as a "soubrette." He further says that "*sa voix étoit fausse, sa manière monotone,*" her manners ungraceful yet with all that . . . a gondola and some coquetry enslaved him at least for a short time.

pilloried in a satirical episode of his play *Don Juan*, and afterwards exposed to the readers of his *Memoirs* in a lengthy anecdote.

The episode is characteristically Venetian. Not precisely good looking, with green eyes, a full-developed figure, and a complexion which required a good deal of making up, Goldoni tells how he only meant to pay a visit to the lady, who was older than she wished to appear, and shrewder than he suspected; and how she persuaded him to step into a gondola, in order to enjoy the beautiful evening. Praise of the gondola has been sung ere now by poets and lovers, its gliding movement, its soothing complicity, the softness of its cushioned seats under the sheltering felze, all this and more have lovers appreciated in every time; and Goldoni was neither the first nor the last young man seduced by the combined allurements of a coquette and a row along the laguna by moonlight.

Only a few days later Goldoni learns that the lady is playing him false with Vitalba, the young actor who impersonates lovers on and off the stage. Goldoni keeps out of the way in proud disdain, until the lady sends for him, plays the grand scene of despair and remorse, without forgetting the dagger aimed at her breast, in the correct attitude for such moments of passion. Goldoni is no monster of cruelty, he cannot witness such despair, he rushes to her couch, bends his knee, swears, kisses, forgives, or is forgiven "*et nous voilà comme auparavant*." Which means that he plays for some days longer the rôle of the greenhorn whom his mistress betrays, openly, with the comrade who knows all the tricks of the pretty play.

Goldoni turned the tables once more. He introduced a pastoral episode in the play that he was then staging, and thus forced the Signora Passalacqua and Vitalba to represent, in the presence of a well-informed audience, just the adventure of which they were the heroes. The profit, in the end, was all Goldoni's. Besides recalling the episode to all the gossips and scandalmongers, who delighted in such anecdotes of theatrical people, this translation on to the scenic stage of a real event was excellent practice for the future realistic playwright.

His style changes, and the flippant intonation of other stories melts in a more delicate mood of mingled sentiment and reticent emotion, when Goldoni tells of his first meeting with Nicoletta Connio,[1] and how he soon succeeded in becoming her husband. No dramatic incidents, no complications, the course of peaceful, honest love tending to marriage, and proceeding by prudent steps toward the happy ending.

[1] Nicoletta Maria was the daughter of Agostino Connio, a Genoese notary, or attorney. She was the eldest of five children. Besides the short but always grateful and affectionate allusions contained in the *Memoirs* and *Letters* Goldoni paid homage to his beloved wife in the preface to vol. xv, ed. Pasquali, dated 1761, though probably written later — a detailed narrative of his first accquaintance with Nicoletta, their discreet lovemaking and marriage. As soon as Goldoni recovered from the smallpox they left for Venice, which they reach on the ninth of October, "landing at Santa Mater Domini at a house over the bridge of this name which my mother had fitted for us and where she and my aunt were already expecting us. Our welcome was hearty; the affection and peace, the perfect harmony which reigned between these three women, was an example."

It reads like the sketch of one of his plays; and, like them, it is pervaded by a homely spirit. Goldoni had gone to Genova with the Imer troupe, and he had seen Signor Connio, a banker of no great means, but of very good reputation. From the window of the lodgings he occupies he observed, behind the opposite casement, a girl just pretty enough to please his eye and elicit from him a tender salute. She curtsies and withdraws, never to reappear again at the window. Such a demure behaviour must have charmed the young man, if only as a change from facile amours. It encouraged him to make his proposals, according to the fashion of the time, to the young lady's father. A whole month for prudent investigations, and finally the wedding.

He could not have chosen better. The Connios were a good Genoese family, well known and well connected. Although Nicoletta did not bring him a *dot*, she secured for him the support of a solidly established father and brothers-in-law. Personally she was a most desirable wife — not the brilliant and flippant Venetian, but the steady and devoted stay-at-home, industrious Genoese, who could put up with scanty means, and yet, when the occasion called for some display, she could hold her own place without clumsiness or presumption in a subdued way that exactly filled Goldoni's requirements and his taste. Her patience and devotion all through their long life was a comfort and a prop for the husband who realised her value, and requited in tenderness and regard his debt of love.

Goldoni spent the honeymoon in a high fever and a serious attack of smallpox. Nicoletta nursed him through it, and fortunately did not take the infection. Goldoni thanks her for this, as for the constant affection and devotion she lavished on him all through their lives. In an epistle [1] to Signor Connio, which prefaces one of his plays — several years later — Goldoni praises Nicoletta. "She knows exactly when I want to be left alone, and when I want to be spoken to. Overwork and worry often make me cross and moody; she then bears with me, takes no notice, yet as soon as I recover my temper she is ready to meet me half way, with some amusing bit of news, some talk so as to sweep clean away all my vexation. We are the best of company to one another, just as we were in the first days of our marriage. I always discuss with her my plans, and ask for her advice about my plays, because I trust her to give me excellent suggestions and previsions."

With even more tenderness and gratitude, in his old age Goldoni pays homage to the "woman who has been my comfort in every moment." How few wives of celebrated men have earned such testimonials! Yet Goldoni was not a perfectly faithful husband; the customs of his time, and especially his profession, condoned unfaithfulness. Yet after every departure

[1] This letter to Agostino Connio is the dedication of *La Donna Sola*, first printed in the "Nuovo Teatro" etc., in Venice, in 1758, but which, like every other preface or dedication, can be read in the classical edition of Goldoni's plays lately edited in Venice, *op. cit.*

COURT OF GOLDONI'S HOUSE IN VENICE, THE PALAZZO "CENTANNI"

Goldoni returned to his dear Nicoletta, whom he set far above all other women. She was prudent enough to ignore these things, and wise enough to avoid complaining. On his part, Goldoni spared her feelings by every possible means.

Nicoletta was also a model daughter-in-law. The young pair settled in Venice, in October, 1736, in the modest house which Margherita Goldoni and her maiden sister already occupied.[1] Nicoletta's highest praise is that she managed to live in perfect peace with both. Goldoni enjoyed the rare privilege of having a quiet home, enlivened by the presence of three women who were rivals in their zeal for his comfort. It is difficult to exaggerate the beneficial effect of such an environment. When we see Goldoni so serenely impervious to the stings of calumny, to the arrows of bitter pamphleteers, so easily appeased after his short crises of wrath, so forgiving, let us remember that the font of his enviable equality of humour, the secret of his unflagging spirits, is not only within his happy nature and healthy temperament, but also in that inexhaustible spring of joy and courage,[2] a happy home.

[1] Goldoni with his wife, mother, and aunt, Maria Salvioni, settled in a house belonging to one Degna, in Salizzada (Salizzada, a corruption of *selciato*, a street paved with flags, not cobbled with smaller stones), San Lio, where he lived until the year 1740.

[2] Goldoni is very reticent about his private affairs. He scarcely mentions his peaceful home life. His *Memoirs* are merely the painstaking rehearsal of incidents written for the public eye, omitting those deeper feelings he holds sacred. When William D. Howells, in his clever introduction to Goldoni's *Memoirs*, speaks of "fulness and frankness" he does not seem to have

In such pleasant conditions, Goldoni made his début in Venice. His first comedy, in Venice, was warmly received, and his success was justified. Goldoni warmly praises his first interpreters; it is a debt of honour to those who have taught him the rudiments of their art. By living with his comedians "as a painter lives with his models" he learned many a useful lesson. These models are not automatons; under his eyes each acts his own rôle. They gossip and dispute and narrate their personal experience, and the quietly smiling author listens and notes every word, every look, and draws their portraits.

After taking them for models he used them as interpreters. He mentions Golinetti, the *Pantalone*, whose expressive physiognomy, he thinks, it is a pity to conceal under the traditional mask. Having noted the grace and elegance of his manners, he decided to employ him in the representation of a character that would be for the greatest part an imitation of the man himself. On this lucky hint, *Momolo Cortesan* was imagined and brought out. Another time Goldoni noticed that another *Pantalone*, Darbes, presented the useful singularity of changing completely his voice, manners, expression, and looks from one moment to another. At times a cheerful, spirited cavalier, at others a clumsy, moody fellow. Goldoni found the way to making it profitable. The old, old theme

rightly interpreted the principal character of this work. All the pretty story-telling, if sifted and weighed, gives but a minimum of information and just the smallest amount of real "confession" such a composition can yield.

of twins, on the stage, could be thus rejuvenated and made as attractive as a novelty.

This method is typical of Goldoni's talent. In temperament, as well as by education, Goldoni was inclined to accept guidance. He adapts external influences to his wants. Players trained to the difficult art of improvised comedy were apt to consider themselves as collaborating with the author, and even as leading in the partnership. Goldoni profited by their experience, and later on he was strong enough to check their presumption and enforce his own method, when he outgrew this first period of preparation.

We try, further in this study, to analyse what influence the "*commedia dell'arte*" exerted on Goldoni's conception of his art; the advantage he derived from the comedians is almost as great.

Some of them were mere *istrioni*, only able to secure popular favour by using indelicate tricks and jokes, some merely repeated their rôles, according to the rules of tradition; but there were others who were not satisfied with repeating hackneyed speeches out of their *zibaldone*, or content exactly to reproduce the traditional personage; they wanted to stamp their impersonation of the old mask, or personage, with some original traits; they wanted to astonish their more learned hearers by classic quotations from poets and philosophers, and, in their improvisation, to interweave their borrowings so aptly as to form a mosaic work of art. Many possessed talent, and some were of superior merit.

Every man, says Goldoni, has a character of his

own; if only the author gives him the opportunity of representing a fictitious character, in complete analogy with his natural one, success is sure to follow. As a general statement this principle is open to discussion; in Goldoni's case it facilitated the reciprocal influence of the author on his interpreters, and it directed the formation of his own talent. Goldoni is an observer rather than a psychologist, he sees his personage from the outside; conceives, in parallel lines, the creation and the impersonation; the abstract personality is identified with the living one that acts and speaks and moves before him. At every step of Goldoni's career the motive of each new inspiration can be traced back to the actor, or the actress, who was first to suggest and then to represent a character.

Goldoni was thus slowly but surely advancing as a playwriter. His name was just beginning to be well known to theatregoers, when, for reasons which he does not mention, he asked for, or accepted, the title and duties of "Genoese Consul in Venice." [1] Doubtless the appointment was due to the influence of the Connios, but there is no evidence whether Goldoni submitted to this honour or sought it.

[1] See Belgrano, "Il Matrimonio e il Consolato di C. Goldoni," in Imbreviature di Giovanni Scriba, Genova, 1882. *Memoirs*, part i, chap. xliii, "When the consulate of Genoa at Venice was offered to me, I accepted with gratitude and respect, without enquiring about the emoluments of the office." Which sounds unlikely. A few lines lower, Goldoni writes, "I increased my domestic establishment, my table, and my retinue . . . ." Of course he was expected to meet Ministers and other official personages but it was not customary to entertain them privately. There were even laws forbidding officials visiting at the houses of foreign ambassadors.

It seems a contradiction to his often repeated assertion that the theatre was his unique attraction, and his vocation at all times irresistible, to find him giving up his prospects and turning to so different an occupation. In fact he was not absolutely obliged to discontinue writing for the stage, but besides a lack of time, the representative of "la Serenissima Repubblica di Genova" commissioned to transact all sorts of affairs with the other "Serenissima" of Venice could not continue to live on familiar terms with actors and actresses in the easy-going fashion Goldoni had adopted ever since his marriage.

He probably expected the place to be remunerative and also a stepping stone to still higher official promotion. Else Signor Connio would not have proposed, and Goldoni never accepted, this charge. Still less would he have enlarged his establishment and his expenses, in proportion to these expectations. Goldoni's is a complex nature. He may have entertained the vanity of the middle classes for social distinction, and succumbed to the temptation of donning a court dress, and having a handle to his name.

Whatever his hopes and aims, he certainly performed with zeal and application all the duties his position involved. His foreign biographers have overlooked the documentary evidence which reveals Goldoni under this aspect. Out of Goldoni's official despatches to the Genoese authorities it has been easy to trace the salient points of this career. He unravelled several affairs of importance, to the satisfaction of all parties concerned, and displayed courage, skill, and activity that will appear unexpected in him, if we were to judge him exclusively from his *Memoirs*.

Thus, for instance, in August, 1741, the consul of Genoa is able to obtain for the benefit of a Genoese skipper redress for an abuse of prerogative. "I found out that a decree of the Senate settles that whenever the captain of a Venetian ship has been licensed by the magistrate of *cinque savi* to load at a certain embankment, no foreign ship is allowed to come near this embankment until the Venetian has finished his loading, for which a whole month is granted. . . . Now the Venetian skippers, even when they were not ready for loading, used to get their license and thus stop the foreigners' loading." Against this ancient abuse a Genoese, Padron Leonardo Caffarelli, appealed "with tears" to his consul. Goldoni, remembering that he could don a barrister's robe, assumed the office of attorney for his party with such success that the case was decided in his favour, the abuse was redressed, and the privilege recalled.

Instances of Goldoni's kindness appear at every step of his career. Sometimes it is a miserable convict, formerly a priest, whom the Council of Ten would pardon, after twenty-two years of imprisonment, if only he could manage to pay the expenses of his trial, amounting to four hundred ducats. The consul does not possess this sum, but he begs for it and hopes, "with Divine assistance," to set the poor man at liberty.

Another time it is the extreme severity of a sentence issued against two Genoese tramps, guilty of no greater sin than begging on the road, and sentenced by a zealous magistrate of Monfalcone in the Friul to eighteen months' imprisonment. Goldoni "declares that the sentence is inhuman, exceeding the bounds of justice; hence he has appealed to the Venetian tribunal and expects to see the magistrate and the chancellor condemned and the poor devils set at liberty."

More important and more complicated was the case of murder of Suzanne Dubic by her lover, René la Fère. The murderer, having taken refuge in the port of Genoa on board a Venetian ship, was apprehended with the consent of the Venetian consul, and carried before the Genoese magistrate. But the Venetian commonwealth was sensitive, and the Genoese did not care to give offence, so Goldoni conciliated the susceptibilities of both the *Serenissime* and saw that, without encroaching on the rights of the one, the other could try and eventually condemn the subject of the other. Goldoni is pleased with himself, and points out that it is due to his zeal that the affair did not drag on for months, but was despatched in a few days.

From December, 1740, to March, 1743, Goldoni held this place of consul. An unfortunate scrape brought this diplomatic career to a sudden end. About this abrupt close of an episode that seemed so promiseful, Goldoni intentionally makes a mess of dates and of motives. He talks of having discovered after three years — rather two and a half — that there was no fixed salary annexed to his charge. It is hard to believe that he did not enquire first, and so suddenly realised that he must give it up. There is also a story about some jewels that were pawned by his order, and then distrained by the broker, thus placing Goldoni in the difficult position of either paying for the larceny or of incurring the charge of complicity.

The story, as he tells it, is incredible, and its consequences remain unexplained; the real significance of the event and its importance in Goldoni's life have been the object of patient researches that throw some light on that which really happened, and some more interesting light on Goldoni's character.

Giampaolo, the scapegoat of the family, has a large share of responsibil'ty in this affair. Giampaolo was then at home, which means living at his mother's and brother's house, after leaving the army, his casual profession. Now Goldoni, sitting quietly in his study, was startled one day by the sudden appearance of his brother, "rather red in the face, rather too bright in his looks," certainly more noisy and rude than either mother or elder son desired. Giampaolo has made a friend in a few minutes, round a table and several bottles of wine, and wants to introduce this friend to his brother. Goldoni listens to the man's story and he keeps him to dinner. Goldoni notes the green eyes, the pale face, the courtly ways that belie his assumed character of a captain, native of Ragusa, and on a recruiting tour.[1]

The green-eyed visitor makes a dazzling proposal; he is commissioned by a State, which remains unnamed, to raise a corps of soldiers, he has letters of credit and other papers which he shows, bearing a royal signature. He allures Goldoni with the title *in partibus* of "Auditeur Général" of the corps; he promises Giampaolo a high rank. Thereupon he is invited to stay with the Goldonis and partake of their hospitality. Merchants of the city are persuaded to provide goods, officers enlist, Goldoni advances six thousand ducats, on the security of a bill which a firm of Venetian bankers have not yet honoured because the usual confirmation of credit by letter has not come.

The day after Goldoni's payment, the captain vanishes. The several dupes he has made in Venice come clamouring at Goldoni's door. Certainly the trick played on him was exasperating. Goldoni had

[1] The personage of the *avventuriero* is not found in Goldoni's plays, but here in these *Memoirs* (chapter xliv) is a prose portrait worth reading: "This man had more the appearance of a courtier than a soldier. He was sleek, sweet spoken, extremely polite; his complexion was pale, his face thin, his nose aquiline, and his eyes small, round, and greenish. He was very courteous and paid great attention to the ladies, holding grave discourse with the aged ones and saying pretty trifles to the young ones. And with all that never losing a good morsel at meals. We took coffee at table and my brother put me in mind of every bottle of liquor there was in the house for the sake of his friend. . . ."

Coffee was never taken round the table, still less was wine called for after dinner in respectable Venetian houses. Goldoni notes this infraction to common use as giving a more special colouring to this unusual visitor.

every motive to be angry, but why does he run away post haste with his wife and brother?

On the shortest notice, just two days for packing, they make their departure, and never stop until they get clear out of the Venetian State.[1] It has been suggested, and almost proved, that the impostor was really the agent of a foreign nation, the Two Sicilies. It seems probable that these levies of troops were sometimes effected with the connivance of some Venetian authority, and only punished when discovered in good time. It seemed preferable, often, to hush the scandal so as not to get the Government entangled. Punishment was likely to come suddenly and secretly, leaving out the bigger fish, but surely catching the smaller fry. Goldoni considered himself as belonging to the category of the smaller offenders, and he saw the advantage of getting quickly out of reach.

When he felt safe in Bologna, he wrote a comedy *L'Impostore*, which is the account he wanted people to believe; he avoided dangerous explanations. For once he found that it was safe to appear a fool, and he played his rôle to perfection. Goldoni may have been so advised, or he may have realised that his position was a dangerous one; he remained away for more than two years, under the most futile pretexts.

[1] Dates get terribly mixed in Goldoni's *Memoirs*. The date, July, 1743, is the most probable, because on the sixteenth of this month Goldoni was in Rimini signing in the register of the *curia vescovile* the baptismal act of Margherita Bonaldi, the offspring of "Colombina, a fresh and attractive brunette, who was the soubrette of the troupe . . . it was my fate."

It appears also that he resigned his consulship at this time. Goldoni prudently refrains from explaining his real motives. He hastened to Rimini on hearing that the Duke of Modena was there "spending the winter at the Spanish camp." Now why did he want so eagerly to join the Duke of Modena, if it were not that he meant to appeal, in his quality of a Modenese subject, to the protection of his sovereign? He admits that an audience was asked and granted; he admits that something was asked and denied. Something about the Modenese Ducal Bank and the payment of some shares he held. Why? The Goldonis' funds in Modena and the management of their affairs were entrusted to their friend and relative, Signor Zavarisi, a notary, who could have arranged things without troubling the Duke. Certainly this special condition of the Goldonis, this double nationality, was an advantage, since they each and all through life paid for it the tax imposed on absentees in order to enjoy this privilege. Probably at this critical moment he sought protection from his presumptive sovereign.[1]

This matter has little other importance except as showing Goldoni's method of telling his own history, with all the reticence and mingling of fact and fiction that he deems fitting and proper. Having adopted this version of a whole affair in the preface of his plays, he did not care later, when he was safe from danger in Paris, to correct his first statement. Yet to leave

[1] About Goldoni's affairs in Modena see the volume edited by the Modenese municipality, "Goldoni a Modena," *op. cit.*

Venice on such a short notice, to break all the ties of affection and friendship, the pleasant habits of social intercourse, and to wander away, with no definite aim, no clear prospect, must have been then a heart-breaking experience. Little wonder, indeed, if Goldoni's health gave way under all the worries then attending all travel, and all the misery and apprehension that certainly embittered this one. The elasticity of his resourceful nature and naturally sanguine disposition helped him to recover his balance. He soon shook himself free of Giampaolo's undesirable company and "endeavoured"—as he says—"to forget past evils and think of a brighter future."

Here begins in the *Memoirs* a long series of anecdotes detailing Goldoni's wanderings across those regions of Italy then disquieted by wars fought by foreigners, for aims that were of no interest to a Venetian. A considerable amount of pleasant reading, of amusing anecdotes, that provide almost no reliable information as to events related, almost no insight into Goldoni's real conditions.[1] Just as in Bologna he tried to

[1] Many pretty little stories of adventures are to be found in the *Memoirs*, referring to these wanderings with Nicoletta. One of the prettiest (*Memoirs*, part i, chap. xlvi) is placed in the neighbourhood of Cattolica, where the Austrians had entered and seized the luggage of our travellers. "The loss was irreparable for me; my wife and myself were very well provided with clothes, we had three trunks, two portmanteaux and boxes and handboxes and now we were left without a shirt." Goldoni undertakes to go and recover his goods. He does not see why Austrians should not be as willing to assist him as Spaniards. He finds a *vetturale*, obtains a passport, and starts with his wife who is quite willing to follow him—"the situation of a woman who loses all at once—her jewels, dresses, and everything belonging to her—may be easily imagined."

assume an attitude, to make fun of his own simplicity, in the comedy *L'Impostore*, so in his *Memoirs* he now describes his travels.

Whether he went to the Spanish camp in Rimini to meet a troupe of players, as he suggests, or whether he hastened there to throw himself at the Duke of Modena's feet, he found a cheering welcome. Spaniards were eminently qualified to appreciate Italian plays and players. They were as lavish of their praise as of their money; they could bend their knees to kiss a lady's hand and were glib in their compli-

"I ordered the driver to stop while we alighted for a moment, but the rascal turned the horses immediately, set off at a gallop toward Pesaro, leaving us in the middle of the highway, without any resource nor any hope to find any. Not a living soul was to be seen. Not a peasant in the fields, not a single inhabitant in the houses, every one feared the approach of the two armies and kept well out of their way. My wife was weeping. I looked to heaven and felt inspired."

They walk on some time and come to a stream.

"There was a small wooden bridge across it, but the planks were broken. The stream seemed rather too deep to be forded by my wife, still I would not be disconcerted. I stooped down, bid her put both her arms round my neck. I rose smiling, crossed over the stream with inexpressible joy, and said to myself, '*Omnia bona mea mecum porto*.' My feet and legs were wet but I did not care. . . ."

Another stream, another ford, and a long walk for untrained Venetians. At last they come in sight of the sea, an old friend of theirs, and a fisherman's boat. "A second circumstance was not less agreeable. A branch of a tree attached to a cottage announced the possibility of getting some refreshment; we procured milk, new-laid eggs, etc."

A branch suspended over a doorstep is even to-day the sign for an *osteria* all over Italy. Hence the proverb "*buon vino non ha bisogno di frasca*" — good wine does not require a branch — meaning that when a place is furnished with good wine the neighbours do not require to be told where it is.

The *Memoirs* tell at length how Goldoni and his wife met with a kind welcome at the Austrian camp. There he stayed and did some work.

ments, and as ready for suppers, dances, and parties as Goldoni, or any other Venetian could wish.

But a few months later, in the same Rimini, Goldoni will be the paid entertainer and playwright of the Austrians; and contrasting them to his former hosts, the Spaniards, he notes that they did not bend their knees to the ladies, that they were noisier and ruder in their love-making and in their pleasures, but withal just as acceptable to Goldoni's unruffled national feelings.

Nicoletta did not enjoy this sort of life. She never cared for social entertainments, and objected to German manners. She may also have objected to her husband's preference for a pretty actress, Bonaldi, a former flame of his, whom he found in Rimini, and employed in the rôles of *servetta*. Goldoni, protesting that he was a most loving husband and that he shared with his wife all his pleasures, records that the only house wherein she would not accompany him was this one. "She did not prevent my going, but she did not like the lady." A wise woman was Nicoletta. She knew where to draw a line, even while she allowed her wanton Carlo as much liberty as was good for them both.

When the Austrians left Rimini, more than a year had elapsed since his flight from Venice, yet Goldoni hesitated to go back. If he longed for his home and for his mother's company, he did not care to recall attention to himself until the unlucky recruiting affair was forgotten by the Inquisitor.

"I wished to see Tuscany; I longed to visit Florence and Siena, and also to dwell some length of time in these cities, in order to improve my style of language, by a greater familiarity with the pure Italian spoken by the Florentines and the Sienese." Both a wish and a necessity, with Goldoni, as indeed with other writers of his own country, not excepting Manzoni. Yet if the need is proved by Goldoni's clumsy Italian, the wish is not so evident. The Goldonis visited several Tuscan cities;[1] they made acquaintances here, and they were welcomed and entertained at several places, and finally settled down in Pisa.

The *Memoirs* contain very little interesting information about this trip in Tuscany. Goldoni has no eye for the beauties of scenery and scarcely notices the social conditions of the people. There is no description of places or persons, no account of literary movements, as evidently none fixed his attention, with the single exception of Perfetti's extempore poetry.

Some affinity of temperament, or simply Goldoni's admiration for extensive and varied knowledge, must account for his enthusiastic praise of a performance that, by other critics, was considered merely a clever trick. Goldoni thus recommends to immortality "le Chevalier Perfetti — one of those poets who can improvise poetry, and who are only to be found in

[1] For Goldoni in Florence see Ademollo, Corilla Olimpica, Florence, 1887, which contains anecdotes about Arcadians and *literati* in Florence at the end of Settecento. Président des Brosses, "Lettres Familières," Paris, 1885, vol. i. For Goldoni in Pisan Arcadia see V. Cian in "Miscellanea di erudizione," Pisa, 1915, fsc. 2.

Italy. He was so far above any other, and he added so much science, elegance, and facility to his versification that he should be entitled to the honour of a crowning in the Capitol, honour which was granted to no one after Petrarch."

Goldoni was invited on the day of Assumption to hear the poet improvising in the hall of the *Intronati* — the Sienese Academy. "Perfetti was sitting on a sort of a chair; one of the Members of the Academy addressed him, and as he could not stray far from the subject that solemnised the day chosen by the Academy for this gathering, he proposed the argument: The Angels rejoicing at the approach of the Virgin's immaculate body."

Goldoni does not draw the obvious deduction that the poet was expecting such a theme to be proposed on this appointed day; but he further extols Perfetti by setting him above "Petrarch, Milton, Rousseau" (meaning, of course, Jean Baptiste) and even above Pindar himself! This extravagant praise, testifying to Goldoni's impulsive, warm-hearted nature, is also evidence of his scanty book learning, of his wretched critical sense, else he could never have mistaken such bombast for eloquence.

Président des Brosses, after listening to one of these extempore recitals, gave some praise to the poet's talent, but limited it by adding "*Vous devez croire vraiment qu'il y a lá dessous beaucoup plus de mots que de choses.*" Posterity has ratified this judgment by ignoring altogether the man Goldoni compared to

Pindar and Milton! Goldoni's excuse being that he could read neither.

A few lines about Florence and a few more for Volterra, a short description of the catacombs, or rather of the impression caused by a visit to these subterranean crypts, and then half a page for Pisa. He says that he did not mean to stop here longer than a few days, but on learning that he could, by resuming his former profession of lawyer and by opening a legal "studio," provide for his wants, he settled down in Pisa and practised law there about three years.

One more turning, one more tacking and shifting round of his sails that plainly contradicts his repeated statement of irresistible attraction toward the theatre, if the circumstance that bade him keep well away from Venice is overlooked. A vocation for the theatre was undoubtedly latent in Goldoni's brain and in his heart, but he also and for not utterly dissimilar motives inclined toward the barrister's profession. The craving for immediate success and popular applause found much the same satisfaction in both callings; the gifts that fitted him for the one also equipped him for the other calling; both offered opportunities for a display of the ready wit, easy flow of language, promptness of repartee that were his natural qualities, and for the subtle interpretation of character and facts, the acute observation of men and events, that were so thoroughly Goldonian.

If we were to study Goldoni as a writer of Italian prose, and were comparing him to his contemporaries, it might be worth the trouble to quote some fragments of his oratorial style, preserved by one of his Pisan admirers, but since we are merely concerned with Goldoni, the author of comedies, the flowery images and bombastic phrasing may be omitted. It was the sort of thing that was expected from a barrister, the sort of language that appealed to the Magistrates. Goldoni used it until he discovered a more suitable and personal style of address, and his growing mastery of his art helped him to discern when it was time to change. His *Memoirs* contain the account of several lawsuits on which he was engaged while in Pisa. Goldoni's literary preparation was rather advanced than hindered by his legal career. A short and honourable career it proved to be, profitable in many ways. It assisted in the evolution of Goldoni's mind by giving opportunity for seeing some of the sterner aspects of life, and further by bringing him into close contact with men of letters, scholars, and even *dilettanti*, of whom there were many then in Pisa.

The greater benefit to Goldoni's literary improvement came through his admission into the Pisan colony of Arcadia. The question is too complex and involves too much that is irrelevant in Goldoni's case here to discuss the merits of Arcadia. It is enough to record that it aimed very high, even while the means adopted appeared ludicrously puerile, and that it produced some good results, even though it did not fulfil the ambitious program first proclaimed in Rome.

In Goldoni's case, initiation to its ceremonies led

to much practical advantage by introducing him to persons that could appreciate and encourage him and direct his choice of models. Thus, if Arcadia did not realise the larger purpose of abolishing triviality, or fighting against classicism, if it could not create any new ideal of art and literature, still it helped to promote the idea of Italian unity by establishing a spiritual bond, linking together many small intellectual groups within cities that, but for their Arcadian colony, would have been almost ignorant of the existence of one another. Of such filmy threads was slowly woven the great ideal chain into which was finally reunited, under one flag, the long severed members of the Italian nation.

It was, as he says, quite by chance that Goldoni happened to walk through an open gate into a beautiful garden, wherein the shepherds of Arcadia were holding their assembly. The sight of several coaches in waiting attracted him, his fondness for society urged him on toward the group of listeners, his taste for improvised poetry kept him on the spot. If surprised, he was not unprepared. A sonnet composed on some former occasion he instantly adapted, and delivered as an improvisation. Goldoni was already a master in this facile art which his contemporaries held in great esteem. His improvisation, or the adaptation of his sonnet, was probably as good as anything produced in the Fegeian colony, wherein he was soon admitted with the usual formalities and more than the usual compliments. He was given the name of Polisseno

Fegeio, duly registered in a diploma; he was also given a charter "investing him with the Fegeian lands." He playfully explains that "We are rich, as you can see, my dear reader; we the Shepherds of Arcadia; we own lands in Greece; we water them with the sweat of our brows, and we reap laurel boughs; the Turks sow wheat, and grow vines on them and laugh at our titles and our songs."

Goldoni, too, laughed at his title and made light of the Arcadian diploma afterward, but at the time he was proud enough and glad enough of getting them; for some time afterwards he liked to inscribe both his Arcadian name and qualification on the title-page of his printed works, and on the tickets of the several theatres that produced his plays. What is even more probant of Goldoni's indebtedness to Arcadia is the trace left in his style by the peculiar æsthetics of the Academy. Not merely in his lighter compositions — sonnets, *capitoli*, and other occasional pieces — can we see the flowered images and ultra-refined sentimentalism of Arcadia, but also in many scenes of his comedies, where they jar discordantly with the general realistic and unconventional intonation.

Neither the charms of Arcadian meetings, nor the society of literati, nor even the profits and reasonable expectations of his career at the Pisan bar could entirely satisfy Goldoni's desires. Venice and the theatre were ever present to his mind; the temptation could be restrained for a time, it was not stifled. It blazed forth irresistibly when Sacchi — the great

Sacchi — asked for a play, anticipating payment, in the thorough matter-of-fact way that ignores refusal, and suggested the argument with the authority his established fame entitled him to. What else could Goldoni do than comply? What else than compose play or scenario and realise that this indeed was pleasure in work, or work in pleasure, for him?

Then when Sacchi wrote back telling of his great success in the farcical comedy wherein he had impersonated *Brighella*, servant of two masters at the same time, and asking for another play in which he meant to appear in a serious character and appeal by pathetic situations to the audience's feelings, what else could Goldoni do than take up an old play of his and rearrange it for Sacchi? Goldoni resisted some time the temptation. The two plays written for Sacchi did not immediately bring a change. He plodded over his briefs, and pored over his codes; but his heart was not in his work, and, for a man of Goldoni's temper, this sort of thing was unbearable.

He tried to persuade himself first, and then his readers, that some sort of wrong was done to him when he was denied promotion after the death of a colleague invested with many charges, Goldoni recording on almost the same page that "he had briefs in all the courts of the town, clients in every rank of society, noblemen of the first nobility, citizens of wealth, merchants of large credit, curates, friars, even big farmers, and also one of his brethren who, being implicated in a difficult criminal prosecution, chose me for his advocate"; it seems that he might have overlooked the real or presumed wrong. What information he may have received from Venice, and what encouragement to prompt his return, he does not record.

As fate would have it, Nicoletta was not at hand when the irresistible temptation walked into Goldoni's room under the burly, pleasant figure of an actor, Darbes. Nicoletta was away, on a visit to her people in Genoa, a visit which had been first planned by both, but eventually given up by Goldoni on the plea of finishing his play for Sacchi. Would Goldoni have listened to her advice if, being near him at the time, she had pleaded against the folly of giving up the honourable career of the law for the more venturesome profession of playwriting and stage managing? There is no telling. Nicoletta was so prudent and sensible that she might have guessed the uselessness of opposition. The woman who possessed tact enough to know "when it was better to speak and when it was better to stand by in silence" could not stake the peace of her household against the formidable enemy of a poetical vocation attended with all the allurements of behind-the-scene life to back it.

With what evident relish Goldoni details the visit of Darbes, "a man nearly six feet tall and broad in proportion, crossing the room with a cane in his hand and a round hat." How playfully he notes all the funny gestures and tricks of the artist, all the comic posture and bombastic talk that sounded in his ear like the hunter's horn to the eager hounds.

"He laid hold of my snuff box while we were talking, took snuff from it, slipped into it several ducats, shut it again, then threw it down on the table with one of those gestures that are meant to betray an action even when they pretend to disguise it."

And then his first introduction to the Medebach troupe. How full of youthful gaiety, with unspoken hopes!

Was it only the prospect of working for a stage manager that thus elated Goldoni's heart? Was it not also the sense of freedom coming upon him with some tidings from Venice and showing him that the path was open for him, that his adventure was forgotten, buried under the dust of police archives, and that he could at last return to Venice, to his mother, to his actors and actresses, to the joys and pleasures of that Venetian life, the equivalent of which he had found nowhere else in Italy, and was never to find elsewhere?

CHAPTER IV

GOLDONI'S LIFE FROM 1747 TO 1753

Contract with Medebach, 1749 — becomes professional playwright — to compose and stage eight new plays each year, and attend all rehearsals — Medebach troupe a family, a clan — Goldoni's method was imitation of the actor that was to impersonate the character — his relations with women — with Theodora Medebach — his first plays had little success — pamphleteer attacks Medebach troupe — Pietro Chiari rival of Goldoni — his character — a plagiarist — Goldoni seeks affection of common people — Chiari-Goldoni quarrel causes commotion — censorship established by government — Goldoni promises to write sixteen plays for next season — magnitude of task — Bettinelli in Venice and Paperini in Florence rival publishers of his plays — signs agreement with Vendramin, which was several times modified 1753 — San Luca theatre too large for his plays — character of Vendramin — money difficulties — Goldoni's mother dies 1754 — his interest in a young man nicknamed Goldoncino.

A VERBAL agreement, soon followed by a regular contract, a short period of probation, ending in a profitable understanding with Medebach, brought Goldoni back to Venice and to a fresh start on the stage of the Sant' Angelo Theatre. Real business was beginning under promising circumstances. The Sant' Angelo Theatre was small enough to allow of the delicate effects Goldoni intended to produce, but large enough to admit a sufficient number of spectators to make it pay. The small apartment Goldoni rented for himself, his wife, and his mother was near by in Calle San Giovanni.

Goldoni took his place in the Venetian world as a professional playwriter. His purpose was to satisfy his employer, to ensure good profits to his actor collaborators, and to direct them toward a higher standard of their art. His mind had not yet formulated a complete plan of reform, although he says that from the very beginning of his career he meditated "blending the comic and pathetic elements in such proportions as to make his plays similar to the classic ones but far more interesting."

The exact nature of Goldoni's contract with Medebach is not known, but his duties were certainly heavy and varied. Besides the tremendous labor of composing and staging eight new plays every year and the adaptation of several old ones, he also wrote "occasional" pieces of poetry, compliments for the opening or closing of the theatrical seasons, sonnets to be delivered at the end of performances, and also supervised the acting, which means attendance at all rehearsals, which was required to correct the bad habits of the players due to improvisation, and to the stage tricks then commonly practised.

There were sallies and repartees, gambols and *lazzi*, a sort of stock in trade, which were in some cases handed down through generations of players, and in others, having been created by one of them, seemed peculiarly his property. While Goldoni probably never intended to deprive either the public or the actors of this customary stock-in-trade of Venetian theatres, still he earnestly proposed to modify the coarseness and triviality of such pranks, and he tried hard to substitute a more æsthetic and delicate sort of fun.

There was also difficulty in teaching actors to appear without the mask which tradition had fixed to some of their rôles. They were to learn how to make their features express the feelings and emotions which heretofore they had indicated by forced attitudes and violent gesticulation. To achieve this task perfect understanding and mutual reliance between the actors and author were essential. It was necessary that Goldoni should proceed with great tact and discernment and his interpreters display unusual skill and docility.

For having so usefully collaborated in Goldoni's first success and exerted such an influence on the forming of his first manner, the Medebach troupe demands special consideration. Medebach himself, though he afterward behaved meanly, was at first a capable and intelligent manager. He spurred Goldoni's ambition, and stimulated his activity by keeping him to the letter of their agreement, and also by his sympathy with his intentions of theatrical reform. The Medebach troupe did not differ essentially from more famous ones. Indeed this company exhibited the characteristic traits of the craft. This was a family rather than a partnership. It was a clan under an autocratic chief.

Gaspare Raffi, like a patriarch, assisted by his wise and prudent wife, Signora Lucia, had guided the troupe through the thorny uphill path from rope dancing and itinerant performances at village fairs on improvised stages to the comparative dignity and more remunerative arrangements of regular acting, in the pay of His Excellency Condulmer at the Venetian theatre of Sant' Angelo. The troupe was increased in number and in importance. Theodora Raffi, who formerly charmed humble audiences with her rope dancing, now successfully impersonated the favourite character, *Rosaura*. Married to Medebach, she transferred to him her rights to rule over the tribe, when the elder Raffi died. Maddalena Raffi her aunt, the spirited *servetta*, annexed Brighella Marliani when she married him. He remained in the company, even during the long and unjustified flight of his wife.

Around this nucleus of relatives, bound both by common interest and the ties of affection, other elements gathered, forming a compact whole which tended to clear and definite aims. And because they were forced to adjust their individualities to the requirements of a common plan they not only increased their own individual value but increased even more the value of the company as a whole. This common effort, which required both comprehension and implicit trust in their leader, the members of the Medebach troupe earnestly attempted and largely achieved.

The importance to Goldoni of this intelligent and willing support can be realised only by remembering how very near in spirit and in time they all were — author and players — to the improvised comedy;

and how very sensitive and easily swayed by external circumstances Goldoni always was and especially so in his earlier career.

Goldoni's method, amply recorded in his *Memoirs*, of imagining a character or modifying an old one, by a close imitation of the actor that was to impersonate it on the stage, was an application of the spirit and tradition of the *Commedia dell'arte*. He sees his personage, and listens to his talk in the person of the player — just as the player used to remodel any classical or historical character, according to his own capacity and means, to his own figure and physiognomy. Hence Goldoni and his actors made collaboration possible; and progress was generally constant. Goldoni's tact, his kindness, his quiet manners, and a modesty that tempered his authority, all helped to reduce friction.

There were many changes in the Medebach troupe before the end of Goldoni's contract. Collalto succeeded Darbes in the rôle of *Pantalone* and two clever actresses died; Signora Marliani came back in time to rouse Theodora Medebach's jealousy, but the importance of his actor collaborators grew less with each passing day, with each new step Goldoni was taking.[1]

[1] *Il Teatro Comico* is a representation of the troupe Medebach, each personage being composed in imitation of the actor who impersonated it, Medebach, playing *Orazio*, utters those principles which he was then helping to enforce. In the preface to this play (see ediz. compl., *op. cit.*, vol. i, p. 142) Goldoni says: "In a decisive moment of his career, the author found in him (Medebach) the most effective support of his ideals."

Though Goldoni's *Memoirs* are often otherwise inaccurate they always record every debt of gratitude he owes to anyone. Many passages describe the influence exerted by his first interpreters, praising their talents, insisting on the value of their advice, and how he imitated their peculiarities. Indeed he only omits mention of their occasional mean tricks. The whole Medebach troupe influenced Goldoni and were influenced by him, but naturally the greater reciprocal influence was due to the women of the company.

In regard to Goldoni's relations with women it would require extraordinary credulity to accept as the whole truth the account in the *Memoirs*. There are so many instances of Goldoni's delicacy and reticence, that in his *Memoirs* he must be credited with having told only that which the Venetian standard of propriety admitted of telling without scandal. To assume that his "friendships" were really quite so simple and superficial as he makes them would be to ignore both Goldoni's

Placida is Theodora Medebach, whom Goldoni praises for her prudent, honest customs, for her delicacy and feelings, while he laments her premature death (in 1761) when only thirty-seven.

Beatrice is Caterina Landi, who the following year left and was replaced by Maddalena Raffi Marliani, Theodora Medebach's rival.

Tonino was Antonio Matteucci (or Matteuzzi), known in art under the name of Collalto. Goldoni was pleased with him up to the time when he tried to appropriate the authorship of the play *I Due Gemelli Veneziani* on the plea that he improvised the principal rôle.

Brighella was Anselmo Marliani, and a great favourite with the public for his acting and also for his singing; in several rôles written for him a song is introduced. When his wife returned to the troupe after seven years' absence he (see Goldoni's *Memoirs*) explained matters as "a juvenile error." More about her will be said *à propos* of Mirandolina.

great susceptibility to feminine charms and the Venetian morality of his times. Theodora Medebach, whom Goldoni "esteemed beyond all other actresses," whose graceful manners, pretty face, and sweet voice conquered even the sceptic and fastidious Venetian audience, did everything possible to ensure the success of his plays. Even if she did not realise the nature of her affection for him, even if she disguised it from herself and from her family, her grief at being supplanted by another woman in interpreting the plays of the youthful and attractive author was certainly deep enough to cause a serious illness which was quickly cured when she perceived she had a fighting chance against her rival and might reconquer the first place in Goldoni's favour.

This first place she secured through untiring application, and the most submissive and comprehensive translation of Goldoni's intentions. As one reads the plays it is easy to see how the stage character of *Rosaura* grows in dignified simplicity, in refinement, from one to another of the impersonations composed for Theodora Medebach and — knowing as we do Goldoni's methods — in imitation of her own sweet self. She was aware of her share of merit in these successive creations, she was aware of Goldoni's dependence upon her, and the natural pride of any woman in such a situation was increased by that special pride that exists behind the footlights. She was the *primadonna*, she was the giver of glory, and then suddenly because it pleased her Aunt Marliani to come between her and the man she worshipped and served, was she to be set aside and left to play second fiddle?

Of course Signora Medebach could not see with Goldoni's eyes the possibilities of the *servetta* rôle. Nor could she judge critically of matters so bitterly close to her own heart. She only saw the tokens of favour, the opportunities offered to that coquettish Marliani flirt, whose reputation had nothing to lose after the easily granted forgiveness of her husband.

Goldoni did not wantonly trifle with the feelings of the two women. He strove to conciliate and to make a comedy of that which he refused to consider as a possible tragedy. He may have really tried to hold the balance straight and reconcile his duty of gratitude to the one, and his interest in the other, with the stronger demand of his artistic methods, which required the fuller development of the second rôle. But all these sentimental complications developed later; on Goldoni's first admission to the official title of playwright of the troupe, the smooth waters of collaboration were unruffled.

The first plays given by Goldoni in Venice were not much noticed. *Tonino Bella-grazia*, *Il Cortesan*, and *L'Uomo Prudente* had indifferent success. Goldoni felt "that he had no rivals to fight, but only some prejudices to conquer."

When Darbes in his impersonation of two Venetian twins obtained a personal success, Goldoni confessed it was due rather to the acting than to any merit of the play. The *Memoirs* mention the "unparalleled ability of *Pantalone*," and also the satisfaction of Medebach, "who felt sure that his enterprise was going to pay," and he modestly adds, "I got my share of this satisfaction on being applauded and congratulated a great deal more than I expected to be."

The plaudits of the audience roused the attention of critics. "During the Christmas holidays some idlers . . . sent forth a pamphlet against the author and his comedians." That was the beginning of the nerve-destroying strife. This pamphlet — whether printed or handed round in manuscript as the fashion was — attacked "my country rather than my work." Parts of the plays were even praised, while other parts were pronounced "too true and too pungent for exhibition in Venice." The whole was seasoned with a certain amount of discernment, says Goldoni, and some compliments, but the pamphleteer violently attacked the whole Medebach troupe, calling them rope dancers and *baladins*. Against this sort of thing chivalrous Goldoni at the time protested fiercely and years after filled a good page of his *Memoirs* with a vindication of these honest actors' merits. Better than by continuing a war of pamphlets, Goldoni supported his players by providing them with good plays.

Goldoni does not name his foes. In the intimate literary sets of Venice, no one was ignorant of whence the blow came. Either of the two great patrons, two theatre owners, their Excellencies Grimani and Vendramin, could easily find some literary hack to do the dirty business of reviling the plebeian lawyer and his acolytes, who presumed to compete with them. Moreover, certain men of letters may have joined in the quarrel from honest disapproval of the new style.

He could not fight either Vendramin or Grimani. Grimani had already proved a kind patron, Vendramin was likely to become an employer, both were too important to be directly attacked. Thus there was a lull in the brooding storm and Goldoni worked on, his sympathy for his own actors growing with every effort he made to understand and interpret their simple souls. Thus he produced one of his most powerful representations of Venetian customs, *La Putta Onorata*, in the attempt to destroy an infamous, now forgotten, play of Chiari's.

By this time the champion whom Goldoni could challenge was conspicuous. Senator Grimani had discovered him in Modena, and brought him out under his protection and in his pay. Abbot Pietro Chiari became the official rival of Goldoni, when he was given, at the theatre of San Samuele, just the same sort of position that Goldoni held at the Sant Angelo. He now possesses a certain sort of immortality as Goldoni's rival. But for this competition his name would have been forgotten by posterity.

Pietro Chiari, born in Brescia in 1711, was first a pupil, then a teacher, in the Jesuit schools. He afterward became a secretary to Cardinal Lante della Rovere, and a shepherd of Arcadia under the name of Egerindo Criptonide. From his untiring pen dripped innumerable occasional poems, translations, adaptations, and many works which were most evident plagiarisms. He possessed a special aptitude for fawning on the powerful and an ability for making the most of every favour, however obtained.

He came to Venice, provided with such letters of introduction as were then equivalent of letters of credit. Grimani, bent on crushing the Goldoni-Medebach partnership, hired him and gave him the support of the great Sacchi's acting. Chiari's extensive reading, his knowledge of several languages, justified him in the eyes of his partisans in assuming the attitude of scholar and critic, passing judgment on Goldoni's plays.

Around Chiari clustered all the anti-Goldonians, who, however, were not all Chiarists. There were those who lived on or around the many other theatres of Venice, there were the clients and protégés of the patricians who owned these theatres, and then, also, there was the swarm of buzzing, stinging literati.

In this Italian *Settecento*, a sort of freemasonry was then knitting together all those who could wield a pen, all those who could boast of some classical education. Italy has seldom wandered so far from the path of classicism, yet seldom have men of letters mouthed so much about the classics, extolled more blindly the beauties of Greek and Latin authors, and more violently discussed the æsthetic principles of the ancients. Of course under this noxious blossoming of weeds a splendid harvest of good grain was ripening. Alfieri, Parini, Beccaria were soon to appear and, by directing Italian literature along lines appropriate to the Italian genius and in accordance with the glorious past, prepared the way for an even more brilliant future.

But just then, especially in Venice, neither Saverio Bettinelli breaking a lance against Dante, nor Gaspare Gozzi starting in defence, nor Giuseppe Baretti proclaiming the superiority of English culture, nor Denina advising to drop Italian and adopt French for daily use, nor Cesarotti and his erroneous philology, knew exactly where they were leading their readers. Unable to appreciate originality, unable to differentiate between pedantism and erudition, these men of letters indiscriminately praised each other, or clustered into groups to discourage outsiders. Frequently these groups formed into "academies," clubs designed to keep out literary intruders.

Chiari, superficial, but with extensive reading and with that self-sufficiency and smattering of letters which the Jesuits imparted to their pupils, was just the sort of man these societies were sure to adopt and support. His intellectual shallowness easily adapted itself to those demands of fashion, to the vagaries of public taste that, in every age and country, have succeeded on the stage. He could borrow from every source, though he could not assimilate; he could plagiarise unblushingly with this incredible explanation, "I am no plagiarist, I am a merchant who takes goods from all hands." His translation of Pope's *Essay on Man*, other translations from the Latin, dazzled the pseudo-scholars of Venice. When the Milanese group of scholars, centring round the brothers Verri — *il Caffe* — discussed him seriously, simply publishing some of the most foolish things selected from his voluminous work, his reputation crumbled.

But in 1747–48, when Chiari, the author of letters on every subject, was standing as the champion of conservatism and orthodoxy in letters against a nameless young lawyer in the pay of a theatrical troupe, who did not side with him? Those who wallowed in cyclopedian knowledge hailed him as a glorious recruit, those whose supreme pleasure was to stand as umpires, watching the jousts at the playhouses, the ceaseless tattle of drawing-rooms, those who considered the coffee houses and *casini* as the only battle field, those who longed for the excitement of literary polemics, this whole little world of letters in Venice was attracted toward Chiari.

Goldoni fought the battle almost single-handed. Almost, because his actors stood by him at first and almost from the first the public of the pit was faithful. Chiari made a great mistake when he slandered the Venetian girls in a play *Le Pute di Castello*, a mistake which Goldoni turned to advantage in a succession of masterpieces, pictures of the lower classes, and Chiari at the same time alienated the favour of a very large part of the audience. "Everything was bad in this play," says Goldoni, "character, plot, dialogue, everything was dangerous; yet it was a national play, it amused the audience, it filled the house and people laughed at nasty jokes."

By *comédie nationale* Goldoni understood comedies of Venetian customs, especially the customs of the lower classes, of the people he best liked, best sympathised with. Chiari's attempt, moreover, pointed out to Goldoni the pleasure of observing and representing these humble friends, without failing in his moral obligation of filling Medebach's pocket, and ensuring opportunities for the whole staff of players. In so far as such delicate flowers of purely Venetian growth can be translated into another language, we will try to show what delightful plays Goldoni created out of this treasure house, the life and thought, the joys and sorrows of the humble.

Chiari's play offended the groundlings — whom Goldoni particularly tried to please; *Putta Onorata*, which interpretates all that is best and most honourable in the common people, won for him their affection. He rejoiced heartily when he was cheered by the boisterous clapping of hands and other noisy signs of approval, which he rightly interpreted as a sign of their preference "for comedy instead of farce, for decency instead of grossness."

Goldoni's foes charged him with flattering the rabble. His having obtained for the gondoliers, in waiting at the theatre doors, the right of free admittance within the house, was interpreted as a mean trick, a sort of bribery, even as the delineation of a most interesting character of gondolier — Menego Cainello — was blamed by those who could not understand the genuine love he bore to his own people, his solidly rooted democracy.

The real battle was fought on the occasion of a second *reprise* of Goldoni's *Vedova Scaltra*. The play was merely meant to afford a pretty actress the opportunity of appearing in different characters, the only difference between this and former plays of the same sort being that the actress in Goldoni's play not only changed her clothes and the arrangement of her hair, but exhibited a difference of manners, from one scene to the other, as she flirted with three different men. Goldoni composed it when still entirely under the influence of players, and in accordance with the standard of the *commedia dell'arte*. It was very well received by the audience for three nights. Then the posters of the San Samuele announced a new play by Chiari, *La Scuola delle Vedova*, and Goldoni was told that this was a criticism of his own work.

Donning the ample cloak, the white vizor, and the three-cornered hat that made a real disguise, he went to the San Samuele and listened to Chiari's play, only to find out that it was an imitation of his own interspersed with irrelevant impertinence. Angered by the performance and by the applause from the public, "which was not my public" as he says, he went home decided to show fight, for it "would be cowardice not to stop the torrent threatening his destruction." With more vitriol than he ever felt before, he at one sitting wrote the *Prologo Apologetico*, a short dialogue that contained a well-aimed attack on his adversary, sent his pamphlet directly to the printer, and arranged for its immediate distribution about town.

Having been challenged, he answered with a body blow.

In the parody of his play were some words that could be construed into an offence to foreigners, the popular nickname of *panimbruo* (something equivalent to milksop) used in reference to an English personage, and knowing how solicitous the Venetian government was not to offend their foreign guests, he made the most of this sally. Goldoni was amply satisfied by the decree of the Tribunal *della Bestemmia* instituting a theatrical censorship. He interpreted this decree as an approval of his retort and he rejoiced at this tightening of legal control.

The quarrel Chiari-Goldoni caused much commotion. His adversaries retaliated with bitterness and malice. The swarm of literary gossips clustered, as in two intrenched camps, within the two book shops; they gathered into coffee houses, thence spread in drawing-rooms and along the "Liston," carrying about copies of sonnets, epigrams, *canzoni*, which now fill many shelves in the archives of Museo Correr and other private collections. Very few of these are signed; none can be safely assigned to Goldoni's pen.

When, some time later, he was attacked with more violence and more talent by Carlo Gozzi, Goldoni disdained to fight. Some commentators have hinted at a moral cowardice which closed his mouth. It seems more in accord with his general character to imagine him placidly unconcerned when personally attacked, though warmed into a short-lived anger by offences directed at his humble colleagues, and easily forgiving, when the storm blew away. His motives were serious and honourable; he would not risk a conflict that might ruin his employer. Goldoni lacks audacity, but he possesses much of that enduring patience, unselfish consideration of other people's rights, which are a rare form of courage.

The *Letters-Prefaces* written at this time, though printed at a later date, are reticent; yet they indicate Goldoni's attitude. Many such expressions as: "My friends wanted me . . . I was eager to satisfy the Pantalone . . . or the Arlecchino . . . the first actress wished . . . the second expected . . ." show that his actions were controlled by his affections for his friends the players of the Medebach Company and the interests of his employer. Goldoni's reaction against the literary polemic raging around his name was practical and dignified. He created better plays. He threw down his gauntlet, under the form of an official engagement to produce twice as many plays as he was bound to give by his contract, the promise of composing sixteen new comedies in a twelvemonth. The Sant Angelo was losing some of its credit, the players losing some of their spirit, the paying public — those at least who rented the boxes for the season — were deserting. Goldoni set his back to the wall and faced the worst.

It was an ancient tradition in the Italian comedy that at the end of the night's performance an actor, or sometimes an actress, should step out of the curtain and announce the play they intended to perform on the following night. When the audience grunted disapproval a change could be proposed; when the audience was peculiarly well satisfied with the evening's performance, they would cry "This one" (*Questa*). When the curtain closed on the last scene of the last play in the season, and the players were expected to take their leave for a time and start on a tour through other cities, it was customary for the actor or actress to deliver a "compliment," expressing thanks for whatever encouragement had been given, and promises of doing better next time the troupe would have the honour of reappearing before these enlightened judges and kind protectors.

When Theodora Medebach stood up alone in front of the closed curtain impersonating in her graceful figure, in her appealing looks, and soft, musical voice all the delicate refinement of a dawning art, the hush that fell on the house was pregnant with the electricity of momentous events. For one short, telling instant the silence was broken only by the melodious voice, delivering its simple argument announcing the joint purposes of author and interpreters; then the audience began to realise the full meaning of this unusual leave-taking; they measured the greatness of the attempt, admired the courage which could devise it. A hearty cheer went through the theatre, a promise of support. The following year at the same date, the same cheers, the same plaudits, by probably the same persons, hailed the accomplishment of the rash promise. And thus the Goldonian party enlarged and spread.

It is a characteristic note of the time that on the memorable evening when the crowd cheered so heartily "some people were frightened and talked of a rebellion" when the box occupied by Goldoni was stormed by enthusiasts, and he was carried away in triumph into the sumptuous halls of the Ridotto where the whole procession rushed. Goldoni says that he was kept out of his bed and his well-earned rest longer than he cared for, and made to listen to more compliments than he wanted to hear.

One of Goldoni's foreign biographers has attempted to calculate the magnitude of Goldoni's task by adding up the pages or newspaper columns and even the number of words he wrote! This commercial estimation gives an inadequate idea of the intellectual effort, of the inventive power, and of the application required to accomplish this feat. Other critics have searched contemporary annals and Goldoni's correspondence to discover how much of this work is entirely original and how much was prepared beforehand. Useless and irrelevant speculations! Goldoni wasted more nerve power and health than any author ever squandered in similar undertakings, and he got very little moral and less financial advantage out of it.

His extraordinary working power was taxed to its utmost. The sixteen plays finally became seventeen, and there were also several lighter compositions, operas, and the usual demand for occasional poetry. All this Goldoni achieved without utterly breaking from those social habits that were considered as an obligation and from other habits of his own liking. No great talker, but an amused listener, Goldoni could not miss the daily gathering round a coffee table, inside a *farmicia*, or a bookseller's shop, nor could he get to the end of a day without some game of cards. He could sit at his desk writing for hours, then rise fresh and good-tempered and join the conversation of friends, or face the paltry annoyances of a rehearsal.

Evidently Goldoni expected to gain something more than his fixed salary when he produced double the fixed amount of work. Medebach saw things differently. He pocketed the large profits due to Goldoni's *tour de force*, but he gave Goldoni not one *soldo* above the salary fixed by contract. Goldoni, too proud or too wise to beg for what he deemed his due, was justly disappointed. Not extravagant or avaricious, but fond of that display which was then understood as lending dignity, with a taste for costly furniture and artistic trinkets, with a fondness for candy and good eating, and a weakness for cards, Goldoni felt the misery of enforced thrift. The terms accepted at first, in the eagerness to get back to Venice and play-writing, proved insufficient for his daily needs.

To supply the deficiency Goldoni composed or adapted works for musicians. He hoped that an edition of his plays might bring him enough to balance his budget. Arrangements were made with the Venetian editor, Bettinelli. But Medebach interfered, pretending that the printed sale of the plays would prejudice the interests of the theatre. Goldoni submitted to this claim, and consented to issue only one volume of four plays a year. By so doing he recognised Medebach's right to limit this production, and thus compromised his position. It seems that a lawyer should have better measured the possible consequences of his acts, and not allowed that the man who paid only for the performance of his plays should also be entitled to regulate the publishing of the same plays.

Thus when, at the end of their mutual engagement, Goldoni declared to Medebach that he would not renew it, he was to a degree prepared for the trick Medebach and Bettinelli had jointly arranged. "Bettinelli having already edited the first two volumes of my plays, I went to his shop with the manuscript for the third volume. My astonishment was great when I heard this phlegmatic man declaring in his coldest manner that he could not accept from me the original text of my plays since he got them from Medebach's hands and since he was continuing the edition by order of this comedian. On recovering from my surprise, striving to smother my anger, I told him: 'My dear friend, mind what you are about; you are not wealthy, you are the father of several children, do not run useless risks, do not force me to ruin you.'"

Considering that copyright was subject to the most arbitrary decisions, it is not certain that Goldoni—as he asserts—was sure to win a lawsuit against the publisher and his late partner, whom he had in some manner already recognised as having the right to print his plays.

Goldoni acted according to his own subtle rather than impulsive nature; he did not attempt a lawsuit which he knew might mean going from one tribunal to another and losing precious time. He did not oppose the Bettinelli edition, but he announced another edition with corrections and variations.

He went straight to Florence, obtained the necessary permission from the Grand Duke — who then happened to be also the Emperor of Austria — secured a contract with the Florentine publisher, Paperini, and eagerly pushed the printing of his plays and explanatory prefaces.

Thus whilst Medebach continued to issue the other volumes of the Bettinelli edition, the Paperini volumes made their regular appearance. Goldoni protested vehemently in a "Manifesto" that the Venetian edition was prejudicial to his work, since the plays should not be printed just as he had given them to the players; they needed corrections in every case and sometimes an almost complete rewriting, and it was even more unfair to have them tampered with by any one else. Considering the terrible haste in which some of them were composed "when he gave forth one act at a time to the stage copyist," and got somehow to the end without having under his eye the beginning, no one could doubt that these corrections were needed. Indeed the comparison of texts shows that Goldoni corrected with the greatest care. Many changes and many cuttings prove how the author tried to better his work.

The strangest feature, and the most typical, of this

affair is the manner in which the Florentine edition was introduced into Venice. "I had five hundred subscribers in Venice, and the introduction of my edition was forbidden in the States of the Commonwealth; this proscription of my works in my own country may seem surprising, but it was business. Bettinelli had secured some patrons to support his exclusive rights, and the union of booksellers stood by him, because this was a 'foreign edition.'" The word "foreign" sounds strange as applied to Florence by a Venetian.

"As soon as one of my volumes came from the press, five hundred volumes were sent to Venice, somewhere on the banks of the Po; they were deposited in a safe place, thence a society of noblemen passed them in contraband and introduced them within the capital, where they were distributed openly. The government did not interfere in this affair, considering it more ludicrous than interesting."

The laws and regulations against contraband were stringent because of growing slackness of trade and the danger of foreign competition, yet the pleasure of getting the better of custom houses brought about an alliance of noblemen and boatmen on the river and gondoliers on the laguna. It is remarkable that it was Goldoni who joined these strange partners in an illegal enterprise. Evidently, though he had foes and rivals among writers and actors, he also had friends in every class.

Even before the end of his engagement with Medebach Goldoni provided himself with another employer. He could not risk remaining without pay and depriving his wife and mother of their small comforts.

The brothers Vendramin, of the most authentic patriciate, were owners and managers of the theatre San Luca, now Teatro Goldoni. With them Goldoni signed a first agreement, which was several times modified. The texts of these successive contracts have been preserved. They state exactly the number of ducats promised, the amount of work to be done, the conditions and the rewards.[1]

[1] *Carlo Goldoni e il teatro di San Luca a Venezia, Carteggio inedito* (1755–1765), *con prefazione e note, di Dino Mantovani*, Milano, 1884. Fratelli Treves, p. 2.

First contract February 15, 1752, Venice, between his Excellency Antonio Vendramin and Doctor Carlo Goldoni, thirty-one pages.

Second contract October 14, 1756, between His Excellency Francesco Vendramin and Goldoni.

Third contract March 2, 1762.

The second and third contracts were signed by Francesco Vendramin after the death of his brother Antonio. These contracts are given in full. We only offer a few extracts. First contract was amended by the second, which allowed:

1. C. Goldoni was to give no less than six plays a year, viz.: two in the cities of *terra firma* during the tour the troupe made before the Venetian season of autumn; a third one in Venice before Saint Martin's day; three others within the month of January. . . . Goldoni could if he liked give two more, but he was never to pass the number of eight a year (the year beginning after the end of Carnival).

2. Goldoni was forbidden to write or compose plays that might be performed in Venice less than three years after they had been performed at the San Luca.

3. Goldoni was to provide all the occasional poems, leave-taking, thanks, introductions, etc.

4. Contract to be continued for ten years — till February, 1767, and even then neither party could be released if both were not agreed.

5. Vendramin would pay one hundred ducats for each play.

To understand properly what these conditions really meant for Goldoni it is necessary not only to fix the valuation of money and the cost of living, but to understand how clumsily his intentions were supported, how his sensitive nature was wounded.

His optimism and high esteem for the patriciate made him very confident of success. He was glad to get out of Medebach's grip, glad to do business with a nobleman, glad to move from a small theatre to a larger one. His letters at this date are overflowing with bright expectation.

But the larger house was unfavourable to the development of his planned reform. The players had no common purpose, and were not bound together by relationship or long-standing friendship; more-

6. When Goldoni has performed all that he is expected to do, Vendramin of his free will condescends to give two hundred ducats to be paid in two portions, one in December, the other in the spring.

The second contract was not annulled by the third, which stipulated that whenever Goldoni returned to Venice he was bound to resume all the obligations of the second contract, which means that he was bound to drudge on for as many years as remained to fulfil the ten years of the stipulation, and to remain further bound by the elastic term: "until both parties were agreed" for his release.

For every play that Goldoni would send from Paris one hundred ducats were stipulated; the maximum number of nine a year was fixed.

There were minute stipulations about the plays performed in Paris and those sent to Venice, Vendramin insisting on their being entirely different. So they were on the title page and in some details, but as a matter of fact there are many resemblances between the comedies given at Paris and afterward at Venice or vice versa. In those last miserable years of Goldoni's career, the unbearable strictness of terms, the smallness of remuneration, the utter uselessness of these restrictions, more than account for Goldoni's breach of a contract that caused such irreparable havoc in his career. How appropriate the axiom *summum jus, summum injuria.*

over that intimacy, that trust and mutual reliance which had graced the first enthusiastic partnership were wanting. The buoyancy of youth and inexperience, the docility of the débutant playwright, as well as the good will of hopeful interpreters, were also wanting. Then instead of Medebach, a clever, enterprising actor whose mind was open to new ideas, whose authority over the rest of the company was undisputed, Goldoni now dealt with an irritable, elderly gentleman who seldom realised the significance of novelties, and exerted no authority over the actors he employed.

Goldoni soon felt the iron hand under the velvet glove of his Excellency Francesco Vendramin who, after the death of Antonio, remained sole owner of the San Luca Theatre. Several letters exchanged between them, published by Professor Dino Mantovani, prove the bondage, the exasperating limitations Goldoni endured.[1] To what extent did they influ-

[1] Even from the first letter of this collection, dated August, 1755, Goldoni complains to his Excellency of Gandini's desertion and continues (p. 8) ". . . let me only have my hands free (to recruit players) and we may do better with fewer persons; if only they are obedient instead of being so beastly" (*bestie di tal natura*).

In a P.S. (*op. cit.*, p. 69): "Medebach has neither in Mantova nor in Milan performed any new play, and there is no telling whether he has any one in readiness. He may have some; but we too will have enough to compete with him, and even to crush him. Let Chiari come to Venice or keep away as he pleases; I don't care. Last year I was quite sure that he would win the victory; this year I flatter myself of just the contrary."

Goldoni has many pretty ways of acknowledging the grumbling remarks which Vendramin sent him. "I often tell you that I can make any change in the rôles as you please — the man who makes a watch knows how to mend it." Occasionally he is stung to answer with resentment (p. 129, *op. cit.*):

ence Goldoni's decision to seek release in an exile to Paris?

A typical Venetian character, representative of his caste and of his time, is Francesco Vendramin, as he is revealed in this correspondence. A patrician who insisted on both the privileges and the duties of his rank, yet mindful of his own interest irrespective of injury to others. His biographers have condensed the history of his life into three dates — birth, marriage, and death. He happened to be just one link in the chain of a family once great.

Goldoni soon discovered that he was to wrangle single-handed with the whims and deficiencies of players; that he would receive no support from his employer. The unfitness of the theatre for Goldonian plays, the unpreparedness of the players for Goldoni's methods, were obstacles that could not be overcome. Moreover Goldoni, by his own interpretation of duty toward Vendramin and the actors, was forced to write plays that would rival Chiari's plays, full of the pathos and the exotism which was the momentary fad. With his usual facility of adaptation he gave the sort of things that his actors could perform, plays which allowed of scenic display and the striking effects of tragedy, just the plays he had condemned with that curt word, *Romanzi! Romanzi!* applied to Chiari's. Precious time and energy were thus wasted on plays

"Your Excellency says that money is for me the most important point. For God's sake do not entertain such an opinion of me! I am a poor man, but a most honourable one!"

that are now utterly forgotten — *La Sposa Persiana*, *Ircana*, and a few others.

In time the players were taught better things. Goldoni never found them so docile and eager to improve as the Medebach staff; he did not win their entire devotion, yet he coaxed and scolded, forced them to learn and to adopt some of his ideas. But it was a sore trial to be always struggling against either their caprices or the blundering of their common employer. Goldoni's greatest difficulty was to obtain from Vendramin the money required for the staging of new plays and that minimum of support which he absolutely needed to guide the actors.

As one reads the letters, the contrast between the personality of the two men is extraordinary. Goldoni, considerate, respectful, the slave of his duty, but careless of details, devoted to his art, and eagerly striving toward a reform that he now clearly conceives, forced to plead for the smallest favour and to beg for trifling changes, worse still, constrained by circumstances to beg for some advance payment and even for a loan of money. On the other hand the elderly patrician who will only adopt some improvement when persuaded that he likes it. He has a sense of honour and would not rob his dependents, but he will squeeze out of them as much profit as he can. When he does not create difficulties he aggravates those which the rivalries of actors, the strictness of censors, are constantly provoking. Thus when Goldoni has sketched a caricature of Chiari in the personage of *Grisolgo*, and the magistrates interfere for fear of complications, Vendramin does not support his poet but insists on a correction. Again when Goldoni proposes an elaborate spectacular performance on which he builds some rosy hopes, Vendramin pleads that the staging is likely to be expensive. Again, when the censors find fault with one of Goldoni's plays, *La Sposa Sagace*, wherein a nobleman is represented as plotting adultery, Goldoni is forced to change the title of his play, the social position of his characters, and turn the wronged wife into a faithful fiancée.

Goldoni supplicates for money, the more pressingly for having opened his house and his heart to Giampaolo, the prodigal brother, and to his two motherless children; he wants money because his health is failing, because his aged mother, "having lived enough to see her long-lost" and probably half-forgotten second born, must be comforted and petted; also he wants money because he is open-handed and fond of nice clothes and jewellery. Vendramin does not understand Goldoni's wants; he insists on the strict observance of his contract. Yet he will not allow Goldoni to leave him.

Vendramin's letters are pompous and stiff, like the brocade out of which his patrician robes were made. In some of the letters there is an assumption of superior morality, a supercilious impertinence, a mistrust that must have been irritating to one so essentially honest as Goldoni. Goldoni writes with irrepressible chagrin: "Now indeed the question of money is the most important for me. I have my brother here with me;

I must pay the debts he left in Modena; I must provide him with clothes and find some sort of employment for him. I have no money; to-day I borrowed six sequins." In one of his minor poems he explains that he was the bread-winner for eight persons. At some unfixed date, probably 1754, his mother died, and at some also unstated moment his brother made his exit, but still his burden was heavy, considering that it must be met out of the minimum of six hundred ducats for six new plays a year, or the maximum of eight hundred for eight plays, with an unfixed surplus offered as a free gift when it pleased his excellency.

We have already said that Vendramin took no pains to make matters easy with the comedians. It was the author's unassisted tact and the players' appreciation of his talent that gradually smoothed the way to pleasant relations. The difficulty of Goldoni's position is very well shown in his management of the Gandini pair, where it was necessary for him to reconcile the arrogance of an elderly leading lady, backed by a bullying husband, and the claims of his art. It is absurd to assert his amorous infatuation for a younger and more clever actress, la Bresciani. Goldoni never allowed personal motives to intrude. He composed adequate rôles for this actress and she contributed to the success of his plays by her exquisite performance.

Another affair brought more pain and did not end so well. His natural kindness, or perhaps some private motive, made Goldoni anxious to secure employment for a young man, Giovanni Simoni, nicknamed

"Goldoncino", whom he sometime kept as his secretary and who wanted to become an actor. Repeatedly Goldoni entreated Vendramin to admit the young man into the company of the San Luca, just give him a chance, just try him as a second or a third rôle. Vendramin was not to be moved. Goldoni appealed to his feelings "as a Christian and as a nobleman." His Excellency does not see why "either as a gentleman or as a Christian" he should relinquish one iota of his obstinacy or run the risk of some small expense for his poet or for the young man whom he brutally designates by the name *figliuolo*.[1]

Thus through the letters it is possible to note a crescendo of irritation; and alas! a growing desire to shake off his fetters. The intonation remains deferential, but the spirit is of rebellion.[2]

[1] Goldoni to Fr. Vendramin, March 10, 1759 (p. 95, D. M.): "Their (the players) having excluded the young man I recommended so warmly is clear evidence of their scanty love and esteem. . . . I am, as a Christian and as a gentleman, under the obligation of providing for that young man; . . . Your Excellency is a gentleman, your Excellency has some affection for me, your Excellency will remember that which you have promised."

Fr. Vendramin to C. Goldoni, March 15, 1759, Venice (p. 98, D. M.): "That you are in duty bound to provide for that young man, I do not see that it concerns my theatre. . . . Of my affection for you, you may judge by all that you can remember; because I am a gentleman I am sure that I never failed," etc. (but Goldoni's protégé was not accepted).

[2] Goldoni to Vendramin, March 17, 1759 (p. 101, following D. M.): Goldoni explains that he has been made offers for Rome and Naples but that he hesitates to accept them. "My hesitation is not the effect of indecision or caprice, not greed of gain or ill will against any one, and still less do I overlook your interest and my engagement toward your Excellency, with the players and the public of Venice whom I love and respect, but from a moral persuasion that your Excellency would gladly set me free. This persuasion being grounded on the unsatisfactory snubs of the players and

(allow me to say so) on the facility with which your Excellency has let them humiliate me on the question of the young man I protected. All this put together induces me to believe that for a whole year I might be left quiet. One year's vacation does not alter the contract 'for ten years' when both parties were agreed on this point."

Goldoni is forced to give up his projected tour in Naples. But the sore point is still the young man. "This young man is not related to me, but I have promised to provide for him and I must keep my promise. He would be the first actor accepted on my recommendation. He could never be so bad as to prejudice the troupe in the rôle of third *Amoroso*. . . . It is God's will that I should be so humbled. Yet everyone knows that I have tried in every occasion to repay the wrong made to me by acts of kindness; and so will I ever do."

CHAPTER V

GOLDONI'S LIFE FROM 1753 TO 1760

Goldoni's fondness for the groundlings — cares only for popular applause of those in the pit — description of Venetian theatres — Goldoni the guest of several patricians — also friend of several men of letters — he accepts patronage but not servitude — friendship with Arconati Visconti, Stefano Sciugliaga, Gaspare Gozzi, and Fr. Albergati — how Goldoni was paid by his patrons — play *Il Cortesan Vecchio* a failure — visits court of Parma and is granted pension — goes to Rome — interview with Pope Clement XIII — his plays a failure in Rome — physical contrast between Goldoni and Gozzi — Gozzi's life and character — Gozzi founds academy of "Granelleschi" — attacks Goldoni in a disgusting poem — payment for literary work considered undignified — reasons for Goldoni's going to Paris — character of the *Théâtre Italien* in Paris — Vendramin permits Goldoni to leave Venice 1762 — he stops at Bologna, Parma, and Genoa and thence on to Paris.

BRAVE-HEARTED Goldoni has his vulnerable point — his fondness for his public, for the Venetian audience, and especially for the groundlings. Malignant criticism, worries of stage management he faces bravely and forgets to record, but a misunderstanding with his fickle audience he resents bitterly and remembers years later. When he fawns, when he turns out of his way, and forgets the principles of his intended reform, it is because he wishes the approval of these judges.

Goldoni did not depend on public favour for his earnings. Both with Medebach and with Vendramin his contract fixed the price of the plays irrespective of their success. Goldoni's craving for applause is not mercenary. It is stronger than pride, stronger even than self-respect; and many times it has led him astray, but fortunately it has more often guided him aright.

Goldoni cares little for Chiari's rivalry and the even more bitter attacks of Carlo Gozzi, but he will do almost anything to keep the only prize he cares for — popular applause. No cynic, no boaster, he wants his friends to really know him in the everyday relations of business and entertainment.

Thus he tells stories of his doings, anecdotes of intercourse with players, but nothing absolutely confidential. He does not desire intimacy, but he is eager to secure many friends. Thus he gives *Il Teatro Comico*, which he calls "a dialogued treatise of comic art," in order to acquaint the general public with his intentions; thus he gives the *Avvocato Veniziano* to remind his audience that he is a barrister and is proud of his profession; thus in *L'Avventuriere Onorato* he relates many anecdotes — true or slightly arranged — which he attributes to himself. His letters to Bettinelli, written as prefaces to the volumes of his plays, have the same character of attenuated autobiography; they all aim to establish a friendly understanding between himself and his readers.

The eighteenth century yielded many such "confessions," even in Italy, although Italians are less than any other people inclined to such exhibitions. Casanova tells all and more than all the truth about his life, but there are many Italians who, like Gaspare Gozzi and Goldoni, only reveal that which any one could know about them; or like Carlo Gozzi, only mention such fragments of their personal history as relate to some particular fact. Goldoni, too, has a clear aim in view, as he writes to his friends, or in the unpremeditated style of his prefaces, or when he uses the actors as his mouthpiece to address the audience.

A Venetian audience, then, had a physiognomy of its own. A Venetian crowd was different from any other. Centuries of close communion with artists that translated the Venetian spirit into every form of beauty had especially prepared the people to judge that most complex art — a comedy. There was no better judge of theatrical performance than the public of a city that contained sixteen theatres at a time when London had only six and Paris ten, no better judge than the countrymen of the best actors in the world. Also, for centuries the Venetians had been flattered and pampered somewhat on the plan of ancient Rome, their favour courted not in the "forum" but in the "circenses."

Instinctively Goldoni relies on the judgment of this Venetian audience. Not on the people who sit in their tiny boxes, for the sake of seeing and being seen, paying or receiving visits, discussing the latest scandal and weaving the everlasting tissue of flirtations and amours. Little clapping of hands or demand for encores came from the boxes, too engrossed in their everlasting *conversazione*. Even music could not enforce silence for anything except the favourite tune or the elaborate *cadenza*.

The audience which Goldoni calls "my public" were those who sat or stood in the pit. It was, and is still, the habit for even fashionable men to stop in the pit either on their way from one box to the other, or simply for the sake of a quiet hearing. Gaspare Gozzi complained of the practice of the aristocracy spitting from the boxes on the heads of those who were underneath in the pit. The fact is almost incredible. The groundlings gave most of the applause when they were satisfied, and certainly the whole of hissing when they disapproved. Goldoni knew that the judgment passed on a play by this part of the public was without appeal. He always feared them. The plays he thought his best he gave first in Venice, then in other cities; those about which he had misgivings, he preferred trying first somewhere else.

Descriptions of Venetian theatres are found in every book of travel.[1] As a rule foreigners moralise about the apparent intimacy reigning in the boxes; Italians

[1] De Vaumorière: *Lettres sur toutes sortes de sujets*, Paris, 1714, for a description of theatres in Venice. "The boxes on the second tiers are generally preferred and specially those in front. . . . Many persons rent boxes for the whole time of carnival; they have them painted and hung with tapestries inside, which is not a small adornment. The pit has this comfortable arrangement: it is almost wholly filled with seats, folding chairs and armchairs, which allow of resting one's shoulders and arms without troubling one's neighbour."

Under the enlightened direction of Luigi Rasi, an ex-actor, a writer, and a

know better. A box is neither worse nor better than a drawing-room, open to a flow of callers, eventually turned into a sort of club by the setting of card tables. The often-quoted story of curtains drawn to close the box from the public is untrue as far as Venice is concerned. Witnesses tell how people crowded quietly into the pit that was thriftily held almost in the dark, just a few candles to prevent stumbling. The first-comers occupied the seats of rough wood. Later in the night payment for these seats was collected by an official coming round; the price differed according to the theatre and the season, but averaged about ten cents. Even in this semi-darkness no violent incidents occurred, though there was often considerable noise. Just before the rise of the curtain, lamps were lighted illuminating the stage but leaving the house almost dark. Inside the boxes chandeliers of white wax candles were lighted by the owners, adding to the brilliancy of the whole.

When Goldoni passed from the small Sant' Angelo to the larger San Luca, he had to win back the favour of "his public," part of which remained faithful to Medebach and his troupe, now performing the plays that Chiari wrote, in close imitation of his rival.

teacher, some very interesting reconstructions are being attempted of Goldonian and pre-Goldonian comedies. The Venetian masks and personages are represented in their historical costumes, the improvised rôles imitated, every detail carefully preserved.

Gaspare Gozzi's *Gazzetta Veneta* contains many papers concerning the Venetian theatres. It should be remembered that Gaspare Gozzi was for several years in partnership with his wife, Luisa Bergalli, acting manager of the Sant Angelo.

Chiari was better read, his mind was padded with books. Goldoni in his attempt to follow him forced his original genius to travel the pathways that suited a literary hack.

Omit, therefore, consideration of the exotic comedies Goldoni composed in this first engagement at the San Luca. The whole world was then pervaded with a fad for exotism. From *Robinson Crusoe* down to Montesquieu's *Lettres Persanes*, a few good works supported much rubbish. With Diderot's *Voyage de Bougainville* and many others it was simply a pretext for satirising their own country and developing their own social thesis. In Venice, where there was so much positive knowledge of distant lands obtained directly from foreign merchants and visitors, the fad came through literary contagion; it inspired the fantastic travels of Seriman and popularised translations and adaptations only mentioned because of the time Goldoni lost in composing the trilogy of Ircana. Its success, however, reconciled Goldoni to his favourite supporters and by bringing forth the actress, Signora Bresciani, smoothed over difficulties with the whole troupe.[1]

[1] Giuseppe Ortolani, *Della Vita e delle Opere di C. Goldoni, op. cit.*, quotes as most likely to have been read by Goldoni two books that may have provided him with notions about distant countries. *Lettere Critiche Giocose dell'avvocato Giuseppe Ántonio Costantini.*

And also *Viaggi di Enrico Wanton alle terre incognite di Australia e a paise delle scimie, dell abbate conte Zaccaria Seriman* — an imitation rather than a translation of Swift's.

Among exotic books tending to satirise the society wherein the writer was then living, a place should be given to Marmontel's *Incas*. Goldoni also doubtless read it.

Unfortunately Goldoni's literary production was unduly influenced by external circumstances, an influence which seldom develops originality. He relied too much on the opinion of others. He grew in his own esteem as he grew in the esteem of his fellow-citizens, and became better satisfied with himself and with his own work.

The aristocratic Venetian spirit did not permit Goldoni to move in patrician circles on a footing of intimacy. It was not difficult for each one to find his right place. Goldoni accepts the patronage of the patrician, since he is able to pay for every favour they may grant. Sometimes Goldoni gave more than he owed; the tarnished glory of many an ancient household, by the ornate style of his dedications, he gilded anew. Yet these patrons failed him in the hour of his need; they did not prevent his departure for Paris, as they might so easily have done.

In the full sunshine of popular favour, in the time of active production, Goldoni was the guest of several patricians—the Loredan, Mocenigo, Falier, Tiepolo, and others belonging to the "Libro d'Oro" or to the even more select rank of the "Apostles." Nor was his circle of patrons limited to Venice; Marquis Albergati Capacelli, senator of Bologna, Marquis Arconati Visconti of Milan, and even several noblemen of Frioul and Carinthia, acquired honour by showing him favour and, in a few cases, a benevolence very much like friendship.

Men of letters presently began to realise his value.

Parmenione Trissino,[1] after criticising severely Goldoni's first unlucky *Amalasunta*, afterward accepted dedications and wrote letters of encouragement and approval; Abbot Giam Battista Vicini,[2] deserting Chiari's party, championed Goldoni; Abbot Frugoni, an authority in Arcadian literature, quarrelled for personal and amorous motives, but was afterward reconciled; dignitaries of the Church, Cardinals Rezzonico and Lambertini, who both became Popes, and many *grandes dames* justified Goldoni's good opinion of his own value.

Unlike every other Italian poet of his time, Goldoni

[1] The Trissino famous in the history of Italian literature lived in the sixteenth century, 1478–1550. His tragedy *Sophonisbe* was immensely admired. Pope Leo X made him his Ambassador and Emperor Maximilian gave him the Toson d'Oro. Goldoni's friend, Parmenione Trissino, was only the author of some inferior plays, and a gentleman whose principal merit is the sound advice he gave to Goldoni, who thus records it in *Prefazione al tomo XI delle commedie: ediz Pasquali*, "Thus as we talked, passing from one topic to another (at the time of Goldoni's escape to Milan) I mentioned my tragedy *Amalasunta*. He (Count Parmenione Trissino) bade me read it; he praised it very coldly, and suggested that I would do better by turning to comedy. I promised that I would some time turn to it; but in the meanwhile *Amalasunta* flattered my pride."

To Parmenione Trissino Goldoni dedicated his *Giuocatore*.

[2] Giam Battista Vicini, whom Von Lonner suspects of being the abbot whom Goldoni saw on the pillory of Modena, was first a partisan of Chiari's but later a supporter of Goldoni. Born in Modena in 1709, he died there, 1782. He is said by Tiraboschi (*Biblioteca Modenese*, vol. vi p. 384) "to have held with honour his place of poet laureate at this court. He might have aimed at higher place amongst poets if his diligence in cultivating his talent had equalled his natural disposition." Though he wrote some of the poetical epistles collected by Chiari in Modena with a view of discrediting Goldoni and his plays, we find several letters of Goldoni's addressed to him, plays dedicated and some light poetry signed by Vicin, in the polemic battles.

never accepted that attenuated form of slavery, attachment to one great house or party. He would not tolerate the collar of servitude, even though disguised under the title of secretary, or the euphemism of confidential agent. Casanova's *Memoirs* and Ballarini's *Letters* reveal how easily this patronage could be obtained, and what enormous advantages it carried.[1]

[1] A very long chapter could be made out of the different *salons* where Goldoni visited. Some names are well known to readers of Vernon Lee and De Brousse. We mention here only the most important ones.

First in importance for the rôle she played in Gaspare Gozzi's life and for the share attributed to her in the unhappy Carlo Gozzi-Grattarol affair is Caterina Dolfin Tron. Born of a noble but impoverished family, married to a Tiepolo, Marco Antonio, the marriage was registered in the Libro d'Oro but not the divorce. Tiepolo was not a good husband and his neglected wife did not submit to such treatment. With wit and poetical talent, after publication of her poems she attracted many suitors and selected Andrea Tron. They were married in 1771. Two years later Tron was elected Procuratore di San Marco. His power was so great that he was known all over Venice by the nickname of *el paron*. It is said that he spent sixty thousand lire for feasts on his accession to his charge. Emperor Joseph II was his guest, foreigners of fame and Italians of birth begged for admission, poets sang the praise of the lady, and pamphleteers penned satires and lampoons. Barbarò openly praised Caterina. Carlo Gozzi dedicated to her his *Marfisa Bizarra Arcadia*. Her *salon* might have rivalled the most famous Parisian *salons* if Venice had not just then lost her splendour and intellectual value. Barbarò confirms the reputation of speculative freedom of ideas admitted in the *entourage* by these lines:

"Da strissimi studiosi
Citevimo Russò
Da Strissimi ingegnosi
Dicevimo bomò."

which freely translated means, "we quoted Rousseau and forged *bomò* (bons mots) without losing our characteristic manners (remaining *lustrissimi*)."

When Carlo Gozzi ridiculed Grattarol, who held a State charge, in a play caricaturing him, Caterina Tron was asked to stop the scandal, but she refused and even encouraged the player who made up his face so

Such a yoke, once accepted, was a life insurance, a protection against all foes, and brought the certainty of daily bread. Goldoni's tact and ability could easily have won for him such a position. Yet his foreign biographers, judging of his character by some ceremonious compliments and flattering expressions, mere formalities then in common use, have pictured him as an obsequious courtier.

In many instances, Goldoni, by appealing to his high-born patrons, might have avoided some unpleasantries or punished his foes. To mention one such occasion, in the year 1752 Goldoni was so much in favour with the Loredans and the Gradenigos that he was invited to the banquet celebrating the alliance of these two semi-royal families by the marriage of two direct descendants of the Queen of Cyprus, Caterina Cornaro. Evidently such personages were able and willing to protect the poet admitted to their table, from whom they accepted the dedication of plays, from whom they demanded a poem on every important event of their houses, yet the swarm of pamphleteers buzzing round Goldoni's ears were left undisturbed simply because he did not care to ask protection against them.

as to perfectly imitate the unfortunate Grattarol, an art practised in Venice to perfection; and Grattarol could sit for an entire evening listening to the laughter and abuse addressed to an almost perfect counterpart of himself.

After Andrea Tron's death his widow retired to private life, rejoicing in the triumph of those philosophical ideas which she had expressed as freely in Venice as anyone did then in Paris. (For more about Caterina Dolfin Tron see in *Nuova Antologia*, June, 1882, Castelnuovo, *Una Dama Veneziana del Secolo XVIII*; Pompeo Molmenti, *Epistolari Veneziani del Secolo XVIII*; Ernesto Masi, *Studi Letterai*, etc.)

One of his earliest and most constant friendships .was with Arconati Visconti. At every turning point of Goldoni's career we find him writing to this great nobleman. Sometimes it is just a short note testifying to his perfect reliance on his reader's sympathy; sometimes it is an exposition of plans, and in some rare instance it is a short outburst of ill humour caused by the perpetual worries of his career. In the preface to one of his plays, *La Putta Onorata*, Goldoni pays homage to his friend and patron's lordly hospitality by describing the princely residence of Castellazzo, where the Arconati Visconti maintained the magnificent traditions of Lombard munificence. This description is typical of the writer's incapacity to appreciate the natural beauty of landscape and enjoy the healthy pleasure of open-air exercise; but it is also interesting as a picture of that characteristic feature of Italian life, *la villeggiatura*.

Goldoni has little to say about the park, rich with game and grand old trees; he is full of admiration for the gardens adorned with plants "so cleverly cropped and fashioned that they give architectural beauty to the grounds." He is also impressed by the presence of tamed wild animals roaming freely about, or kept in cages.

But, for him, the most wonderful place is the library with its many volumes and its annexed lobby for experimental astronomy. At this time Newton's works were the fad, and ladies prattled about science, and Arconati Visconti lectured to his guests about *la mécanique philosophique*.

This sort of castle life varied in the different parts of Italy. It imitated city life and customs, was stamped with the ceremonious formalism of the time, but differed in different districts. From his early boyhood Goldoni was always a welcome guest in such places. He knew how to make himself useful and agreeable. At Count Widiman's [1] country seat of Bagnoli, the mania for private theatricals was carried so far that Goldoni's best praise to the master of the house is to represent him as a good pupil of Sacchi's, an excellent Arlecchino.

Goldoni directed the amateur performances, manipulated the scenarios, or wrote the rôles. He presided at rehearsals. The ladies made much of him, and insisted on his taking a part. He complied, but with little success; the ladies made fun of him, and he retorted by setting up a fair, in which he represented four different characters and set the audience in roars

[1] Locovico Widiman was a patrician and also a count of the empire. (See *Memoirs*, chapter xxvi, second part and also in *Componimenti diversi.*) The poem in *ottave, Il Pellegrino*, composed in 1763–64 to solemnise the entrance into a convent of Vittoria, daughter of Widiman, is a long praise of the family, and contains descriptions of Bagnoli, Count Widiman's country seat near Padua.

"Twice every year, in gleeful company of ladies and cavaliers and goodly friends, in cool autumn, and in summer season — he (Widiman) enjoys and bids others with him enjoy blissful days," etc.

In the second part of the poem written after the patrician's death Goldoni has accents of genuine emotion when he tells "*Oh quali grazie*" about a present received. Further on Goldoni says: "But the greater profit, the more priceless advantage, — was ever for me his voice, his advice — candidly I opened to him my heart . . . he did not speak much, but from his lips poured forth pearls and lilies. His saying was clear and strong, dictated only by sincere friendship, and a heart of justice. . . ."

of laughter by his impersonations of a mountebank, a trickster, a street singer, and a stage manager. It was a splendid imitation of all these characters as they could be seen any day on the Piazzetta, a sample of that naturalism which Goldoni alone possessed. Moreover he managed to ridicule in his improvised speeches the persons who had laughed at him.

The list of Goldoni's friends covers almost every class, every shade of opinion. On the lowest social round was Giacomo Casanova, whose mother was one of Goldoni's first interpreters. It is a question whether this friendship began in some Freemason Lodge. Anyhow Casanova was charged with belonging to the secret society, and imprisoned just at the outset of the Goldoni-Chiari quarrel, and he had been heard to promise *un cargo de legnæ* (a volley of blows) to the presuming abbot. Many years later Casanova slandered Goldoni in an interview with Voltaire, discovering thus the essential incompatibility which made friendship impossible between them.

A far better man remained faithful to Goldoni even after a prolonged absence, Stefano Sciugliaga[1] in Garbugliesi, on whose sympathy and support Goldoni

[1] Stefano Sciugliaga in Garbugliesi (*Memoirs*, chapter xxvii). Both Sciugliaga's and Gaspare Gozzi's names are to be found side by side with Goldoni's in occasional poems celebrating some event of the same patrician households.

Very few letters to Sciugliaga are found in Goldoni's correspondence. It is regrettable, since Sciugliaga was a confidential friend, and also because even as late as 1780 . . . we know that he kept pleading his cause in Venice, acting as intermediary between Goldoni and Vendramin.

could always rely. A man of importance holding a diplomatic office in Milan, who could also write a defence of his friend when the opportunity demanded.

Gaspare Gozzi,[1] the most justly famous, is also the most constant and active of Goldoni's friends. With great tact he avoided the polemics between Goldoni and his own brother Carlo, even while he at every opportunity praised and encouraged Goldoni. Between his mind and Goldoni's there was a spiritual relationship that proved stronger than family affection

[1] Gaspare Gozzi came of a very ancient family of foreign—Ragusean—origin, descending, however, from a branch that settled in Venice, in 1592, and was in the course of centuries allied to the Tiepolo, Cornaro, Morosini, and other Venetian patricians. Gaspare was the eldest of nine children. His mother, *née* Tiepolo, represented the worst type of Venetian *gentildonna*, extravagant, domineering, spiteful, quarrelsome, yet unable to manage either her financial affairs or to bring up decently her many children.

Gozzi's wife was Luigia or Luisa Bergalli, a poetess, in Arcadia "*Irminda Partenide*," who was almost as great a trial as her mother-in-law. After 1758, impoverished Gozzi started writing and translating as a means of living and paying off debts. In 1777 his health broke down from overwork and he attempted suicide. Caterina Dolfin Tron came to his assistance and made life easier for him. Gaspare's second wife, Giovanna Cenet, outlived him. He died in Padua in December, 1786.

Gaspare Gozzi's *Difesa di Dante* is the best known of his writings. It was the rallying cry of the defenders of classicism against Saverio Bettinelli's *Lettere di Virgilio*.

Besides an enormous amount of other writings there were his literary reviews: *La Gazzetta Veneta*, in one hundred and three numbers, February, 1760, January, 1761; *L'Osservatore*, one hundred and four numbers, February, 1761, January, 1762. They did not pay. Yet they are a precious font of information and are still interesting reading. See about G. Gozzi: Tommaseo, Firenze, *Le Monnier*, three vols. E. Masi: *Sul Teatro Italiano de Secolo XVIII Fierenze*, Sansoni, 1891. G. Zanella: *G. Addison e Gaspare Gozzi in Parallelii Letterarii*, Verona, 1884, and of course the *Manuali* of D'Ancona e Bacci, and of Mestica, the *Storia della Letteratura Italiana*, edited by Vallardi, which are standard works, often quoted.

or literary polemic. From the high position which Gozzi's literary review held in the world of letters, his support and approval, even if mildly expressed, was an enormous encouragement. When Goldoni wished Voltaire's praise of him to be made known, Gozzi printed in his *Review* Voltaire's verse and Goldoni's translation and answer; when Goldoni left for Paris, Gozzi assumed the heavy task of revising and correcting the Pasquali edition of his friend's plays.

A characteristic figure of aristocratic epicurism and literary dilettantism was Goldoni's friend Albergati [1] Capacelli, of ancient Bolognese family, a man of importance, honoured by many, flattered and incensed by many more. Common gossip discussed his magnificent establishment in Bologna, and his famous villa of Zola, writers and critics mentioned his authorship

[1] About Fr. Albergati see: *La vita, i tempi e gli amici di Francesco Albergati*, di Ernesto Masi, Bologna, 1888. A clever book which outlines the unimportant figure of the noble marquis, senator of Bologna, *chambellan* to his Majesty the King of Poland, the host of Cardinal Lambertini, the correspondent of Voltaire, etc., most fitly by leaving him in the shadow and grouping around him more interesting personages. Of his several love affairs only one need be recorded. Elisabetta Caminer Turra was that exception, in her time a woman of letters who was not a dilettante but who really wanted to earn some money. She began by writing contributions to a literary review, *L'Europa Letteraria*, that succeeded the *Giornale dei Letterati* of Zeno and the *Gazzetta* of G. Gozzi. She afterward translated French plays, Beaumarchais', Saurin's, and Goldoni's *Bourru Bienfaisant*. Her romance with Albergati lasted long enough to endow the petite bourgeoise with the manners, the tact, the conversational ability that years later in Vicenza, when she had married a Doctor Turra, permitted Elisabetta Caminer to become the centre of a literary salon. Something like a *salon* on the plan of Mesdames du Deffand et Geoffrin in Paris or Isabella Albrizzi and Giustina Renier in Venice. See E. Caminer, *Teatro*, in four vols., edited Colombani.

and performance of plays. A regular correspondent with Voltaire, an entertainer of Cardinal Lambertini and many other great men, he provided endless argument for moralists and magistrates by the multiplicity and scandal of his love affairs, that sometimes ended in marriage and — once at least — ended in suicide; yet he would be forgotten nowadays but for the part he played in Goldoni's affairs.

Albergati's relations with Goldoni are worth serious study, as they show many different aspects of contemporary life. The marquis and senator was so sorely affected with the stage craze that he eagerly sought from Goldoni not only the manuscript of new plays, but as much good advice and direction as possible. Suggestions that certainly were not lost by the receiver. Even more interesting would it be to follow through Goldoni's letters the reflection of Albergati's jealousy of the compliments Goldoni paid to the *Contessina*, the lady who for some time reigned in Albergati's heart and over his household. Yet Goldoni's relations to Albergati remained friendly even to the last and Albergati is almost the only Italian subscriber to the Parisian *Memoirs*, a notable instance of fidelity in one who had proved himself fickle to three wives and many mistresses.

Two other of Goldoni's early and faithful friends were the brothers Cornet,[1] in whose quiet and hospitable

[1] In a letter to Gabriel Cornet, April 20, 1759, Goldoni, lamenting his friend's absence from Venice, exclaims: "I wish you may be coming back in time to see my new plays. I wish it most earnestly because when you are

house, in Venice, Goldoni caught a first glimpse of French politeness and gentle manners. The letters that have been saved out of a correspondence that evidently was intimate and active make it doubly regrettable that so many have been lost. They are more free from reticence than any other of Goldoni's. Some of Goldoni's most important statements about his plans or about his intentions are derived from these epistles. There is a confidential intimacy that indicates a certainty of being understood and approved. To Gabriel Cornet, Goldoni entrusted the care of some delicate family affairs when he left Venice.

It is easy to reconstruct Goldoni's position in the intellectual sets of his time. The simplicity and straightforwardness of his nature attracted those spirits who inclined toward the simple beauty of realism in art, of common honesty in daily life. Thus Pietro Longhi vies with Piazzetta in repeatedly reproducing the features of the poet, which Marco Pitteri found pleasure in engraving, and others in moulding in medals.

It is difficult to know what sort of support Goldoni accepted from his friends and patrons. Honest pay for honest work was not by any means the standard of the time. Judging by his expressions of gratitude one might think that he received more than he gave;

not here I miss one of my best friends, one who is a champion of my fame. . . . In your absence I rejoice in the affection of your family to whom I beg to be commended, entreating you to remember often even from afar he who swears to be forever your friend and servant. Goldo."

judging by results one must rather think that he got very little for the great pains he always took for satisfying every demand of poetical homage. Either he was too proud or else too indolent to ask for protection against slanderers and pamphleteers, though his rivals and detractors were certainly bitter in their attacks.

His *Memoirs* tell of one episode which was probably not the only one he could remember. It was in the first year of his engagement at the San Luca, when, not realising the obstacles to a reform of the old comedy, Goldoni attempted a bold novelty. The idea was so true to life that one wonders why it so startled and shocked the Venetian audience. Goldoni chose for the central figure of his play, the lover, a man no longer young.

It is a foible of southern nations and an axiom of the stage that the part of *amoroso* should always be performed by a very young and handsome actor. Prejudice against middle-aged stage characters had the sanction of tradition through every classical imitation; it had gained in intensity and vulgarity through the *commedia dell'arte*.

Goldoni, who studied out of two books, "the world and the stage," who had already elevated the mask of Brighella and the character of Colombina, attempted now to present the gentleman of wit and pleasant manners whose hair was turning to grey while his heart remained youthful.[1] The San Luca company

[1] *Il Vecchio Bizarro*, performed under the title of *Il Cortesan Vecchio*, was violently hissed. Goldoni, dedicating it to his Excellency Bonfadini, Governatore of Chiozza (Chioggia) in 1727–28, when Goldoni was Coadjutore, and

was just then enriched by the excellent actor Rubini, whom Goldoni knew well and pronounced to be one of the most amiable men he ever met. The play composed for Rubini, on the plan that served so well of adapting the rôle to the actor that was to enact it, is a jewel of characterisation and an exquisite picture of customs; yet it failed. Whether, as Goldoni says, Rubini was not at his best, nervous at appearing without a mask, or whether the novelty was too great an anticipation of public taste, the failure was complete. The disapproval was so violent that Goldoni left the theatre in a distress and exasperation which demanded solitude. Where could any man be so perfectly alone as in the midst of a crowd under the shelter of a mask? Where could he expect to learn the real causes of such a startling failure as in the very centre of Venetian life, in the Ridotto? [1]

ever afterward, as in Milan, a generous patron of Goldoni's, acknowledged this failure "*non caddeno precipitò del palco*" — a parody of Tasso's line in *Gerusalemme Liberata:* "*non scese no precipitò di sella*" (it did not fall; it tumbled down).

[1] For his experience at the Ridotto on that evening see in preface of *Il Contrattempo* (1754): "This Ridotto is an ample place wherein among many wise persons, meeting for their decent amusement, a number of idle, sour men are allowed to crowd in. Having covered with a mask their faces, they persuade themselves that their voices too are disguised and will not be known when they speak. They thus confide their own affairs to people who do not care to know anything about them; and besides their own they even discuss other people's affairs, adding freely invented stories, or jokes which they suppose to be very witty. They pass sentence on a man, and do not know that he may be standing behind their back."

Il Caffe, published in Milan by the brothers Verri and their friends, contains many praises of Goldoni's plays and a bitter word battle with Baretti, "*Il caro Barretti*," whom Goldoni scorned to answer.

There under the impenetrable disguise of an ample *tabarro*, a white vizor, and the three-cornered hat that went with this dress, Goldoni lingered long enough to hear the talk of those who came in, as usual, after the end of the play. So severe were the opinions he heard that years afterward he remembered the tone of the voice, the very words spoken. A man who spoke through his nose, the noble born, low-souled pamphleteer Zorzi, declared "that Goldoni was finished, that he had emptied his bag and could do nothing more."

Goldoni went home in a rage. He dismissed even the sweet company of Nicoletta. He vented his anger in the only way that he conceived adequate: he composed and versified a play in which all the absurd criticisms spoken at the Ridotto were ridiculed and repeated by the comic characters. Goldoni sketched the character of *Grisolgo* in the *Malcontenti*, and though he consented to the cutting out of the rôle to please the censors, he did not destroy the manuscript and probably read it to some friends.

If ever Goldoni's equanimity was shaken by Chiari's attacks there was balm for his spirit in the growing favour shown to him by the great. A bourgeois by birth and education, a democrat by natural instinct, Goldoni was too much of his time and too much of a Venetian not to appreciate the magic of princely or royal acknowledgment. In Parma and from a prince of the Bourbon family he got a first draught of this intoxicating nectar. Du Tillot, the great minister of this petty State, thought that it would add lustre to the glory of a grandson of *le Roi Soleil* to encourage poets and artists. Goldoni, having already written some books for operas and other poems for that court, was invited to Parma and to the Versailles of the State, the ducal residence of Colorno. There he was granted the official title of "Poet of the Court," which implied a small pension. Voltaire, forgetting how he used to fawn and flatter the royal mistress of Louis XV and how he trimmed and shifted to earn the title of *chambellan* of Frederic II, made sarcastic reference to Goldoni's acceptance of this chain. Favours that came unasked, that did not require any real *diminutio capitis*, he accepted with the courteous thanks, the long sweeping bow, that were part of the Venetian etiquette, and he did not omit the ornate phrasing and incense burning that politeness then demanded.

The three thousand Parmesan lire did not seriously enlarge Goldoni's budget, but his stay at this miniature French court greatly influenced his future. By his own confession he did not understand French at the time. Yet he was attracted by the French manners, the gay magnificence, the talk, and even the theatrical performances of the French court of Parma. Some of the persons he met there, like Signor Duni, the musician, spoke a good deal about Parisian life and opportunities. Goldoni dreamed of larger gains and more repose, as contrasted with the worries of his actual situation with Vendramin. After his visit to Parma there was a growing interest in French persons. Goldoni enjoys the homely gatherings in the residence of Madame Cornet, his friend's mother. Two years later he is enthusiastic about the *esprit* and Parisian amiability of Madame du Bocage, whose drawing-room was a French intellectual resort.

This time, which was the brightest for his literary production, the most fruitful of masterpieces, and which shows him possessing a full mastery of his art, might have been the happiest and most productive if, instead of a tattling, shrewish employer like Vendramin, Goldoni had served an enlightened and generous patron, and received financial advantages corresponding to public favour. From the disconnected account of the *Memoirs*, from other information gleaned by his biographers, one discovers Goldoni making the most of professional opportunities for quitting Venice. He eagerly accepted an invitation to visit Rome, and probably hoped to prolong his stay there.

With the elevation of one of their family to the throne of Saint Peter, the Venetian Rezzonicos were spreading their influence over Rome. A Count Rezzonico encouraged a direct invitation to Goldoni from the manager of the Tordinona Theatre. Vendramin was silenced for a time by the shadow of such a patronage. He did not forbid Goldoni's going, but grumbled in his letters almost from the first.

Goldoni's stay in Rome was made very pleasant by the favour of the Rezzonicos, by Cardinal Porto Carrero, and other great personages. Even the Pope found pleasure in his Venetian chat. The account of his papal audience is typical of Venetian manners, contrasting with the solemn etiquette of the court. Goldoni was well known to the Pope; they had met in the palaces of Venice and Padua. Goldoni had even composed a poem celebrating the elevation to the Roman throne of this pope, Clement XIII.[1] Naturally the audience lasted longer than customary for such ceremonies, as the two Venetians exchanged gossip and information. They may for a moment have forgotten where they were; Goldoni certainly did. "His Holiness touched the bell on his table: it was for me the signal of departure. As I moved away I performed many bows and signs of reverence and gratitude; but still the Holy Father did not seem satisfied. He moved his feet, his arms; he coughed; he glanced at me significantly but said nothing." At last Goldoni understands! He was forgetting to kiss the papal foot! He kneels down, pays the ritual homage to a much bejewelled slipper, and makes his exit.

Though he was by this time fifty-two, Goldoni has no real appreciation of Rome. Just a few lines of admiring prose about Saint Peter's and he passes to a pretty sketch of the family he lived with, a married

[1] Interview with Pope Clement XIII (*Memoirs*, chap. xxxvii, part ii). Goldoni was bearer of letters from the Minister of Parma for Cardinal Porto Carrero, Spanish Ambassador; of a letter from Prince Rezzonico to his brother, both nephews of the reigning Pope. He lodged with Abbot Petro Poloni, whom he has very pleasantly described in his *Memoirs*, Chap. xxxvii, part ii. With him besides Nicoletta was the young man, Giovanni Simoni, nicknamed Goldoncino, whom he was so eager to provide for. (See extracts of *Letters*.)

abbot who is proud of such a famous guest; then he gives his experience with the Roman actors.

This Roman experience should have enlightened Goldoni as to the impossibility of transplanting his plays into an alien atmosphere and to the difficulty of having them interpreted properly by actors differently trained. The Neapolitan actors who made such a disgusting muddle of his *Vedova Spiritosa* should have been a warning against their brethren of "*la Comêdie Italienne*." Think of a Neapolitan *Pulcinella* impersonating nimble-footed, nimbler-tongued *Arlecchino!* Think of a close-shaven Roman lout impersonating the witty, coquettish Venetian widow! The shock for Goldoni and also for his patrician protector was great. They should have remembered that women were not allowed on the stage of Roman theatres; and certainly they should have known the sort of fun expected from Neapolitan *comici*.

Goldoni did not remonstrate. From the first *Pulcinella* impertinently declared "that everyone has his own notions of art; these are ours." With the docility and good will that were predominant qualities of his nature, Goldoni did his best for the Roman manager and actors by selecting from operas and popular songs some representations that, bringing no honour to him, filled the house at night. It was a sin against his own art thus to lose his precious time and energies, but he was resolved that ill-mannered, clownish *Pulcinella* and the other actors should not be losers, if he could help it.

The more aristocratic theatre of Capranica took up

Goldoni's plays and provided him with a certain success, a compensation which cheered his spirits just then wounded by Vendramin's refusal to admit his protégé, Simoni, on trial, and encouraged him so far as to make plans for a trip to Naples. Here, however, Vendramin interfered and forbade this tour, although Goldoni pleaded that an interruption of even one year — part in Rome and part in Naples — could in no wise alter the terms of the contract binding him to the San Luca.

When Goldoni, reluctantly obeying Vendramin's orders, retraced his steps toward Venice, he knew what was in store for him. He lingered in Pisa and other cities bidding farewell "unconsciously," as he says, to this Italian country that he did not "then think of leaving." Goldoni did not fly from the spectacle of his rival's success, but before the combined misery of insult on one hand and of wrangling incomprehension on the other.

Personal antagonism between Count Carlo Gozzi and Avvocato Goldoni was as complete and unavoidable as racial, social, personal differences and contrasts could make it. Carlo Gozzi is so completely the antithesis of Carlo Goldoni that between them they cover most of the characteristic traits of their time and country, the one having that which the other lacks. Goldoni is the representative of the middle class and the forerunner of a more democratic and national spirit, Gozzi is an embodiment of that which was passing. He is the representative of aristocratic prejudice, of Venetian separatism.

Contrast between Goldoni and Gozzi was noticeable even in their appearance. Gozzi tall, gaunt, loosely built, his hard features unrelieved by any shadow of kindness, the sourness of his expression growing with age until it became the darksome, strained stare of incipient mania, a slovenliness of attire that later degenerated in antiquated singularity — the exact opposite of Goldoni's figure, face, and manners. The sixth of a family of eleven, Carlo spent his childhood in a dilapidated castle under the misgovernment of his vain patrician mother, *née* Tiepolo, and the mismanagement of ill-paid servants. The miracle is that his elder brother Gaspare escaped the worst influence of this education. It may be that things went from bad to worse and that the younger children were even less cared for than their elders. Also that family discord gained in bitterness in proportion with increasing poverty, Countess Gozzi insisting on her birthright to direct. Yet she was even more inclined to extravagance, gambling, and display than the average Venetian gentlewoman. Of her many children she took no care, providing the traits of Gaspare's picture of a young nobleman entrusted to the care of servants, "as were the puppies," initiated to the most undesirable aspects of life by the gossip in the servants' quarters and afterward guided to the most disreputable haunts by these same teachers. Worse still, Countess Gozzi, by her extreme partiality, provoked the quarrels and litigation of her children.

They were a curious brood of talented, mad people,

these Gozzi — an hospital of poets, as one of them has said. Like every Venetian of the time they could "indite" poetry or improvise scenes of comedy; they could perform their own compositions and amuse even grown-up people with their acting. That the habitual amusement of these children was composing plays and masquerades is a sign of the time; that they were allowed to parody their neighbours and the guests, and that without reproof they should have made their own parents and the family quarrels the object of their clownish performances is significant.

From this disrespectful childhood they passed on to so many entangled lawsuits that the residue of a once prosperous estate dribbled away. Gaspare found comparative peace and self-respect in hard toil; Carlo never recovered a healthy mental balance. After spending some years as an official in the colonies (or, as they were called, "*stati di terra firma*") in Dalmatia, he returned to Venice a confirmed grumbler. Thus while Goldoni developed in pleasant social intercourse, in naturally sweet disposition, Gozzi grew more bilious and ill-tempered.

Thus while Goldoni made friends everywhere and had many small love affairs that caused no greater harm than a few tears, or some regretful sighs, Gozzi's stern maturity only exploded in a passion and a jealousy for an actress that drove his rival Grattarol away from Venice a ruined and discredited diplomat. Thus while Goldoni scribbled autobiographic prefaces filled with pleasant anecdotes, or in his serene poverty and old age retraced the history of his life in fragments of amusing memories, Gozzi only wrote with some malignant aim in view. When he wrote his *Memoirs* he merely aimed at explaining his share of responsibility in the Grattarol affair. It is a long pamphlet, full of venom and falsehood.

His old age was further embittered by the change in public affairs. Count Carlo Gozzi lived to sign his own name "citoyen C. Gozzi"; he lived long enough to protest, even on his death-bed, even in his last will, against the new notions of a philosophy that was destroying the old order of things. This was bitterest pain for a man of Gozzi's violent and stubborn conservatism, the last act of the gloomy tragedy of his life.

Carlo Gozzi possessed sufficient book learning to champion correctness, purity, Italianism, against the novelty of Goldoni's reform. His title of count somewhat excused his supercilious contempt; his small means allowed him the petty satisfaction of taunting the poet who was obliged to live by his pen. While in Dalmatia he was snubbed by his superiors. Gozzi resented this humiliation. He took no interest in the natives. On coming home after seven years, he discovered that between his mother and sister-in-law the ruin of the family was almost complete. He set about quarrelling and litigating. As a diversion he joined his brother Gaspare and a party of literati in founding the academy ingloriously known under the untranslatable name of "Granelleschi."

This academy would have been as completely ignored

by posterity as all such mushroom growths deserved to be but for the scandal of Gozzi's attacks on Goldoni. A group of idlers with some pretensions of scholarship who presumed to fight for the purity of the Italian idiom by insisting on servile imitation of Tuscan trecentists. Unlike other such attempts which, in imitation of Arcadia and the Tuscan Crusca, aimed at delicacy and refinement, these Granelleschi affected the utmost grossness of feelings and expressions.

The principal activity of this society, besides some foolish ceremonies at their meetings, was the publication of a sort of literary review, "*Atti dell'Academia dei Granelleschi*," issued at the "Libreria Colombani." Carlo Gozzi wrote for this review a number of pamphlets against both Chiari and Goldoni. At first he had supported Chiari, and indeed pitted him against Goldoni, but he soon realised that the pedantic abbot was a useless ally.

Coarse and unscrupulous Gozzi was, but not dull. A mock heroical poem, *La Marfisa Bizarra*, though it chiefly owes its celebrity to its insults against Goldoni and Chiari, "*Marco e Matteo del pian di San Michele*," as they are nicknamed by "*Dodon della Mazza*" in imitation of Ariosto, possesses some rudeness, force, and imagination.

Two years later, in 1750, Gozzi gave out an almanach, *La Tartana degli Influssi*, for the year 1749, in which Goldoni and Chiari were caricatured, presented as two mountebanks fighting with wooden swords, then, after having amused the onlookers for a while, dividing the profits of their performance. Gozzi's conservatism and his caste prejudice embittered the quarrel. In his eyes Chiari was an unworthy priest who could pen a profane comedy after celebrating mass, and Goldoni was an impertinent scribbler who dared observe the degradation and represent the folly of the aristocracy. In his eyes both these writers were also degraded by accepting money for their literary work. For a noble-born dilettante this was a desecration.

The poem *Il Teatro Comico all'Osteria del Pellegrino*, entirely devoted to crushing Goldoni, was the most disgustingly personal of all his pamphlets. First Goldoni is represented as a three-headed monster speaking by turns with each one of his three mouths. This is a parody of the several sorts of plays Goldoni was then producing: the sentimental, the romantic, and the popular comedies. There is some wit and a real comprehension of the aims and objects of the reformer. But the satire becomes disgusting when it proceeds to show Goldoni, "*il Teatro Comico*," enticed within the drinking house "*il Pellegrino*," drunk, made a laughingstock, and finally driven to a desperate appeal. The burlesque of that appeal is unparalleled in Italian satire. Goldoni is pictured unbuttoning his *culotte* and discovering a fourth mouth in the middle of his belly; out of this mouth is uttered a whining entreaty, explaining that whatever the three other mouths have been attempting to do had no other object but filling this one.

Now, not only in Gozzi's opinion, but according to a

generally admitted notion, and even in Goldoni's eyes, the fact of selling the produce of one's brains was considered undignified. In order to depreciate Goldoni's work, Carlo Gozzi, when he was forty-two, wrote the first of his *fiabe*. He tauntingly said that people went in crowds to see Sacchi, Tabarin, Goldoni, or a dancing bear and that they would be sure to come to see his plays. At worst, he added, the author who writes these *fiabe* gives them as a present.

Certainly the production of these plays of Gozzi, that were the antithesis of his own and which tended to overthrow all his plans of reform, caused more grief to Goldoni than he would ever confess [1]; yet the critics and biographers who have charged Gozzi with the entire responsibility for Goldoni's expatriation go too far. How far this rivalry influenced Goldoni's decision it is not easy to decide. Goldoni could shrug his shoulders at Gozzi's insults when, in the same family, in the same aristocratic circles, there were champions to defend his fame; when from the "oracle of

[1] For all this matter see *Modena a C. Goldoni*, *op. cit.*

In Goldoni's *Letters* or *Memoirs* very little is to be found of these polemics. In a letter to Arconati Visconti, April 5, 1755, accompanying a short poem by Padre Roberti, Goldoni says: "It is not a small honour for me that a Jesuit writes about a play, and benignantly praises its author. He does not follow the style of the Modenese in their Epistles in Martelliani; nor does he set me above great authors as they have done for their versifier" (Chiari).

(Two of these Modenese letters came from the pen of G. B. Vicini; they were addressed to Chiari and bore the title in the printed edition, *La commedia dell'arte e la Maschera*, and were outrageously bitter against Goldoni, yet Goldoni forgave them and never mentioned Vicini's name otherwise than with respectful admiration.)

Nations"[1] came the verdict that proclaimed him a great poet and the painter of Nature. Goldoni was not so unconscious of his own value as to run away at the first shifting of the wind in public favour.

In addition to Carlo Gozzi's persecution, niggardly Vendramin[2] must bear his full share of responsibility in

[1] The expression "*L'oracolo delle genti*" is to be found in Goldoni's answer to Voltaire's well-known lines.

En tout pays on se pique
De molester les talens:
De Goldoni les critiques
Combattent ses partisans.
On ne savait á quel titre
On doit juger ses écrits;
Dans ce procès on a pris
La Nature pour arbitre.
Aux critiques, aux rivaux
La Nature a dit, sans feinte,
Tout auteur a ses défauts,
Mais ce Goldoni m'a peinte.

Gaspare Gozzi printed both in his *Gazzette Veneta*, No. 45, July, 1760.

[2] From *Letters:* Dino Mantovani, *G. e il Teatro S. Luca*, *op. cit.*

Vendramin to Goldoni, August, 1759 (page 135): ". . . Thus for the disposition of things before or in the performance of plays, I must tell you that it would be well if you were in Verona, because they (the players) complain of you from a distance when they think that they have a right to do so. But with me they complain *viva voce*, charging me with all their grievances. . . . I have been made to undergo laments, discussions, tears, and all that which I have not thought fit to tell you, wishing to spare you a share of my annoyances. . . ."

In the same letter Vendramin objects to sending the one hundred ducats.

A few days later (page 141) Goldoni writes: "Now indeed the question of money has become the most important one since on every other point we are agreed. I have got my brother here with all the debts he has made in Modena for his living, I must provide him with clothes, and find for him some sort of employment. I am without cash, to-day I borrowed six sequins. Your Excellency has some kindness for me and may reach further

driving Goldoni from Venice and Italy. The stolidity of the government in refusing him a place or a pension must also be taken into account, and also racial instincts, the tastes, the social habits of Goldoni help to explain how the desire for change finally became irresistible.

The *Memoirs* become at this vital point not only incomplete but even misleading, and fail to give a true revelation of the growth of discontent and the dawn of new prospects. Contradiction between the *Memoirs* and the *Letters* is more than inaccuracy; it is too constant and too significant not to suggest a purpose. He naturally wishes to conceal his disappointment in his countrymen from the knowledge of his foreign readers and his tendency to forgive and forget unpleasant experiences made this even easier. Goldoni will not depreciate his own value and make himself cheap by recognising defeat.

with your hand than your steward could with his foot" (meaning that Vendramin could write a cheque as easily as send round a servant).

On December 4th (page 145) Goldoni was exasperated past all endurance, and from Bologna he asked to be released from his contract. "With all due respect and humility let me tell Your Excellency that I understand clearly that you are annoyed with me, anyhow your players are tired. With the same submissiveness that made me accept the honour of serving you, I am ready to accept the release which it may please you to grant me, or which I may be forced to take after this year."

From Vendramin to Sig. Fontana, *segretario dell'Ambasciata Veneta à Paris*, on receiving some information about Goldoni's intentions of going to Paris, his Excellency insinuates that "C. Goldoni, a comic poet who now serves and must for five years more serve in my theatre, as according to contract which I here enclose, is said to be taking steps for going to Paris," and he entreats Sig. Fontana to serve him with the utmost discretion and secrecy. Why if the contracts were binding does he not say so? Why does he condescend to Goldoni's departure if he could prevent it?

That he came to this decision slowly is inferred from the account of his doings up to this momentous date of 1761. From the first allurements of the court in Parma, from the first glimpse there of the munificence and amiability of a French sovereign, contrasted with the disappointment at the San Luca theatre, the players' malice and incapacity, the manager's supercilious ways and niggardly support, we can see how the thought of quitting Venice gradually took form in Goldoni's mind.

Even far back in a letter to Cornet, Goldoni expressed a wish to accompany his friend to Paris; and in all his correspondence with Albergati there is the infatuation that Paris promised both profit and honour, comfort and pleasure. Goldoni's notions about French customs were slight, his ignorance of the language almost complete, his ignorance of the French spirit profound. But Paris was a change, it was release from unprofitable, unpleasant duty, and also it was escape from malignant satire and rude rivalry.

One of Goldoni's most undisguised contradictions is between his often-quoted letter to Albergati and the corresponding passage in the *Memoirs*. To the friendly patron who supported his plans Goldoni writes: "Oh, what good news will this letter bring you! Goldoni is going to Paris! He will, so please God, leave in Lent of next year; he will pay you homage in Bologna, then pass through Ginevra so as to embrace Mr. de Voltaire." This double promise of visits is significant. Goldoni's first thanks go to those who aided his plan of release. "You will say what are you going to Paris for? I have been two years in correspondence with the Théâtre Italien, to go and take the management, that is to say, to have my works there performed according to the taste of the people. There were difficulties on the side of the French players that are partners in the troupe (the Italian troupe). But now everything is settled. . . ."

Thus there had been discussion of terms, difficulties raised and settled, trial plays performed to probe public opinion, terms fixed. "Messieurs les gentilshommes de la Chambre have written to the Venetian Ambassador. My salary will be six thousand francs a year, and the thing is settled for two years; my travel expenses to be refunded. . . ."

How different all this reads from the *Memoirs;* from the story of an almost casual visit to the French Ambassador and to the surprise of receiving from him a letter, ". . . a letter just received among other official despatches from his court. . . . The letter was written by Signor Zanuzzi, the actor . . . who introduced my play *Il Figlio di' Arlecchino perduto e ritrovato*. . . ." Then, adds Goldoni, the French Ambassador offers his good offices to overcome any difficulty that could arise with the Venetian Government and mentions that the Duc d'Aumont is very eager to have him in Paris. Even if the sad sequel of events did not contradict this statement of the case, the account thus offered could hardly be accepted. Two years, planning and discussing, invitations and encouragement coming from the many Italian friends of Goldoni that were already in Paris, seem a more likely version of the truth, or at least of that comparative truth which alone can be discovered.

Lelio Riccoboni, Favart, Duni, the father and sisters Veronese, and many more who in some manner were attached to the theatre and friendly to Goldoni, may have been active in forwarding a plan that promised to be profitable to the Italian Theatre in Paris. A further indication of lengthy pourparlers may be gathered out of Vendramin's letter to Signor Fontana asking for information and insinuating that the thing should be stopped "prudently."

Did Goldoni then contemplate remaining in Paris longer than two years? In his letter to Albergati he writes: "If I gain some praise, I may remain on better terms; if I do not, I will have to come back to Italy; having gained no further advantage than enriching my imagination by the novelties I may have seen, and having given to my edition an impulse that alone would justify my undertaking the travel. . . ."

Goldoni's arrangements were just those that his habitual prudence and kindness would make for the greater advantage of everyone concerned. Besides Nicoletta he proposed to take Antonio his nephew with him, trusting to provide some employment for him in France. Petronilla, Giampaolo's daughter, Goldoni sent to the safe protection of a convent, further providing her with the guardianship of a steadier man than her own father.[1] Though Giampaolo was not to be trusted with the management of his own children, yet his brother did not leave him unprovided; some relics of the Modenese estate were transferred to him, so that he might end his life in respectable comfort. Friends were at hand, willing to do their best for Goldoni in his absence. Cornet would supervise some affairs, Gaspare Gozzi would attend to the publication of plays, Stefano Sciugliaga was ready to interpose with all the authority due to his position between Goldoni and Vendramin.

How and by what arguments Vendramin was persuaded to grant those terms which admitted of Goldoni's departure, Goldoni does not say, and no letter of either party has been found. The *Memoirs* say that Goldoni obtained "with some pains" (*avec un peu de peine*) this permission. For all we know of Goldoni's euphemisms this may mean a long and exasperating wrangle, as it certainly meant the bugbear of a hard yoke awaiting him in Venice, if ever he came back.[2]

Leave-taking from his beloved Venetian audience was quite another thing.[3] Even while he was preparing

[1] Giampaolo's children: Petronilla Margherita was born in 1749 and Anton Francesco Paolo Mariano about 1750. Petronilla married in 1781 and at that time it appears that her father was dead.

[2] For text of contract see D. Mantovani's *Goldoni, e il Teatro, op. cit.* The arrangements imported that Goldoni interrupted, did not break, his engagement of ten consecutive years with Vendramin. Also that he should send every year some new play. This agreement was signed in March, 1762.

[3] Anzoletto's adieu in *Una delle ultime sere di Carnovale* (act iii, sc. 13) is often quoted.

"That I could forget this country! This my beloved native land!

for departure, even while he seemed to be deserting them, Goldoni's heart craved sympathy. He could refrain from complaining, he could disguise disappointment, he could not permit any misunderstanding between the people of Venice and himself. The play which he composed uniquely with that aim in view is the cry of a soul appealing to other souls, the pleading of a man forced to break away from home and associations and desirous of having his motives understood. It has a force, a pathos that no other of Goldoni's works possesses. If tragedy ever flapped her black wings above Goldoni's heart, it was at this turning point of his career.[1]

According to promise, Goldoni and his party halted first in Bologna. There his health broke down. Malice interpreted this prolonged stay in Bologna in many ways. He condescends to explain, in his *Memoirs*, that if he also composed an *opera comica* he

Forget my patrons, my good friends! This is not the first time I have gone away, and wherever I have been I have always carried the name of Venice engraved on my heart. I have always remembered the favour, the kindness I received; I have always longed to return, and whenever I did come back it was with the greatest joy. Every comparison I have been able to make has shown me my country more beautiful, more magnificent, more worthy of respect; whenever I came back I discovered new beauty; so will it be this time, too, if God grants I come back. I confess and I swear on my honour that I leave with a broken heart, and that no attraction, no pleasure, no fortune I may meet, will compensate the grief of being away from those I love. Do not deprive me of your affection, my dear friends; may Heaven bless you: I say so with all my heart."

[1] Goldoni left Venice April 15, 1762. The *Gazzetta Veneta*, May 22, gives the strange particular that Goldoni was told just at that moment that one Signor Teodoro was already performing the office of playwright in his place at the San Luca.

did not stay on purpose. Zola was a delightful abode, the hospitality of *casa* Albergati proverbial. What wonder if Goldoni lingered on his visit?

A visit to Parma was imperative.[1] Goldoni was pensioned by this French petty sovereign and must not only take official leave from his royal patron, but also obtain letters and commendations for the French court. Something in the Venetian customs predisposed Goldoni to become a courtier and to rely on the favour of princes. In Parma, on his first visit, Goldoni, having caught a glimpse of French manners and of French actors, was eager now to practise his French there. "I speak much and blunder along unblushingly; people understand me or at least they never ask me to repeat my words; and I enjoy wonderfully the fine conversations, '*à la façon française.*' My wife, poor thing, is not quite so well pleased; she does not understand one word of French, yet it is good for her to train her ear to their talk and also to fall into their ways and offer her cheek for '*se laisser embrasser.*'"

Thus Goldoni to his friend Gabriel Cornet.[2] Evi-

[1] Goldoni himself in a letter to Gabriel Cornet — Parma, July, 1762, (see *Lettere di C. G. di E. Masi, op. cit.*, page 164) thus describes their party. ". . . My nephew is enjoying himself fully. He stutters some French, but I am afraid he will have a weakness for the *mesdemoiselles*" (sic).

"O the worthy son of such a great father! Tonino (the servant boy) will find it hard to learn French, when he thinks that he has understood, he brings water when one has asked for wine. He is eager to serve, his excessive good will makes him frantic. He is like one possessed. Yesterday he dropped two cups of chocolate on my bed. . . ."

[2] Goldoni to Gabriel Cornet, *Let. di Gol.*, E. Masi, *op. cit.*, p. 163, Parma, July, 1762.

"What a fine life! What a delightful trip! . . . I have been already

dently the courtesies and encouragement they lavished on him, in Parma, and at the royal residence of Colorno, have elated Goldoni. He is lodged grandly, at the palazzo Rezzonico, in the absence of its masters; a household of servants are at his orders, and from the reigning duke he receives promises of patronage for the royal court "*de mon grand'pere.*" More favours, more promises, Goldoni receives in Corte Maggiore from the Landgrave of Darmstadt and the Princess Dowager of Parma and then onward toward Genoa so as to bid farewell to the Connios; onward then through French cities, along French roads, toward that Paris where he was expected by a company of second-hand comedians in a theatre of less than second rank.

ten days in Parma; only one day have I been able to *dîner chez moi.* I have seen the court in Parma; and now in half an hour's time will see them again in Colorno to take my leave. . . . I am staying in the house of Signor Conte Rezzonico, who is for the moment in Milan, having left his orders to his gardener that I should be lodged and provided for. What a splendid house! What a fine garden! This is indeed a pleasant way of travelling. . . ."

CHAPTER VI

THE END OF GOLDONI'S LIFE

After his departure from Italy his *Memoirs* are especially inaccurate — reasons for this — Italian comedy in Paris had greatly degenerated — French plays and French actors admitted to the Italian theatre — *Figlio d'Arlecchino* played before court at Fontainebleau — a failure — Goldoni rents apartment in "Rue de Richelieu" — his judgments of Parisians are superficial — his friendships not profitable — did not make headway in the Paris *salon* — he aims at royal favour — is a natural courtier — his visit to Diderot and to Rousseau — he fails to understand the French — his play *Il Ventaglio* a success — *Les Amours d'Arlequin et de Camille* a great success — is appointed teacher of Italian for Princess Adelaide — eyesight injured — is lodged at court at Versailles — Nicoletta not happy at court — perpetual difficulties with Vendramin — receives a pension — Italian theatre in Paris comes to an end 1781 — his *Bourru Bienfaisant* a great success — fight against poverty — nurses Nicoletta through illness — his niece Petronilla marries — longing for Venice — stops writing when eighty years old — dies at age of eighty-six, February 6, 1793 — in politics was a conservative democrat — *La Convention* granted his widow a pension — she did not long outlive him.

THOUGH Goldoni's *Memoirs* from beginning to end are frequently inaccurate as to facts, and are never a sincerely confidential account of their author's feelings and sensations, they do give us a picturesque and in the main a correct idea of his life, if we allow for his histrionic viewpoint. But from the moment his narrative reaches his departure from Italy for Paris until the end of his narrative, Goldoni seems almost to have been intentionally inaccurate. Several possible reasons may account for this apparent insincerity.

Goldoni's memory was poor. We have noted many errors, and there are many more in his narrative. His dates are seldom right, sometimes he forgets to mention some of his own plays, often misspells names of persons or places familiar to him. These mistakes, frequent in his youth, increased with old age, semi-blindness, and a heavy heart. Goldoni was almost eighty years old when he undertook to fulfil his engagement toward subscribers to his *Memoirs*, knowing that a certain amount of manuscript must be sent in to the printer daily, and he was in financial and mental distress. So long as he could fashion his narrative from material accumulated in his prefaces and his other published anecdotes, his work was easy. Without correcting or improving, he took everything as it was in the Italian and turned it into his colourless French. But when this Italian material was exhausted, he tried padding. Sometimes he analyses his works, sometimes he describes Paris and its monuments, sometimes he drifts into long enumerations of "friends," though some were scarcely acquaintances, sometimes he describes books and plays, but above all he gossips about pompous trifles of court life. Not certainly in the style of a Pepys, or a Saint-Simon, who could make trifles interesting, but in the timid style of one who needs favour, and cannot afford to be quite sincere.

Things began to go wrong even before he reached Paris. At Lyons [1] he received a letter from Zanuzzi

[1] From Lyons Goldoni writes August, 1762, to his friend Gabriel Cornet, — *Lettere editeda*, E. Masi, *op. cit.*, page 168: "To tell the truth, after

saying that the comic opera had been united to the Italian comedy and the Italians reduced to the rank of accessories. Goldoni, who had not sufficiently understood the conditions of the Théâtre Italien at Paris, failed even now to realise what this union with "l'Opéra Comique" was likely to mean.

He knew that public taste was tending to music rather than spoken comedy and also to spectacular performances. The tendency answered to the spirit of the times, to that same spirit which in Venice advantaged Carlo Gozzi's *fiabe* over his own plays. Moreover he knew that the Italian comedy had been fast declining. Ever since Lelio Riccoboni,[1] answering the Prince Regent's invitation, had valiantly endeavoured to galvanise it, *la Comédie Italienne* lived a poor and indecorous life, holding on by expedients which brought no real glory and only a small financial return. Riccoboni attempted to direct public taste by giving classical pieces, Scipione Maffei's *Merope*

Marseilles and after Aix, which is a pretty city, all the rest of Provence and the Dauphinais disgusted me sorely for the ugly and dirty towns one meets there. On reaching Lyons I breathed and felt comforted, and I now begin to appreciate France. The city is very fine, well situated. . . . I have thought it wise not to stop at Geneva, where I first intended to go, as I did not want to appear impertinent or to take advantage of the great love and anxiety they show for me."

[1] Madame Riccoboni, widow of Francesco Riccoboni, under the pseudonym of Laboras de Mézière, published several novels. Goldoni praises them in terms that seem unjustified. The last days of his life were employed in the translation of one of these novels, *Histoire de Miss Jenny*. She imitated Fielding in a novel *Amélie* and presumed to give a sequel to Marivaux's *Marianne* (see Ademollo, *Una Famiglia di Comici Italiani nel Secolo XVIII*, Firenze, 1885).

in 1716 with free entrance, and Ariosto's *Scolastica* a few months later. Yet with all his ability and with a good repertoire of plays he failed and was reduced to repeating stock plays, and to courting public favour by allowing full liberty to his players in the way of *lazzi* and clownish tricks. His successors did worse. They admitted French plays and French artists and produced heterogeneous comedies of the so-called *genre forain*, and they catered to the growing taste of their audience for *grivoiseries* by intermingling dances and songs with their plays.

At the end of Carnival season in 1739, in a *complimento*, Signora Riccoboni says, "*Sifflez plutôt, messieurs, mais revenez nous voir,*" a program that should have disgusted Goldoni from attempting to collaborate with such artists. The troupe drifted lower still under the direction of "le sieur Brécourt," who made his Pierrot — an addition to the Italian staff of masks — announce to the audience that "*il recevra des acteurs à tous prix — mais il veut que surtout les femmes soient jolies,*" closing this significant speech with this *boniment*, "*il permet les amants et les tracasseries.*" We can only guess how much of this Goldoni knew.

That his half-forgotten play, *Il Figlio d'Arlecchino perduto e ritrovato*, arranged by Zanuzzi, had met with some success was not in itself a serious encouragement. From plays of that sort Goldoni tried to wean the Italian public. Against this unæsthetic conception of comic art he fought vehemently in his critical prefaces. He knew also that his *Pettegolezzi della Donne* in a French adaptation by Riccoboni was favourably received, an adaptation so different from the original that it should have discouraged him, by showing how the taste of the Parisian public differed from the Venetian.

His reasons for leaving Venice must have been great, if such slender encouragement from Paris influenced his decision. Optimism, however, or the dignified reticence of the man who hides his fears, dictates the playful narrative of his travel both in his letters and in his *Memoirs*. "I even imagined that my countrymen would consider their honour at stake, would emulate their new French comrades, and I supposed them perfectly able to sustain the competition."

He travelled leisurely, saying, "If the Parisians are fiery and impatient, I am too phlegmatic to trouble about them," stopping at Bologna to write an opera-buffa, stopping at Parma to take his leave from his princely patron, avoiding Ferney, since he was now courting favour from kings and princes and did not boast of the exiled Voltaire's friendship. Across France he progressed with more speed, failing to observe and describe the unfamiliar country and strange manners of life. In his earlier days, when wandering through Italy, he noted typical individuals, dialogues, and other traits and customs, which he afterward described. But now in travelling through France he neither describes a landscape, a city, or a monument, not even the Roman ruins of Aix. But he contrasts French and Italian custom-house officials, and indulges in a little etymological dispute with his nephew.

His first walks in Paris were enthusiastic. Madame du Bocage describes him as so *enchanté* with everything in Paris that he liked even the noise of its streets. He certainly liked Signora Riccoboni,[1] who, having retired from the stage, provided him with information about the actors; and he also liked Camilla Veronese [2] who was to interpret his plays and win for herself — and partly for him — the favour of Parisian audiences. Even the Italian actors [3] did not then disappoint him. He would not be discouraged, though he noticed that on the days of *opera comique* with the French actors the house was crowded but that the Italian actors failed to attract people. He hopefully discussed plans with his comedians, and only realised his danger when

[1] Also, and for everything about Italian comedy in Paris, see E. Campardon, *Les Comédiens du Roi de la Troupe Italienne*, Paris, 1880 (vol. i, p. 38, for Goldoni).

[2] About Camilla Veronese, Grimm in *Correspondance Générale*, *op. cit.*, vol. v, Janvier, 1764, says: "Si vous voulez savoir quels sont les meilleurs acteurs de Paris, je ne vous nommerai ni Lekain, ni Mlle Clairon, mais je vous enverrai voir Camilla et l'acteur qui joue d'ordinairement Pantalon et qui fait dans cette pièce le rôle d'un honnête homme."

[3] For the Italian players of the eighteenth century in Paris see Saint-Evremond, *De la Comédie Italienne*, 1677: "Pour les grimaces, les posture, les mouvements, pour l'agilité, la disposition, pour les changements d'un visage qui se démonte comme il lui plaît je ne sais s'ils ne sont pas préférables aux mimes et aux pantomimes des anciens . . . et ce serait un goût trop affecté de ne passe plaire à leur action parce qu'un homme délicat ne prendra pas plaisir à leurs discours."

The best known of Goldoni's troupe were Charle Bertinazzi-Carlino who impersonated *Arlecchino:* Du Hesse, valet; Collato who impersonated the Goldonian twins; Zanuzzi, first *amoroso*, surnamed Vitalbino Balletti, son to the celebrated Flaminia Riccoboni; Camilla Veronese; Mme. Favart; and two other ladies "who had no ability but were young" (see *Memoirs*, iii, chapter iii).

he attended the performance of his *Il Figlio d'Arlecchino* at Fontainebleau before the court.[1]

It was a repetition of that which he had endured in Rome when a close-shaven *trasteverino* impersonated his *Vedova Scaltra*. Had he indeed left Italy to collaborate with these Philistines who mingled the jokes of *Le Cocu Imaginaire* with his always decent dialogue? To have his play thus mangled! To have come so far in quest of honour and to be thus presented to an audience of king and princes! "I returned to Paris [2] with a firm and determined mind; but I had not to do with my comedians of Italy. I was no longer the master at Paris, as I had been in my own country."

He was not the master because the Paris public would not support his ideas of reform. Otherwise he was, at first, satisfied with his interpreters. He writes

[1] Goldoni to Sciugliaga, Paris, December 9th (D. M., 227): "The first of these three plays (*Arlequin et Camille* in French) was performed Wednesday last at court. I was there, and was very much annoyed. They started performance at seven — French hours — the king having sent word that he wanted supper by eight. In one hour they strangled my comedy. I was in despair to see it thus mangled. Withal the play was well received, but I have entreated that the others may not be given unless the court grant the necessary time required for performance. This will not be easily obtainable, because there they only give '*des petits pièces italiennes*' specially in this season."

[2] *Memoirs*, part iii, chap. iv: "On returning to Paris, I looked with another eye on that immense city. . . . I realised that curiosity and impatience had caused my first bewilderment; and that one could enjoy Paris and amuse oneself there without fatigue and without giving all one's time and one's peace."

From his window he could see among other novelties this most Venetiah meeting of *nouvellistes* around the '*Arbre de Cracovie*.' "They traced with their sticks in the sand trenches and camps, military positions, divided Europe according to their own particular view" (part iii, chap. iv).

to Gabriel Cornet (September, 1762) that he is pleased with *Arlecchino* and *Scapino*, though they speak French "so as to make the play better understood" and that the manager allows him to take time to study and observe before giving a new play. "Is it not," he adds, "a fine difference from the time when I drudged like a dog for one hundred ducats, embittered by reproaches and cutting words?" But in December, 1762, he confides to Albergati Capacelli that these Italian comedians are *des paresseux*. "They have not yet learned the first play I gave them. I have prepared two others *a soggetto* to suit their negligence."

Thus after toiling so many years in Italy to raise Italian comedy above the level of improvisation *a soggetto*, Goldoni was forced to resort to it in his very first Paris season. Worse still, he forces attention by giving a French synopsis of the Italian play, *L'Amor Paterno*, to be distributed at the door of the theatre on the first night. This first night was delayed from October to Christmas, then from Christmas to the end of Carnival, and was a failure.

When in his *Memoirs* he relates this lamentable history of his début he adds that he wished to leave Paris at once, but that the charm of the city proved stronger than the desire of returning to Venice.[1] But listen to

[1] For all these unofficial impressions of Paris see the volume of *Letters* edited by Ernesto Masi, *op. cit.*, page 191, for a letter to Albergati Capacelli, January, 1763. . . . "Rue de Richelieu à côté du Café de Foy, I have taken a pretty apartment with windows on the gardens of Palais Royal which is the finest walk in Paris wherein the great world and finest world are to be found. I cannot as yet decide whether I stay or not, as my first

this confession: "I never went to see my own plays; I was fond of good comedies, and went to the Théâtre Français." When such a man has lost pride and joy in his work there is little left for him.

Deciding to remain in Paris, Goldoni settled in an apartment elegantly furnished, "Rue de Richelieu,"[1] spending four thousand francs in adorning the nest for himself, Nicoletta, and his nephew. He explains that if he wanted to dispose of this extravagance he felt sure of a profit. From his windows he saw the Palais Royal, then the rendezvous of fashion. At that moment he was eager to mix with French people and to familiarise himself with the language, the manners, and the spirit of the country.[2] Evidently he failed. His judgments on Parisians are superficial. "Politeness," he says, "is the predominating character of the nation," a truism which he corrects by commenting that not all are sincere but none are disagreeable. "There is a certain uniformity of customs and manner of life which deprives one of the pleasure of making particular observation. Nowadays all vice and virtues are middling (*mediocri*); there is no typical original to be seen in anyone. The *petit maîtres* are lost in the crowd. Whoever has money to spend is a

piece has not yet been performed. When it was ready the soubrette fell ill, then the prima donna was confined. Now the former is all right, the latter almost out of it. It may be given next week." (It was only given much later.)

[1] In September 6, 1763, Goldoni gives to Gabriel Cornet his first address, rue Mauconseil; in January 24, to Albergati Capacelli this second and definitive address, Rue Richelieu à côté du café de Foy.

[2] See letter to Albergati Capacelli, October 23, 1762.

gentleman, and who has none appears satisfied. No misfortune afflicts them, they find comfort in considering that they might be worse off. Whenever they lose a battle or a city, they do not grieve, but rejoice at the idea of what is left."[1]

This astonishing picture of the French in 1762 is to be found in a letter to Albergati, hence it cannot be accounted for as can a similar bland characterisation of the French nation which he inserted in the *Memoirs*. It corroborates the general impression of Goldoni's rapid decline. Even before losing his eyesight, he lost the power to read character and detect the significant diversities that stamp on each individual a physiognomy of its own. Many things have been written about the French of this unique epoch that prepared the Revolution; yet no one has described them as lacking individuality.[2] Madame du Bocage,[3] who liked him, rightly judged, *Goldoni n'aura*

[1] Letter to Albergati Capacelli, Paris, October 25, 1762, E. Masi, *op. cit.*, page 18.

[2] Compare Goldoni's several descriptions of Paris to Sebastian Mercier's *Tableau de Paris* of the same time.

[3] Madame du Bocage (Marie Anne Lepage, b. 1710, d. 1802) travelled in Italy and made many valuable friends, amongst others Gaspare Gozzi and Algarotti, with whom she exchanged an active correspondence. She also published a *Voyage en Italie*. (See P. J. Guilbert, *Notice Biographique et Littéraire sur Mme. B.*, Rouen, 1807.)

Goldoni met her in Venice in 1757 and was captivated by her "conversation, sweet and intellectual," and flattered by some ready compliments she gave him. To her Italian friends she wrote frequently about Goldoni when he came to Paris. In February 1763 she tells Algarotti, "*Goldoni ne nous a encore rien donné*," and prophesies that he will not be understood and that he will not have time enough to understand and represent French manners. In March she gives further account of his doings: "Je l'ai

pas le temps ni les moyens de voir les nôtres (*mœurs*) *de façon a nous faire rire de nos ridicules ressemblants.* It was not merely time that he wanted, but a better knowledge of the language, of its subtleties and "finesses," and, above all, sympathy between him and his adopted countrymen.

Goldoni tried to persuade himself and his readers that he liked Paris, yet he was puzzled and astonished rather than attracted. His impressions resemble those of a simple-minded tourist on sight-seeing bent. "Every day I felt more perplexed as I tried to distinguish the ranks, the classes, the manner of living, and the different modes of thinking. I no longer knew what I was, what I wished for, or what I was becoming. I was absorbed in the vortex."[1] The more so because Goldoni, unlike Hume or Galiani, was not extolled and exhibited by any of those half-score ladies who from their *salons* guided the opinions of the people *le plus spirituel.*

In his misconception of this Parisian world, Goldoni failed to understand what support these women might have been for one who so needed tactful guidance and the protection of undiscussed authority. Madame Geoffrin, or du Deffand, if properly courted and en-

prié à dîner; nous avons parlé de vous, monsieur, de votre santé de vos talents, et des siens peu propres pour Paris, qu'il aime à la folie; jusqu'au tapage des rues meme lui plaît; hors la cherté des vivres et l'Opéra, tout le ravit; il me paraît même content de la maniére dont il a été reçu. On est à la vérité bien prévenu en sa faveur; mais si peu d'auditeu l'entendent que leur suffrage doit peu le flatter (*Opere di Algarotti*, p. 98).

[1] *Memoirs*, part iii, chap. iv.

listed as a champion, might have influenced critics and through them the taste of the larger public. At that moment, in Paris, the line between society and "literary shop" was not easily drawn. Goldoni's failure to penetrate within the sanctum of some coterie was one cause of his failure both to win favour and also to understand the French spirit.[1]

His friendships and acquaintances were not profitable. Favart [2] was always loyal, but neither his poetical mediocrity, nor the disputable propriety of his life, could promote that triumph over national prejudice which Goldoni needed. The other members of the club which Goldoni describes as *les Dominicaux* [3] were respectable writers. Some, like Joseph Saurin and Crebillon fils, have even conquered a little place in

[1] It is almost useless to mention here names that are in everybody's memory. Madame Geoffrin's celebrated *salon* was the habitual resort of all the Encyclopédistes, besides the aged and most influential Fontenelle. Abbot Galiani, a great favourite of this set, used to say that the armchairs of that house "were like the tripods of Appolo, and inspired people to say sublime things."

In the *salon* of Madame d'Épinay, where Diderot was a frequent visitor, Grimm held a privileged position.

There were also the Thursdays at Baron d'Holbach and the Tuesdays of Helvétius, known as "*les synagogues de l'Église philosophique*," and many lesser centres of conversation, "*bureaux d'esprit*."

[2] Favart, Charles Simon, was born in Paris, 1710. He died in 1792. His wife, Marie Justine Bénédicte Duronceray, 1727–72, is only too well known for her amours with Maurice de Saxe. For more piquant details about her see in *Le Mercure de France, 1915, La véritable Histoire de l'abbé de Voisenon.* Favart wrote an enormous amount of verse, mere doggerel. His *Memoirs* and correspondence have been edited by his nephew in 1808.

[3] Goldoni sometimes spells Dominiqueaux and gives this note of Members: M. de la Place (privileged to print le Mercure de France), M. de la Garde (a contributor to the same periodical, who also dabbled in theatricals),

the temple of fame, but, even had they made the effort, they had not enough authority to lift their friend to the same honour. Goldoni, describing in a sonnet[1] these weekly dinners and meetings, proclaims that "our meals are brightened by gaiety without nonsense — by discreet and salutary criticism — simplicity of heart and truth on every lip." A woman just once was admitted to this symposium, a clever and charming woman, crowned with the fame of a great artist and a passionate lover, Sophie Arnould. She tried to open Goldoni's ears to French music. For obvious reasons she could not introduce him into society.[2] Poor Nicoletta was not a help to her literary husband. "She does not enjoy Paris," writes Goldoni, "because she cannot speak French." A terrible handicap.

We have said that the Parisian *salon* was then the highway to fame and fortune. Goldoni did not gain admittance; perhaps he did not earnestly try; but

M. Saurin (the author of several tragedies), M. Louis, M. de la Ports, M. Crebillon fils (better known for his most shocking *Sopha* than for his tragedies *larmoyantes*), M. Favart, and M. Jouen.

"Each member of the society used to invite his colleagues and give them a dinner, and as these parties met on Sundays we adopted for them the name of Dominicales and we called ourselves les Dominicaux.

"The only statute we observed was obedience to the customs of good society, but we were agreed that women would not be admitted in our assemblies. We realised their charms and feared the sweet enticements of their sex."

[1] The sonnet is quoted by Malamanni in *Nuovi Appunti Goldoniani*, page 133. It begins: *Noi siamo nove: a ognun de noi le porte — sono schiuse dell'altro. . . .*

[2] Goldoni does not give here the name of Sophie Arnould, but mentions her as "*unica sorella dominicale*" in dedication of "*Il Curioso Accidente.*"

he certainly courted the critics and writers. Even before coming to Paris he had secured Voltaire's support. The philosopher of Ferney went with Goldoni as far as his wit and his command of Italian and of Venetian dialect allowed. In Italy, and especially in the literary set centring round Albergati Capacelli, these praises were taken for pure gold, translated, published, commented upon seriously; in France they were discredited by a better knowledge of Voltaire's willingness to give almost as much to anyone who asked for it, and perhaps also by some contradictory opinion uttered by Voltaire. Casanova has registered one such derogatory opinion. How many more did the wonderful *causeur* express? [1]

Then Goldoni aimed at royal favour; even from his first admittance to Fontainebleau, he was dazzled with courtly magnificence. Hence his reticence in answering Voltaire's compliments and his delay in paying him the visit announced in 1761 until Voltaire was in Paris receiving the homages of the en-

[1] Goldoni in a letter to Albergati Capacelli (Paris, June 13, 1763) gives this account of Voltaire's epistle: "At last I have got a letter from Voltaire. He writes *à propos* of the works I promise: 'Quand j'aurais l'honneur de vous faire parvenir mes rêveries, qui ne sont pas encore prêtes, je ferai avec vous le marché des Espagnols. Avec les Indiens ils donnaient de petits couteaux et des épingles pour de bon or.' I have every reason to retaliate the argument, and to believe that I am the Spaniard and Voltaire the Indian, but I fear the gold he could give me will be so long coming that he may forget everything about little knives and pins. I like well the end of his letter: 'Je recois quelquefois des lettres de Lelius Albergati, l'ami intime de Terence. Heureux ceux qui peuvent se trouver à table entre Lelius et Terence.' "

tire city. Goldoni was also befriended by Marmontel,[1] then director of "Le Mercure de France." A few words of praise and encouragement Goldoni repaid with the dedication of *La Casa Nova* and by many complimentary lines in his *Memoirs*. There was a similitude of temperament between them that might, under favourable circumstances, have given better fruit. Fréron [2] sided with Goldoni merely because Goldoni was then a fit in-

[1] Marmontel (Jean François de Bort), 1725–1799, holds a considerable place in French literature. His *Contes Moraux* and his *Incas* were then immensely admired and afterward immensely imitated (see Sainte-Beuve, *Causeries du Lundi*, Paris, 1880). When Goldoni knew him he was already a member of the Académie, of which later he became Secrétaire Perpétuel; he was also the directeur and principal contributor to Le Mercure de France, hence in a position to lend great assistance to a foreigner.

Goldoni in a letter to Conte Agostino Paradisi, March 28, 1763, writes: "Monsieur de Marmontel honours me with his friendship, he has subscribed to the edition of my plays, we meet very often and he speaks of me with kindness. He has lately printed an *Art Poëtique* wherein he does not speak ill of the Italians; he even praises them." Which shows that Goldoni was easily satisfied.

The dedication of *Casa Nova* is a logogriph lately explained by Carletta in the *Nuova Rassegna:* "*Un logogrifo di C. Goldoni*, May, 1893. Carletta suggests that Goldoni thus disguised his friend's name because the dedication was composed when Marmontel was imprisoned, or in disgrace. Other Goldonists suggest other rather far-fetched explanations. In fact logogriphs were just then the fad in Paris, especially in Le Mercure de France (see *Memoirs*, part iii, chap. xxxiii).

[2] Élie Catherine Fréron, the most biting antagonist of the philosophers, who always valiantly attacked even Voltaire and Diderot, was Director of *L'Année Littéraire* from 1754 to 1776. About his polemics with Diderot for *Il Vero Amico*, see chap. vi, p. 10.

Goldoni (*Memoirs*, part iii, chap. xxxiii) says of Fréron: "He was a very learned man and very sensible; no one could give a better summary of any book or any play than he did; he was sometimes bitter (*méchant*), but that is the fault of his profession."

strument for the pen of the pamphleteer to use against Diderot.[1]

Goldoni's visit to Diderot has been often told.[2] It is one of the most amusing anecdotes in this last part of his *Memoirs*, and just sincere enough to show Goldoni's good nature and the ill humour of one who was habitually above such petty bickerings. Diderot was annoyed, if not at Goldoni's success, certainly at Fréron's criticism. No writer likes to be convicted *flagrante delicto* of plagiarism. Diderot was such a hard worker, such an active contributor to every form of literary criticism, that he must be excused for having severely judged Goldoni's plays, "some sixty farces," as he lightly declared. To be found out and pilloried by Fréron aggravated his hasty temper. Goldoni thought to conciliate Diderot by an outstretched hand and an open heart, and to set things right with a smile and the apt quotation of two rhymed lines. He forbears to tell us Diderot's answer; he simply concludes

[1] Diderot was dead when Goldoni published his *Memoirs*, yet he preserves the respectful attitude toward him that he had assumed in the preface — "*L'Autore a chi legge*" — printed years before in Pasquali's edition of his plays (vol. vii), where we find: "In this great city (Paris) a piece has been printed under the title *Le Fils Naturel*. Its author is well known in the republic of letters for his talent and erudition and for being one of the principal contributors to the great Encyclopédie. . . . There seem to be, specially in the first scenes, some resemblances . . . there is a letter somewhat like mine . . . but these things can easily happen . . . two writers may very well hit on the same idea, just as two musicians may chance on the same tune. . . . He has paid me the honour of writing a *poetica* merely in order to show that I am not a great poet. . . ."

[2] For the visit to Diderot see Black's translation of *Memoirs*, pages 358 to 360.

with "both M. Duni and myself parted from him very well satisfied with what had taken place," which is no proof of Diderot's real reconciliation.

Goldoni's failure to conciliate Rousseau is even more typical. It shows his failure to comprehend the movement of ideas in Paris, and marks the abyss between his conception of honour and dignity, and that which gleamed bright in the conscience of poor Jean Jacques. The scene as it is narrated in the *Memoirs* almost equals some of the best in his plays.[1] It is complete and admirably finished, even from his first knocking at the door of a small apartment on the fourth floor, and his first glance at the woman, "neither young nor pretty nor prepossessing," who shocked his Venetian notion of a mistress of the house by answering the visitor's ring. We can imagine with what courtly bow Goldoni apologised for his mistake, and how Thérèse Levasseur, unused to such courtesy, must have stared at him. But imagine Goldoni's bewilderment at seeing the lady of the house "acting as a servant" and putting wood on the fire, while her "husband" looked on, and even bid his visitor "not disturb himself, and let her attend to her concerns."

Sound and reasonable advice Rousseau gave his visitor. "What are you doing here? . . . You came to France to work for the Italian comedians, who are lazy fellows and do not want your plays. Return again to your own country; I know that you are wanted there." Excellent advice, too, about the play

[1] Visit to Rousseau, see Black's translation of *Memoirs*, pages 393 to 396.

Goldoni was then preparing for the French Comédie; but it was not listened to, or at least not followed, because circumstances were beyond Goldoni's control. Grimm [1] several times mentions the Italian playwright and gives contradictory opinions about him, in his *Correspondance*. Grimm has written so much and about so many things and persons that he could not well omit this passing mention.

When, at his début in Venice, Goldoni aimed at the conquest of his public, circumstances were favourable. He spoke both their language and their dialect, imitated their manners, and read their hearts, could ridicule their faults, and detect their latent virtue; his players were at the same time his teachers and interpreters. Here in Paris everything was changed. The writer's own spirit was less elastic, his mind embittered, and he was growing old. There was the nightmare of possible failure. The French language he knew imperfectly, and must, when allowing his players to speak in French, rely on their standard of propriety and exact interpretation of his ideas. These players were just the sort of professionals that would grow in impertinent self-assertion under the system which then regulated

[1] Grimm's *Correspondance* was written for "*les cours du Nord*" and specially for Germany. It is a good sample of honest reporting. Grimm could never lose the abruptness and essential rudeness of his origin, he could never write lightly and *finement*, but he took pains to register every literary event and to give some account of everything that was then going on. In analysis of Goldoni's plays we quote some of his opinions. Charles Rabany, *op. cit.*, gives a great many more. In 1770 Grimm was made a baron and a minister of some petty German court.

the French theatres.[1] Goldoni was neither their master nor their partner; he worked for them. They flattered the public by following it. Goldoni's system had been just the opposite. Hence, in Paris, this initial misunderstanding which aggravated every difficulty and embittered every momentary triumph.[2] With the public matters went still worse. Goldoni's letters for that first year are filled with such expressions as: "So few people understand me. . . . In France women do not understand Italian and when they do not come to the theatre few men will come. . . . In a city containing one million souls or thereabout, I feel that those who understand and favour me are indeed too few. . ."

Goldoni did not, however, lose heart. He worked earnestly this first year in Paris. Work that brought little satisfaction, however. His *Letters* show him turning from Vendramin's perpetual demands [3] to

[1] For Italian players in Paris see E. Campardon, *op. cit.*, Riccoboni's *Histoire du Thé. it, op. cit.*

[2] About Goldoni's disagreements with Parisian actors see his letter to Melle Sylvestre, October 15, 1765 (In *Soccoriamo I bambini Rachitici*): "Oh miserable Italian comedy! I would gladly have paid out of my pocket the right to go away when my play was performed. You cannot imagine anything worse. They have chosen one of my worst plays and they have made it ten times worse by cutting it down from three acts to two. Then, as it was even then too long, they stopped when the *gentilhomme de la Chambre* said 'that will do.'"

[3] Sciugliaga to Vendramin, January, 1765 (D. M., 231). Sciugliaga resents fiercely certain unjustified assertions that extracts of Goldoni's plays had been shown. Such a charge, he says, is unsupported by evidence. While Goldoni complained of Venetian players discrediting the play even before its presentation to the public, he complained of their exacting caprices and petty rivalries. "If they are satisfied, well and good; if they

Albergati's more polite but not less insistent claims, from the toils of directing the many rehearsals of the plays to the composition of a variety of pieces to suit varied tastes. How painful to witness this great man groping in blind efforts to satisfy public caprice!

It is sad to see him in *L'Amor Paterno* flattering his audience with the praises of their own city. Sad to read Grimm's supercilious lines in pointing out this flattery. Sad to realise that the Parisian public was right; poor Goldoni, in his desire to conciliate, has flattered abjectly. One of his attempts was fortunate. If not a real masterpiece, it answered perfectly to its purpose of lightening the task of lazy artists and an uncomprehending audience; it was hardly more than a sketch, and yet a solidly constructed comedy, *Il Ventaglio*. Yet even that failed, even that minimum of effort was too much for audience and players.[1]

His patience was almost at an end, when, in August,

are not, no one obliges them to use the service of a poet they do not approve of, of whose doings they are always grumbling. If they are tired of him I can tell you that he is more than tired of them, and if they go on in this way I know that the author, as he writes, will be able to get out of it all with honour."

[1] In a letter to Albergati Capacelli, April 18, 1763, Goldoni writes: "Now I am trying a new sort of play to see whether these players can be made to perform something good. They will not learn written scenes, they cannot perform long and well constructed scenes; so I have composed a play made up of short, lively scenes, bristling with life and movement, so that the actors have nothing to do but to perform them more by acting than by speaking them. . . . A woman's fan starts the play, brings about the end, and supports the whole plot."

A month later to the same he wrote: "My play entitled *The Fan* has been performed, but not with the success I expected. It is too involved (*inviluppata*) for the ability of these actors."

1763, he detailed to his friend Albergati the whole series of his strenuous efforts and the scanty support received from his players. "They do not learn written comedies, and they cannot improvise well on outlines. I do my whole duty; if they cannot do theirs, it must be the worse for them. The end of this month closes my first year in Paris. If the second is not better, I will leave. '*De solo pane non vivit homo.*' Reputation is a man's food, and in search of reputation I will return to Italy as soon as I can."

Goldoni, however, made one more great effort. One of his plays had a clamorous success, supported by the talent of Camilla Veronese, and also helped by the morbid sentimentalism that was just then current in France and more especially in the French theatres.

Goldoni, knowing the hollowness of such a victory, yet rejoiced because it brought a reprieve to the hard problem of his staying or going. To Albergati Capacelli he wrote joyfully: "A week ago my play, *Les Amours d'Arlequin et de Camille*, was performed. The success obtained is so general and so full, that now I may say that my reputation is made in Paris. They granted me two years to find my way to their favour, I have found it in half the time. You know that the French like to weep at their tragedies and object to pathos in comedies. At this play of mine they wept and laughed with equal pleasure; its fun amused them, and its story interested them. This new sort of composition has pleased them all round. They say that their own theatre has nothing so good. In this play I have so managed that even those who do not understand Italian can follow the incidents, the pantomime, the truth, the life-likeness of the plot."

The second and third comedies, forming the trilogy of Camille's loves and pains, proved even more successful than the first. "The first two have done much; the third one everything. . . . If I transcribed here all the praise they are giving to my work, with all your kindness, you must tax me with exaggeration."

Even in these days of triumph Goldoni writes to Albergati (January 10): ". . . if I could, I would leave at once for Italy. Not because I dislike Paris but because I do not feel at home here (*Fuori del mio centro*) and I realise how difficult it is to satisfy when one is not understood. . . . Then six thousand francs a year, in Paris, do not cover the expenses of a gentleman; and I cannot swallow that even second-rate artists are pocketing fifteen thousand when I have to be satisfied with six." The gentlemen of the royal chamber interfered and Goldoni's gains were, if not increased, made a little more certain by their action, but as Goldoni wrote, "In Italy I was accustomed to something better."

The mirage of a royal court had haunted him ever since in Parma he saw the possibility of obtaining admittance "*auprès de mon Grand Père.*" This mirage he entertained from the time of his first coming to France, when he carefully recorded every word of compliment dropped by princely lips at Fontainebleau, when he adopted the "*deuil de cour*" for a princess he knew nothing about. He asked his friends to assist him in finding a permanent position. Favart,[1] the faithful and trusted, believing that the court of Vienna was then the best harbour for an Italian playwright, wrote to Vienna and planned for an engagement there. But this plan failed.

A Venetian Ambassador [2] offered to take Goldoni back to Venice in his train. Such a return might have restrained Vendramin and silenced the critics; but Goldoni hesitated. The ambassador was in bad health, he might not reach home — as indeed he did not — and the best effects of his protection would not outlive him. "A star," says he, "rose in my sky!" A lady in waiting or a reader of the dauphine and, like her, a foreigner in the court of France, introduced him to the dauphine and obtained for him the place of Italian teacher for the Princess Adelaide.

Goldoni was neither prepared nor fit for the task of teacher. Doubtless he did his best, and tried to earn his salary. He did not spare his trouble and accept the place as a sinecure, even though this first and the second and third royal pupils proved dull and idle. He took pains; he divided the lesson hours into exercises of pronunciation and translation, the reading

[1] Goldoni makes no mention of this plan of Favart, but part of the correspondence between Favart and the court of Vienna is to be found in E. Maddalena, *Goldoni e Favart*, *op. cit.*

[2] *Memoirs*, part iii, chap. vii: "On the other hand Le Chevalier Tiepolo, Ambassadeur de Venise, was always encouraging me to return to my country that loved and desired me; he was at the end of his embassy and would have taken me in his train."

of Muratori's *Annals* and of his own plays, besides some remarks on the differences between French and Italian literature, which he wrote overnight and then gave his pupil in the morning, that she might copy and memorise them.

When Goldoni turned to teaching as a means of support he renounced intellectual, sceptical, philosophical Paris, so filled then with new ideas, with confused but splendid ideals, and he slipped into the dull atmosphere of a court that had lost contact with the world. While the élite of French thought despised court honours, simple-minded Goldoni rejoiced in the slightest favour granted by princely ennui. Madame Adelaide [1] could rightly say: "*Vous verrez, nous sommes de braves gens.*" Like her sisters, and many other members of this court, she satisfied Goldoni's ideal of middle-class honesty, politeness, and that facile kindness of mere words.

Goldoni is grateful for a few kind words, for the present of some medicine when that accident happened which left him nearly blind.[2] Suddenly he

[1] Madame Adelaide was the fourth of Louis XV's children. Goldoni always hoped but was never asked to teach "*les enfants de France.*" Madame Adelaide and her sisters were known under the name of "*Mesdames tantes*" and considered as bugbears by Marie Antoinette.

Bacaumont in his journal, January 12, 1769, mentions that "un sieur Goldoni has been given a pension of four thousand livres."

[2] For this accident to his eyes, see chapter vii, third part of *Memoirs* and also his short poem, *Il Pellegrino*, where he tells the story as airily as he can; but another poem, *La Piccola Venezia*, written the following year, 1765, is a cry of distress. "My poor eyes are in sad condition — I swear on my honour very sad — on account of having spent over my inkstand whole days and whole nights — and my eyesight is all my capital — if I lose it I lose all my earnings."

felt as if a dark veil covered all the world around him. His dismay, his physical and moral distress, must have been great; yet he does not lose his sense of professional duty, but totters forward, and, after groping for a seat, he takes up the book and begins his lesson. His concern is for the trouble others may take on his account; his pain is for the inconvenience his infirmity may be to others; his anxiety is to express his gratitude in the many ingenious, pleasant ways familiar to Venetian politeness, but open to unlucky interpretations when translated into French.[1]

Six long months of service were rewarded with lodgings at court in Versailles. "A large and comfortable apartment with a view on la grande rue de la Surintendance,"[2] as he describes it to his friend Albergati, and as he wants his other Venetian friends to know. A favour that he was expected to repay by that perpetual attendance was then euphemistically called *faire sa cour.*

In one of his pretty short poems, *La Piccola Venezia,*

[1] In chapter above mentioned Goldoni enumerates his little infirmities, always preoccupied with the trouble they are likely to give to . . . other people.

[2] Five days a week for two hours and a half and even three each day. See letter to Albergati Capacelli, March 18, 1765.

Goldoni, promised by la Dauphin "Il ne manquera rien," expected to have lodgings in all the different places where the court was going. But though he followed his pupil to Marly in the spring, to Fontainebleau in summer, to Compiègne in autumn, he only got in Versailles the rooms that were those of *l'accoucheur de la dauphine,* the place being then vacant "owing to the sad condition of the Dauphin's health." After the Dauphin's death and the marriage of future Louis XVI with Marie Antoinette, an *accoucheur* was named and Goldoni was asked to vacate the rooms.

he gives an amusing description of the many duties of his position: to attend the meals of dauphin and dauphiness, of princes, king, and queen . . . to observe every form of etiquette with ministers of the court and foreigners, to get information about everything that happened, to run from one to another room in order to make believe in one's importance. Then if one stays at home there is no escaping invitations nor the obligation of giving parties; nor can one keep away from card tables, else one would be left out of every conversation.

And Nicoletta, how did she like this sort of life? She submitted to it because she was a prudent and loving wife, but she avoided it as much as possible. Once when she was cornered into a short talk with Madame Adelaide and her *dame d'honneur*, her shyness and dismay were so great that her husband writes, "Thank God neither I nor she have ever entertained the slightest amount of pride." [1]

[1] From Marly, May 13, 1765, to Gabriel Cornet Goldoni writes that in Versailles his wife was presented to Madame Adelaide, "who benignantly entertained her for almost half an hour." And that here, owing to some mistake, they happened to come into the room where the princesses and the dauphin were sitting. "My wife was somewhat surprised but soon comforted by the kindness of the royal personages. I took advantage of this moment for introducing and commending my nephew."

On returning from a terrace, where he assisted in some court parade, Goldoni found near the railings Princess Adelaide speaking Italian to Nicoletta. "You may imagine how happy the dear little woman was; how her heart was beating with shyness and pleasure."

Madame de Narbonne was formerly *dame d'honneur* of the Duchess of Parma, a French princess. In 1760 she came to the French court, and was attached to Madame Adelaide.

Truly there was little to be proud about, and less to live on, if, in May, 1766, the present received of a gold snuff box and one hundred louis is hailed as a providential stroke of good luck. And there were perpetual difficulties with Vendramin, whose grumblings could not even be stopped by the intervention of Sciugliaga,[1]

[1] Giovanni Fontana to S. E. Vendramin: Paris, May 2, 1763 (D. M., page 169):

"In obedience to orders your Excellency gave me in last letter; I have seen Signor Goldoni and spoken to him in the manner that befits your dignity and your interest. . . ."

Same date as above, Goldoni's answer to Vendramin after seeing Signore Fontana: "My letter from Bologna testifies to my good intention of serving you ever since last year: my letter from Paris is evidence that I have not been able to do so. The past is past. I beg your Excellency to allow me to speak of the future only. I am most willing to serve you and also I think that I can do so. I entreat you to grant me three things besides the terms that are registered in the contracts you honoured me in making. First that I may use the plays that I will compose for Paris, using the argument and the construction but, of course, rewriting the whole play for your theatre according to the system of your players and the practice of our country. Secondly, that you will pay the postage expense of the plays, since I find that it is not so easy as I expected to send my plays into Italy post free. Third, that if I contrive to send you six plays in time so that they may be performed in Venice in the autumn and in Carnival, you will give me the two hundred ducats as a present as you used to give me. I entreat your Excellency to take no offence, but to consider that I am in a country where the cost of living is high, and consequently literary work is paid dear. After my duty toward the Italian players is done, I can employ all my spare time in librettos for music, which, being translated into French, I expect to bring me good profit. I have done some already, and they have been accepted by several persons. One hundred ducats for a play is here considered a very miserable price. Yet I will not on this point change the terms of our agreement. I merely want the players, who have grumbled at granting them (the one hundred ducats), to realise that here they become a mere pittance. By granting me my demands your Excellency may in part make up my loss and I may, leaving out some other work, find more time to serve you and keep my engagement of giving you as many of my plays as I can. . . ."

and little pleasure to Goldoni in his collaboration with the Italian comedians in Paris.

Tossed between these annoyances, not knowing "whether I will go on writing for any theatre, it is difficult to write for the Parisian comedians, who will not learn their rôles. For Italy, I am bound to Vendra-

Franc. Vendramin to Giov. Fontana, Venice, May 19, 1763 (D. M., page 172 and *pas.*).

After summing Goldoni's three demands Vendramin bitterly comments: "I observe that he considers it possible (to work for me), if I grant his demands, and impossible if I refuse. This I do not understand, nor will I ever understand."

Vendramin stands on his contract. To the first of the three demands he knows that he could not control the originality of plays. To the second he makes infinite restrictions about "the play being copied in very small" so as to cost as little as possible for postage. He positively refuses to grant the two hundred ducats which he used to give as a present when Goldoni had directed the rehearsals, made all the necessary changes, and the play had encountered favour, but offers to grant one hundred ducats, and in conclusion appeals "to the justice and vengeance of that Lord who knows and weighs everything in his Truth."

Goldoni accepts the terms offered: he will not have plays printed earlier than three years after performance at San Luca, plays not to be shown to anyone else, manuscript to be copied in small handwriting, and lastly "that payment in Venice will be made into the hands of Stefano Sciugliaga when play has been accepted." "As for the hundred ducats, I do not accept his Excellency's offer, but I will accept with thanks whatever in his conscience he thinks proper to give me, promising not to complain."

Goldoni to Vendramin, Paris, October, 1763 (D. M., page 202):

"I cannot tell whether at the end of the two years I will return to Venice. The great success of my last play in Paris (*La Trilogia Camilla e Lindoro*) is likely to alter my plans; but you may be sure that as long as I stay in Paris I will send plays to no one but you and that if I return to Venice I will serve no one but you. I do not mean to boast of this declaration. It is my duty. . . ."

Sciugliaga, the true friend that he is, speaks more boldly than Goldoni. Thus, even after receiving from Paris a letter which did not absolutely claim the present of two hundred ducats but simply pointed out that the plays sent to Venice had been successful, Sciugliaga writes to Vendramin (D. M.,

min by a hateful, unendurable bond (*laccio odioso insoffribile*). If I cannot release myself from him, I will undertake some other sort of work that will keep me busy, without having anything to do with the theatre and comedians."

"I was at court, yet I was not a courtier," repeats Goldoni, unconscious of the contradiction. A courtier, a hanger on at court he must be, or else starve. Only a courtier could have accepted the duties of an office without fixed payment, or swallowed the offence of being asked to teach royal infants. Only a courtier could have discovered the exact moment for asking and obtaining a place for his nephew. A courtier Goldoni was, every day a little more, because circumstances were stronger than his will, but not because he liked it.

But Goldoni still maintained his self-respect and his industry. Witness his gallant attempt at writing a French play, the many Italian comedies he arranged or composed during these years. The pains he gave

page 210): "Il Signor Goldoni . . . will not write any play unless he receives the two hundred ducats. . . . He is in a position to dictate his will, his plays are in great demand, he is well paid in Paris. An author of his worth will always find players ready to perform and to pay. . . ."

Stefano Sciugliaga was not only the trusted intermediary Goldoni wished to stand between Vendramin and himself but also a man of letters whom he thought both able and willing to revise his works (Let. to Vend., July 13, 1763, D. M., page 192): "Signor Sciugliaga has authority from me to make whatever changes may be required; he is gifted with the necessary talent and ability, and I think that your Excellency could trust him to see the play (enclosed in a packet addressed to Sciugliaga, so as to spare post expense for his Excellency) and also others; considering that he is the wisest and most prudent man in the world, my most faithful friend deeply concerned in my affairs and my good name."

to the editions of his works, to the translations and adaptations of some of his plays, the trouble he took to find employment for his nephew,[1] the plan he partly realised for starting an international literary review, all prove Goldoni a hard-working, honourable man who drifted for a time into the ways of court parasites.

Under all the flowery eloquence of his gratitude to his benefactress, or to his patrons, Goldoni's gain was small. His rooms at Versailles he did not keep long. They were reserved for "*L'accoucheur de la Dauphine*" and when this dauphine died an accoucheur was appointed to the young and newly married princess, and the rooms were occupied by a physician.

Three years later, by the intercession of the three *Mesdames tantes*, Goldoni received a pension. Six thousand francs were asked, only four granted by the minister, and only three thousand six hundred were actually paid.[2] In what proportion they dwindled in darker years until the pension was suppressed entirely is not recorded.

Later in 1775 Goldoni resumed his service as court teacher. He was asked to prepare a French princess

[1] In December, 1763, Goldoni wanted to send Antonio to Canada with a cousin of Senator Albergati — see *Fogli Sparsi, op. cit.*, page 63. In 1781 this unlucky Antonio was still on his uncle's hands — see in *Lettere inedite del Goldoni*, pubblicate da E. Maddalena, Napoli, 1901.

[2] Choiseul, granting him the pension of four thousand livres — reduced to thirty-six hundred through Goldoni's simplicity in paying a *retenue* that no one else paid — told Goldoni that "*C'est bien autre chose qu'il vous faut.*" Kind words and good intentions that buttered no parsnips.

to become a Piemontese Queen of Sardinia.[1] This time he adopted a more literary method and gave his pupil some notions "of classical Italian authors, and some anecdotes about them as a means of familiarising the princess with Italian manners." Then some more teaching to Madame Elisabeth, who carried so bravely to the block the giddy head Goldoni could not keep attentive to the reading of Italian poets, not even when Metastasio was the author chosen.

For all this, Goldoni was granted an extra gratification of six thousand livres. What exactly was then the cost of life and the value of money it might be possible to find out; but what were the requirements of a man of Goldoni's tastes and habits, of his age and failing health, is less easy to determine. From his few letters during these last years, it clearly appears that he was in constant pecuniary embarrassment. He borrowed one hundred ducats from Sciugliaga and was anxious to pay him back. In May, 1780, he wrote an affecting appeal to Vittore Gradenigo,[2] then attached as secretary to the Venetian Embassy, in which he explains as fully as he can the causes of his distress. That letter is the counterpart of the *Memoirs*. "Six

[1] Madame Elisabeth, sister to Louis XVI, was beheaded in 1794. Marie Clotilde Adelaide, sister to Louis XVI (Goldoni's third pupil), was married, 1775, to the Prince of Piedmont (afterward King of Sardinia) in 1796. She was so sweet-tempered and devout that after her death she was proposed for "*La canonisation.*"

[2] Letter to Vittore Gradenigo, May 5, 1780. Like other letters quoted to Albergati Capacelli see *Lettere scelte del Goldoni*, edite da Ernesto Masi, Bologna, Zanichelli.

years' attendance, six expensive years in Versailles: house rent, travels, inconvenience, all that I have done for these two princesses, all for nothing! Will the Italians believe that two princesses, sisters of the King of France, instead of making my fortune, have brought about my misfortune? Yet, unhappily for me, it is so. Trusting in expectations that seemed so reasonable, I have neglected more remunerative employment. Also I may have spent more than I should have done but for these expectations; in one word, I am ruined. . . ."[1]

Nor did Goldoni find any compensation for this situation in such artistic triumphs as would have elated his spirit. That same year he registers the end of the Italian Comédie. Goldoni had written for the comedians six plays that were not performed. One can guess with what disgust he pocketed the price paid to him by these players, before their final exit from Paris.[2]

When Goldoni retired from court, he dropped out of the current of life. Though he mentions friends and acquaintances, his *Memoirs* suggest that he submitted

[1] Goldoni to S. E. Gradenigo, secretary of the Venetian Embassy in Paris, Versailles, May 5, 1780:

"Yes, sir, I have sent in my resignation from the office I held in Madame Elisabeth's house, in favour of my nephew; I have introduced him and taken my leave. But in what manner am I left? With a broken head." (proverbial Italian expression meaning in a sore strait).

[2] Plays composed in Paris will be reviewed in another chapter. There is very little originality in any of them. *Les Amours*, etc., *de Camille* was an outline. The written text is a second revision meant for the Italian stage. So is the *Fan*. As for *Il Matrimonio per Concorso*, it is probably the same play. For Vendramin or for Albergati Goldoni used the material given to Italian players in Paris.

to the routine of a very quiet existence, and anticipated senility by leading the life of a veteran before being really an old man. The few words he says about a literary society [1] or *pique nique* are just sufficient to demonstrate how indifferent he was about such things. The longer pages he grants to the description of his sedentary daily habits are more probant of his mental attitude.

He did not trust the unexpected success of his *Bourru Bienfaisant;* he probably knew that such a *tour de force* could not be repeated. In his *Memoirs* he notes that action, life, the study of characters were less cared for than style and purity of language. That the good French of *le Bourru* is due to some unnamed corrector is evident, if the original text of the *Memoirs* and the few, faulty French sentences in the letters are compared to it. Goldoni was attracted by the Opéra Comique; he felt sure of his ability in arranging and inventing plots, in writing appropriate couplets for that special sort of play. Moreover he was in close intimacy with Favart, a master of this questionable form of art. These pieces are not equal to his plays; but they are evidence of untiring industry, and a gallant fight against poverty.

In Chapter XXVI (third part) he describes the Italian opera-buffa in Paris; how he expected to be asked to work for them, how he was ignored and only called when it was too late. "I do not remember having felt a deeper grief for a long time. Those who

[1] For this second "*société littéraire,*" *Memoirs*, chap. x, part iii.

wanted to comfort me said that the managers thought the place unworthy of me; the managers did not know anything about that. If they had taken the pains to ask me, I would have told them that they wanted an author and not a cobbler. . . . I would have worked for nothing if asked to do so, or I would have asked my full price; but certainly my work would have saved their undertaking. I make bold to assert that this spectacle would be still going on in Paris."

Thus debarred from employing his talent in either the French comedy after the failure of *L'Avare Fastueux*, or in the Italian opera-buffa, Goldoni made several beginnings which he has recorded, without complaining of their failure.

The plan of an international *Revue Littéraire* was a genial anticipation doomed to failure because Goldoni lacked the indispensable intellectual preparation and could not interpret the movement of ideas either in France or in Italy; yet he gave this plan much attention, he secured correspondents in Rome, Naples, Florence, Milan, Bologna, and Venice, found a contributor in Paris and some funds. Yet his disappointment is disguised under a little anecdote. He passes lightly over his collaboration in translations of his plays; mentions lightly his painful attempt to prepare a dictionary of the Venetian dialect; entirely forgets his effort to establish in Paris a colony of Arcadia, and gives only a few words to the last of his toils, a translation of Madame Riccoboni's novel. Thus a man, pensioned by the court of France, was reduced to literary drudgery even when nearly blind and only with an effort could command the attention of his tired brains.

Neither age nor sickness nor literary failure could deprive Goldoni of that treasure of kindness and amiability that softened the decrees of harsh fate, and left him the enjoyment of sweet affections and pleasant companionship. If the intellectual groups ignored him, a few friends comforted his declining years. He mentions them in his *Memoirs*, indeed this last part of his toilsome work is very much like a record, giving praise and thanks with full heart.

Goldoni says something kind about every book, invention, and institution that he mentions. His indiscriminate praise makes slight distinctions. *Le Mariage de Figaro* gets its few lines of approval and the work of some long-forgotten author gets the same. Marivaux is overlooked and Florian mentioned side by side with an amateur actress. Buffon is praised in exactly the same style as a Count de la Billarderie. His descriptions of Paris are tame as the pages of a Baedeker, but they reveal his sweet disposition in this closing of a chapter (xix): "Paris is very beautiful; its inhabitants are most amiable; yet some people do not like it. They say that one must have much money to enjoy it; that is not true. No one has less money than I have, yet I enjoy myself, I find amusement and satisfaction. There are pleasures for every purse: limit your desires, measure your forces, and you will be happy here, or else you will be miserable everywhere." Thus does Goldoni proclaim the philosophy of the balance of human desires and opportunities.

His affections kept warm even to the last. His tenderness for Nicoletta was unflagging. When she fell ill, and was threatened with more lasting trouble after recovering from pleurisy, he nursed her, and kept her as good company "as she always kept him."[1] He was grateful for her devotion; he knew that she preferred staying at home to mixing with the world she did not like and did not care to know better. "But for taking out the dogs she would never go for a walk," he writes from Fontainebleau (he spells it Fontanablo). Now when they are brought closer together, he takes unusual care of her. He keeps early hours, shares her bed in winter, and, before asking her assistance as a secretary, he reads to her in the evening.

He was constantly occupied in finding employment for his shiftless nephew, who was soon dismissed from every place secured for him. At the last this nephew may have been of some assistance, of some comfort; but certainly in a very small way.[2]

[1] Chapter xxxviii, part iii, *Memoirs*, Goldoni writes that Nicoletta "*a eu une maladie considérable*," which he afterward mentions as a pleurisy, adding that he was afraid of leaving her alone. This suggests the absence of all servants.

[2] All Goldoni's biographers record a document first published by E. Campardon, *Les Comédiens du Roi de la Troupe Italienne, op. cit.* It is the *declaration* of a woman, Catharine Lefebure, or Lefèvre — alias Méry — charging le sieur Goldoni demeurant rue de Richelieu with seducing her and leaving her with child. This document, however, has a sequel; the

Goldoni was happy to arrange, even from this distance, the marriage of his niece Petronilla.[1] Whether the girl, tired of her convent life, was quite as satisfied as she pretended to be with the proposal of her middle-aged guardian, Goldoni could not discover; and probably he rejoiced at this solution of a problem that might have become troublesome if the girl had remained unmarried and unprotected. With the generosity and patriarchal benevolence of one of his paterfamilias, and like Pantalone, he gave all that was left of his Italian stocks and possessions to his niece, and with it his blessing and good wishes. "This event was necessary to my quiet. . . . I would have been perfectly happy if I could have been present at her marriage, but I was too old to undertake a travel of three hundred leagues."

woman was paid and she withdrew from the lawsuit. "*Ayant été pleinement satisfaite par le dit sieur Goldoni.*"

Now the culprit mentioned as "le sieur Goldoni" may have been either our author or his nephew. Both gentlemen lived in that same street. On one hand a middle-aged, perfectly honourable married man, whose behaviour up to that day and ever after was always as decent and prudent as the general rules of decorum and the sense of personal dignity then required. On the other hand a good-for-nothing youth, who could never keep steady in any employment, about whose amorous tendencies his uncle wrote in October, 1765, from Fontainebleau (see *Fogli Sparsi, op. cit.*, pages 72–73): "He speaks some French (*borbotta in francese*) but I fear he likes too well *les mesdemoiselles* (French in text) oh! the worthy son of his great father! (*oh degno figlio di si gran padre*)."

Presumption points to this second *accuse*. In which case *parce sepulti*. But why repeat the stupid charge against Goldoni without trying at least to explain such a strange lapse of his habitual honesty? Or was it simply blackmailing?

[1] Maria Petronilla married Signor Chiaruzzi in October, 1781.

Though his *Memoirs* show him satisfied with Paris and the Parisians, his letters reveal his constant love for Venice and his own people. He spared neither time nor pains when asked for information; he gave assistance and advice to every Italian who came to him. In many ways he proved his lasting affection for his country.

In short poems, either composed or published during these years, this longing for Venice finds delicate expression. The lines "*da Venezia lontan do mile mia*" are quoted by all his biographers: they tell how the music of his own dialect, the charm of his own people's manners, are always present to his mind. A passage in *La Piccola Venezia*,[1] describing his casual

[1] "*La Piccola Venezia — Ottave per le felicissime nozze delle Eccellenze loro Zorzi e Barbarigo — in Componimenti Minori*," Biblioteca Universale, No. 143, page 77.

I me poveri occhi xe stai mal
Zuro sull'onor mio mal assae;
Frutto d'aver passà col caramal
Le intiere note, e le intiere zornae
E la mia vista xe el mio capital,
E se le perdo ho perso le míe entrae.

Further on he explains that la Piccola Venezia is a place in the park of Versailles where

Zonti a la riva del canal se trova:
Quattro o cingue barchette, e una cavana . . .
E el batelo co la pope, e prova
E le forcole, e i remi a la nostrana,
E veder a vogar da barcarioli.
E no come in galia voga i marioli
(not as the slave rows in a galley).

Goldoni is Venetian even in his prejudice against rowers who ply their oars in a sitting position — whilst the gondolier rows standing on the *prova*.

Further on Goldoni sees the gondolier himself, in a little hut:

meeting with a Venetian gondolier who plied his long oar in the waters of a royal pond in Versailles, evinces his deep emotion. If ever Goldoni read the episode of Virgil and Sordello in Dante's *Commedia*, it was present in his memory when he wrote how, in the name of Venice, he hailed the Venetian gondolier.

Faithful to the friends who remained, Goldoni maintained a cordial acquaintance with Favart, Madame Riccoboni, and a few others. They met in small dinner parties and drank each other's health in doggerel verse which, if they add nothing to Favart's reputation as a librettist, add a trait to his moral figure. "*Au Molière de l'Italie — digne nourisson de Thalie — A toi mon cher Goldoni — dont le goût au talent uni — fit le charme de ta patrie*" . . . and so on, until all the rhymes seem to have been exhausted.

He visited Voltaire in Paris in 1778 and was lost in the crowd of visitors, after being entertained just for a few minutes in Italian by the illustrious polyglot. Alfieri called upon him, and found him uninteresting. The two men and their ideals were far too different to understand one another. Of the infinite variety of Italian characters they may be considered as the extremes, in violent contrast of temperament and ideals.

Vedo un omo senta che ha mal un pié
Ma col viso bronzin robusto e san.
Una di quelle tale fisionomie,
Da galantuomo da vero cortesan.
Quando el me vede, el vol levarsi in pié
No, ghe digo, ste là son venezian.
Ceremonie no fe, no ghe ne fazzo.
Patria, Patria! El m'abbrazza, e mi l'abbrazzo.

Goldoni could never have appreciated the rising sun of tragedy, Alfieri never could have realised the simple beauty of Goldoni's spirit and the excellency of his intended reform. Both would have been surprised if told that for one performance of Alfieri's tragedies a hundred of Goldoni's comedies are now given.

Few events of his last years are recorded beyond that which he says of himself[1] when informing the readers of his *Memoirs* that he was aged eighty when he finally laid down his pen in 1787, having finished the work he never hoped to finish; and when he declared that he did not care much "if any writer should think proper to employ his time on him, for the sole purpose of vexing him." He was then past all ambition, past all vexation, past all terror and all hope. He died at six o'clock in the evening, February 6, 1793, at his home, number 1 rue Pavee Saint Sauveur, at the age of eighty-six.

A question arises in the mind of every reader of Goldoni's *Memoirs* and no answer has ever been given. What was Goldoni's attitude toward the revolutionary movement, and how did he escape persecution and enjoy the posthumous honour given to him by *La Convention Nationale?* Goldoni's general ideas considering his time and country are steadily, prudently, but consistently democratic — singularly *avancés*. Yet such ideas availed little to save from popular fury persons attached to the court. How

[1] Gorani in his *Memoirs* gives some notices about Goldoni, but they do not seem reliable. The adventurer spoke by hearsay and confuses dates.

many others, guilty of being pensioned by the royal budget, guilty only of the attachment to the royal family that Goldoni expresses in his *Memoirs*, were dragged to prison and violent death!

In his letter to the king, prefacing his *Memoirs*, Goldoni says: "In the midst of your kingdom's notables, in the sight of the whole universe, your Majesty has explained views and announced intentions for the welfare of your States and the comfort of your people. . . . How many profitable decrees for the present! What happy prospects for the future!"

Thus Goldoni sees the dawn of reform in the timid and half-hearted concessions granted to threatening difficulties. Even at this supreme crisis of the ancient régime Goldoni is faithful to his old ideal — Reform. In his eyes royal condescension could still cure the age-long evils caused by abuse of royal authority. In a time when passion overruled justice in France, there must have been extraordinary reasons for the French National Convention to not only vote a pension to Goldoni, an Italian, long attached to the Court, but to decree and attend a memorial performance of one of his plays. Never under such circumstances has a nation so honoured a foreign writer.

Marie Joseph Chénier's most eloquent pleading for him *à la Convention* hardly tells the exact truth. A poet pleading to obtain redress for the shameful neglect of a poet's rights is permitted some exaggeration. Clavière's letter, both documents carefully recorded by Charles Rabany,[1] is more important. Clavière is not speaking before an audience that he seeks to inflame with his own zeal. He writes to a society of players that Goldoni was sorely aggrieved "to accept a pension from the late king," that he wanted to throw into the fire that "annihilated all royal prerogatives" the decree fixing his pension. Such a deliberate declaration must rest on some basis of fact, of which we have no other information.

To imagine Goldoni disguising his real feelings in order to flatter the new democracy would be to misrepresent his essential honesty. Probably Goldoni was so far favourable to the first explosion of *civisme* as to take some share in public festivities, in ceremonies or meetings. He may have approved of theories that sounded so liberal and generous. He may have applauded the proclamations of those "rights of man" that he unconsciously advocated all through his voluminous works. Moreover it was in Goldoni's nature to make friends with the humblest that passed within reach. It would be characteristic of the amused and amusing companion of Venetian gondoliers, who always sought "his public" among the humblest auditors of the "pit," to have a kind word for the *pauvres diables*

[1] *La Convention Nationale* the day after Goldini's death voted to restore his pension, and then on learning of his death, on the demand of Chénier, they voted his widow a pension of 1500 livres (February 10, 1793). She also received 1859 livres realised from a benefit performance of *Le Bourru Bienfaisant* which was attended by *La Convention* (June 18, '93). For all documents relating to Goldoni's death, for speech uttered by M. J. Chénier, letter of Çlavière, and several other matters, see the Annexes of C. Rabany's often quoted book.

of his neighbourhood. He says somewhere that he could manage even the Parisian *cochers de fiacre*. Now when these poor devils became the masters and boasted the title of *sans-culottes*, probably they protected the old man, whom they may have honoured for his intellect and loved for his kindness.

Though nothing is positively said about her, Nicoletta was sure to conciliate further good will, and alas! to awaken pity in the hearts of those who saw her so patient, so devoted, and so destitute. *La Convention* granted her a pension and *la Comédie* added the profits of a representation to refill her empty pockets. But what comfort could money bring to one who wept over the companion of her whole life! Possibly Antonio, the nephew she had mothered for so many long years, the only heir of his uncle, Carlo Goldoni, paid in some measure the great debt of gratitude they both owed to sweet Nicoletta, and that comfort and quiet lessened her grief.

If Goldoni's great and tender soul hovered near the place where his last days were passed, he may have overlooked the homage paid to his memory by official powers, he may have scorned the denunciations uttered, in his name, against the perversion of public customs by the theatre, he may have smiled at the shutting of the Comédie Française claimed by an unsuccessful playwright, Barrière, and granted by an inflamed Assembly; but certainly as he watched over his long-loved companion he must have rejoiced to see her provided for.

Nor was the parting long; though history has not recorded or official registers fixed the date of Nicoletta's death, it is presumable that she did not long outlive her husband.

CHAPTER VII

THE PLAYS (1734 TO 1749)

Goldoni's "vocation" — his life reflects his environment — his plays mirror the Venice of his time — Goldoni was a poor scholar — but a good lawyer — did not care for books — Goldoni and Machiavelli compared — Machiavelli's *Mandragola* the greatest Italian play — common traits in the plays of Goldoni and Machiavelli — the soul of Venice is revealed in her palaces and paintings — Venetian craving for splendour, which covered but did not hide her poverty — passion of Venetians for theatre — Goldoni meets Bonafede Vitali the mountebank in Milan — who performs Goldoni's first play *Il Gondoliere Veneziano* — *Belisario* his next play — his first teachers were his players — character of "improvised comedy," in which discordant elements are mixed, and coarseness — yet these players possessed merits — they were heirs of the past, and Goldoni was their pupil — period from *Belisario* to *La Putta Onorata* (1734–1749) copied from ancient *commedia dell'arte* — success of these due to simplicity of aim — *La Donna di Garbo*, 1743, marks an epoch — Goldoni flees from Venice to Pisa — advance in his intellectual evolution — influence of *Arcadia* on his style — engaged by Medebach — *Due Gemelli Veneziani* copied from improvised comedy — *La Putta Onorata* (1749) first purely Goldonian play — a representation of Venetian lower life — the character Menego Cainelloa picture of Venetian gondoliers — *Cavaliere e la Dama* an attack on "serventism" — *cavaliere servente* described — at first a privilege of highest class — finally became generalised — due to Venetian social habits — Goldoni's viewpoint of the custom — this play examined — his innovations best seen in *Il Padre di Famiglia* and *La Buona Moglie* (1749) — *Il Teatro Comico*, a play of this second manner, illustrates Goldoni's reform.

WHEN Goldoni insists on the inevitableness of his vocation, he disregards how largely this vocation was affected by the peculiar social and political conditions of his time, of the intellectual atmosphere he breathed, and of all the surrounding circumstances which encouraged and directed his natural gifts.

The story of his life, as related in his *Memoirs*, evidences his responsiveness to events and his adaptability to every vicissitude; the entire story of his career shows in extraordinary degree the action and reaction of his own ego to the spirit of his world. No man has ever more accurately reflected in his own self or more accurately revealed in his writings the thought, the atmosphere, the soul of his own environment. To know Goldoni the man and to have read his writings is to know Goldoni's Venice.

His propensity for the stage was characteristically Venetian. His æsthetic standard, his conception of comedy, he accepted from contemporary writers and artists. He appropriated from every attainable source, he mirrored his time because he had first absorbed its every vital element. Instinctively a writer of plays, his bent was encouraged because the stage was then the lodestar of Venetian spirits. He educated his natural talent by adopting all that survived of both classical and popular comedy, blending them with additional realistic traits which were his own.

Goldoni's classical education was, for an Italian, meagre. He passed from school to school without regular promotion. Admitted by favour at college, dismissed before the end of his last term, his schooling was sketchy and slipshod.

In the autobiographic preface to the second volume of his plays, he tells of having been at the top of his form in Perugia, of having been raised to the honourable title of King of the Romans. The frontispiece of the book, corroborating this information, shows a little Goldoni standing in front of other schoolboys and carrying a banner inscribed with the letters S P Q R. Now the register of the school for that same year mentions Carlo Goldoni among the boys who were not found worthy of promotion to the higher form. That course of philosophy which he should have attended in Rimini he deserted, in order to follow a company of players, and evidently never resumed.

Goldoni's most serious study was the law. Though he makes light of the manner in which he secured his degree in Padua, he appears to have mastered the several codes, of having memorised the comments and glosses. He practised law in Pisa with some success. His eloquence was admired; the exaggerated style, the intricate sentence charmed at that time as much as they now annoy the reader. Though his talk was inflated, yet he fenced cleverly in the word duel that in those days passed for a trial. His plays contain further evidence of this professional training. The plots of some of them, *Uomo Prudente*, *Avvocato Veneziano*, *La Donna di Governo*, are founded on lawsuits; other plays contain juridic arguments and discussions which are not only adequate and witty, but also ingenious and learned.

Goldoni never experienced that hunger for books that was so common a trait among Italians of his time. The few books he mentions were apparently lent him casually. He never mentions buying them.

When visiting Signor Lauzio, on his way to the college at Pavia, he used this gentleman's library containing several Latin plays. He read them, yet he dismisses a subject of such capital importance to him with a few commonplace observations. He purposes to "imitate them in their plots, in their style, and exactness, and not to rest satisfied unless he could make his own plays more interesting, richer in marked characters, in comical spirit." He also purposes to give happy endings as a rule.

Thus in a little more than two lines he dismisses the Latin classics, and before the end of the page he discards not only all the Italian classics, but presumably all other Italian playwrights, without exception. This is ignorance rather than presumption. He did not care for books and for printed plays. When he afterward became better acquainted with classics in the popular form in which they had come down to his time, through the interpretation of players, he appreciated them better, and borrowed freely from them. The few words he gives to Machiavelli's *Mandragola* show his lack of literary appreciation. Machiavelli was the one precursor whom he should have worshipped and acknowledged as his direct master.

Between the great thinker-statesman and the easy-going, talented writer of plays there are few common traits; yet between their conceptions of comic art, their applications to the painting of life, and also between their interpretations of dramatic morals there are important affinities and resemblances.

Like Goldoni, Machiavelli adopted all the elements of

the past to compose a new sort of comedy. His plot, characters, episodes, as well as the stage directions, can all be traced back to some old play or to some popular *novella*. Yet, with all those loans, Machiavelli creates something that is entirely new. He eliminates none of the classical elements, not even the coarseness and immorality of the plot; he introduces no new character. The short witted though honest wife, the lustful debauché, the miserly old woman, even the unscrupulous friar, are old acquaintances. But, like Goldoni, he touches all these dead leaves with the magic wand of truth and they live. Even Friar Timoteo becomes palpitating flesh and blood; just a few words discovering the scruples of her simple conscience and the doll wife became a woman.

What modern psychologist could better describe remorse than that delivered in a monologue by Friar Timoteo? Not that conventional, almost indispensable form of remorse which, for morality's sake, other writers introduced at the last fall of the curtain, but the restlessness and physical torment of the genuine rascal of mixed emotions. He tells how he could not sleep for thinking about the success of his intrigue, how he got up and went to arrange the veil in front of the Madonna, how by so doing he discovered that his lazy brethren allowed candles to burn out, and how he piously repaired the omission. And again what realistic satire ever better interpreted the casuistic arguments of an intrigant than does Machiavelli in the exhortations of the friar to the woman he would decoy?

It is no worse deed then eating flesh on Fridays. There is absolution ready for such sins. Even so does Goldoni revivify his borrowed characters; even thus, when he employs his Venetian dialect as Machiavelli used his familiar Tuscan, does the sincerity of his observation appear clearly in the talk of his personages.

Another less generally recognised trait common to Machiavelli and Goldoni is the type of morality which informs all their work. It is a social not a religious morality. Its standard of ethics is concerned only with the public welfare. In Machiavelli this ideal is the result of much experience and of an uncommon power for generalising; in Goldoni it is an effect of his unbiased, unsophisticated clear-sightedness. Both writers, so separated by time, circumstances, and intellectual preparation, have discerned that the only possible way to the recovery of their people from decadent corruption rests in a greater respect for the marriage bond.

Machiavelli's intention is clear enough in the *Mandragola*, but it becomes even more explicit in his second play, *La Clizia*, and still more so in the song that he composed to serve as epilogue to both these plays. The statesman who learned scepticism by observing the crimes of men, and Goldoni, who skimmed lightly on the surface of social wrong-doings, meet on this same platform of social reform. Goldoni seems unaware of his great debt to Machiavelli; he praises with reticence and remarks about the immorality of the plot.

Like all Venetians of his time, Goldoni was drawn

to the theatre, yet this inclination was rather for stage life than for dramatic literature.

When he abandoned his lawyer's office and the proud title of *Avvocato Veneziano*, his unpreparedness was complete. He blindly staked all his worldly prospects on the chance of a dramatic success in Milan. The objections and corrections of the Milanese players found him utterly unprepared to answer them.

His ideas about literary forms were vague. Having penned a certain number of sonnets and other occasional compliments, having acted a part in some amateur performance, having directed the staging of some theatrical entertainments, he concluded that he could construct a tragedy that might, like Metastasio's, be either an opera or a drama.

The players' refusal to accept his play astonished and discouraged him, and for a while he relinquished his purpose; but he could not eradicate that longing for the theatre which was his inheritance.

The soul of Venice, at every period of his history, is expressed through the plastic arts. In lines and colours of almost unequalled beauty, Venice has recorded the aspirations and glories, the mystic cravings and unlimited ambitions of her people. In her monuments and palaces, in the vast series of paintings and groups of statues, the history of Venice and the very soul of its people are revealed.

One character predominates — magnificence. No display of magnificence seemed too splendid for the magistrates of "La Dominante," no splendour of picture and sculpture adequate to express their ambition.

As long as power and wealth equalled the aspirations of genius, there was harmony in Venetian painting, sculpture, and architecture, between intent and achievement. But when, with the dawn of the eighteenth century, decadence began to enfeeble the Venetian spirit, when Venetian artists dwindled from antique greatness to virtuosity, then the discord between love of splendour and drab reality diminished spiritual authority, and encouraged expressions of art that gave brilliancy rather than splendour.

The successor of Tiziano and Veronese was Tiepolo. Strange aërial perspective, extraordinary foreshortenings, contrasts of light and shade, flowing draperies that seem to be unfurled by some pre-romantic wind, are liberally used to compensate for the loss of simple greatness.

Public and private ceremonies present the same phenomena of disguised decline. The reality of power was fast slipping away, yet every official assertion of power was surrounded with all the ancient ritual. Sea trade was choked by the active competition of other nations, the war galleys of Venice were not able to retain the distant lands which the last great Venetian admirals conquered; yet with the same antique pomp, amid the same gorgeous train of ships and boats, the bucentoro glided on, bearing her freight of crimson-robed patricians to witness the traditional symbolic wedding of the doge to the sea.

The natural craving for splendour exaggerated by some intuition of approaching decline assumed a mannerism that aimed merely at startling the onlooker. The pageantry that gilded with borrowed brilliancy the decline of arts and of power was for the Venetians as necessary as the intoxicating draught craved by palzied age desirous of ignoring his decrepitude.

It suited the Venetian spirit, and answered to traditional habits to cover under the flowers of gaiety the symptoms of approaching poverty, the warnings of diminished authority in the counsels of nations. Every class of citizens, imitating the policy of the state, resolved to disguise under a gay mask whatever might bring discredit, and to ignore such evils as it was not possible to conceal.

Even as the state ceremonies preserved all their ancient splendour and offered to the admiring gaze of princely visitors and foreign ambassadors the same magnificent display, the patrician houses whose estates on the mainland were cut off by the disastrous treaties of Carlowitz and Passovitz, whose sources of gain were dried up by the limitations of trade, still retained their habits of profuse hospitality, still disclosed to the stranger guest or to the admiration of fellow-citizens the treasures of their art collections, the beauty of their gilded halls. The middle class imitated patrician example. Merchants would not restrict their expenses, lest they betray the change from the enormous profits formerly made in business; they rather developed a new spirit of competition in spendthrift extravagance.

From such a conception of life to a general propensity for the art of the theatre, that summary and epitome of all the arts of make-believe, there was but one step. As Goldoni traced to his grandfather his infatuation for players and private theatricals, so every other Venetian boy could find in his earliest recollections some similar example. Boys were encouraged to practise the art of acting as a part of their education, quite as much as for amusement.

In every social rank, from the patrician villa to the humble *campiello*, play-acting was customary. And there is evidence that these amateur performers were often as good as or even better than professional players, and not less thoroughly trained.

Great as may have been Goldoni's natural gifts, he was doubtless first prompted to write for the theatre by the desire of partaking in the pleasure of stage life, and it was only after his first failure that he realised the possibility of attempting a reform and gaining for himself glory.

While in Milan acting as secretary to His Excellency Bartolini, Goldoni confesses that he met many actors of both sexes and attended their performances as frequently as possible. Goldoni says in his preface to volume ix of his works that he discussed Scipione Maffei's comedies with Parmenione Trissino. Also at this time began his friendship with Count Arconati Visconti, an amateur playwriter and actor of unusual discernment, and with Count Prata, a man of good counsel.

Thus when he met that extraordinary mountebank, Bonafede Vitali, Goldoni first admired the cyclopedic knowledge of the man who solved impromptu questions on every branch of science, letters, and arts; but afterward came more practical encouragement and the turning point was passed. Goldoni's first play was performed and applauded.

A trifle, a duet, *Il Gondoliere Veneziano*, yet a first step that carried Goldoni behind the curtain, and to the reality of collaboration with real players.

Goldoni's unpreparedness and the confusion in his mind is shown in his next choice, a tragic and historical subject, *Belisario*, while he entirely lacks both the sense of history and the pathos of tragedy. *Belisario* was a success, but the following tragedies of *Rosmonda*, *Griselda*, *Rinaldo di Montalbano* were mere pot-boilers, and as little worthy of notice as many other mistaken incursions of Goldoni's into a field of an art not his own.

Goldoni's first teachers were players. The effect of their teachings may be traced through all his first, and through many of his best later works. He says, "I was with my players like a painter with his models." Models indeed and also sweethearts some of them.

To succeed in the so-called improvised comedy it was necessary that the player possess gifts superfluous to the modern actor, as well as an amount of reading not now required by those of his craft. Improvisation was the assembling with taste and discernment of most varied elements, and forming them into a mosaic work, appropriate to the player, the play, the audience, and such eventual circumstances as required to be considered.

This selection may have been prepared leisurely before the rehearsal, it may have been repeated and refitted from one play to another or selected out of those collections of sayings *il zibaldone*, which every actor kept as an aid to his memory. Some of these jokes and repartees may have been traditional, and clownish tricks may have supplemented the gaps in the dialogue; nevertheless the ability, promptness, and literary taste indispensable to the successful actor of improvised comedy required very real ability. Goldoni pays homage to the extensive reading of Sacchi, and acknowledges that from him, and from other players, beside the order for writing a play, he accepted also its title and plot.

By studying the manners of his interpreters Goldoni often composed a character. Golinetti, who could pass with astonishing rapidity from the most vivacious mood to the most torpid, suggested the idea of entrusting to him two parts in the *Gemelli Veneziani*. Rubini's pleasant and well-preserved middle age gave him the idea of composing *Il Vecchio Bizzarro*, an anticipation of the present fad for white-haired lovers. Smart, coquettish *servette* helped him to a better insight of feminine nature when he gave up flirting with them, but in the meanwhile they suggested to his responsive spirit how best to exhibit their charms and to display their talents in rôles written expressly for each one of his favourites by turn.

All these players brought some contribution to the technical preparation of their poet, learning every day more of that special technique which prepared the way to his better work. He took from the players and from the plays they performed a more extensive knowledge of the past than he could ever have taken from books.

Both the classical and popular forms of comedy had come down to this time, overlapped and mixed even in the minds of the more enlightened writers. In the hands of players they blended into strange compounds. In the palmy days of the Renaissance no one would have thought of mixing Ariosto's exquisite prose or lofty verse with the rustic pastorals of his contemporary, Angelo Beolco, alias *il Ruzzante*. But since then the Florentine classics having drifted into familiar language, having borrowed some of the makeshifts, the dialects, and the masks of the popular muse, and, moreover, the performance of both sorts of plays having become the privilege of the same players, the distinction was no longer visible.

From Flaminio Scala to Lelio Riccoboni every director of itinerant companies transformed the old-fashioned scenario into something like regular comedies and adapted ancient comedies of the classical type to the lighter and more enjoyable construction of a modern scenario. In addition to this generous provision of national plays, the actors possessed also a certain number of foreign cosmopolitan subjects, some imitations from the Spanish, some translations from the French, which they adapted to the taste of their different audiences, to the capacity or ambition of those players who claimed to be stars.

These favourites of the public being generally the players who held the masked rôles, comedies were manipulated so as to display their abilities. Thus Goldoni's *Memoirs* tell of a Don Juan (Goldoni spells it Don Jouan) lavishly padded with some of the more popular tricks of the *arlecchino*. One of these harlequins, Florindo, earned his nickname of "Florindo dei maccheroni" for having eaten a dish of real *maccheroni* at the last supper with the ghostly guest and the doomed profligate. Another trick, or *lazzo*, of Arlecchino consisted in turning somersaults with a lighted candle in his hand just at the last impressive scene of Don Juan's disappearance.

These instances of improper mixing of discordant elements are often quoted to support the conventional charge of wholesale coarseness and corruption of the popular comedy. The charge has some foundation. An art that had been exerted for almost three centuries by professionals only, whom no genial writer had guided and enlightened, whom the undiscerning favour of foreign audiences, the contempt of almost every other social class, had all tended to lower in their own esteem, and allure into unæsthetic, unbecoming tricks, could hardly have preserved the pure elegance and refinement of other more favoured forms of art.

Yet notwithstanding this fault against good taste and literary fitness, these players possessed merits which proved useful to Goldoni's education. They were the heirs of the past and they bequeathed to Goldoni all of this past that had survived. Dusty textbooks and ponderous critical essays could never have taught Goldoni how to reduce the representation of multiform life within the limits of a comedy; how to sketch a plot and develop an intrigue in the balanced measure taught by Greek classics to Latin imitators and perfected by Italian classics into sincere and vivid realism. The experience and tradition of past ages came to him embodied in his amiable comrades, willing not merely to give for him their best acting on the stage, but also to let him use them at his pleasure, in every attempt at the correction or reproduction of their performances.

Goldoni was a brilliant pupil; with genial intuition he borrowed that which was most valuable and congenial, adding his own excellent touches.

The first of these imitations of the ancient comedy was the little masterpiece, *Momolo Cortesan*, an excellent subject and wisely treated. Unfortunately the first version was not preserved, and thus the printed text, composed years later, though delightfully unpremeditated, does not allow of a critical study of Goldoni's first conception of his art.

It is almost proved that he corrected some of the more realistic traits, and modified the whole dialogue when, having outgrown the first phases of imitation and achieved a manner of his own, he recomposed the entire text of the play, which in the beginning he had been satisfied with directing and outlining when Golinetti, after suggesting the character of Momolo, was allowed to give his own interpretation of the character.

This first period of production from *Belisario* (1734) to *La Putta Onorata* (1749) ought to be classified as a first manner, almost entirely taken from the ancient *commedia dell'arte.* Notwithstanding his assertions to the contrary, he was during these years only dimly conscious of his aim. An analysis of such plays as *Le Trentadue Disgrazie d'Arlecchino* (1740) or *Il Servitore di Due Padroni* (1745), like the dissection of a bright butterfly, would fail to reveal the gaiety and spontaneity, the fun and briskness of the plays; while the secret of their delicate construction could not be thus discovered. The receipt is simple. Take the familiar masks, plots, staging, and give them new life by the application of well-worn tricks and manners. Only a genius could, with such scanty preparation and with such insufficient models, compose these little jewels.

Goldoni's success in these his first compositions is the result of the simplicity and limitation of his aim. He did not then dream of correcting and reforming the fundamental confusion and abasement of the comedy. He merely noted that the players drifted into coarse jokes and overcharged their performances with tricks and *lazzi.* But the observation being right, and his ambition of correction not above his power, it proved successful even beyond his anticipation. Lacking knowledge of higher standards he saw only the more gross and superficial imperfections of the popular plays and only the coarser mistakes of the players.

Thus he undertook to remake the tragedy of *Belisario* without understanding the principal character, the historical moment represented, or the necessity of choosing between a comic and a tragic interpretation and the consequent choice of style.

It was a dogma of the classics to separate entirely these two sorts of composition. Apostolo Zeno, Scipione Maffei, Martelli, all the contemporaries whom he most admired, insisted upon the distinction. Metastasio indeed blended the sentimental and musical elements of poetry, yet even he disdained the comic style.

Goldoni, however, ignoring classic and contemporary usage, imitating only the practice of players, thought that he might mix them in the composition of a tragi-comedy provided he avoided extremes. Though his riper judgment afterward refused to print this *Belisario*, he appears in his *Memoirs* to have been pleased with it, as he says: "The principal fault in my play was the appearance of *Belisario* with bleeding and empty orbits. Barring that, my play, which I entitled a tragi-comedy, was not deprived of good points; it was interesting and in conformity to nature." The fact is that *Belisario* was only slightly in advance of former plays of that hybrid sort, only a little less bombastic and coarse and unnatural; but it was a step in the right direction.

La Donna di Garbo, composed in 1743 and rewritten in 1747, is sometimes considered as marking an epoch because it was entirely written. Yet, like *Momolo Cortesan*, this play is not essentially different from the improvised comedies. It was composed for one of Goldoni's favourites, La Baccherini, who died before playing the character, on the plan that was then usual among the *commedianti dell'arte*, a personage appearing under several disguises by transforming not only his clothes, but his manner and talk. When the artist was a woman, there was also opportunity for showing a pretty face and figure under several aspects.

Goldoni innovated nothing when he composed the character of the clever girl whose wiles enchant a whole household of most different people. She talks *cabala* to the gambler who meditates the lottery numbers; she teaches the extravagant lady the newest fashions; she bewitches the paterfamilias who wants to marry her; she chaffs the Venetian youth, and allures the high-born fop; she even argues on legal points, and finally wins back the lover who had deserted her. *La Donna di Garbo*, like *Momolo*, is a happy hit, but Goldoni's conception of continuing the ancient comedy with just a few changes is still simple and rudimental. He was still a pupil of the players.

In a play partly written, which he composed after his appointment as Consul of Genoa, he introduced some traits imitated directly from that experience of business affairs which he was constantly gaining at his office. *La Bancarotta* is a poor play, but it is a promise; though well received it did not create a sensation.

Trouble came like a thunderbolt from a blue sky. Entrapped by a false or genuine foreigner who levied troops in the Venetian state, Goldoni fled in haste, wandering about the Peninsula. Playwriting was of little use in his wanderings. When he settled down in Pisa he remembered that he was a lawyer. He was proud of his title of *avvocato* and he was gifted for the bar. Pisa was then a prosperous mart as well as a city of learning and refined social customs.

Goldoni's stay in Pisa marks a new advance in his intellectual evolution. He mingled daily with men of letters, and developed a desire for scholarship, and that wrought an important change in his dramatic composition.

In Pisa he entered the Alphean Colony of Arcadia. The sins of Arcadia are clamorous. The puerility of emblems and mottoes, of poetical surnames and allegorical ceremonies, has been justly ridiculed. Yet this far-spreading order rendered important service to Italian literary and political unity, through the literary correspondence between the hundred colonies. Writers and poets obtained fame and found support in this association.

Arcadia influenced Goldoni's style; some of its extravagant *concetti* passed into his occasional compositions and into the talk of his fops and snobs. These traces are evident to anyone who has read Frugoni or other minor Arcadian poets. But they were largely compensated by the awakening in Goldoni of the literary vein. Henceforth he rises above the tuition of players; though he uses them still as instruments for his art, he is the master. Thus when after two years he reviews the manuscript of his

Uomo Prudente, he does so with a new eye for its faults.

Pisa, with the opportunities for intellectual conversation, a tour through Tuscany, a short stay in Florence, transformed Goldoni into a playwright conscious of the nobility of his art, and prepared to seriously pursue his career.

Medebach engaged him on reasonable terms. The company was not so ambitious as to disdain direction, yet not so raw as to mar the intentions of the writer. His loved Venice smiled a welcome; the public welcomed the returned prodigal; the critics mildly attacked the débutant who was as yet too obscure to be envied or feared.

Evidence of Goldoni's evolution must be discovered from his own writings. Since he does not indulge in self-investigation, but prefers to give his readers a huge amount of inaccurate biographical information in which fact and fancy, that which he purposed and that which he accomplished, are so mixed that the difficulty is to discover the real facts.

Thus the letters to Bettinelli prefacing the first edition of his plays must be compared with the plays they introduce, and dates must be compared to discover in what direction Goldoni's mind was developing.

Thus the comedy of the *Due Gemelli Veneziani* was copied from the conventional tradition of improvised comedy, at a time when its author cared little for classical lore, yet the introduction to this play, composed many years later, displays an erudition which betrays the hasty and undiscriminating recapitulation of recent reading. To illustrate the spontaneous burlesque, adapted freely from the worn-out scenario familiar to every company of players, he summons all the dead-and-gone plays he can discover, all the performances recorded in stage annals of twins, amusing the most different audiences with the obvious trick of the same actor impersonating the two rôles. It took a Shakespeare and a Molière to really rejuvenate the subject.

The first purely Goldonian original play which marks a date in his career and in the history of the Italian comedy is *La Putta Onorata*, produced in December, 1749.

Three short acts in prose, mostly Venetian. A plot of slight novelty: an honest girl beloved by a fool, desired by a middle-aged protector, pursued by a high-born profligate, misused by an unscrupulous sister and a boorish brother-in-law, finding courage in her own simplicity to face all these evils, conquer all obstacles, and marry the fool she has loved all the time. The episodes are even more threadbare. A nurse has changed her own son for her master's so as to bring about the surprise of recognition at the end.

With such old-fashioned ingredients, Goldoni created a genial representation of lower Venetian life, a picture of customs and manners, an intuition of deep feelings, and withal, such an amusing story, supported by the unflagging liveliness of dialogue, by a flow of witty sayings, as to make, even in our days, a delightful play.

The best traits of Goldoni's art are found here, as also the first hints of what will be, later, his worst faults.

The contrast between aristocratic vice and popular virtue is strongly delineated in the representation of Marchese Ottavio and his wife Marchesa Beatrice's household, in opposition to the group of plebeians centring round Menego, the gondoliere; and in the contrast between the honest behaviour of the heroine Bettina and her sister's complacency.

Ottavio is shown in the darkest colours. He ignores his wife's acts provided she does not interfere with his own plans for seducing Bettina. Brighella, his servant, plays the go-between gladly, as he is the boon companion of Arlecchino, the husband of Catte, Bettina's sister and chaperon.

Act i, sc. 2. Ottavio — Can you manage to introduce me by means of these people?

Brighella — I'll see to it. Mrs. Catte is a tender-hearted woman; I expect that she will lend us a hand.

Ottavio — I like the girl. I mean to keep her under my protection.

Brighella — She is already provided with a protector, a middle-age merchant, who goes by the name of Pantalone dei Bisognosi.

Ottavio — A merchant must give way before a nobleman.

Brighella — He means well. It is all pure charity with him.

Ottavio — I don't believe in such charity. That will do! To-day I mean to see the girl.

Brighella — You must know, my lord, that I have discovered something.

Ottavio — That she is in love?

Brighella — You guess right.

Ottavio — I expected it. The sly little rogue.

Brighella — Do you know who is her sweetheart?

Ottavio — Some good-for-nothing wight.

Brighella — Pasqualino, Menego Caianello's son, the son of your own gondoliere, my lord.

Ottavio — Well, well! And does he respond to her affection?

Brighella — He's head over ears in love with her.

Ottavio — Why, then, we could bring about that marriage. . . . Then under my protection. . . . Yes . . . that's it; go at once for Caianello. Send him to me.

The respective position of characters being thus cleverly explained, Goldoni moves them briskly.

Bettina is discovered on her balcony, and Pasqualino below in the street vainly asks to be admitted. Bettina loves him, but she is prudent and sends him to her sister Catte, as to her natural guardian.

Catte comes in presently. She talks to Pasqualino and finds him pleasant enough. "I do feel pity for young people. Indeed if I were not married already, I'd willingly steal my sister's sweetheart."

A lifelike and comical quarrel between the two sisters

reveals that Pantalone is providing so largely for Bettina's wants that Catte and her husband Arlecchino live on his bounty. Catte, the unscrupulous worldling, suspects Pantalone's intentions, yet she welcomes him warmly "since he pays." Obligingly she leaves him alone with Bettina.

Pantalone is shocked. He realises the dangerous position of his ward and offers to marry her. In the ancient comedies this situation was not new. Nor the fact of father and son being rivals, as happens here when Pasqualino is discovered to be Pantalone's and not Menego's son. But Goldoni turned this situation into something quite different. Pantalone is not made a laughingstock. His love has a fatherly tenderness which saves him from ridicule and prepares the happy ending. This situation is made lifelike by the truthful rendering of the manners and language of the principal characters. Critics pronounce the psychological study superficial because there are no complex feelings. Evidently this simplicity is adequate to the moral and social standing of the characters; it is consistent with the whole picture. Everything holds together — language, customs, plot, everything is true, in that measure of truth which the footlights admit. The episodical personages are naturally more faithful to tradition; Arlecchino, Brighella, Catte, Lelio come in directly from the ancient stock, but Bettina, so sweetly loving, so prim and yet so clever in word fencing; Pantalone so humane, yet so shrewd; Marchese Ottavio, the fashionable debauchee, each have a life of their own. They stand out the first in date of a long series of Goldonian characters.

The most popular character in this *Putta Onorata* is Menego Caianello, the gondoliere. Goldoni may have selected this model in order to secure the sympathy and the applause of the whole craft, a powerful craft in seafaring Venice, an important class standing midway between their aristocratic patrons and masters, the merchants they served as boatmen, and the popular class they belonged to. In the theatre the gondoliere were a power. They came in numbers because they had to stay up till the end waiting for their masters or for customers; when the house was not crowded, door-keepers winked at their entering without tickets, and in some theatres there was a place reserved for them at the back of the pit.

Goldoni may for this reason have flattered them; but it seems more likely that he pictured them because he liked them, because he sympathised with their free-and-easy manner of judging their betters, with their simple feelings and witty talk, because he saw them as the characteristic embodiment of the Venetian plebs. Thus guided by his sympathy in interpreting the feelings of the gondoliere, by his keen observation to reproduce exactly their language and manners, by his painstaking application of his principle of faithful imitation of life, he enriched the Italian comedy with this excellent model of popular characters. In *La Putta Onorata* are some symptoms of lachrymose sentimentalism. Goldoni was infected by some French "*comédies larmoyantes*" lately translated and performed in Venice.

The same year, 1749, Goldoni produced his *Cavaliere e la Dama,* his first daring attack against one of the most objectionable fashions of his time, *Il cavaliere servente.*

A classification of Goldoni's works is almost impossible. He suggests the most plausible when, in the preface to Pasquali's first volume, he says that some were written under genial impulse, others were composed as a duty. In another of his writings he divides his whole production into two sorts of comedies — those of characters and those of manners. His biographers and critics have each and all adopted some method, but none are satisfactory. Plays that paint one or several characters contain also an elaborate plot; plays that present a picture of popular life contain also a certain number of aristocratic personages; plays in dialect have some rôles in Italian and vice versa; some dialect intrudes in plays that are mainly Italian. Of course there is a possible distinction to be made between comedies in prose and others in verse, but this is a superficial distinction, as will be seen further.

Without attempting any new classification in order to trace Goldoni's evolution and to consider those plays that have some bearing on the growth of his talent, let us consider *Il Cavaliere e la Dama*, one of his almost forgotten plays, and certainly not one of his best. It is loosely constructed, the plot being planned to expound a theory. The characters are not lifelike:

they represent types rather than distinct individuals, and one aspect of each rather than a complete and finished type. All these faults are redeemed by the importance of the play as revealing Goldoni's character, his purpose of social reform, his attitude in regard to much slandered and misunderstood cicisbeism.

It is an evidence of that real courage that, though then little more than a novice, he boldly challenged the favourite sin of those whose favour and support were necessary to him. It shows how he loved and understood his people, how temperate and clear was his judgment, that instead of a ranting satire, of a violent and ineffectual attack, Goldoni drew a masterful outline of the picture of cicisbeism as it was considered, practised, and discussed by the Venetians.

One must understand this Venetian custom from the Venetian standpoint. For modern and non-Italian minds the idea of the *cavaliere servente*, a duplicate of the husband in almost all social and familiar transactions, a hybrid between the lover, the friend, the chaperon, and the lackey, is incomprehensible. The grosser interpretation of this complex personage being the most obvious is generally adopted. Moralists have ranted, critics have withered with scorn, historians with a turn for generalisation have passed judgment on the whole morality of the Venetian people, on the plea that in this peculiar trait was mirrored the average standard of honour, morality, self-respect, and all those social virtues which every nation at every passing period of its existence shapes and moulds for itself.

Now those who practised cicisbeism were not aware of committing any sin, or even an impropriety. They believed, and those around them believed, that the custom honoured both the lady and her cavaliere.

Something of the chivalrous spirit which in the Middle Ages animated the champion in the lists and inspired the songs of minstrels for some "*Dame de Beauté*," some of the spirit which curbed the proud "hidalgo," who though he kept his hat on in the king's presence yet caused him to bow low before his lady-love, some of the arcadian refinement which trifled and simpered in the salon of Madame de Rambouillet and wandered along the meanders of "*le fleuve du tendre*," some of the Oriental jealousy grounded on racial experience of woman's helplessness against the brutality of crowds — all these and other causes joined to produce this phenomenon and to create the atmosphere in which it prospered.

Like many other customs, serventism was at first a privilege of the highest caste. The patrician, whose state duties left him no margin for social pleasures and attendance on his wife's amusements, sought among the most respectable and fit of his friends one to whom he could entrust the care of attending his lady in that fatiguing and difficult round of ceremonies which made up the life of patricians. The attendant knight was chosen then, even in the contract of betrothal, because he was considered as a necessary appendix to the social belongings of the newly married pair. The young lady was not consulted, but she was expected to accept the choice of parents and of her future husband.

As with all fashions, in time the practice of having a *cavaliere servente* was aped by lesser dames, and finally the wives of merchants and professional men began to exhibit a chaperon of this ambiguous sort. As it generalised and democratised, the fashion admitted some alloy of vulgarity and grossness. It also gathered a large share of ridicule. But the grossness, vulgarity, and ridicule were not, in the opinion of Venetians, inherent to serventism; they were accidental deviations, individual mistakes, liable to be corrected. They did not dream of abolishing the institution itself.

The high-born fashionable lady could no more dispense with the attendance of that ever-ready servant than she could walk about unattended in the streets. It was not mere coquetry or fashion, but a consequence of many causes. The use of high pattens, never entirely discarded, the necessity of tripping in and out of her gondola, encumbered with tight and stiff-waisted gowns, ample panniers, toppling headdress, made the help of a hand necessary. The limitation of space, which gave to the parade on the *liston*, to the rush in the *ridotto*, to assemblies at every public ceremony, such a picturesque gaiety, also necessitated for her the presence of a cavaliere.

The very habit of living always on exhibition, always surrounded with the buzz and fuss of perpetual company, was at the same time the extenuating reason and the regulation of this custom. In fact for the lady who spent her whole life in accomplishing the round of social duties which a high rank demanded, the presence of one responsible attendant was rather a guarantee than a danger. Thus it was understood by the best part of the patriciate. The nobleman who accepted the charge recognised the duty; he realised that if he tolerated the compromising attentions of any other man he would look foolish, and if he himself presumed to behave improperly toward his elected ward he would appear brutal and unworthy of his trust.

The most delicate and refined prided themselves on constancy in this almost legal bond, and it is needless to say that no such situation could have survived long without a certain amount of mutual trust and respect. Président des Brosses, a very good judge of Venetian manners, records his own and other French personages' opinion, that there was little real harm committed in these apparently compromising connections.

Such evidently was Goldoni's viewpoint. In his careful, comprehensive picture of Venetian society he seems to have discovered a test of character in the interpretation and practice of serventism. Thus, for him, a woman of noble feelings would develop the highest features of her character in her intercourse with the man who serves her. The delicacy of her conscience in accepting that which it is honourable for her to accept, in refusing that which it would be dishonourable to both even to mention, has its counterpart in the duty, which she recognises, of giving gratitude, constancy, and every proper show of attention, politeness, kindness for the service she receives.

On the other hand the vulgar-minded woman, even if belonging to the highest rank, will reveal all the lowness of her real character in her exacting, peremptory ways toward her *cavaliere servente*, or, if she had impure inclinations, hidden by fear for her reputation in her social intercourse, she is sure to betray her natural depravity in her treatment of her cavaliers. For she will not be constant, but always changing either because she asks too much or because she sets her vanity in trying her fascination over several men.

Goldoni in several plays introduces a number of these peculiar pairs. The different shades in their reciprocal attitude, the different way of considering their obligation to each other, he turns to the best advantage for illuminating the whole character of each one, and their respective standing in the social group.

Only those who have failed to penetrate the very spirit of Goldoni's picture of his times have mistaken him for a decided opponent of serventism. Instances in his own life, as the interest shown to Albergati's contessina, are evidence of Goldoni's sanction of the custom. This play, *Il Cavaliere e la Dama*, is both an attack against offenders and a glorification of the votaries, a picture of the noblest feelings fostered by the cult of love, and a few strong and impressive dashes against those who turned it to unworthy use.

The plot is simple and not interesting. Goldoni prudently locates the scene in Naples, a thin disguise which was not meant to deceive anyone. Donna Eleonora, of noble birth and poor, is a sort of widow in anticipation, her husband being in exile and afterward dying to make way for the inevitable happy ending. Around her the hostile group of Donna Claudia and her *cavaliere servente*, Don Alonso, Donna Virginia, and her *cavaliere servente*, Don Flamminio, who is the husband of Donna Claudia. These, like the antique chorus, perpetually comment on the attachment of Don Rodrigo for the poor and proud Donna Eleonora. The pair stands for the idealised picture of serventism, he, a sort of Sir Galahad, she as virginal and shy as any heroine of romance.

Donna Eleonora is so poor that she cannot pay Anselmo what she owes him, and even accepts from the honest merchant the loan of some objects and the gift of others, thus offering the opportunity for Anselmo's views to be exhibited. The merchant, who might as well have worn the black mask of Pantalone, has the true Venetian attitude; toward the aristocratic caste he is respectful and devoted.

She is the poorer for being entrapped by a lawyer, il Dottore Buonatesta, a secondary figure forcibly drawn by one who, appreciating the honour of the profession, despises those who disgraced it.

The first act and half the second are a presentation of these personages. Delicate love scenes between Eleonora and Don Rodrigo, he timidly offering, she refusing even a disguised gift. On the other hand the other ladies with their *cavalieri* are going about, playing cards, very exacting and wayward, very vulgar and inclined to interpret Donna Eleonora's position according to their own standard of morality.

They support Don Flamminio's ribald wager of reducing Donna Eleonora to accept him as a protector. A plot is laid, a false letter from her exiled husband rejoices her, and induces her to show some politeness to the bearer of good news, who also pretends to be a friend of that husband. When Don Flamminio has by these illicit means won a place in Donna Eleonora's drawing-room, and the scandal mongers are busy discussing his chances, in comes Don Rodrigo to unmask the felon cavaliere and challenge him as a liar for having given Donna Eleonora false hopes and carried to her a message as coming from her husband, who has been dead two days.

The third act drags in scrupulous hesitations. Don Rodrigo seems to care more for his own and Donna Eleonora's reputation than for her love. He will surrender her rather than let people say that their marriage is forced upon them to regularise their position. In the end, however, things are arranged to the satisfaction of everyone.

Don Rodrigo, acting here as Goldoni's mouthpiece, has his theory about serventism, in a scene with Donna Eleonora (act ii, sc. 7).

D. El. — Would you be a jealous husband?

D. Rod. — No, Donna Eleonora, I would not. I am at heart very fond of society, and I would not hinder a discreet wife from being becomingly attended. Simple attendance (service) is not reprehensible. Let me point out to you a fine example. I have the honour of serving you, I have done so for some time. You are a beautiful lady, you are young and adorable; I am free, I am a man, I know how to appreciate your merit. What of that? Can you charge me with any impropriety? Can your husband complain of my friendship? No one can say it better than you can, and I ask you to speak now, when there is no object in disguising the truth.

D. El. — Yes, Don Rodrigo, your delicacy, your chivalry cannot go any further. Yet what merit is there in you, if you only feel indifference for me?

D. Rod. — Without offending the honour of his lady the wisest cavaliere may harbour some love for her. It is enough that he never allows the phantoms of his passion to trouble the purity of his intentions.

D. El. — Who can promise to be so virtuous?

D. Rod. — Anyone who is not in the habit of being a roué. I do not deny that even the purest heart may be assaulted by dangerous and dishonest ideas, but then by means of some opportune diversion they can be stopped, as by starting to do something, or calling a servant. . . .

D. El. — Colombina. (*She calls.*)

Don Rodrigo takes the hint and pretending that some important affair calls him away, he goes out, leaving Donna Eleonora to remark "on the difference between taking such wise and honest resolutions and living up to them."

Contrasted with these high-flown sentiments is a typical scene (act i, sc. 8). Donna Claudia has been bullying her servant Brighella, giving him twenty orders at a time, calling him names, and at last, turning to her *cavaliere servente*, Don Alonso, she says: "Oh, these servants are really unbearable.

D. A. — You might use him more kindly.

D. Cl. — All right, sir! I see that you side with the servants. What a dear man! Indeed I'm very much obliged to you; oh, very much!

D. A. — I beg your pardon. I should not have interfered.

D. Cl. — Quite the contrary. You should interfere; it is your duty to interfere and to oblige my servants to obey me.

D. A. — No, that is your husband's duty.

D. Cl. — My husband takes no care of such things. He may be taking care of them in some other place; but here, in my house, it is your duty to keep my servants in good order."

Perhaps the less acceptable scene for a foreign audience, and yet that which must have looked most lifelike to Venetians, is the following (act i, sc. 9), wherein Don Flamminio is discussed by his wife and her friend Virginia who is avowedly his lady-love.

D. Claudia (*to D. Virginia*) — Now, tell me, have you seen my husband this morning?

D. Vir. — Yes, he favoured me with his visit early this morning.

D. Cl. — And he did not attend you in your drive?

D. Vir. — No, because Marchese Ascano was there, and you know that your husband is not wont to insist on precedence; he willingly yields his place to any stranger.

D. Cl. — What have you done with the marchese?

D. V. — After attending me here, he went about some important business of his own at court.

D. Cl. — Who, then, will come to fetch you?

D. V. — He may, or your husband, or the baron, or the Englishman. I cannot tell! Anyone!

D. Cl. — You have plenty cavalieri.

D. V. — I have so many that I do not remember them all.

D. Cl. — Who's your favourite?

D. V. — No one. I do not care a fig for anyone.

In later years, when Goldoni's experience of more select circles enlarged the field of his observation, he takes up this theme and gives variety of portraits and sketches. In this first essay at a picture of customs in a world which was not then familiar, he displays a greater violence of satire, and more bitterness in condemning manners and principles that he has not yet in any wise adopted or even fully understood.

In the contrast between the honesty and delicacy

of the merchant, as opposed to the indelicacy and unscrupulousness of the aristocracy, he brings about a situation which, according to the idea of honour then current, could only be unravelled by a duel, and then he makes his hero, the personage he evidently holds up as a paragon of virtue and manly perfection, to avoid it and send arguments to his rival instead of the *stoccata* prescribed by the code of honour.

(Act ii, sc. 11), Anselmo and Don Flamminio.

Ans. — You seem to be surprised that a vile merchant should dare to teach a man of noble birth, such as you are, how to behave.

Fl. — Of course I am surprised, and also I think that you are foolhardy.

Ans. — Let me tell you: noblemen who know how to keep their own rank, behave themselves accordingly; they are in no need of being taught lessons by anyone, but those who wear a noble name and take advantage of their birth to behave very badly are unworthy to stand face to face with an honourable merchant such as I am.

D. Flam. — Hush, you impudent fool! I'll make you repent of your impertinence. I am a cavaliere, and you are a vile merchant, a plebeian.

Ans. — A vile merchant, a plebeian? If only you knew what is meant by the word merchant, you would not speak so. Trading is an industrious profession followed even to-day by noblemen of higher birth than your own. Trade is useful to the world, necessary to the relations of peoples; and whoever attends to it with honour, as I do, must not be called a plebeian; the real plebeian is the man who, having inherited a title and some acres of land, wastes his days in sloth, and thinks that he can trample under his foot everyone and overrule everyone. The vile man is he who does not know his duties, and would have his pride respected unjustly, thus betraying that he is only noble by accident, but ought to have been born a plebeian.

Il Padre di Famiglia and *La Buona Moglie,* which belong to this same manner of Goldoni's, also reveal the ripening of his talent; the best of his innovations are there. Some of his qualities, indeed, are carried further in these early plays than they will be in latter ones. There is more crude naturalism, more open assault against vice, more powerful contrast between evil and good, between vice and virtue. At that moment of his evolution he could almost be mistaken for a moralist, which he was never meant to be. He toned down his pictures, as he better understood the art of playwriting, as he better understood the secrets of the human heart.

At this moment of his career, on the eve of battle preceding the challenge of the sixteen plays in one season, Goldoni grows conscious of his aim and, at the first opportunity, he announces his intentions.

Goldoni's definitions are faulty. His formulas answer but loosely to his idea. He proposes to reform the Italian comedy by a return to nature.

The abstract noun "reform" was most popular in the eighteenth century. Its very vagueness made it acceptable to every variety of mind. When reactionary patricians cried reform as a panacea for threatening dissolution, it meant a return to antique simplicity. Stylists and grammarians wrote "reform" when they thought of invigorating the language by additions from the French; readers of Voltaire's books were busy building air castles out of this magic word. For many Italians the notion of "reform" was summed up in such superficial worldly wisdom as Gaspare Gozzi ladled out in his many writings. Thus Goldoni understood the word, but with the addition of sincerity, honesty, decency, a careful sifting and retention of the best from the old order, and rejection of the rest. It also meant the return of comedy to its original plan, a picture of society.

When Goldoni speaks of nature he means society such as he saw it. Nature is another of those abstract words dear to his time. Another of those protean expressions that enchanted an epoch stirring to a new sense of life, to the consciousness of new wants. Rousseau meant something very different when he wrote nature from that which Goldoni meant. Yet both men are equally earnest and veracious; it is their entirely diverging viewpoint which changes their conception of the same word. With Goldoni, nature means civilised humanity as he sees it daily revealed in the streets and public resorts of Venice.

His knowledge of the past was by this time extensive,

for he had perfected by some slight study of the classics that which he had already learned from the players. His mastery of the theatrical technique was faultless; no playwright ever better knew how to make the most of his interpreters, how better to adapt his own and his interpreters' abilities to the wishes of his audience. Above all he was ideally situated in the midst of a people that could both inspire and understand his every intention. This communion between author and audience was a happy return to the spirit of ancient comedy. Goldoni relied on the opinion expressed by the audience; not so much by that part of the audience that, sitting in the boxes, almost uninterruptedly pursued their habitual conversation and lent a careless ear to the play, but by that audience crowding the pit, whose sympathy was not easily won.

In his eagerness to secure the favour and even the collaboration of "his public," Goldoni took his audience into his confidence. As often as he could he introduced a personage made to his resemblance, and used him as a mouthpiece to announce his motives or his intentions. He appealed to the popular favour, at the same time seeking to guide public opinion.

Thus he remained faithful to the oldest and best traditions of the *commedia dell'arte.* He established a communion between the pit and the scene, which experience had proved most beneficial, all through the evolution of this form of art.

In many of the earliest plays of this second manner, more specially in the play entitled *Il Teatro Comico*, he tried to illustrate the reform of comedy, such as he understood it.

Il Teatro Comico, in three short acts, carries us behind the scenes to see the players rehearsing a new play, and discussing with a manager, Orazio, the new method. Orazio represents Goldoni, and the players are portraits of members of the Medebach company, some of them approving of Goldoni's reform, others lamenting.

Thus Pantalone complains that for one trained to extemporise, the effort of learning his part by heart and of following the author in the interpretation of a character is embarrassing. Moreover, though retaining every other trait of the mask, he has been deprived of his pasteboard vizor, and, in consequence, he has to learn the art of facial expression, and must also refrain from the exaggerated gesticulation which a covered face encouraged.

A poet is introduced as foil to Orazio. He would like the manager to take his play. It is a scenario in the style which Goldoni ridicules.

(Act i, sc. 9.)

Orazio — Well, signore, let us hear your canvass.

Lelio (the poet) — Ready; I begin at once: Act the first. A street, Pantalone and the Doctor. A scene of friendliness.

Orazio — That's out of fashion.

Lelio — Please just listen awhile. The Doctor asks Pantalone for the hand of his daughter.

Eugenio — And Pantalone grants it.

Lelio — How clever of you. Pantalone gives his promise. Doctor goes to the house door and knocks, calling Rosaura.

Orazio — And Rosaura comes into the street.

Lelio — Just so, signore, Rosaura comes down.

Orazio — If you please, signore, I have heard enough. (*He rises.*)

Lelio — But why? What is the matter?

Orazio — It is an enormous impropriety to have women coming down into the street; it has been tolerated too long in Italy, to our discredit. Thank Heaven we have corrected it, abolished it; this sort of thing must not be admitted to our scene.

Lelio — Well, let us arrange it thus: Pantalone goes inside the house and the Doctor remains in the street.

Orazio — Whilst Pantalone is inside, what is the Doctor to say?

Lelio — Whilst Pantalone is inside . . . the Doctor says . . . what he likes. In the meantime Arlecchino, the Doctor's servant, comes in stealthily and gives his master a blow.

Orazio — Fie, fie! Worse and worse. . . . It is a scandal to see a servant knocking about his master. This foolish *lazzo* has been but too often practised by our players, but now it is abolished. How perfectly stupid it was. Arlecchino beats his master; his master endures it because it is funny? Signor Poeta, if you haven't got something more modern, you may spare the trouble of reading any further.

Lelio — Listen to this dialogue, at least.

Orazio — Let us hear the dialogue.

Lelio — First dialogue: Man entreats. Woman sends him away. Man: You are as deaf as the wind and will not hear my complaint. Woman: Hello, go away, you are as insolent as a fly or like a butterfly. Man: My beloved idol. . . .

Orazio — I cannot stand it.

Lelio — Have pity.

Orazio — Go and sing such nonsense on the *colascione*. . . . (*Exit Oraz.*)

In the second act and in the third scene Orazio expounds his opinions about the difference between French and Italian plays, naturally preferring the Italian. Goldoni at the time could neither speak nor read French. Readers of his life know also that he never clearly understood the spirit of the French people.

Further on, Orazio delivers his own comment of Aristotelian rules, adding by way of conclusion that "if Aristotle were now alive he would revoke his canon about the unities, as being the font of much incongruous absurdity. There are two sorts of comedy, the comedy of intrigue and the comedy of character. One is simple, the other is more intricate. The former may be performed in a fixed scenery; the latter cannot be so represented without incurring inconsistency. The ancient classics did not enjoy our facility for shifting the scenes, and that is the reason why they held to the rules of unity. It is enough for us if we obey this canon by locating the play in one city and, better still, in one house."

Having thus disposed of Aristotelian canons, Goldoni does not omit to display his acquaintance with Horace. Lelio has a notion about Horace's forbidding the presence of more than three players at the same time on the stage.

(Act iii, sc. 9.)

Orazio — I beg your pardon, whoever told you so did not exactly understand Horace's intention. He said: "*nec quarta loqui persona laboret.*" Hence some people think that he meant: Let not more than three persons act at the same time. He only meant: if there are four of them, let not the fourth overexert himself, lest the four actors come into each other's way, and create confusion, as so often happens, in improvised plays. . . . Before presuming to talk about the precepts given by the ancient classics it is well one should consider two things: first, their intended meaning; secondly, whether their rules are adaptable to our times. As the world has greatly changed as to the fashion of dressing, eating, talking, so has taste changed in the matter of play acting.

Lelio objects that the new method will grow old and appear antiquated, but Orazio is ready with his confutation. "Plays will indeed grow old; but the method for composing them will, I hope, last and be perfected. True and well-observed characters must always please, and even if they are not infinite in genera, they are infinite in species, each virtue, each vice, each custom assuming a different appearance under different circumstances."

Orazio does not disapprove of monologues, yet he contemplates a reform of this favourite device of the ancient comedy. "The player is supposed, when he is alone on the scene, to believe that no one hears him and no one sees him. If he talks to the public, he drops into an unpardonable absurdity which has been too long tolerated."

Lelio objecting that it will then be very difficult to acquaint the audience with the situation, Orazio gives his notions about the best way of explaining the situation. "It was the fashion formerly with our players to have, in a first scene, Pantalone and the Dottore, master and servant, or lady and maid talking so as to inform the audience of the subject of the play. I think the best manner to inform the public is to divide this exposition through different scenes, and so, little by little, elucidate things to the greatest amusement and surprise of the hearers."

The technical advice contained in the *Teatro Comico* is not only good in itself and practically useful, but it was excellent for training the members of the Medebach company and correcting them of some clownish tricks, some unrefined ways formerly practised.

Goldoni's capacity as a teacher and stage director must have been very great. Here, in the *Teatro*

Comico, when asked by Lelio if he would altogether suppress the masks, Orazio declares that he does not wish to run against the ingrained taste of the public, but that players must keep the place which tradition and common sense assign to the characters they embody.

He knows well that people crowded the theatres merely to see the antics of the popular actor impersonating one or the other of the favourite burlesque personages, and that every Arlecchino will have his part, but it must be short and unimportant; he will be allowed to play on words, to skip and dance about moderately. Pantalone must not always quote poetry. He is meant to rise high among Goldoni's characters. Brighella must talk common sense, and show the kindness of his rustic disposition.

Finally Goldoni, by Orazio's voice, delivers to all a neat lesson.

(Act iii, sc. 3.)

Orazio — Mind how you utter very distinctly the last syllables that must be understood. Speak slowly, but not too slowly, and in moments of passion force your voices and accelerate your declamation, but still remember to speak naturally, as if you were talking; since comedy, being an imitation of nature, everything in it should be lifelike. Your gestures, too, should look natural. Move your hands according to the sense of the words you speak. . . . Whenever you are acting with another personage, never divert your eyes nor your attention from him; do not look about you and steal glances at the tiers of boxes; this inattention leads to three undesirable effects: First, the audience is aggravated, condemns the absent-minded player as a fool; secondly, you are guilty of offence toward your comrade acting with you; and lastly, whenever you lose the thread of the talk, the prompter's voice coming unexpectedly startles you and you cannot perform your part with the required naturalness.

Goldoni does not forget that most important item — morals. He makes no pretence of saintliness, but champions decency and propriety. He does not tolerate coarseness or vulgarity.

Goldoni's private life was not guileless, nor was his conception of comedy absolutely idyllic; yet he detested scandal, he protested against licentiousness. He wanted his players at least to appear respectable, and his plays must at least be decent.

Orazio expounds this in the *Teatro Comico*, from which Goldoni tried to expel the musicians, those at least of the craft who interpolated their intermezzi between two acts and sought applause by complying with the national inclination for music of some sort.

CHAPTER VIII

THE PLAYS, 1749–1750

Chiari's antagonism — deep elements of discord — *L'Avvocato Veneziano*, 1750, is an earnest of his ripening power — new, original, a tragedy of common life — plot is simple, the supremacy of duty over love — an intense spiritual drama — Venetian dialect used fits the characters — it is a microcosm of Venetian society — sins of aristocratic caste denounced — in *La Famiglia dell'Antiquario* the "masks" take their proper place — character of Italian masks — Arlecchino, Brighella, Colombina, Pantalone represent the Venetian middle class — a favourite with Goldoni — certain aspects of Venetian life were forbidden to the stage — play of *Pamela* a great success — contrasted with Goldoni's English model — Goldoni is a conservative democrat — upholds Venetian customs and respects the aristocracy — learned something from French writers — *La Bottega del Caffè*, 1750, a masterpiece, is purely Venetian — directly borrowed from the *commedia dell'arte* — described — Goldoni's method of creating a character — Don Marzio the central character.

ABBATE CHIARI'S character, his pedantry, his plagiarism have been sufficiently exposed by all those who admire Goldoni and consider Chiari as responsible for the suffering and the many deviations of talent which he directly caused or willingly encouraged. Yet this antagonism of Chiari's was not entirely hurtful, since it roused Goldoni to exert his power to the utmost and in every direction.[1] Easy-going Goldoni needed the goad to urge

[1] Abbate Chiari's notoriety is due to his rivalry with Goldoni and not to his character or his works. For Chiari's life and works, one may consult Niccolò Tammaso, *Storia civile della Letteraria*, Torino, 1872, page 260, *passim;* G. B. Marchesi, *I Romanzi dell' abate Chiari*, Bergamo, 1900; G. F.

him; he needed the sting of malice, the assault of unfair competition to shake off his mental placidity which made him so easily satisfied with himself. Now Chiari and his employers and supporters provided Goldoni with this spur. He was roused from his leisurely complacency to a better comprehension of the comic art, to a better appreciation of his own capabilities.

The struggle was embittered by the circumstances of time and place in which it was fought. Goldoni, who could easily ignore every other Italian playwright, would not have troubled much about Chiari's success if the unavoidable rivalry had been restrained to a literary competition.

Deeper elements of discord than the two writers were aware of underlay the literary quarrel, and other motives also added fuel to the strife.

Goldoni brilliantly repulsed a first attack against *La Vedova Scaltra* by charging his opponents with insulting foreigners, and especially English Protestants, because one of the characters, a servant, in Chiari's

Sommi-Picenardi, *Un Rivale del Goldoni*, Milano, 1902, and also the often quoted volume of G. Ortolani, *Della vita e dell'arte de C. Goldoni*, page 53 and *passim*. This hero of plagiarism, Chiari, was born in Brescia and he died in that same town in 1785. After opposing Goldoni for several years, he managed a reconciliation and obtained Goldoni's pardon, but he betrayed his insincerity when, after his rival's departure for Paris, he protested that they had only pretended to quarrel in order to advertise their plays. Goldoni never condescended to deny such an absurd statement. The only allusion to Chiari in the *Memoirs* is in vol. i, page 323: "If my readers were curious to know the name of the author of *The School for Widows*, I could not satisfy them. I will never mention the persons who have tried to wrong me."

parody used the word *panimbruo*. In fact nothing was further from Chiari's mind; he never intended to insult the guests that Venice always gladly welcomed. But Goldoni did not scruple to wield this weapon though it was dangerous.

Whether Condulmer or Grimani or Casanova were his powerful patrons is not important. Goldoni won his fight, and was encouraged to pursue his career both by the applause of the public and by the official support through the institution of the theatrical censorship,[1] which Goldoni welcomed. In the battle that was just beginning, the magistrate was a protector; though he was often assaulted, Goldoni exhausted all the fire of combat in this first encounter. The petty malice of polemics, as they were then practised, was alien to his nature; besides he was not prepared to fight any real literary battle because of his lack of scholarly arguments. His only weapon was his creative power, his faculty for intense application. His answer to his opponents was an increased production of good plays, a strain of extraordinary activity, culminating in the achievement of sixteen plays represented in one year.

Whether some of these plays were already prepared, whether the argument of some of them was freely borrowed from earlier foreign or Italian works, matters little; that most of them were good and some excellent is evidence of Goldoni's power and energy when he

[1] *Mem.* i, 323: "*The School for Widows* was immediately suppressed and two days later a government decree established censorship for all theatrical performances."

was goaded to intense action by a sense of duty or pride.

Neither personal ambition nor greed prompted the effort. He was surprised by his triumph, and Medebach paid him only the scanty wages agreed upon for the year.

During the carnival of 1750, even before he took the engagement of the sixteen plays, Goldoni gave a splendid earnest of his ripening power with the *Avvocato Veneziano*.[1]

The influence of the past, the imitation of either classic or popular comedy, the tricks and makeshifts of players, everything that by accumulation had fostered and fed his genius, is outgrown. Here everything is new, original, lifelike, and plausible. The grosser elements are discarded, the burlesque reduced to the limits of decent comic style. Here an element of real emotion, of restrained feeling, is introduced with taste and measure. The tragedy of common life is there, as it is in real life, not blatant and ranting but half disguised under the forms and manners of polite society.

The passage from the ancient moral standpoint to that which was to become dominant for more than a century dates from this interpretation of dramatic art. The early moralists encouraged playwrights to paint vice in its darkest colours, so as to frighten the audience

[1] *Mem.* i, 325: "This was a terrible year for me, I cannot recollect it without shuddering. Sixteen plays each of three acts, according to the Italian fashion, each requiring two hours and a half for their representation."

from imitating it, or to paint virtue under incredibly bright hues to make it attractive, while the description of sin was supposed to be amply accounted for by a finale of unconvincing punishment. A new, and nicer, sense of morality suggested to Goldoni that the best teaching he could impart must be the genial reproduction of the lessons taught by daily experience, in the acts and sayings of honest commonplace men and women, striving to make their lives both honourable and happy, fighting against the passions within and the temptations without that might drag them down.

This was indeed a reform, and let it be noted, Goldoni did not then know that which Diderot and other non-Italians were formulating in critical essays.

The plot is simple, and contains few episodes.[1] The

[1] *Avv. Ven.*, act iii, sc. 2, Alberto pleading, thus explains the position of parties: "Mr. Anselm Aretusi, father of my client, having been married ten years and being still childless, considering that which others might call a blessing as a most unfortunate circumstance, wished to have a family that he might have worries. He had a friend more really unfortunate, since he was father of three daughters and greatly troubled about supporting them. Anselm proposed to adopt one of these girls (*I figlia d'anima*) and the father gladly gave her to him; indeed he would have given the whole lot if they had been asked for. Anselm takes this child home, three years old and gifted with all the innocent charm of that age; two years later he gives her his entire fortune. Please note with what prudence and wisdom and consideration the wise and prudent man has made this donation . . . considering that in ten years of married life he has never had any offspring . . . and fearing that he might die without knowing to whom he might leave his fortune having adopted Donna Rosaura Balanzoni . . . he has made her a gift of all his possessions. . . . He never revoked this act, but the law must annul it. Because the law says that if a father by giving away his fortune wrongs his children, the gift is void and null. Does this donation wrong his son? Indeed yes! A trifle? It deprives him of his entire paternal inheritance."

interest of the play is concentrated on the two principal characters, and on the struggle between love and duty. The idea of such a struggle was not new to the eighteenth century; the novelty lies in the supremacy of duty over love. Love was then accepted as a supreme law. Almost everything and anything was justified and excused if committed in the name of love. Goldoni stood for the victory of professional honour, of simple duty, over the impulse of passion.

Alberto Casaboni, an impersonation of Goldoni, is the *avvocato* feed by Florindo Aretusi to plead for him in a lawsuit against Rosaura Balanzoni, whom the late Anselmo Aretusi, Florindo's father, had adopted and made the heiress to his large fortune.

The scene is in Rovigo. Alberto is studying the contested point and finds that Anselmo Aretusi, being childless, could well adopt a child and could dispose of his whole fortune in her favour, but when later Anselmo became a father both the former act of adoption and the will were annulled and void. He explains to Florindo Aretusi how matters stand;[1] in another scene he confides to a friend Lelio that he is in love with Rosaura.[2] He has been walking under her balcony,

[1] Act i, sc. 3, the legal deeds are given full length and discussed by Alberto and Florindo: "Flor. — Do you mean that a man is not free to dispose of his own money? Alb. — I beg your pardon, I never said such a foolish thing. A man is free to give whatever he has, but he cannot deprive his children. Flor. — When he gave he had no children. Alb. — Just so, and that is why, on the coming of children, the donation became void."

[2] Act i, sc. 1; "Lel. — Now tell me, have you ever seen your opponent? Alb. — I have seen her at her balcony almost every day. I have met her in the street. Once she stopped to talk with the doctor who was with

courting every opportunity to make her acquaintance because "he has every reason to esteem her very highly." Yet since he is persuaded that Florindo's cause is just and since he is engaged to plead for him, he means to do his duty and exert all his ability in order to deprive Rosaura of everything.

Lelio and Beatrice, friends of Rosaura, arrange things so that Alberto meets her. The scene is prettily conducted. A drawing-room with the inevitable tables for the *tresette;* a set of amiable, witty persons chatting and playing, with just one grotesque personage as a foil to the good manners of every one else. Alberto plays the prominent part, holding the *banco* with that graceful indifference to gain that was one of Goldoni's social virtues. Rosaura makes the most of her opportunity for pleading her own cause; she entreats without ever exceeding the limits of maidenly modesty, yet with a charm most trying to Alberto's love. He answers with gentleness, with admission of his tenderness, but also with firmness. All these asides, going on while the cards are dealt and played, are cleverly managed.[1]

me, so that I was able to consider her attentively, and I have formed a very high opinion of her. Lel. — Is she not a pretty girl? Alb. — Upon my word, she is indeed of no common beauty. Lel. — Do you like her? Alb. — We all like that which is beautiful. Lel. — I guess you would rather plead for her than for Signor Florindo. Alb. — Well, as far as intercourse with the party goes, I certainly would prefer to talk with the Lady Rosaura than with Sig. Florindo, but as to this suit I prefer standing for the party who has justice on his side."

[1] The whole *conversazione* in Beatrice's house, comprising scenes from four to ten, is a pretty picture of Venetian manners. Alberto on coming in (sc. 9) finds the card players sitting round the table and is introduced to Rosaura. "Alb. — My dear lady, I'm sorry that I must be your antag-

Alberto is suspected by his employer, insulted by a rival who offers him a bribe,[1] and further tempted by a visit of Rosaura, chaperoned by Beatrice, who wisely slips out of the room when she has brought things to this climax. The scene between Rosaura and Alberto rises almost too high for comedy. It is the very tragedy of life; with the allurement of mutual love in opposition

onist; but you must find comfort in this, as it is an advantage for you, since my insufficiency will help you to prove your rights. . . . Beat. — Would it be presuming to ask your opinion? Alb. — If my opinion were not favourable to my party, I would not certainly plead for him. Beat. — Then Rosaura is lost. Alb. — Signora Rosaura cannot be lost. Beat. — Why, if she loses what has she left? Alb. — If she loses the inheritance, she still retains a fortune in personal merit which no lawsuit can take from her. Ros. — Signor Avvocato, you make fun of me. Alb. — I am not so impertinent."

Beatrice manages to detain Alberto a little while longer by inviting him to sit at the gaming table. "Ros. — The Signor Alberto is in a hurry to go away; he must have time to consider how he can best ruin me. Alb. — You make me blush. I protest that I am not always thinking against you. Ros. — That may be; yet certainly you do not think in my favour. Alb. (*after tenderly regarding Ros.*) — What would you like us to play? Ros. — He shifts the subject of his talk very cleverly." There is a Count Ottavio, foil to Alberto, who grumbles and quarrels, but still the play proceeds and Alberto is holding the cards. "Beat. — Well! You are winning, winning everything. Alb. (*with a side glance at Ros.*) — Would to goodness I could win everything! Ros. — What would you gain worth having? Alb. — Why, the stakes and the stakeholder. Ros. — The stakes are worth little and the stakeholder even less. Alb. — The stakeholder is worth a fortune. Ros. — If it were true, you would not be her enemy. Alb. (*drops purposely the cards he holds*) — Oh! I've dropped my cards. I have lost and must pay. Here are two fillippi and two lire. Beat. — You are an adorable croupier. Ros. — To-night you play in my favour and to-morrow you will play against me. Alb. — Have you yet unburdened your mind? Ros. — To-night I unburden my mind, to-morrow you will unburden yours. . . ."

[1] Scenes 1 and 2 of second act may have been copied from life. Conte Ottavio, a bully, tries first to bribe, then fights Alberto in a duel. Alberto is as clever with his sword as with his tongue.

to the strict duty of the one and the obligation of the other to respect her lover's honour more than any worldly consideration. The dialogue is the more forcible for being free from the formal Italian, Alberto's part being in idiomatic Venetian, more familiar and more effective to Goldoni.[1]

[1] Act ii, sc. 2, is the capital scene in the play (*le clou*). Rosaura has been persuaded to visit Alberto, and Beatrice, her chaperon, has slipped out of the room. The situation, according to Venetian ideas, was rather *risqué;* the young lady is embarrassed, but not a bit silly. She asks a plain question simply and frankly: "Have you only been philandering, or do you feel for me, if not love, at least pity? Alb. — Signora Rosaura, I must answer as a man of honour, hence I cannot conceal my feelings. Unfortunately from the first moment I saw you my heart was wounded. When I strolled under your window, and courted every opportunity to see you, I was a sick man in search of relief. Oh, dear me! how scanty the balm to the depth of my wound! It only irritated it, and increased my pain. Last night! Oh, last night! What agonies I endured! Your reproaches were like arrows piercing my heart. Your looks that spoke of tenderness and indignation! My heart was so heavy, I could hardly speak. That I am constrained to appear publicly as the foe of one whom I secretly adore is a new sort of torment never before suffered by men, never before invented by demons, never before imagined by the cruelty of tyrants. Ros. — Do you indeed love me? Alb. — With the dearest love of my heart. Ros. — Then I ask no more. Let fate do its worst with me; I will suffer anything without complaining, if only I am assured of your love. Alb. — Yes, dear Lady Rosaura, but the certainty of my love can in no wise assist your desire for your fortune. You see that I am under the dire necessity of doing my utmost to ruin you; my heart weeps for you, my blood is frozen when I think that it is my duty to dispel all the bright hopes of my passion. Ros. — I pity you more than I can tell and more than you can think; though I have shown indignation at your manly firmness, still I admire it. I realise that you are the worthier of my love the more ready you are to prefer your honour to your love. If you had given up your client for my sake, I would have enjoyed my good fortune but I could not have esteemed your merit; while I would have rejoiced at the effect of treason, I could not have trusted the traitor. . . ." Sc. 11 is also very effective. Florindo tells Alberto that he does not trust him and Alberto has to beg in order not to be discharged and dishonoured.

The play never flags, never loses the dignity of the spiritual drama under discussion. A crescendo of emotion leads up to the ending; Rosaura understands and, though she expects to be entirely ruined by Alberto's eloquence, she swears that she will still love him and endure with joy a poverty that will be the proof of his honesty.

The third act shows Alberto pleading against Doctor Balanzoni. Both speeches are good evidence of Goldoni's competence in his legal profession. The thesis was certainly one that he had particularly studied, having discussed it at Padua for his examination. The arguments on both sides are supported with a knowledge of the law, Balanzoni quoting a number of texts, Alberto refuting them with others, while he strives to give a basis of common sense to his argument. In this, as in many other instances, Goldoni forestalled his contemporary colleagues.[1]

The Venetian dialect used serves well, fitting the character and clearly expressing the ideas of the author.

In the end, of course, Alberto, having caused the ruin of Rosaura by gaining his patron's cause, makes compensation by marrying her.

This play, though not especially popular with Italian

[1] The third act pictures a trial before a Venetian court of justice, the proceedings, the formalities, everything true to life and indicated with care for every detail. The pleadings also are interesting. Doctor Balanzoni's is not so much a caricature as an imitation of the speeches uttered by barristers in Goldoni's time. Every argument is ponderously supported by Latin quotations. Alberto's is delivered in simple and apparently unpremeditated style.

audiences, is worthy of high rank among Goldoni's works. The construction is good, the scenes coherent. Though the interest in Rosaura lags after Alberto's avowal of his love, there remains as a higher theme the conflict of emotions warring within his heart. A modern actor could make much out of the situation.

In this same season of carnival, 1750, Goldoni gave *La Famiglia dell'Antiquario*, a play of great importance in the history of his theatrical works which reveals the spirit of the times, the ruling ideas, the degree of current morality in that special world which is here represented. It is the borderland between aristocracy and bourgeoisie. The daughter of a merchant has been admitted into a family of impoverished nobility, wherein, somewhat in the spirit of Madame de Grignan's impertinent reply, *Il faut bien engraisser nos terres.*[1] Now the manure brought in, under the name of a *dot*, by Doralice, adds a ferment to the evil tendencies of the noble household, which is on the verge of dissolution, only to be rescued by the common sense and honesty of Pantalone, her father, the embodiment of industry, thrift, shrewdness, and other social virtues of the Venetian merchant. This is indeed a microcosm of that which was going on in Venetian society, the downfall of the recently ennobled, decadent class of the *barnanotti*, and the rise of the merchant class. This situation Goldoni often

[1] Madame de Grignan, daughter of the celebrated Madame de Sévigné, having squandered her own fortune and that which her husband accumulated when he was governor of Provence, married her eldest son to a wealthy heiress.

represents, but perhaps in no other play with equal vigour, with equal realism and logic.[1]

The most obnoxious sins of the aristocratic caste are here denounced, each one being impersonated in an appropriate character. The paterfamilias, Conte Anselmo Terrazzani, spends all his time and as much of the family money as he can get in buying ancient medals and objects of art. He is a caricature of the genuine amateur; he has no taste, no discernment, and also no scruples. The immorality of his character is further shown in his toleration of his wife's misbehaviour. Countess Isabella, though past her prime, has a *cavalier servente*, whom she torments; she gambles and otherwise contributes to the ruin of the family. The quarrel between her and her daughter-in-law, Doralice, is carried on with the petty malice, the irrepressible wickedness, and the senseless impudence which, as Goldoni well knew, characterises such family strife. Just because he knew how venomous such disputes are sure to be, how impossible it is to conciliate two exasperated women, rivals in everything yet constrained by circumstances to live under the same roof, he laid aside the rule of managing a happy ending, and

[1] *Mem.* i, 335: "The name 'Antiquario' is given in Italy both to those who learnedly study antiquity and to those who foolishly collect imitations which they mistake for originals, and trifles which they believe to be valuable objects; it is among the latter that I have picked my model. Count Anselm, with more money than knowledge, becomes an amateur of pictures, medals, engraved stones, and of everything that has appearance of rarity or antiquity. He is fooled by knaves, and purchases at a very high price a ridiculous collection."

caused the curtain to drop on the last vain efforts of Pantalone to bring about a reconciliation.

The characters of the two women are drawn in outline, but in very broad and effective contrast. Contessa Isabella is impertinent, violent, rude as one who has been overindulged in her youth, and taught to consider herself as the centre of the world. She is dumbstruck with surprise when, once, her husband tries to assert, even for a short moment, his authority; she scolds her *cavalier servente*, and exacts from other visitors the homage of serventism, which they would rather offer to the younger lady. She excites her son, Conte Giacinto, Doralice's husband, against his wife. She treats her servants like slaves. Doralice, on the other hand, is sly; she says biting things without raising her voice; she exasperates her mother-in-law by her coolness and impertinence.

One of the most typical features of this play is the part in the family squabbles taken by both ladies' cavalieri. Only Pantalone is shocked at their interference; to everyone else it seems perfectly proper that each lady should be supported, attended, and advised by her ambiguous chaperon, and that they should quarrel for the possession of one of them. Il Dottore Anselmi is the typical *cavalier servente*, tamed by years of slavery and parasitism. He fawns, fetches, and carries, but he makes his profit out of his abjection. He lends money at usury, he acts as legal adviser to the spendthrift son of his lady, yet he submissively retires when a visitor is announced whom the signora intends to captivate. He is the middle-class manikin, feeding on the crumbs of decaying nobility, carrying the infection of mean intrigue and avarice into the ancient palace, and adapting to his own aims the manners and customs of the aristocracy. The profile traced is masterful. Every personage in this play is adequately proportioned to the general ensemble. Thus the other cavalieri, without being quite as abject as the Dottore Anselmi, are tainted with the same docility and intrigue. They carry their compliments and attentions from the one or the other lady of the family according to what they deem to be most profitable for their own chances of securing free entertainment in the house.[1]

[1] The last scene thus resumes the situation. The whole family is assembled, comprising also the *cavalieri serventi:* Cav. del Bosco, the trimmer, who desires the favour of both ladies, and Dottore Anselmi, a veteran of serventism, whose liaison with the mature countess has degenerated into parasitism:

"Ans. — My dear wife, my dear daughter-in-law, let me tell you that I am no longer the head of this family. Isa. — I expected as much; now the care will be mine. Ans. — Don't worry; the care will not be yours. Signor Pantalone has agreed to take charge of my household. My son and I have transferred to him all our possessions and obligations, we have signed certain articles which shall now be read to you. Isa. — This is a wrong you inflict on me. Dora. — Why? Failing the head of the family, it was my right to rule the house. Isa. — I am the principal mistress! Ans. — Brava! Panta. — Please be quiet a moment: I am going to read the articles ready accepted and signed. Please listen, all of you. There's something for everyone of you. Article I. Ans. — That I may amuse myself with my medals. Pant. — Primo, that Pant. dei Bisognosi is entitled to receive the entire income belonging to the family of Count Ans. Terrazzani, annuities and rents of every sort. Isa. — And deliver the money into my husband's or into my own hands. Dora. (*apart*) — The good housewife! Pant. — Secondo, Pant. engages to provide the whole household and every member of the family with victuals, clothes, etc. Dora. — I am in want of everything. I am utterly unprovided. Pant. — Terzo, that Pant. has authority to employ all means in order to ensure peace between the mother and daughter-in-law. Isa. — That's quite impossible. Dora. — She is a devil, — a devil! Pant. — Quarto, that neither the one nor the other of these ladies be allowed to entertain continued and fixed friendships. If either insists on having one of these attachments, she shall be obliged to go and live in the country. Isa. — This is too bad. Dora. — This article offends propriety. Cav. del Bosco — This article offends me. I understand it, gentlemen, I do understand it, and since I am forced to realise that my services to Lady Doralice are not well accepted I will leave the house immediately; since a cavaliere of good birth should never add to the dissensions of a family. (*Aside*) I swear that never will I set foot in a house where there are mother and daughter-in-law. (*Exit cav.*) Dora. — Since the cavaliere is gone, I expect that the doctor also will go. Pant. — What do you say to that, Signor Dottore. You have seen how prudently the cavaliere has behaved. Isa. — The doctor shall not leave my house. Dot. — Our friendship is an old one. Pant. — All the more reason to put an end to it. Dot. — I'll put an end to it; I'll leave the house; but I would like to know for what cause with such pretty words a gentleman of my sort is dismissed. Pant. — If you don't understand, I'll tell you. Because you philanderers are good for nothing but encouraging nonsense. Dot. — I upheld my lady countess because when one respects a person one cannot contradict her. Isa. — I always said so; you are a doctor without wit and without science. Dot. — Do you hear her? Ever since I had the honour of attending on her, she has paid me such pretty compliments. (*Exit Dot.*) Pant. — Let us go on with the articles. Quinto, the two ladies, mother and daughter-in-law, in order to keep peace shall live in two distinct apartments, one in the lower, the other in the upper story. Isa. — I want the upper one. Dora. — I'll take the lower and climb fewer stairs. Pant. — Hear! They are beginning to agree! Sesto, that Colombina shall be dismissed. Isa. — Yes, let her be dismissed. Dora. — Yes, let her go away. Pant. — All right. Here also you agree! Now in the presence of your husbands exchange a kiss in token of peace. Isa. — Oh, never! Dora. — Never! Pant. — Come along! The first who rises to embrace and kiss the other will have this diamond ring. (*He shows a diamond ring. Isa. and Dora, both partially rise but stop midway and sit down again.*) Isa. (*Aside*) — I would rather die! Dora. — I'd rather go without any ring all my life. Pant. — Not even for a diamond ring? Ans. — If it is antique I take it. Pant. — I see that it is impossible for them to kiss; if they did, it would only mean that to-morrow they would quarrel again. Now you have heard the articles. I am the head of this

Goldoni did not entirely break with the past. Sometimes he dispensed with the masks or — as in the *Avvocato Veneziano* — gave them a small place in the background; but when he wanted them he knew better than anyone before or since how to use them.

In the *Famiglia dell' Antiquario* the masks take their proper place according to the traditions of classical comedy.

From the classic model Goldoni adopted the plan of having a group of intriguing menials entangling their masters in embarrassments and disputes; on this plan the Greeks, Romans, and early Italians constructed their plays; on this plan the *commedia dell' arte* arranged every performance. In this play Colombina, Arlecchino, and Brighella ape their masters, encouraging their fads, and excite them one against the other, and so they remain faithful to their traditions even though they are slightly modified by Goldoni, the reformer.

A learned disquisition on the origin of masks and their derivation from Greek and Latin personages would please the writer, but it is a mere *hors d'œuvre* for

family. It will be my care to provide for you all. Signor Conte, you may amuse yourself with your medals, I'll let you have one hundred sequins a month for that. Signor son-in-law, you must assist me in the direction of the household and so learn. You, my ladies, have quarrelled at the instigation of a foolish maid and of foolish cavalieri serventi; the causes being removed, let us hope that the effects may be removed too. You may have two maids and also have your meals served separately; thus, if you don't meet, perhaps you won't quarrel."

The scenes 12 to 15 of act ii make a vivid picture of the most abject rôle played by the cav. ser. Dottore Anselmo is bullied by Countess Isabella in the intervals of Colombina's mischief-making reports.

About *cavalieri serventi*, see Chapter VII.

the understanding of Goldoni's plays. For Goldoni knew little and cared less for such investigations. He understood the characters as they had come down to his time and possibly may have formed some plan for making them more individualised and lifelike in the future; but he had no fanatical reverence for antiquity.

Arlecchino,[1] descended from the German Herlen König or from the French Harlequin, or from both, was to Goldoni a mere Bergamasc mountaineer who, having come down to Venice to earn a living, exerts his clownishness, his stupid docility, low instincts, and greed in his place as a confidential servant in a large household, or of *facchino*, sort of Jack of all trades, in a smaller family. He has no morals, only a wholesome terror of punishments which may keep him from gross crimes, without preventing him from using his wits in every profitable way. He is servile, but without respect for the masters who confide their intrigues to him and tolerate his impertinence.

That many-coloured, tight-fitting suit of clothes, wherever derived, is by this time connected with his

1 Brighella persuades Arlecchino to put on the disguise of an Armenian merchant, and offer to Sig. Anselmo some worthless rubbish as precious antiquities. Ambrogio Mondino, in a comment to Goldoni's *Famiglia* (Livorno, Giusti), at page 28, gives in a note a strange origin of the name Arlecchino. At the court of France, during the reign of Henry III, there was, says he, an Italian actor of a lithe figure who, being under the patronage of Harlay de Chauvallon, assumed the name of his patron and made some jokes about this name: *Il y a parenté entre nous au cinquième degré, vous êtes Harlay premier et moi je suis Harlay quint.*

About Arlecchino, Brighella, etc., see chapter on the Italian comedy.

For the character of Corallina see chapter and analysis of *Locandiera* and *Serva Amorosa*.

lithe and nimble figure, wherever he has got that rabbit tail of uncertain origin which adorns his soft shapeless hat, emblematic of his cowardly quickness in escaping the blows he well deserves. The noisy bladder he wields is as blatant as his impertinence. Those who would have his name of *zanni* derived from the Latin *senex* ignore the graceful puerility of his spirit, his susceptibility to love, his facile affections. Easily frightened, easily comforted, he jumps from one extreme to the other. His language is a corrupt Venetian, mixed with some Bergamasc idiotisms, some expressions gathered from the mariners and many proverbs. Though unlettered, he twists the meaning of words and misapplies them cleverly. Having mingled with all sorts of people in cosmopolitan Venice he successfully imitates every accent and intonation. Thus in this play he pretends to talk like an Armenian merchant in order to deceive the antiquarian.

Brighella has redeeming points which make him essentially different from Arlecchino. Though he too has come from the mountainous inland and has entered the service of rich men, he has preserved some of his native honesty and directness. Clumsy in his ample pantaloon and long jacket of white cloth trimmed with a green border, he is clumsier in his talk, he is susceptible of better feelings. Goldoni has transformed him more radically than any other mask. Though here he shows him cheating his master and saying, "Well, if he must be ruined by others, let me have my share of the profits," in Goldoni's later plays he has developed from the traditional personage the latent germs of faithfulness, of common sense. He is warm-hearted, falls in love and is faithful, remembers a benefit and forgets injuries. He shares certain traits with Pantalone. Brighella's sins are due to the poverty of his origin that brought him in contact with decadent nobility, and made him a servant. When he escapes from servitude, or is employed as clerk and confidential help in smaller households, he shows all the simple virtues of the people.

Colombina is the feminine counterpart of both *zannis* with added pertness and coquetry. Goldoni, who had a peculiar fondness for the *servette*, could not redeem Colombina from the traditional lowness of her character, so he created the type of Corallina, which he has immortalised. His Colombina mirrors each mistress's manners. She is adept at starting quarrels, at tale-bearing, and at providing the most scandalous interpretation of facts. She has a prominent part in this play, being the confidante of both the ladies, and betraying them both. Of course she manages to get money out of both, though she prefers mischief-making to coin of the realm.

Goldoni's favourite character, Pantalone,[1] gives

[1] It is the whole history of Venice that should be considered in order to trace back the growth and rise of Pantalone. *Chronique de Geoffroy de Villehardouin* provides interesting information about the share taken by the Venetian merchants in the second crusade.

One of Callot's engravings representing Pantalone is thus described by Riccoboni (see Riccoboni): *La robe de dessus est la zimarre que les marchands portaient dans leurs magasins, et qui étoit encore en usage an dix-huitième siecle parmi les avocats dans leurs cabinets. Cette robe étoit noire, l'habit*

significance to the play. He shows that honesty, thrift, and industry are surer means to success than inherited titles, and also that obedience to one chief is a necessary condition for the welfare of a family.

He is common sense and righteousness in the midst of absurdity and vice. He is the third social power, the citizen, who averts the ruin of aristocracy and from the enfeebled hands of former leaders seizes the reins of government. He is a symbol, the more significant for having grown gradually and slowly taken shape and colour through all Goldoni's works, just as the real citizen he stands for was assuming definite shape and colour, importance, and value in the wide world outside.

What is the origin of Pantalone, and what does he represent? Neither the comedy personage, nor his living model can be traced back very far into the past. He is the *pianta leone*, the Venetian pioneer of trade who planted the ensign of San Marco, the winged lion, in Eastern countries conquered by the Crusaders who had sailed under Venetian flag, in Venetian ships, to subdue the infidels and open new marts for European trade. Even in those distant times he was the collaborator who provided funds and forbore to claim his share of

de dessous ou pourpoint rouge dans son institution. Cet habit devint noir en signe de deuil après la prise de Constantinople parles Turcs (May 29, 1453, which makes Riccoboni's statement rather startling) *puis le noir prêvalut par habitute et fut le plus gênêralement en usage pour le pourpoint comme pour la robe. . . . La culotte et les bas sont d'une piece . . . le masque n'a rien d'extraordinaire.*

(The word *zimarra* may be the italianised form of "zimmer rock.")

glory. In the days of triumphant celebration, he allowed precedence to the knight who had fought, but at the right moment he claimed the financial profit of the expedition. It was power and influence as well as profit on his money that he wanted. His was that large spirit of industry and thrift, that sense of commercial honour which characterised the Venetian merchant.

He was called the *Magnifico*. His costume was gorgeous; his manners wanted refinement. In Venice he flourished with the caste of merchants he impersonated. Like them he became sober in his garb when the effects of the Catholic reform restrained his taste for magnificence. He put on the black, well-fitting clothes of rich material, the comfortable slipper, the ample cloak so appropriate for the climate and habits of Venice. He covered his face with a mask because this vizor facilitated his constant association with the aristocracy.

The relative position of Pantalone, the wealthy merchant, toward his aristocratic patrons and associates is typical of Venetian society. By tradition he appreciates the peculiar service which, through centuries, the aristocracy have rendered to Venice, he glories in the splendour of ancient families, considers inscription in the *Libro d'Oro* as something above common mortality; but individually he judges and weighs any man, whether he wears a scarlet robe or a peaked cap.

From his original "magnificence," he has gained an air of elegance and courtly manners that suggest equality with those that stand above him in social rank. In his youth he may have been a *cortesan* and practised all the graceful arts and sports that made the Venetian youth so gay and amiable. He has become a sober merchant, a kindly father, a long-winded speaker.

Goldoni found the mask of Pantalone sadly inferior to this standard. Somehow he had caught the infection from the ancient dramatic person of the old man in love with a young woman, ridiculed for this senile passion, or for his general imbecility, or for his avarice. Goldoni at first in *La Bancarotta* adopted the character almost as he found it; but as soon as he began to copy from life he created a new Pantalone, in *La Putta Onorata* and its sequel *La Buona Mugier*, a middle-aged man, with kindly manners.

In this *Antiquario* Goldoni added some traits that individualise him, and complete him as a representative figure.

Pantalone has married his daughter to a nobleman. The hard-earned ducats go to gild the coat of arms of a fool. His one object is to make his only daughter happy. "You are the wife of a count," says he, "you are a countess, but this title is not sufficient to ensure for you the respect of other people, unless you can gain their love by your obedience and humility." When he hears that his daughter has boxed the ears of Colombina, he insists that she must beg pardon of her mother-in-law, since she is the mistress of Colombina and of the whole household.

Pantalone is firm yet respectful toward the antiquarian. He scorns him for closing his eyes to his wife's *cavalieri servente*, for being so credulous that even Brighella and Arlecchino cheat him; but still he does not use harsh words.

Pantalone, the embodiment of the Venetian middle class, has none of the rebellious spirit that marks Beaumarchais's *Figaro*. He bides his time. He gets many of the advantages reserved to the higher class — money, pleasure, influence — but he does not try to deprive those who are in possession. Like Goldoni, he would reform, not destroy; he places himself in the sunlight, but he does not try to push anyone else into the shade.

He recognises the authority of the aristocracy in public affairs, yet he distinguishes clearly the point where his and their interests divide, and where their authority must not interfere with him. In Goldoni's representation of his character, Pantalone is also a personality that is rapidly evolving. In the succession of the plays, from year to year, as Goldoni's experience in life enlarges, as his comprehension of social problems grows, the figure of Pantalone appears better finished, more complex, every time nearer to our modern conception of the citizen.

From the very first Goldoni raised him above the vulgar but always effective *lazzi*. In each of the following plays he set him progressively higher, using him as a mouthpiece for the teachings which common sense, honesty, and simple family affection have to impart to giddy youth or extravagant pride.

In this first and most democratic phase of Goldoni's career Pantalone assumes a distinctive character; in later plays he loses some of his significance as a symbol, but none of his importance as a representative of a common type.

Pantalone is neither misanthropist, nor *rustego;* he grumbles sometimes, and scolds often, yet he is sociable, has pleasant manners, and enjoys all those amusements peculiar to the gaiety and refinement of Venetian life, he is free with his money, yet not extravagant, he enjoys a good dinner, delicate wines, but he lives simply.

He most hates effeminacy. Pure Venetianism stood opposed to the mannerism and exaggerated delicacy imported from Spain. He approves of the *cortesan* and his bold gallantry, gay impudence in affairs of love and honour, but he hates the *cavaliere servente* and his flaccid servility. Thus in *Le Femmine Puntigliose* (Act ii, sc. 14) he says: "Men nowadays are reduced to such a point that they have nothing left but the name of man. Women order them about like puppets. Everything is done for them, and whoever wants to obtain a preference must bow low to a woman. As a consequence, women are grown very proud, persuading themselves that they are made to rule. I laugh to see how women behave to their *cavalieri serventi* in society! They sit there as stiff as stones, expecting men to worship them. One man sighs at her elbow, while another kneels in front of her; one hands her a

[1] *Le Femmine Puntigliose. La Putta Onorata* and *La Buona Mugier* form part of the group of dialect and popular plays.

saucer and the other picks the handkerchief she has dropped to the ground, one kisses her hand, the other tenders his arm for her to lean upon, one proffers his service as a secretary, the other as a footman; some sprinkle perfumes, and some fan them; they are fondled and cajoled all around. Then they incite one another, they plot together, and in the end they trample under their feet all the men; the female sex is domineering and men are slaves in chains, worshippers of beauty, polluters of their own honour, a scandalous example for youth."

In the same play, the same Pantalone expresses himself on another obnoxious but characteristic Venetian custom, the practice of taking revenge for an offence on the shins of the offender's servants. Florindo has been insulted by a Count Lelio and orders his servant, Brighella, to pay one sequin each to four men who will "thrash all the servants that come out of that house." He adds that "This sort of thing is practised everywhere. Thrashing a servant is the best way to insult a master."

(Act iii, sc. 5) Pantalone is shocked. "Oh, the fine vengeance. Really heroic and manly! . . . Because the masters have insulted you, you beat the servants? Is it the servants' fault if their masters do wrong? Do you call that compensation for an insult? You talk of vengeance; what sort of vengeance do you mean? Is it so difficult to find four men willing, in cold blood, to beat the poor servants? My dear Signor Florindo, this is foolishness, a trick of imagination, to make men believe that to punish the culprit it is sufficient to oppress the innocent."

But Pantalone's real importance is when he becomes Goldoni's mouthpiece, and at the same time represents the Venetian point of view when he explains why it is unbecoming for a merchant's wife to try to enter into the aristocratic circles.

His advice to the wealthy merchant and his wife, who have vainly sought admittance into exclusive social sets, is to make a better use of their money than squandering it on some impoverished nobleman. "Go about with honest people of your own rank . . . and, when the opportunity serves, tender some service to a nobleman; pay reverence to them, and respect them without forgetting yourself. By such means they will all be able to say 'though I have not been admitted in the society of cavaliers and ladies, yet cavaliers and ladies have shown me much favour and paid me compliments in private.'"

The year 1750 was a milestone in Goldoni's career. He challenged his rival by promising to give sixteen plays in one year; he undertook to do an appalling amount of work.[1] Yet he did not change his tenor of life. His duties behind the scenes, his engagements to provide other theatres with lighter compositions were all observed.

He went about his business quietly, finding time for arrangements with his first editor Bettinelli, finding

[1] His letters to Bettinelli (see U. de Ghe, *Lettere*, and A. G. Spinelli, *op. cit.*) contain some expressions that may be either of complaint for his crushing labour, or the usual apologies of authors late with their prefaces. His letters to more intimate friends show him active and cheerful (see Letters to Arconati, etc., in collections quoted).

THE PIAZZETTA OF SAN MARCO AND THE ISLAND OF SAN GIORGIO IN THE TIME OF GOLDONI

From a painting by Francesco Guardi in the Correr Museum, Venice

time for social pastimes, especially for the favourite Venetian amusement, a stroll on the Piazzetta, to enjoy the spectacle of that perpetual fair and listen to the blarney of mountebanks, to the quarrels of gondoliers, to the lisping, mincing talk of masked gentlefolks, to look on the popular dances and note everything in the wonderful memorandum of his observant brain, there to be melted in the crucible of imagination and reshaped into a new play. His great preoccupation was to avoid monotony. He knew his public well, realised that they must be amused, they must have variety.

Goldoni ranged the entire field of permitted subjects. Certain aspects of life, certain classes of persons, were forbidden; others could only be presented under a veil.[1] The classical Italian comedy offered but a limited number of subjects which frequent repetition and re-adaptation by the comedians must have made stale. Goldoni's acquaintance with foreign authors could not compete with Chiari's extensive readings and brazen plagiarism. He imitated his opponent's method even though he openly condemned it. Thus while he scornfully swept aside all Chiari's plays with the epithet *Romanzi*, he selected Pamela[2] and transformed her into an Italian heroine.

[1] Magistrates, priests, nuns, and senators were forbidden stage characters. Adultery could only be pictured under the guise of cicisbeism; a stage kiss was shocking.

[2] "He (Richardson) was contented for many years to print books without writing them, and he was past fifty when a commission or suggestion from two well-known London publishers, Rivington & Osborne, for a sort of model letter writer led to the composition of *Pamela*, published in 1740, and which became very popular. . . . *Pamela, or Virtue Rewarded*, gives the

He merely knew a translation and adopted the general plot and characters. But he could not reproduce the shade of maidenly reserve and common sense, the blend of simplicity and archness which characterise the English girl; nor could he reproduce the atmosphere of homely propriety and stiffness of his model. He could not read English, had no insight into English manners and mentality.

The play was applauded in Venice. It created a sensation in Paris; it was honoured later with a discussion at the *Convention Nationale*, which caused the *Comédie Française* to be suppressed for a time.[1] It has been revived often, both in public theatres and in private theatricals; it has been translated into many languages, thus establishing a right to be taken in consideration even though the long, sentimental speeches, the wearisome adventures, have little interest for modern readers, and would appear dull indeed to a modern audience.[2]

history of a girl of low degree who, resisting temptation, marries her master, and in the second and inferior part reclaims him from irregular courses." From *A Short History of English Literature*, by George Saintsbury, Macmillan & Co., 1908, page 508.

[1] Charles Rabany, *C. Goldoni, Le theatre, etc.* (*op. cit.*) gives at full length the discussion at the *Assemblée Nationale* about Goldoni's play — or the French adaptations of it.

[2] *Pamela* is "a simple, common theme, and quite unlike the subject matter of the heavy affected licentious romances which had hitherto supplied readers of fiction with poisonous amusement in their leisure hours. . . . Few read Richardson's novels in this fast age; for their extreme length and minuteness of description — in which there appears something of a womanish love of gossip — repel any but earnest students of English fiction." *History of English Literature*, in a series of biographical sketches, page 309, by W. Collier, LL.D., T. Nelson & Sons, Paternoster Row, 1888.

Goldoni did not attempt to settle a point that had been learnedly discussed a century and a half. Can a good play be made of a novel? Is there an essential difference between these two forms of literary fiction, or is there a fundamental affinity in the common aim of both representations of life? The frequent success of such adaptations is undoubted, but popular applause of the crowd is not final argument. It is probable that the form of any artistic work is so intimately connected with its content that no such reshaping can produce a real masterpiece.

In this case the difficulty of adaptation was aggravated by the original form of the novel — a series of letters. The timid outpourings of a sentimental heroine were transplanted into scenes, enacted before an audience. The charm of mystery, all that was hinted rather than stated in the English novel, evaporated out of the Italian play, while some new elements of emotion, of fun, were introduced. The imitation was something quite different from its model, because Goldoni did not know how to copy.

The contrast between Goldoni's play and his English model is interesting. To begin with, there is an entirely different viewpoint. The struggle between love and the prejudice of birth is the keynote of the whole plot, as it was in Marivaux's *Marianne*, and in hundreds of other romantic tales of the time. Pamela's love is shown in contrast with that rigid division of caste that was the basis of the Venetian life, the principle of Pantalone's creed, and Goldoni never dreamed of infringing such a law. That a nobleman could, by marrying a servant girl, accomplish an action worthy of approval and likely to inspire applause from the audience would have seemed preposterous to the Venetian idea that nobility was a divine right, an inheritance of which it would be detestably sinful to deprive one's yet unborn children.

Had Goldoni been burdened with critical scruples, he might have known that the whole book was originally intended to reach, through many windings, this precise goal, that all Pamela's virtuous humility and all her lord's splendour of "fine laced silk waistcoat of blue Paduasoy, and his coat of a pearl-coloured fine cloth, with gold buttons and buttonholes" were but the ornamental decorations, the gay streamers and pennons that heralded and proclaimed one homely conquest of revolutionary ideas. Now, Goldoni had no sympathy with revolutionary ideas. Pantalone is always ready to explain the difference between the philosophical upheaval first brooding and then exploding, in France, and the progressive "reform" of order and justice demanded by the Venetian. Goldoni took the plot, some of the characters, such of the petty details as suited his conception of a dramatic work — half sentimental, half realistic — and left the perplexing problem altogether out of his plan. He avoided the difficulty and so arranged matters as to obtain the necessary happy endings, by recurring to an old, but always successful, trick of the ancient comedy that shifted the ground entirely by making

Pamela a noble lady, the only child of an exiled nobleman.

He did not realise what this shifting of the fundamental basis of the English model meant for his adaptation, else he would have contrived to *escamoter* the trick in a few words; on the contrary he lingered over the situation purposely. "After the recognition scene," says he, "where, according to the rules of the art, the action should terminate, there are ten scenes which, instead of boring people, amuse as much as the preceding ones, and perhaps still more." Of course, they amused the Venetian audience still more. They lifted the weight of a mésalliance from their spirit!

Yet those critics who, fascinated by an obvious and simple theory, detect the influence of French ideas in every foreign writer of the time, have twisted a short speech uttered by one of the minor characters into a declaration of Goldoni's adherence to Rousseau's most extreme ideas.

The passage is delivered by Madame Jefre, Lord Bonfil's housekeeper. "I have often heard it said that the world would be more beautiful if it had not been spoiled by men, who for pride's sake have upset the beautiful order of Nature. That common mother regards us all as equals, though the arrogance of the great does not deign to consider the small. The day will come, however, when one pudding will again be made of both great and small."

Probably an examination of some of the *zibaldoni*, in which the comedians collected their ready-made speeches, would reveal many of these outbursts culled from ancient authors and only intended to convey the classical expostulations of the menial grumbling at his master's tyranny.

Through all his works, even occasional miscellaneous poetry, Goldoni upholds the principle at the base of every Venetian law, custom, and idea, respect for aristocracy and for its rights. In this play of *Pamela* he clearly shows how jealous he was of the privilege of birth, yet for one sentence of radicalism he has been mistaken for a democrat! [1]

Goldoni was not impervious to the influence of new ideas and viewpoints that were then spreading over the thinking world, but this influence did not come to him directly from Paris and the groups of philosophers and Encyclopédistes, but was a gradual change, that his receptive mind adopted in the measure and in the manner that suited his natural disposition, and fitted with his mental attitude.[2] He rejected instinctively that which was opposed to his own and his own people's mentality. None of the abstract notions of right, none of the French philosophical problems which contained in embryo a social transformation, were then contemplated by Goldoni. It is doubtful whether his

[1] To present Goldoni as a Republican in Venice, and as risking the Venetian jail, contradicts both the real conditions of the time and Goldoni's real political opinions. Clavière's "I have heard him warmly express the regret that he was unable to throw into the fire the patent of his royal pension" was written in an apologetic letter for the sake of obtaining a pension for Goldoni's wife; in such a case exaggeration might be pardoned.

[2] This gradual change in Goldoni's manner will be shown in an analysis of his plays.

long residence in Paris, breathing an atmosphere, as he needs must, quivering with intellectual and social unrest, brought any alteration in his ideas or increase in vision. It is certain that during these first years of his career he had not even considered the great social revolution that was even then at the threshold. All his love and comprehension for the lower and for the middle classes of the social fabric do not allure him out of that which seemed to him "the necessary order of things."

Nevertheless Goldoni learned some other lessons from French writers. Gradually some of the tendencies that were developing in France came down into Italy and even found their way into Venice.[1]

Lachrymose sentimentalism was the first of these

[1] About Goldoni's vivid painting of life and the influence that foreign writers may have exerted over him, more will be said presently. Goldoni's realism is not a fixed principle; it is a shifting tendency, a manner of interpretation; the proportion and perspective differ in every picture. Thus in Goldoni's works a clever critic might discover at what epoch of his career each play has been composed by the manner in which realism has been employed. We purposely say "composed" and not performed, or printed, for these disputed dates have no real value for the analysis of his evolution.

Considered in its ensemble Goldoni's work appears most realistic in the beginning, toning down as more perfect composition, more delicate balance is attained, and, later on, when the turning point has been reached and passed, when Goldoni loses touch with his surroundings, without taking spiritual contact with the French movement of ideas, his realism becomes blurred, his rendering of it is weak — in the *Bourru Bienfaisant*, or studiously elaborate — in the *Avare Fastueux*. Worse still in the fantastic creations of his wearied pen, *Il Buono e Cattivo Genio*.

In *Momolo Cortesan*, the episodical figures of Arlecchino and Smeraldina, in *La Buona Moglie* the nursing of a baby, scenes in *La Famiglia dell' Antiquario*, the whole rôle of the old *cavaliere servente* — may be quoted as the most unfinished and unpleasant of Goldoni's realistic descriptions.

doubtful acquisitions. In *Pamela*, as in some of his other plays, Goldoni drifts into sentimental pathos, but never to the degree that became fashionable soon after his time. His sunny nature, the Venetian habit of reticence in the expression of feelings, the racial tendency to discover the absurd side of serious things, saved him from that pathos which infected the theatre of other countries and in some measure even the Italian. *Pamela* was his one successful achievement in the direction of a homely and pathetic conception of the drama. Goldoni could not follow Richardson further, and he did not attempt the deeper tragedy of *Clarissa Harlowe*. In some later plays, circumstances and not his wish forced him to follow the whims of his employers and collaborators.

Goldoni's best plays are those which owe little or nothing to foreign influence, especially those which represent Venetian manners. One of the first of these genuine Goldonian masterpieces was performed during the memorable year 1750–1751 and is still a favourite with Italian playgoers, though it is doubtful whether it would succeed in translation or adaptation. What a delightful blend of idle gossip, imprudence, and withal kind-heartedness and easy wit make up this delightful comedy, *La Bottega del Caffè*.

Its untranslatableness is itself evidence of its appropriateness to its special birthplace. Sympathy with Venetian manners, insight into that predisposition to investigate each other's affairs, then to discuss, with humour, indulgence and sympathy are necessary to understand *La Bottega del Caffè*. It is purely Venetian, directly borrowed from the *commedia dell'arte;* everything has the spontaneity, the *brio* of Goldoni's improvisation. The single scene not only enforced the resemblance with old familiar comedies, but fitly represents the character of neighbourly intercourse so typical of the Venetian coffeehouse and emphasises the unity of the episodical adventures. The place open to every visitor, the man, Don Marzio, with a tongue ready for gossip and eyes peering in every corner, ears listening to every breath of rumour, give to the interwoven plots the significance and interest of a symbol.

Goldoni's suggestion that his plays be divided in *comédies d'intrigue et comédies de caractères* overlooks that some of them, like this *Bottega del Caffè*, are at the same time a construction of dramatic episodes and a study of character, and also a picture of customs. Hence the play can be studied under three different aspects.

It is typically localised in one of these Venetian *campielli,*[1] which are appendages of the houses rather than a street. People perpetually go in and out of the doors, and are equally at home. Doors and windows are never closed; conversation does not stop between those that stand on doorsteps or in front of their shops

[1] Scenes in the typical Venetian *campiello* will be further analysed in *Il Campiello* and other Goldonian plays. For a better acquaintance with these peculiar customs see Molmenti's *Venezia nella Vita Privata*, etc., in the *Edizione Illustrata*. Vittorio Malamani is also a faithful interpreter, if a more severe one, of Venetian customs (Vit. Malamani, *Il Settecento a Venezia*, 2 vols., Turin, a collection of verse).

or at the house window. The intimacy of home stretches over the whole *campiello*. This manner of living under the eyes of one's neighbours at every hour of the day and most of the night may seem unreal to foreigners; it was perfectly familiar to Venetians. The shops stand close together — the barber's; the gambling house, and the *caffè*. An inn and a small private lodging house are in the background. Everything is in the small proportions that answered to Venetian reality and served the theatrical intent of compactness.

The three shops have one common Venetian character — there people enjoy talking. For all Venetians, social intercourse is a craving of their sunny, cheerful nature. When great affairs of state kept them busy in the halls of council, or active trade in the open-air "Change" on the Rialto, when political intrigue caused them to crowd round a leader in earnest dispute, this national propensity found its vent; but when in the eighteenth century business slackened and grew uninteresting, when the only prosperous branch of business was money-lending, when affairs of state dwindled to the proportions of a petty State, when political and clerical censure gagged all free discussion of ideas, then the Venetians developed their propensity for gossip. The average of conversational excellence in Venice was high. Venetians perhaps surpass the Parisians in the art of *causerie*, in the ease of suggesting as much as is expressed in the delicate insinuation, the politeness that covers even impertinence with a veil and adds a charm of kind feeling for the sense of propriety which kept even malice within limits. If the Venetian dialect were more familiar to foreigners, the whole character of Goldoni's plays would be better appreciated.

The three shops here form the background, and at the same time the *raison d'être*, of the whole comedy. From the one to the other, from shaving and listening to that which happens just outside the open door, from drinking a cup of coffee to taking one's place at the gaming table, the round was familiar to every middle-class Venetian idling aimlessly in search of diversion.

Truly a useless and lowly sort of life, yet less wicked than its equivalent in other conditions. Gaming was, as Goldoni knew, a great evil, but as it was practised in Venice its harm was in a degree limited. The gambling house, so close to the street or the *campiello*, was under public control. The sharper, the crook, the money-lender, all the parasites that thrive on vice, being forced to negotiate under the eye of many gossips, were held within bonds. Violence was unknown in Venice. No firing of pistols, few drawings of swords; the very profanity which bad luck suggests to the fleeced lamb was tempered by good breeding or habits of piety. A gambling house where no more intoxicating drink can be had than coffee or chocolate loses some of its peril.

Other things, too, that are objectionable were, in the *campiello*, carried on under the observant eyes of many, and thus restrained in their worst effects.

Thus Pandolfo the *biscazziere*,[1] who makes profit by lending money to the losers, by levying a heavy toll on the winnings, by aiding the sharpers, and sometimes also by gambling himself, is confronted by Ridolfo,[2] the rather too prosy, honest fellow who owns the coffeehouse. Close neighbourhood and the habit of talking on one's doorstep bring about between these two an exchange of ideas which, even from the first scenes, strikes the right chord and reveals the whole situation. Ridolfo, well-intentioned man, wants to help his fellows, Pandolfo represents the several temptations that would destroy them, and Don Marzio impersonates the critical, observant, mischief-making choir that looks on and comments.[3]

As he stalks into the coffeehouse, Ridolfo introduces him, in an aside, as "the man who can never sit still, and will always carry his point." He at once quarrels about the time of the day and insists on the exactness of his own watch. Don Marzio, the central character,

[1] *Biscazziere* is not merely the gambler but also the man who, like Pandolfo, keeps a gambling house.

[2] Ridolfo is rather too good to be quite satisfactory. He is a tame repetition of Brighella (as for instance in *Il Giuocatore*), formerly a servant in a family, and for ever after devoted to every member of it. Brighella in his bucolic characteristics of clothes and language, in his blundering rustic simple mind is more effective than this wise man of affairs, whom Pandolfo estimates properly when (sc. 2) he calls him *un principiante*, equivalent to greenhorn, and "unlikely to make money." Yet Ridolfo's, like every other coffeehouse, has its *cabinets particuliers*. He protests that the doors are never closed. To which Pandolfo objects (with what a wise wink) that he cannot deny coffee to any sort of customer. "What of that?" says Ridolfo, "the cups take no taint."

[3] The personage of D. Marzio is said, on the play direction, to be a Neapolitan gentleman; a thin disguise which deceived no one.

is a compound of many petty sins which Goldoni has cleverly managed to give him in a number of deft pencil strokes. Don Marzio makes mischief for the pleasure of attracting notice, of getting into the limelight as a well-informed person. He is no Iago plotting the ruin of those he hates, and weaving a net to catch the innocent; he is the man who longs to be somebody and finds out that he is nobody. His ambition, his activity, might have been turned into some useful and honourable channel had not every aspiration been frustrated, every energy twisted out of its natural course by circumstances. He is not wealthy; *Le sue a facoltà* (a lucky impropriety of language) are limited, meaning that he is spared the trouble of managing a fortune.

His only occupation, money-lending on a small scale, is rather an enticement to go lounging about the coffee-house and the gambling den than a real diversion. He loans money as he does gossip, with loquacity, with self-assertion rather than with any cold malice.[1] He has lent a few sequins to that scapegrace Eugenio and he must tell everyone of this great affair, partly because, in his empty life, the little things assume importance, partly because he wants to make sure that he is guaranteed by the earnings pawned to him, partly because he wants people to know that he is generous yet

[1] *La Bottega* contains several witty repartees and interesting information about the practice of money-lending and usury. Don Marzio does this as he does everything in a blustering, foolish way. Pandolfo is the low money-lender and knows all the tricks of the trade. In reviewing other plays we will compare him to other money-lenders and show how Goldoni has vividly painted this hateful sore of his time and native city.

shrewd. If this boasting, this telling of Eugenio's affairs brings complications and misery to others, Don Marzio willingly ignores it. Indeed he is so unconscious of this failing that he scolds Trappola, a substitute of Arlecchino, for talking too much: "It is very wrong to blab; if you do so, you will lose all credit and no one will trust you." The next moment he is asking the same Trappola to inform him about a dancing girl, Lisaura, who lives close by. The low-bred lackey gives a bad outline of the woman's life; yet when the higher-born gossip presently repeats the information he makes it worse, just to prove his own shrewdness. First he guesses, since no one visits the girl or enters her house by the front door, there must be a back door, and that people "ebb and flow by the back door"; and he repeats it at every opportunity.

Presently a deserted wife pursuing her wanton lord chances to come under his observation. He first doubts whether he has ever seen her, then he says that he noticed her last year, then he persuades himself and others that he did, and still proceeding in the same manner by accumulation, he gives it out positively that she is an adventuress who decoys young men.

Thus self-asserting, imprudent, and mischief-making Don Marzio grows under the eye of the reader into a solid figure of real humanity. A stroke which goes deeper still, and gives a modern physiognomy to the tattler — he presumes to be scientific. He gravely informs Ridolfo that "warm water is debilitating for the stomach," and to the timid suggestion of the latter about the tissues of the stomach, he pompously answers with a random assertion about the "diastole and sistole which cannot under its action triturate the food."

No less wise in discerning the quality of snuff, he shouts that there is nothing like rappee, and no rappee like that which he has prepared for his own use. His political gossip is typical of the time and of Goldoni's viewpoint. He sees only the absurdity of people bothering about events that happened far from their quiet Venetian world. Don Marzio, here — like Agapito in *La Finta Ammalata* — talks nonsense about the war in . . . Russia. The listeners are above such curiosity. What can it matter to a Venetian whether somewhere in the far-away world armies are fighting, or wintering? They felt so safe behind the liquid rampart of their laguna, they relied on the wisdom of their Senate; only a busybody would trouble about such distant things.

Don Marzio is the central figure of this play. How Goldoni proceeded to the creation of such central figures he has told in more than one passage of his *Memoirs*. He first says he imagined a character; then comparing his imaginary creation to the reality under his observation, he made sure that every trait was true to life. Other realistic writers have proceeded differently; they have first copied reality, then added a few imaginary touches to finish their picture. The two elements, reality and imagination, are bound to be there, though in their integration into a work of art the exact proportion of each may vary. Goldoni did not always hold to this method. Sometimes he took the suggestion from the outside, depending on observation of reality rather than on his own creative imagination. Thus was created *Momolo Cortesan d'après*, a popular type of Venetian youth; thus was outlined the double character of the *Gemelli* in imitation of Golinetti's different moods. It is, apparently, when he starts to paint a complete figure, to create an original character, that he first demands inspiration from his fantasy, then controls its promptings by comparison with nature. Thus was Don Marzio first cast in the mould of imagination, then carefully finished by touches that were in every detail true to life.

He is the embodiment of idle Venetianism; he acts and talks just as any habitual idler and gossip might have talked in Goldoni's hearing. Goldoni's art is to have set him in the right place and to have surrounded him with the right persons to provide opportunity for the development of his personality. To throw the fitting light on his peculiarities, to exasperate his idle gossip into quarrelsome petulance, his mischief-making disposition into the actual crime of "informing the police." And this is art. This is something more than the clever technique Goldoni possessed even from the beginning. This is real art delicately appropriated to the object in view, progressing by genial gradation like the swell of a musical theme, that gathers new melody, new adornments, and variations and motives, until it bursts out into a genial *crescendo* like one of Mozart's or Zingarelli's that carry on victoriously to the last note of the finale without one break, without one discord to mar the stupendous effect.

Yet, even like some of Mozart's best sonatas, the style is here remarkable for its simplicity. An art which had but recently escaped from the bonds of mannerism, still retained a daintiness that, by some, was mistaken for superficiality.

Don Marzio, after living out his short day on the scene so well suited to his exploits, among the persons so well appropriated to mix with him, meets with the punishment that would best satisfy the instinct of justice in an Italian audience. A tragic punishment for his petty sins would have offended both with the general playful intonation of the play and the genuine unconsciousness of the sinner. Yet to let him go free, after he had sinned against the great law of sociability, after he had committed that unpardonable crime in the eyes of Venetians, of annoying and slandering his comrades, was not to be thought of; so Goldoni deals out the fitting punishment for the offender. As he stands all alone on the scene, one by one all the characters of the play come and mock him and apostrophise him. He has talked at random and a police agent has seized Pandolfo. No one cares for Pandolfo, but everyone jeers and insults the man who has turned spy. From every window or threshold they put out their heads or they step out to cry *racah*[1] on the culprit. Spy, informer, are the terms thrown at his

[1] The word "spy" is one of the most offensive in the Italian dictionary, but it was then, in Venice, a most dangerous word to use.

head like stones. He is lapidated with words, as he had used words as weapons against others.

The other characters of this play, being intended especially to set off Don Marzio, are coloured and lighted on that side suited to the general effect. Taken as a whole they are funny, lively, and satisfactory, but they lack individuality and originality. In fact they are the usual stuff of the ancient comedy, only slightly "reformed" according to Goldoni's plan. It is said that a first representation of *La Bottega del Caffè* contained four masks. Whether Trappola was then covered with Arlecchino's variegated hose and jacket, or Ridolfo wore the garb of Brighella, whether Eugenio, went under the familiar name of Lelio, and Placida was Rosaura, with or without masks, they were neither more nor less than the personages of the *commedia dell'arte* with all their traits perfected by repetition. The son and heir, the Lelio (here he is named Eugenio), shows the usual laxity and recklessness which was due to the Venetian custom of centralising all authority and responsibility in the paterfamilias and of indulging young men in the sowing of very wild oats. Gozzi gives a clue to this character when he says that the education of patrician boys was generally entrusted to the lackeys, "just as the bringing up of pet dogs." Both the classic and popular comedy made a large use of this personage as the centre of the plot, but he seldom took an active part in promoting events. He was generally, as he is here, the ball which the plotters batted up and down, while some good Samaritan tried vainly to protect him. In the end he was rescued by the love of some good woman, either his wife, as in this play, or his fiancée, as in the *Giuocatore*.[1]

Leandro is here the more degraded character of a gambler, such as Venice then very plentifully produced. Pretending to be high born, he decoyed the provincial or new-fledged young man with an art that Goldoni had experienced to his own cost often enough to find pleasure in putting him in the pillory of the scene ever afterward.

[1] Lelio will be found in other plays

CHAPTER IX

THE PLAYS (1750 AND 1751)

Playwrights as debtors and creditors — eighteenth century encouraged imitation — Goldoni borrowed but did not plagiarize — Corneille's *Menteur* and Goldoni's *Bugiardo* contrasted — latter an original work — Corneille echoes a tragic moment, his style is ponderous — Goldoni's play is pure Venetian comedy — comparison between Goldoni's *La Finta Ammalata* and Molière's *L'Amour Médecin* — both writers borrow from the *commedia dell'arte* — cause of Madame Medebach's hysteria — her love for Goldoni — *Il Vero Amico* imitated by Diderot — comparison between Goldoni's play and Molière's *L'Avare* — *Vero Amico* presents problem of conflict between love and duty — importance of Goldoni's dialect comedies — *La Dama Prudente* describes unhappy effects of jealousy — it is a mirror of Venetian customs — one feature of this play is courtship of the two *cavalieri* — gambling universal in Venice — hence frequent in Goldoni's plays.

THAT excellent chapter of Rabelais' about debtors and creditors is never more true than when applied to writers, especially to playwrights. It is take and give, along all the endless chain of time. Few things are quite new under the sun, and certainly there are none in the playhouse. But the manner of borrowing differs. The plagiarism which is plain piracy is far removed from the discernment of the scholar who receives inspiration from some classic model, and between such theft and such inspiration there are many intermediary degrees.

The whole nature of the writer will encourage, restrain, or otherwise modify his manner of borrowing.

The wolf writer who ravenously seizes anything and everything is a world removed from the one whose excessive delicacy proclaims and apologises for the slightest borrowings. Goldoni even persuades himself that he takes more than he does really borrow, forgetting how great is the transformation which the material undergoes within the crucible of his own original mind.

This delicacy in Goldoni is almost exceptional in his time. The eighteenth century encouraged imitation; Venice, during the first half of the eighteenth century, cultivated imitation and smiled at plagiarism. Goldoni was surrounded by authors of different value and character who scrupled not to borrow from foreign or ancient writers. Honest Gaspare Gozzi and dishonest Chiari were contemporaries. Even more than any other branch of literature, the theatre was infected with this practice. Gerolamo Gigli's clever and courageous imitation of Molière's *Tartuffe* won him fame, and Albergati Capacelli's amateurish adaptations were applauded.

Goldoni borrowed especially during this fruitful year of 1750–1751, when, according to his own confession, "he was casting about for subjects." He may be excused if he abbreviated the work of construction and invention of plot and characters when he was so terribly pressed. *Pamela*, *Il Giuocatore* were not the only loans nor the last. His scanty scholarship and limited reading restrained his choice, and sometimes waylaid him into adopting models unworthy of his talent, as, for instance, that Madame Françoise Graffigny, whom no one would remember but for Goldoni's reproductions.

Sometimes, however, his perception and taste guided him to select a pattern worthy of his application, as when he recalled to his preoccupied mind the performance of Corneille's *Menteur*, which he had heard in Florence, in an Italian translation produced toward 1743 or 1744. Goldoni noted the possibilities of the plot, the dramatic value of the principal character. He admired, yet he immediately perceived what changes would improve the work and make it suitable to the Venetian stage, to the capacity of Venetian actors, and to his own talent. The changes introduced were so great that *Bugiardo* is indeed an original work.[1] Vol-

[1] As it was first performed the *Bugiardo* showed one characteristic trait of both the popular and the improvised ancient comedy: the use of several dialects. Florindo's servant, Brighella, spoke his rustic Venetian mixed with Bergamasc terms and the colloquialisms borrowed from the mountain people. Tart and impudent, Arlecchino dropped his spicy Venetian and spoke Tuscan when he wanted to parody his master's pretence and copy his master's philandering. "*Chi sta col lovo impara a urlar*" (who goes with the wolf learns to howl), as he says wittily, after a love scene with Colombina, this parody of the master by the servant, this counterpart of the principal intrigue by the lesser personages, being also a trick of the improvised comedy, that can be traced back to the earlier classics.

Pantalone, Lelio's father, spoke his usual Venetian, and Doctor Balanzoni, faithful to his origin, the harsher dialect of Bologna.

Goldoni himself changed the doctor's part to Tuscan Italian. In the *Autore a chi legge* prefixed to the Paperini edition of the *Bugiardo*, Goldoni complains that Bettinelli, printing this play without his approval, had made no mention of the sources, while he protests "that on this point he is *assai scrupuloso e nemicissimo di qualunque impostura.*" He further explains that he might claim priority for some novelties introduced in the play. He is rightly proud of the invention of the sonnet, and its comical appropriation by Lelio, who twists the timid entreaties of Florindo's muse to fit his own reckless love-making. In Gigli's *Giudice Impazzato* there is an episode

taire has rightly said: *Le caractère du Menteur de Goldoni est bien moins noble que celui de Corneille. Le pièce Française est plus sage, le style en est plus intéressant: la prose italienne n'approche pas des vers de l'auteur de Cinna.*

Though Voltaire perceived the essential difference, he failed to realise that the difference was not casual but was deliberate with Goldoni.[1] From Corneille to Goldoni, from the early seventeenth century in France

slightly resembling this trick. A poet hears from a countryman he meets on the road a sonnet which he learns by heart, and afterward gives as improvised by him. Goldoni may have read this comedy.

In a comparison between Corneille's and Goldoni's play attention is called to the charming and purely Venetian opening of the play. A serenade is sung by a woman's voice; the singer is in a *peota* filled with musicians that play the accompaniment. Rosaura is at her window; Lelio and Arlecchino on the balcony so near by that without detection Lelio can pretend that he has given the serenade. The poetry is better than these things usually are. "*Vorrei spiegar o cara, La mia passion, amara, Ma un certo non so chè . . . Non so se m'intendè, Fa che non so parlar.*" The "*certo non so chè*" has remained proverbial.

Book iii, Pantagruel, 2, 3, 4: The celebrated paradox of Panurge about debts is well known. "*Je me perds en cette contemplation. Entre les hommes paix, amour, dilection, fidélité, repos, banquets, festins, joye, liesse. Or argent, menue monnaie, chaînes, bagues, marchandises, trotteront de main en main. Nul procès, nulles guerre, nul débat, nul n'y sera usurier, nul leschart, nul chichart, nul refusant.*" Goldoni is strict only toward himself; when others commit plagiarism at his expense he overlooks it with just a smile of contempt. This is further illustrated when Diderot's shameless appropriation of Goldoni's *Vero Amico* is considered.

Le Menteur was performed in 1642. In the *Épitre* Corneille says: . . . "*quan je me suis hasardé de passer du héroïque au naïf, je n'ai osé descendre d'aussi haut sans m'assurer d'un guide; et me suis laissé conduire au fameux Lope de Vega, de peur de m'égarer dans les détours de tant d'intrigues que fait notre Menteur.*"

[1] Voltaire's friendly feelings for Goldoni do not imply a clear comprehension of his merit. On the other hand Goldoni did not understand Voltaire.

to the Venice of 1750, the dissimilarity was so essential that if Goldoni had simply translated, or adapted, his work would have been on a par with that of Gaspare Gozzi and his wife Luisa Bergalli.

A parallel between Corneille and Goldoni should not even be attempted, the vital divergence between them being further accentuated by the enormous difference in their surroundings and their inspiration. Corneille, great poet that he was, is the faithful echo of a tragic moment, pregnant with the passions of political and religious strife that breathed heroism, but which was so weary of violence that it smiled on the sentimental mannerisms of Scudéry and Benserade.

Corneille was "*l'auteur de 'Cinna'*"; he could not drop the grand style, the ponderous accent. Even when he lisped madrigals *en style précieux* he remained a tragic poet. Nor did he lose that character when he adapted a Spanish play.[1]

His *Menteur* is imitated from *La Verdad Sospechosa*, a play belonging to Alarcon. "*J'ai entièrement dépaysé les sujets pour les habiller á la Française*," says he in the preface. They needed no deeper transformation than the French "dressing." The French spirit and literature were then entuned to receive almost any

[1] As an example of *style précieux* Dorante's address to Clarice, *Menteur*, Act i, sc. 2.

"*Aussi ne croyez pas que jamais je prétende*
Obtenir par mérite une faveur si grabne;
J'en sais mieux le haut prix; et mon cœur amoureux,
Moins il s'en connoît digne, et plus s'en tient heureux" . . .

amount of chivalrous spagnolism. The author of *le Cid* knew how rapturously the French admired and shared the chivalrous valiance of a hero. Hence he need only dress in French clothes and high-sounding French alexandrines the dramatic explosions of a Geronte discovering that his son has sinned against the law of honour.[1]

Altogether this excessive eloquence and emphasis in Geronte is incompatible with the sin attributed to him, in the character of Dorante, the Liar. Literature may attempt to imitate nature and make use of contradictions to give significance to a character, but there are contrasts which shock common sense and literary taste, because incompatible with truth. A high-born warrior who has already achieved prowess on the field of battle, who has won the respect of his peers in a society that set *el punto do onor* above every other virtue, could not utter the petty falsehoods attributed to him in Corneille's play. This habitual practice of falsehood, this double series of feelings, is artistically incoherent in the character of a brave man.

Goldoni perceived the incongruity. No reminiscence of tragedy encumbered his mind, nor did the spirit of his audience thirst for heroic sentiments and grandiloquent phrases. Both his talent and his audience demanded the demi tint and attenuated feelings of

[1] Act v, sc. 3: Geronte — "*Je jure les rayons du jour qui nous éclaire.*
Que tu ne mourras point que de la main d'un père,
Et que ton sang indigne à mes pied répandu
Rendra prompte justice à mon honneur perdu."

pure comedy, seasoned with light ridicule and suggested satire. Then he shared the traditional reverence of Venetians for the patrician caste and would not have satirised that essential quality of the noble born honour. Hence Geronte and Dorante became Venetian, and the trickery and indelicacy which were shocking in the young hidalgo became funny and lifelike in the son of a Pancrazio, the merchant — a substitute of Pantalone — whose scoldings could naturally assume the character of homely common sense and blundering tenderness suitable to the faults committed by his offspring. The majestic alexandrine verse is replaced by dialect prose of Goldoni, more appropriate to familiar intercourse, more likely to amuse the audience, and even more certain to impress the simple lesson intended.[1]

Compare the beautiful Cornelian scene, act v, scene 3:

Géronte — *Etes-vous gentilhomme?* . . .

Dorante — *Etant sorti de vous la chose est peu douteuse.* . . .

and compare it to the same explanation between Lelio and Pancrazio. The surprise and shame of the father forced to realise that his son has committed a series of dishonourable acts is tragically expressed by the

[1] *Bugiardo*, Act iii, sc. 2: Pantalone — "Where the devil do you find the matter of so many inventions? If you have no shame, no loyalty, if you do not care for your reputation, you will always be a suspected man, a bad merchant unworthy of my family, unworthy to bear the honourable name of Bisognosi."

French poet; its very power jars with the intentions of a comedy; it calls for a punishment that Corneille did not think fit to bring about. Because, as he says in the Preface of *La Suite du Menteur*, it is sufficient to paint vice in its true colours without enforcing the moral lesson with a final chastisement.

Goldoni, more consistently with his "bourgeois" education and homely sense of duty, closed his comedy with the most adequate punishment for the liar. He has slandered the girl who trusted him, he has branded her with the name of *donna di mercato*, and in the end he must marry her. Real life is made of such logical consequences of one's sinful acts. Fortunately for Lelio his slander was unjustified; perhaps the girl he deserted and then married proved a good wife.

Corneille's principal scene when compared with Goldoni's reveals the different methods of the writers. When asked by his father to explain his doings, Dorante begins a witty, fluent, fanciful story of adventures. He glibly elaborates from one extraordinary hoax to another. In the hands of two good players the growing astonishment of the fathers and the unhesitating blarney of the son must have produced a most amusing effect. A stage effect which answered to no human possibility.

Goldoni, trained to the realism of the *commedia dell'arte* and educated to the sincerity of direct observation, proceeded differently. Lelio begins his story with half truths; then, when his father interrupts him with searching questions, he seeks for some likely falsehood. Entangled in his own lies, and worried by his father's incredulity, he forgets what he has just been inventing, and adds new lies to justify the first. Then also there is some sort of excuse for the young man's double-dealing in the father's assertion of excessive parental authority. "In my time," says Pancrazio, "sons used to obey their parents," meaning that they married according to their father's choice. To which Lelio, with some reason, answers, "It is the son who has to live with the chosen wife and not the father." [1]

Pancrazio is stunned rather than persuaded by the stories he has been told, but he ends the scene by expressing the desire of having grandchildren to rejoice his old age, and to this wish Lelio replies, "If my father only wishes grandchildren he'll get as many as he likes!" Thus Goldoni remembers that the audience must be amused.

As a foil to his bold-faced Lelio, Goldoni introduced Ottavio, the timid lover. When Ottavio serenades Donna Rosaura, Lelio obtains the credit, and when Ottavio composes a sonnet Lelio persuades the lady of

[1] Act ii, sc. 3: Pancrazio — "Know then, my son, that this morning I have arranged your marriage. Lelio — Why! Without telling me? Panc. — It is an excellent opportunity, a well-bred girl, belonging to a good family of Bologna. She has a comfortable *dot*, and also good looks and some spirit. What else can you wish? I have her father's promise, and thus everything is settled. Lelio — I beg your pardon, sir, it's all right for fathers to provide for their sons; but when all is said, it's the son who has to live with his wife that must be pleased with her. Pancrazio. — I did not expect such disobedience from you. You used to show more respect for my wishes. Remember that I am your father. If it is because you have been brought up abroad that you have not learned how to obey me, I'm in time to teach you. . . ."

his own authorship and ingeniously explains its meaning, comical tricks which served to preserve the general playful intonation of the play.

Corneille, aware of the excessive solemnity of his comedy, introduced a personage which is not without importance in the history of the comedy and not without importance in the history of Goldoni's reform. Cliton, Dorante's valet, acts as the classic chorus and comments on the actions of the liar. Cliton is the descendant of those intriguing and amusing valets of all classical plays, a traditional character, gross and vulgar, the slave of Roman comedy. Corneille improved the antique model by endowing him with a rudimental conscience, and with more wit and more shrewdness than his predecessors possessed. It is almost possible to trace through him the evolution of the personage culminating in that unique *Figaro* of Beaumarchais' masterpiece.[1]

Goldoni on parallel lines transformed both the

[1] Follow the narrative of adventures continually broken by Pancrazio.
Menteur, Act i, sc. 5: Cliton (*à Dorante à l'oreille*) — *Vous ne savez, monsieur, ce que vous dites.*

Dorante — *Tais-toi; si jamais plus tu me viens avertir . . .*

Cliton — *J'enrage de me taire et d'entendre mentir.*

Act iii, sc. 6: Cliton — *A chaque bout de champ vous mentez comme un diable.*

Dor. — *Je disois vérité.* Clit. — *Quand un menteur la dit,*
En passant par sa bouche, elle perde son credit.

The last words of the play are spoken by Cliton; like a final moral.

Comme en son propre fourbe un menteur s'embarrasse!
Peu sauroient comme lui s'en tirer avec grace.
Vous autres qui doutiez s'il n'en pouroit sortir,
Par un si rare example apprenez à mentir.

personages of Arlecchino and Brighella. He developed the latent honesty of both the Zannis, teaching Arlecchino to remain funny without triviality, making Brighella clumsy without imbecility, in one word reconducting them not only to the decency of their first appearance in the *commedia dell'arte*, but also toward an entirely new impersonation of that humbler class which he loved and understood so well.[1] This transformation of Brighella and Arlecchino deserves further study. Here it is enough to indicate what he may have learned from the great Corneille he reverently called *mon maître*.

Goldoni, always ready to recognise his indebtedness to those he honours with the name of his masters, wrote to Count Annibale Gambara in his dedication of *La Finta Ammalata*, "Molière, the famous French playwright, in his little comedy, *L'Amour Médecin* has treated this subject, on which mine is wrought."

The parallel might be pushed further. Both *L'Amour Médecin* and *La Finta Ammalata* were written in a tremendous hurry. Molière says that his was done in five days.[2] Goldoni probably employed less time. Both authors were suspected of having their

[1] In Goldoni's *Bugiardo* the rôle of Pasqualino, the servant and confidant, has no importance. It is in other plays that the personage (usually under the name of Arlecchino) is developed and transformed.

[2] Molière. *Au Lecteur: "Ce n'est ici qu'un simple crayon, un petit impromptu, dont le Roi a voulu faire un divertissement. Il est le plus précepité de tous ceux que Sa Majesté m'ait commandés; et lorsque je vous dirai qu'il a été proposé, fait, appris et représenté, en cinq jours, je ne dirrai que ce qui est vrai."* (Cf. "*Les Grands Ecrivains de la France.*" Nouvelles editions, publiées sous la direction de M. A. D. Régnier. *Molière*, V. p. 293.)

stock of plays ready and pretending to improvise them. Grimarest says so, *à propos* of this comédie ballet. "*Il en avoit, un magasin d'ébauchés par la quantité de petites farces qu'il avoit hasardées dans les provinces,*" an assertion which the best Molièrists consider absolutely unjustified.[1]

Goldoni and Molière both borrow from the ancient font of the *commedia dell'arte*, and they both insert speeches that have graver origins than the comedy.

Molière's comedy is partly imitated from Tirso de Molina's *Venganza de Tamar* and partly from the *Don Juan* of the same author, with suggestions from the Italian improvised comedy. In ancient comedy sickness and disease were objects of fun. Both the medical profession and their pseudo science were part also of the laughingstock. The topic was old in Molière's day, but he added the bitterness of his own experience and that mixture of cruelty and wrath which are part of his genius.[2] Because Molière was personal in this attack, he only altered slightly a real

[1] A. D. Régnier (*op. cit.*, p. 263): "*Au lieu d'une provision d'impromptus dès long temps faite, Molière avait dans l'esprit un trésors d'observations profondes ou piquantes, toujours à la disposition d'une prompte application comique,*" which words could be exactly applied to Goldoni. A further comparison between Molière and Goldoni will be made.

[2] Maurice Raynaud: *Les Médecins du temps de Molière*, Paris, 1862, page 409, confirms the opinion expressed by Gui Patin with this specious reason, worth recording as showing the difference in public opinion between Goldoni's and Molière's times: "*Un médecin* (G. Patin was a doctor) *comme un magistrat, serait fait montrer au doigt; et se fut perdu dans l'opinion, s'il eût paru au théâtre.*"

name, or translated it into Greek, or reproduced even a physical defect of each one of those he pilloried.[1] His contemporaries understood every allusion; serious writers like Guy Patin, libellists like the author of *Elomire Hypocondre* (Boulanger de Chalussay?) or Grimarest took good care to indicate the originals in their indiscretions. Thus, mixed with dance and songs and pantomimes, a great battle was waged.

Goldoni has no such satirical intentions. He ridicules three doctors, but he presents one so perfectly honest and discreet as to reëstablish the balance in favour of the profession. There is no personal allusion made or meant, no name is mentioned.

This bitterness of Molière's satire extends to every part of the play. In the first scene all the friends and relations of the sick girl suggest remedies that can only be profitable to the giver of advice. "*Vous êtes orfèvre, M. Josse*" is proverbial. Molière's father was an upholsterer, and he shows a *tapisser*, M. Guillaume, suggesting that the best remedy for the suffering young lady would be "*une belle tenture de tapisserie de verdure, ou à personnages, que je ferais mettre à sa chambre, pour lui réjouir l'esprit et la vue.*"[2]

[1] The doctors in the play bear the names of Desfonandrès which stands for des Fougerais and De Bahis — from the Greek, for a stammerer which was understood to caricature Esprit, — médecin du Roi, who stammered. One of the brothers Béjart of Molière's troupe being lame, he was entrusted with the rôle of one of the doctors so as to imitate the lameness of one of the victims aimed at.

[2] *Am. Méd.*, act i, sc. 1: Sganarelle — "*Tous ces conseils sont admirables assurément, mais he les tiens un peu intéressés, et trouve que vous me conseillez fort bien pour vous. Vous êtes orfèvre, M. Josse, et votre conseil sent son homme*

Goldoni on the contrary pays posthumous homage to his father when he traces the noble character of Doctor Onesti.[1]

To the misery of his childhood can be referred Molière's insensibility to parental emotions. Father and son stand in his plays either as rivals or as antagonists; worse still the mothers have no tenderness for their children.[2] With Goldoni this chord is always quivering. Here are sweet memories easily stirred, here are quick sympathies readily awakened, and an atmosphere of domestic affections hovers over most of his plays.

Even in this unpresuming *Finta Ammalata* Pantalone overflows with tenderness for the wayward invalid, he is credulous and fussy, but constant in his purpose of satisfying his daughter's whims, securing for her medical attendance, and lavishing on her all the fondling and spoiling he can think of. Thus to bring about the happy ending there is no need for the trickery used by the Molièrian lovers; consent is not obtained by persuading him that the marriage per-

qui a envie de se défaire de sa marchandise. Vous vendez des tapisseries, M. Guillaume, et vous avez la mine d'avoir quelque tenture qui vous incommode."

[1] *Mem.*, i, 349: "I am son of a doctor, for an instant I have been a doctor myself, and I accordingly blame the folly of people who either praise or criticise medicine wholesale."

[2] Act i, sc. 3: Sganarelle — "*Va, fille ingrate, je ne te veux plus parler . . . C'est une coquine qui me veut faire mourir . . . Je l'abandonne . . . je la déteste . . .*" This cruelty is covered by the fun of Lisette's repetition of her young lady's wish: "*Un mari . . . Un mari.*" But still the words are cruel, and Sganarelle does not relent. In the end Sganarelle is tricked into consenting to his daughter's marriage.

formed under his eyes, and with his approval and signature, is mere foolery, but it will be granted after just a moment of hesitation, and mainly with the object of ensuring the happiness of his beloved child.[1]

Sganarelle grumbles (act i, sc. 5): "*Ast-on jamais vu rien de plus tyrannique que cette coutume où l'on veut assujeuttir les pères? rien de plus impertinent et de plus ridicule que d'amasser du bien avec de grand travaux et élever une fille avec beaucoup de soin et de tendresse, pour se dépouiller de l'un et de l'autre entre les mains d'un homme qui ne nous touche de rien? Non, non: je me moque de cet usage, et je veux garder mon bien et ma fille pour moi.*"

But Pantalone strives and entreats his dear invalid to eat (act i, sc. 13): "I have spent much money for her, but I'm ready to spend every farthing I have in this world to see her cured." When told that the girl wants a husband, he is at first surprised. "Marry her whilst she is ailing? Why, if she is taken away from her father she will die at once. Is it not so, darling? Don't you wish to stay with your father? A husband would not be ready to assist her when she faints. My poor dear; she is better with her father."

No comparison is possible between the rôles of the doctors. Molière aimed mortal blows at the whole caste, and especially at certain individuals. Whatever

[1] Pantalone gives his consent with a homely simplicity, act iii, sc. 17: "Sig. Dottore Onesti, since I see that my daughter loves you, and that she was in bad health for your sake, and that nothing but marrying you will cure her, here I am asking you to accept her for your wife."

its cause the bitterness and violence in the attack sprang from his soul with the force of genuine hatred. Moreover Molière used long, masterful passages borrowed from Montaigne,[1] so uncompromising and so stringent that the medical profession still lies under the tremendous accusation of charlatanism and scientific cruelty.

In Goldoni there is no bitterness, no hatred, hence no deadly wounds and no lasting scars. Nothing can be quoted resembling the cruel "*Un homme mort n'est qu'un homme mort, et ne fait point de conséquence; mais une formalité négligée porte un notable préjudice à tout le corps de médecins.*" Nothing half so deep and philosophical as Molière's, or rather Montaigne's, comment: "*Le plus grand foible des hommes c'est l'amour qu'ils ont pour la vie; et nous en profitons, nous autres, par notre pompeux galimatias, et savons prendre notre avantage de cette vénération que la peur de mourir leur donne pour notre métier.*" (Act iii, sc. 1.)

Goldoni goes no further than the mild fun current among men of the same profession, in the talk of the three doctors that meet in consultation round Rosaura's chair.

(Act ii, sc. 11.) Doctor Onesti explains he believes this malady of the young lady to be imaginary. He analyses the symptoms and wisely traces them back to the reaction of the mind on the different functions

[1] See Montaigne, book ii, chapter 37, of the *Essais*, and compare it to *L'Am. Médecin*, act iii, sc. 1, where Filerin exclaims: "*Quel tort ces sortes de querelles*," etc. "*Ils décrient à tous les coups le métier*," etc.

of the body. Doctor Malfatti, having no opinion of his own, consents to everything that the others say. Doctor Tarquinio, a surgeon, believes in nothing but bleeding. Doctor Buonatesti is the genuine pedant.

Malf. — For me I adopt the opinion expressed by the learned Doctor Onesti.

Buon. — If you do, I do not accept it.

Tarq. — Mark me, Signor Dottore, this oppression is certainly caused by superabundance and thickness of the blood that is coagulating.

Buon. — Please let me feel your pulse. Ah! (*He shakes his head ominously.*) Doctor Malfatti, please feel this pulse.

Malf. (*Feels and shakes his head.*)

Buon. — Do you say that this pulse is good? (*Doctors hold each one of Rosaura's wrists.*)

Malf. — I do not think it is.

Buon. — The pulse is bad.

Malf. — Very bad.

One. — Why, it cannot have changed in a few minutes? Please, Signora Rosaura, let me feel it. (*He feels it.*) It is all right; it could not be better. Doctor Malfatti, feel this pulse better; it is all right.

Malf. — Certainly it is.

One. — Could it be more regular?

Malf. — It is very regular.

One. — Feel it, Doctor Buonatesti.

Buon. — So I have, gentlemen, and it is not good. Now allow me, gentlemen, with methodical observation to expound the agnosis and the prognosis of this disease. Hypocrates says: *si sufficerit medicus ad cognoscendum, sufficit etiam at curandum.*

Pant. — Bravo!

Buon. — Madam, what is your name?

Rosa. — What has my name to do with my illness?

Buon. — *Interim medicis nominum inquisitio omnino necessaria.*

One. — I beg pardon, doctor. *Intelligitur de nominibus rerum, non personarum.*

Buon. — We are here to decide, not to discuss.

One. — And talk nonsense.

It would be stretching Goldoni's intentions to find here an allusion to the questions of "nominalism"; though in the ensuing discussion there certainly is a display of all the scanty medical knowledge and scientific terms that Goldoni had gathered from his apprenticeship to his father, from comradeship with students of medicine, and mostly from his constant preoccupation for his health. His was a case most like Onesti's diagnosis of Rosaura's ailments.

In a later play, *Il Medico Olandese*, he gives a more extensive, if not a complete, picture of that which he realised to be rather an affection of the mind than of the body, but which still caused him great depression and anxiety. He studied his case and seems to have come to a clear understanding of it. There is very little morbid apprehension in him; but just enough personal experience to make him considerate in his representation of sickness.

But when he wrote this *Finta Ammalata* he had not yet personal experience of, or sympathy with, illness. His own constitution did not, as yet, feel the reaction of the strain he was going through; and moreover he was irritated against overindulgence, or simulation of bodily pain, by the behaviour of Signora Medebach.

Was there nothing but infatuation on Madame Medebach's part? Nothing but artistic rivalry when she fell into hysterics, fainted, and grew ill enough to frighten her relations? "It was enough," says Goldoni, "to talk of giving a fine rôle to another actress and the sick woman was instantly cured."[1] Does his memory serve him well after so many years, and when age has chilled every remembrance of youthful folly?

Goldoni was essentially an honest man; he followed the code of morals of his time. That code did not forbid an intrigue with the wife of his employer, nor flirtations with every other woman that showed inclination for him. But this same code forbade telling outright how matters stood, hence Goldoni's account of the situation may be *ad usum delphini* and reveal only part of the truth. Madame Medebach was thus protected; her tears, her hysterics are recorded, not the

[1] *Mem.* i, 348: "Madame Medebach was an excellent actress, devoted to her profession, but she was '*une femme à vapeurs*' who was often really ailing. More often she persuaded herself that she was, and sometimes she had only pretended suffering. In such cases it was enough to talk of giving a new rôle to a subaltern actress, and the sick woman was immediately cured. I took the liberty of playing Madame Medebach herself. She was partly aware of it, but finding her part charming she willingly accepted it, and played it to perfection."

secret of her heart which may have been guessed by her husband, who, in such case, may have taken a sort of vengeance when he cheated Goldoni out of his copyrights.

La Finta Ammalata is not the only one of Goldoni's plays that owes something to Molière, although his indebtedness to his acknowledged master is far less than his contemporaries and he himself have said. Indeed the parallel between the two authors is forced upon Goldoni's modern critics by their predecessors, rather than confirmed by a study of his works. Ferdinando Martini, in one of his bright improvisations, has happily said that this "comparison must be made through negatives."[1] The often repeated misnomer, "Goldoni, le Molière Italien,"[2] has hypnotised Goldoni himself;

[1] This parallel by negatives could be pushed very far. Goldoni with a healthy constitution, a petted childhood, a happy and careless youth, and finally settling in life with a tender mother and a devoted wife; Molière growing up in a troubled household, leading for years a loose life, embittered by unruly passions, ending in a miserable marriage that brought shame and grief to a body racked by disease. Molière a scholar, almost a philosopher, was totally different from easy-going, light-hearted Goldoni. Utterly different, too, were their working conditions, their atmosphere, and the degree of intellectual and moral evolution of the society they painted. There was, however, superficial resemblance: they both borrowed much from the *commedia dell'arte.*

What Goldoni owes to it and to its representative players is shown all through the present study; Molière owes not less to the ancient art and its disciples. Moland, *Molière et la comédie italienne,* 1867; Ch. Comte Brunetière, *Etudes critiques,* tome 1 and 4; also his *Epoques du Théâtre Français,* a conference, and, of course, the splendid edition of Ch. L. Livet enriched with excellent notes (*op. cit*) and the chapters in Petit de Juleville's *Histoire de la Littérature* (*op. cit.*).

[2] The epithet "Molière d'Italie" is so often applied to Goldoni, and by so many contemporary and later writers, that it is difficult to discover who

and of course a crowd of critics have repeated it. Under shelter of a paradox we may say that Goldoni is quite different from Molière — in merit, in depth of thought and feeling, no less than in the quality of their intellectual faculty, in the artistic reaction on their spirits and feelings of the external world, hence, in the interpretation of truth as they saw it, of their own sentiments, as they were swayed by them.

Certainly when, in 1750–1751, Goldoni hurried through his sixteen new comedies with no time to analyse foreign or ancient models, with only a most imperfect knowledge of French and an entire ignorance of French customs, he can have borrowed no more than the outline of a character, the episodes of an intrigue.[1] Within these limits of truth stands Diderot's assertion that he copied from Molière's *Avare* the personage of Ottavio in the *Vero Amico*, a play which Diderot certainly took great pains to read and to imitate.[2]

first said it. Though generally attributed to Voltaire, it is not to be found in the gushing compliments paid to "caro Goldoni." Voltaire is guilty of having applied the names of Terence and Plautus to Goldoni and Albergati; but not of this literary blunder.

[1] *Mem.* ii, 164. "*La première fois que j'allai à la Comédie Française, on y donnoit le Misantrope . . mon oreille ne s'étoit pas encore familiarisée avec le langage Français; je perdois beaucoup dans les sociétés et encors plus au Théâtre.*" Thus Goldoni's acquaintance with Molière's works dates from the first year of his Parisian life, when he was past fifty, and had done most of his work. When he mentions Molière in the *Memoirs*, or in the prefaces, there is nothing personal or convincing in the praise given him. For the play *Molière* see chapter X.

[2] *Mem.* ii, 166: "M. Diderot had given a few years ago a comedy entitled *Le Fils Naturel;* M. Fréron reviewed it in his periodical, pointing out that the French play showed certain resemblance to M. Goldoni's

There are essential differences between the character of Harpagon and Ottavio, as there are essential differences between the two plays. Molière's plot is loose and almost inconsistent. Harpagon's son and daughter both make love behind their father's back. He would like to marry Élise to an old man, who does not care for a *dot;* and he is himself in love with the portionless girl whom his son, Cleante, wants to marry. In the end things get straightened and Valère, Élise's lover, and Marianne, the contested bride, are found to be the

Vero Amico; he even transcribed the French scenes side by side with the Italian ones. The one and the others seemed to flow from the same source. . . ." Followed some insinuations about *le Père de Famille.* "I justified M. Diderot, and I endeavoured to persuade those who believed his *Père de Famille* copied from mine." (As a matter of fact *le Père de Famille* is a bad imitation of *Pamela.*) "But I said nothing about *Le Fils Naturel.* The author was angry with me and with M. Fréron. His wrath must find its vent, it must fall either on me or on M. Fréron; he gave me the preference." (Naturally since Fréron was a journalist, and held a very pungent pen.)

Diderot in his *Discours sur la Poésie Dramatique: lettre à Grimm* (*op. cit.*): "*Charles Goldoni a écrit en italien une comédie ou plutôt une farse en trois actes qu'il a intitulée L'Ami Véritable. C'est un tissu de caractères de L'Ami vrai et de L'Avare de Molière. La cassette et le vol y sont; et la moitié des scènes s'y passent dans la maison d'un père avare. Je laissai là toute cette portion de l'intrigue, car je n'ai dans le Fils Naturel, ni avare, ni vol, ni père, ni cassette. Je crus que l'on pouvoit faire quelque chose de supportable de l'autre portion et je m'en emparai comme d'un bien qui m'eût appartenu.*"

And further he asserts with more violence than truth: "*Dois-je au poète italien une seule idée qu'on puisse citer? Pas une. Celui qui dit que le genre dans lequel j'ai écrit le Fils Naturel est le même que le genre dans lequel Goldoni a écrit l'Amie Vrai dit un mensonge. Mensonge encore que la ressemblance des caractères. Mensonge que la ressemblance dans la conduite de la pièce. Mensonge que la transposition de détails et de mots importants.*"

Professore Toldo in *Giornale Storico della Letteratura Italiana* (*op. cit.*), in the year 1895, has reproduced and explained Fréron's essay and the

lost children of this same Anselme who wished to take Élise for his second wife.

transcription of scenes in their original text. Act i, sc. 1, in both show the lovesick Florindo or Dorval declaring in almost the same terms "*que l'amitié doit prévaloir . . . il faut sacrifier toutes les passions a l'amitié.*"

Goldoni, act i, sc. 3, Florindo	Diderot, act i, sc. 3, Dorval
Ma andrò via senza veder Rosaura? Senza darle un addio? Si queste due passioni bisogna trattarle diversamente. L'amicizia va coltivata con tutta la possibile delicatezza. L'amore va superato colla forza e colla violenza.	*Et Rosalie? Je ne la verai point? Non l'amour et l'amitié n'imposent point les mêmes devoirs; surtout un amour insensé qu'on ignore et qu'il faut étouffer.*
Act i, sc. 3, Beatrice —Florindo	Sc. 4, Dorval — Constance
Beat. — *Ben levato il Signor.* Flor. — *Non e piu tempo di dissimulare. Voi conoscete il mio cuore, voi sapete la mai passione.*	Const. — *Ce moment est donc le seul qui me reste, il faut parler . . .*

Lelio and his French counterpart Clairville each asks his friend to speak to Rosaura or Rosalie, their respective wayward fiancées. Both the unwilling messengers protest in almost the same words.

Diderot's second act begins just as Goldoni's by Rosaura (or Rosalie) telling her sorrow to Colombina (or Justine). In both cases the servant speaks practical common sense; in both the same interruption; enter Dorval (Florindo), the culminating point, the asking of advice from one friend to the other is evidently copied.

Goldoni, act i, sc. 19	Diderot, act iii, sc. 2
Lelio. — *Che cosa mi consigliereste fare? Sposarla? o abbandonarla?* Florindo — *Non so che dire; su du piedie.*	*Clairville — Voyez et décidez. Songez Dorval que le sort de Clairville est entre vos mains . . .*

In the same awkward position the two loyal, but lovesick, champions of friendship sigh their despair in almost the same words.

And again Florindo, wishing to rid himself of Beatrice, just as Dorval will want to get rid of Constance, hit on just the same stratagem.

One assertion of Diderot remains true, however; *le genre* is not quite the same. His pseudo-philosophical, pedantic sermons in this play belong to the only *genre* condemned by Boileau's well-known line, *Tous les genres sont bons; hors le genre ennuyeux.* Goldoni's falls on the right side; there is too much of suffering for a comedy; suggestions of tragedy that go too deep.

Ch. L. Livet points out the weakness of this plot by demonstrating that the trouble in Harpagon's household is not caused by his avarice. "A miser," says the learned Molièriste, "does not keep three servants, two horses, and a well-furnished apartment; a miser does not think of marrying a girl who has neither ready cash nor expectations." A man is not a fool because he laments the loss of three hundred thousand francs. True that he lends money at a rather high interest, but that may be a sin, branching out of avarice, as well as out of other sins. Goldoni's genial nature could never interpret so cruelly human frailties and deduce with such pitiless logic their ultimate consequences.

Even if he never opened Molière's book he may have known the *Avaro* as a common character in the Italian comedy. The classic *Aulularia*, or improvised reproduction of the type, became at each adaptation one shade more gross and more vulgar, without losing the first outline of its detestable blend of lewdness, imbecility, and avarice and hateful old age. Every collection of *scenari* contains some reproduction of this character.[1]

[1] There is an interesting comparison between Goldoni's Ottavio and Molière's Harpagon. The latter owes more to the *commedia italiana* than the former. Harpagon is in love, like the classical old miser of Giambattista Gelli's *Lo Errore*, who, in rivalry with his own son, gains admittance into the house of the coveted woman. He had put on woman's clothes, and stealthily, though not unperceived by a jeering, mischievous boy, Fellino, stolen in and spent some time in what he supposed to be illegitimate amours, only to discover, by daylight, that his own shrewish wife had been the object of his caresses.

Worse still is *Il Vecchio Amoroso* of Donato Gianotti, who wants to marry

Unlike Molière or Gelli, Goldoni's miser is not the centre of the plot. Though C. Rabany pretends that such a character cannot be *épisodique*, the result of this shifting of places is commendable.

Il Vero Amico is a *comédie d'intrigue*, as its author insisted on qualifying these tightly constructed plots; yet it is also a *comédie à caractère* because, besides Ottavio, there are several psychologic studies, developed even as far as any other in Goldoni's gallery. There is also a moral thesis which is interesting, even though not convincing. Goldoni's disciple, Gianino Antona Traversi, says of Goldoni that "he wrote great comedies without presuming to introduce in them great ideas; whilst modern playwrights write little comedies and presume to put in great ideas."

Yet in this *Vero Amico* Goldoni proposed the great

the fair slave whom his own son has made a mother. Byron notes that even Congreve was scandalised by Susannah Centlivre's imitation of this hateful character. In her play the *Busybody* an aged guardian, Sir Francis Grip (aged 65), insists on marrying his ward Miranda who prefers Sir George Airy to him, and mocks him freely. Sir Francis — "Humph! Prithee leave out years; change ye. I'm not so old as thou shalt find. . . . I'm young, here's a caper for you." (*He jumps.*)

Examples might be multiplied and some very shocking, too. Goldoni's miser comes more directly from Lorenzino de Medici's *Aridosio* (the word *aridosio* meaning pumice stone to indicate that the man is as dry as a pumice stone) and also from Gelli's *Ghirigoro de Macci* in *La Sporta*. The Tuscan word *sporta* means a small basket, such as housewives carry on their arm when they go to market. (A second, very improper, meaning may have called a smile to Florentine lips.) Ghirigoro is a full-sized figure in the play. He has a daughter and he would marry her to anyone who will take her without any *dot*. Like Ottavio he would make sure that his future son-in-law will not claim any portion, act iii, sc. 1. "Ghirogoro — *E vedi non m'andar poi ingarbugliando con consigli di notai, che l'abbia aver la legittima, o la tribiliana. Il non t'ho a dar nulla.*"

problem he had already attempted to solve, must love triumph over duty? In the *Avvocato Veneziano* the duty in contrast with love was professional correctness, and in the end a compromise was managed so as even to reward the consequences of virtuous consistency. In this *Vero Amico* Goldoni stoops to no such half measures; love must be crushed at every cost of suffering, and friendship must triumph in hearts broken by the strife.

The plot is almost too dramatic for comedy, a fault which Goldoni did not always resist. Lelio and Florindo are the two friends. Both love Rosaura; but Lelio is the accepted fiancé and Florindo, the late comer, is the hopeless confidant who is expected to act as the peacemaker in a quarrel between the lovers. Florindo knows his passion is reciprocated, though maidenly reticence and social propriety prevent Rosaura from speaking out. Florindo, a guest in Lelio's house, is discovered in a desperate mood, ordering a coach for his immediate departure and giving evasive answers to the *avances* made toward him by Beatrice, a faded beauty, the aunt of Lelio. Lelio stops Florindo and asks him to visit Rosaura and clear some doubts which are tormenting him as to her affection for him, a situation that Diderot accepted and reproduced in *Telle quelle.*

Rosaura, the only daughter of Ottavio, is presented in the dreary home her father fills with his grumblings; she is bullied by him, told that she will get no money from him at his death, and that anything she may have heard about a box containing gold is a cursed lie.

Rosaura knows this is all false, but she does not care. She would rather be poor and portionless as her father says, since, in that case, Lelio would set her free, and freedom means marriage with Florindo.

The scene between Florindo acting as Lelio's messenger and Rosaura trying to read his thoughts is delicately conducted in the tone of a madrigal; some mannerism, well seasoned with delicate sentiment, Lelio's entrance, and Rosaura's prompt exit change the atmosphere. Florindo speaks out with manly sincerity, in so far as he gives sound advice to his friend about managing his own love affairs, with Venetian reticence as to the application of this advice.

Rosaura writes Florindo a love letter that he can hardly see to read for his tears. He recovers from his emotion and begins an answering letter to Rosaura. In guarded terms he tells of his love and of the barrier that stands between them. He is interrupted by a call from Lelio's servant, crying out that his master is in the street, assaulted by two blackguards and in great danger. Florindo runs out, leaving his letter on the table, where Beatrice, Lelio's old maid aunt, finds it. Supposing it is addressed to her and imports a regular proposal she quickly shows it to Lelio. The equivoque is cleverly worked out. Florindo admits that he is in love with the person to whom he wrote, and Lelio is delighted that his doubts are dispelled.

Romance has full swing in the complications that follow, and Florindo's loyalty is put to the severest test. Rosaura having persuaded her father to pretend that he has no *dot* to give her, Lelio frees her. His wife must bring a conspicuous *dot* into the family. Florindo is accepted by Ottavio, who will not only keep his own money but receive a dowry from him.[1]

[1] *Il Vero Amico*, act iii, sc. 15: Florindo and Ottavio. Ott. (*takes out of his pocket a bit of paper previously picked from the ground*) — "This paper will do; see how everything comes of use in good time. Flor. — In that paper there is but little space for writing. Ott. — I'll write small. There's place enough for everything. Let us draw the table nearer. There's a draught coming through the chinks of that window, which makes the candle burn down. (*He draws the table.*) Let us sit down. (*He writes.*) Signor Florindo degli Ardenti promises to wed Signora Rosaura Aretusi without *dot*, without any *dot*, without any right to a *dot*, renouncing every and any proceedings or reasons for claiming a *dot*, protesting that he does not want any *dot*, and that he wishes for none. Flor. (*aside*) — With all these *dots* he has filled the paper. Ott. — Item! he promises to wed her without any gowns, or linen clothes, without anything at all; taking her and accepting her just as she was born; promising also to settle on her a *controdote*. . . . Hey, how much do you mean to settle upon her? Flor. — I never meant to settle a *controdote*. Ott. — Unless you settle a *controdote*, there's nothing done. Flor. — Well, then, how much do you require? Ott. — Let it be six thousand scudi. Flor. — Signor Ottavio, it is too much. Ott. — If I judge by that I see, you are a miser. Flor. — Yes, sir, so I am. Ott. — I will not marry my daughter to a miser. Flor. — Right you are; she has such a generous father. Ott. — If I were rich, I would be generous; but I am so poor. Let us go on. How much do you mean to settle? Flor. — Well, let it be six thousand scudi. Ott. — Promising to give her six thousand scudi, to be paid, in cash, on signing the marriage deed, to Signor Ottavio, her father. . . . Flor. — But why should I pay them to you? Ott. — The father is the legal manager of his daughter's goods. Flor. — The husband is the legitimate manager of his wife's goods. The *controdote* is never paid down but in case of separation or death. Ott. — I must be supported on my daughter's *controdote*. Flor. — Why should you be? Ott. — Because I'm poor. Flor. — I do not want to give the six thousand scudi into your hands. Ott. — Well, then, keep me. Flor. — You are welcome to come and stay with me in Venice. . . ."

Goldoni's knowledge of the law adds to the humour of this scene, that compares with Molière's more famous "Sans dot" in the scene between Harpagon and Valère. (Act i, sc. 5.)

Then suddenly the tables are turned; Ottavio's box, filled with gold and silver coins, has been discovered, and loyal Florindo persuades Rosaura that Lelio's withdrawal is only a lover's ruse to test her affection. "Why," says Rosaura, "he has already tested my heart and found out that it was yours." Florindo sighs, but to Rosaura's cry of despair he answers that he has just now married Beatrice, and thus bound himself to a wife he does not love in order that he might now force her to bind herself to a husband she does not love. At such a dear price is bought the triumph of friendship over love.

Goldoni did not, however, understand the value of contrasts which are here softened by the gaiety of incidents, by a certain homely intonation. Thus Ottavio wants his daughter to be happy. The final catastrophe is avoided, but he makes an absurd exit, as if no family concern could stop him when his money is in danger.

There is no tragedy in Ottavio, but there is excellent comedy. His coming in and picking up stray bits of tape, the measuring of eggs through a ring; his attending to every detail of housekeeping and preparing knitting needles and a distaff for his womenfolk, his gloating over his money, and the draughting of the articles of his daughter's marriage settlement so as to ensure keeping his own money from his son-in-law, — yet the complex unity of the character is always preserved and presented with verisimilitude.[1] *I Puntigli*

[1] Ghirigoro de Macci, Ottavio Aretusi, and Harpagon are exactly alike in their treatment of their servants; and so they should be, having been copied, all of them, after the great classical model of Plautus' *Aulularia*.

delle Donne, another of the sixteen plays, is supposedly inspired by Molière, merely because a pair of merchants dream of making their way into the aristocratic set,

For instance, in *La Sporta* (act i, sc. 2), Ghirigoro tells Brigida his servant that in his absence she must admit no one into the house, that she must lend no drop of water, no bit of lighted charcoal, "put out the fire and say that the bucket has dropped into the well." Hear him preaching that the best cure for his daughter's illness is diet. "You women are always ready to eat too much; a sick person must be kept fasting." He will have the door secured in his hearing, the latchet drawn, the bolt pushed in place.

Harpagon's orders to his servants are too well known to be quoted; Goldoni's Ottavio is even more natural when he stops Trappola on his way to the kitchen and scolds him for having lighted a fire (for cooking). Act i, sc. 7: "Ott. — You ass! Who taught you to light a fire so early? I put it out and now you would light it up again! Trap. — Confound your avarice. . . . Ott. — My avarice, yes! If I were avaricious, we should not eat as well as we do. Come, let me see what you bring home from the market. Trap. — I have searched all Bologna to find eggs at half a farthing each. Ott. — Dreadful! Everything is so dear. One cannot manage it. How many have you taken? Trap. — Four farthings. Ott. — Four farthings! What the deuce are we to do with eight eggs? Trap. — For four persons they are not too many. Ott. — One egg for each person is quite enough. Trap. — Why if there are any left they'll keep. Ott. — They may tumble down. Get broken. That confounded cat has broken some others. Trap. — We can put them in a pot. Ott. — A pot can get broken, you are always breaking them. Nay! Give them to me, I'll put them in the flour cask; they will be safe. Let me see these eggs. Trap. — Here they are. Ott. — Hi! You blockhead! You know not how to spend, these eggs are too small. I do not want them. You must take them back to the seller. Trap. — They are the biggest one can find. Ott. — The biggest! You are a fool! Look here, this is the measure for eggs. Those that pass through this ring are too small, I will not have them. Trap. — Curse the miser. A measure for eggs! Ott. — This one passes; this one does not, this one passes . . . four of them pass and four do not. I'll keep these."

He puts them in his pocket and presently they tumble down and Trappola laughs. "Ott. — You laugh, these eggs were worth two farthings. Do you know what two farthings mean? Money is sown like corn; two farthings fructify as many other farthings as in an ear of corn."

(Farthing is given as the translation of *baiocchi*.)

and adopt some of the makeshifts accepted by Mr. Hourdain. Molière's viewpoint is so utterly divergent from Goldoni's that this parallel is not justified.

Goldoni says this play was successful in every Italian city except Venice, where the privileges of titled women were not disputed, and no one would have tried to force admittance in their circle; yet this intrusion of the bourgeois within the circles of aristocracy, when gold paved the way, was always good matter for comedy everywhere in Italy, and Goldoni was sure to use it, especially in those plays that have the *Villeggiatura* as a background. A group of these plays will be considered separately, as they represent a characteristic Italian complement of the picture of city customs.

Another group of Goldonian comedies that will be considered are the popular pictures, generally in dialect, which he wrote for his own amusement rather than for profit, for the last days of carnival. It was understood that these were meant for the humbler class of spectators. He considered them of small importance. Modern critics find them delightful bits of life painting, which announce one masterpiece, *Le Barufe Chiozote.*

Among the sixteen plays composed and performed in such haste are some that cannot stand the test of criticism even though favourably accepted by the audience at the time. One of these Goldoni introduces, in his *Memoirs*, as inspired by *Le Flatteur*, which he seems to have attributed to Jean Jacques Rousseau, though written by Jean Baptiste Rousseau. Hypnotised by the notion that this play was written by a famous philosopher, Goldoni finds that "the French poet had treated his subject as a philosopher, rather than as a playwright; I endeavoured, even while I inspired horror for a vicious man, to brighten my play with comical episodes and funny traits." He mentions also *Le Méchant de Gresset,*[1] which provided part of the subject-matter and perhaps the outline of the principal character; but in that case Goldoni has clumsily imitated.

His *Adulatore*[2] is a poor play. Another bad play

[1] *Le Méchant de Gresset* borrows much from *Le Médisant de Destouches.* They both expose a common character in French and Venetian circles. A Frenchman of great wit, D'Argenson, aptly qualifies them, *les paralytiques du cœur.* Wickedness as a system, carried on in cold blood as if by principle.

In *Le Méchant* Cléonte domineers over Géronte's household, ready to marry either Florise, the sentimental, coquettish, overbearing sister of Géronte, or Chloé, the ingénue: one of the most successful impersonations of this type. There is a Valère to fill the useful rôle of lover, with the usual traditional weakness. Petit de Julleville, *Hist. de la Lit. Fran.* (*op. cit.*), page 582, vol. vi, says that *Le Méchant* is the last *comédie classique.*

[2] Goldoni's *Adulatore* does not want to marry; he only courts a lady by foul ways, with the worst intentions, and is repulsed. He makes mischief by encouraging the folly of the mother of Isabella, Donna Luigia, who pretends to take for her lover (the term is always *cavaliere servente*) the young man who is in love with her daughter; she is the counterpart of Florise. Isabella is more silly than Chloé because Goldoni never could draw an ingénue. (Query: Did he lack models?)

In this play *L'Adulatore* some interesting scenes might be selected to show the intrigues about monopolies, such as the privilege of manufacturing velvet and the gathering of customs (*dritti di gabelle*). Goldoni, as a consul, may have known much of what was going on behind the scenes, in both cases. Also as a secretary to a minister in Milan. This might be compared to other such pictures in *I Mercanti, La Bancarotta, L'Impostore,* that contain sidelights on the business world.

produced by Goldoni at this time was written in order to triumph over his rival Chiari. "I will compose a play out of which a novel might be made," said Goldoni. "I want," said I to myself, "a good deal of intrigue, startling and wonderful incidents, and withal some fun and pathos. A heroine must be more interesting than a hero; where shall I pick her? Time enough to find her out, let me take in the meanwhile for my protagonist an unknown woman; here I set down on my paper *L'Incognita:* Act the first, scene the first. This woman must have a name; well, let her be called Rosaura. Must she come all by herself to explain the subject of the play? Of course not. That was a fault in the ancient comedies; let her come in with . . . Why, yes, with Florindo . . . Rosaura and Florindo.

"In this way I began my play *L'Incognita.* In this way I went on with it, building a very huge edifice without knowing whether it would turn out to be a temple or a market."

Neither Chiari nor Goldoni, however, understood how the transformation of a novel into a comedy might be successfully effected. They did not see that the psychology of the novel is not at all that which the theatre requires. A simplification of characters, a bolder colouring, a stronger contrast of light and shade are needed to ensure an appearance of reality in the representation of life on the stage. Goldoni missed this point in other plays than this *Incognita.*

In his *Memoirs* Goldoni writes that while the *Finta Ammalata* was only meant to amuse, the *Dama*

Prudente[1] was meant only to interest. In the preface, *L'Autore a chi legge*, which was printed some years later, he further explains, confusedly, that his intention was to give a comedy of character, describing the unhappy effects of jealousy in a person of high birth; and his most competent commentator, Ernesto Masi, believes this play attacks *serventisme galante*. Thus three distinct purposes are claimed for this play: intrigue, picture of customs, and psychology of one personage.

All three explanations are true. Goldoni had the genial intuition of a study in character; he gave it greater relief by surrounding it with the customs that were in bitter opposition to it, and also, as he must perforce cater for the applause of the crowd, he charged his plan with an intricate plot. Here is a page out of the history of Venetian customs, here is also a full-sized portrait or rather a *caractère* not unworthy of La Bruyère's delicate penetration, and finally a story of intrigue.

Don Roberto and his wife are both victims of the customs and prejudices of the world they live in. Don Roberto is jealous; but, since he fears to appear ridiculous, he encourages the visits and attentions of two *cavalieri serventi*. He prefers two to one for obvious reasons. Donna Eularia would rather be

[1] *La Dama Prudente* is edited with notes in *Scelta di Commedie de C. Gold. con prefazione e note*, di Ernesto Masi, Firenze, Le Monnier, 1897, vol. i, *Mem.* i, 350. "In order to explain this play one should follow it scene by scene. It is so artfully worked out that the dialogue is necessary in order to judge of it."

left alone, but she, too, is a slave to public opinion and tolerates the visits and accepts the presents of the two gentlemen. She wastes much "prudence" in holding the balance nicely between the two rivals, in quieting her husband's anxieties; but cannot prevent the two gentlemen from quarrelling in her own room and beginning a duel which Don Roberto's entrance interrupts. She explains the matter, but does not satisfy his jealousy. So that when the duel is resumed in the street and the police interfere and arrest the fighters, Donna Eularia conceals the event from her husband. Her excessive prudence is itself compromising. Before daybreak she visits the two champions in their prison in the governor's house, reconciles them, and obtains their pardon and release. Then she recovers the common sense which Goldoni's characters seldom lack, and she persuades her husband that if they went to live in the country they would both be happier.

In this ill-constructed, inconsistent play is the character of the jealous man who is ashamed of, and yet cannot conquer, his weakness.

Goldoni's detractors say that he has only a gallery of *demi caractères* showing hesitation and contradiction. True, Goldoni's characters are complex and their passions or inclinations are often contradictory, but is not that human nature? The heroes of Greek tragedy knew no weakness; Greek statues reproduce only faultless limbs. The aim of the artist is perfection.

But Goldoni aimed at no such æsthetic transformation; he merely wished to reproduce nature as he saw it under the accumulated veils of education, civilisation, refinement, and also of corruption. He did not attempt to lift life beyond the realms of everyday experience and homely morality. Severe critics smile at the words on the tablet that adorns his birthplace, "*plaudentibus Musis,*" yet a muse certainly presides over the work of Goldoni; it is the Greek *eucolia* that cheers and comforts, that laughs at evils, and strips disguises from sin.

The naked truth is too primitive for Goldoni's Venetian spirit; but her half sister presides over Goldoni's soul and guides him to that representation of life which, while it is sincere, is also pitying and considerate. Goldoni sees jealousy not as a tragedy but as a compound of petty and ridiculous impulses, as a miserable attitude of the spirit, too weak to fight yet not sufficiently passive to remain silent. Because Don Roberto's jealousy is just such a contradiction between affections and feelings as is the common portion of so many men, Don Roberto is an interesting figure, one that has not grown old in the gallery of Goldonian personages.

Scene 5, act i, is a microcosm of delicacy, showing the man of the world tortured between his terror of appearing unmannerly and his horror of leaving his wife in the company of a professional philanderer. He invents an excuse for going out, because he knows that it would be an offence to remain; but he comes back under a pretence, because he cannot stay away.

Yet when Donna Eularia snatches at the first plausible opportunity for retiring, he desires her to remain, and he finally goes out.

In the second act, after a pathetic scene (sc. I) in which Donna Eularia vainly tries to soothe him, after the sky has been cleared by her proposing to go into the country for a while, a new storm breaks out because one of the *cavalieri*, Marquis Ernesto, sends a present, a basket of pears. Donna Eularia is for simply rejecting the gift; but polite Don Roberto, for fear of offence, orders it to be accepted. Roberto hates the sight of the pears. He fidgets, finds fault with Donna Eularia because she has sent back a present of truffles; he grumbles and makes her weep, then he begins throwing the pears out of the window. One of these missiles hits the Marquis Ernesto. All through the intricacies and humour of the plot his attitude is thus one of real agony, which gives to this otherwise tame composition an interest verging on tragedy.[1]

[1] Act ii, sc. I: "Donna Eularia and Don Roberto. Don Eul. — You seem dissatisfied. What is the matter? Rob. — One cannot always be in the same mood. Eul. — I see you have been in the same sad mood for some time. Rob. — How long have I been so? Eul. — If I must say truth, it seems to me ever since we were married. Rob. — Why, madam, you must be mistaken. You think so, because ever since you have been my wife you see me with other eyes than you did formerly. Eul. — For my part I certainly have not changed. Rob. — Then I have! Eul. — That may be so. Rob. — Have you not given me cause for this change? Eul. — Indeed I cannot say. Rob. — Yet if this change is more visible to you than to me, it evidently means that you find in yourself a cause for it. Eul. — I know nothing of having displeased you. If I go to parties, if I receive visits, it is for your sake. . . . Rob. — Here you are, you can only talk

The drama of jealousy has frequently tempted Goldoni's imagination and here he came near creating a masterpiece.

of visits and parties, as if I were a jealous husband. Eul. — I do not say that you are jealous; since you have no occasion for it. Rob. — No occasion? Eul. — Indeed, no. Firstly, because I have neither beauty nor grace to attract suitors. Rob. — *Perbaco!* Even an ape with all this finery on her back would appear attractive. Eul. — I do not think that I dress too finely. Rob. — I do not speak for you. I well know that whatever you do, you do it to please me. I speak for those who want to please other people. Eul. — I do not. . . . Rob. — I am not speaking about you, I insist that my words are not intended for you, yet if you appropriate them, it means that you know how they fit you. Eul. — My dear Don Roberto, if you think that I do not know how to behave myself. . . . Rob. — Let us talk of something else. My aunt is much better. She will soon be all right. Eul. — Yes, she is all right. Rob. — How do you know? Eul. — I sent yesterday and they said that her fever was gone. Rob. — Yet this morning she was dying. Eul. — She was dying? Indeed! (*She laughs.*) Rob. — You do not believe it? Eul. (*still laughing*) — Why, yes, I believe it. Rob. — You make fun of me. You think that under the pretence of visiting my aunt I took you away from the *conversazione?* You want to make me out as a jealous husband? Damn jealousy! Damn whoever says so, whoever believes it, whoever is jealous, whoever is not. Eul. — You would damn every living person then? Rob. — No one but myself! Eul. — But why? Rob. — Because I am a fool. Eul. — My dear Roberto, what ails you? Rob. — Nothing, I am troubled about business. About a hundred things. The management of the household, family cares, lawsuits, letter writing, my wife, and a thousand other worries. Eul. — Is your wife one of your worries. Rob. — Don't you think that you fill my mind? Eul. — I hope that your thoughts of me give you no pain. You know that I love you dearly. Rob. — No . . . you give me no pain. Eul. — Well, then, let me see you of good cheer. Let us live by ourselves and enjoy the good things we have. . . . Let us go for a month in the country. . . . We will only have a few visitors; the doctor, the magistrate. Rob. — No, I won't have doctors and magistrates; in the country I want to be quite by myself. Eul. — So be it, we will stay by ourselves. Rob. — Cannot you live without seeing people? Eul. — Those persons are our dependents. Rob. — Didn't you say that you would stay alone? Eul. — Of course I did and I do. Rob. — Well, all by ourselves. A month all by ourselves! At least one month! Eul. — A month! Always if you like."

A feature of this *Dama Prudente* which reveals the peculiar character of Goldoni's Venice is the courtship of the two *cavalieri.* The *cavaliere servente* was generally a model of effeminacy. At a time when in France and in England a certain looseness of customs connived at irregular attachments, at a time when Mademoiselle de Lespinasse, Madame de Warens, Madame du Châtelet, Lady Montagu, and others reaped honour rather than shame for ruling hearts of illustrious men, the Venetian dame asserted her new freedom by chaining a slave.

Il cavaliere servente was originally meant to protect. Fashion turned him into a sort of unpaid lackey; mannerism and affectation of sensibility curbed him into this posture of servility. But the taming of the brute was never so complete that the vulgarity and grossness of the man did not sometimes break out.

Brutality, only held in check by polite manners, then broke out. Goldoni, having pictured in the *Cavaliere e la Dama* the genuinely chivalrous pattern of serventism, also painted the tinsel copy. These two philanderers are always drawing their swords. They are not really in love, they would not care for an undisputed prize, but as long as one of them is admitted, the other insists on the same favour.

Goldoni's gallery of portraits grew with each new comedy. These two are certainly not the last of the *cavalieri serventi* he selected for models. We note them progressively as they came on the stage, sent to hold the mirror, and teach a lesson.

Goldoni had extensive personal experience of both the gambling house and the drawing-room card tables. He knew the ways and manners of different types of players. The Italian proverb, that character is revealed *a tavola e a tavolino*, when eating or when gambling, he applied frequently. The sin of gluttony is small in the roll of Venetian faults. Hence Goldoni has comparatively few scenes round the table, but he has many scenes round the *tavolino.*

They are as nicely differentiated as the caste of the players required. Every detail is appropriate, and Goldoni's theatre gives an adequate idea of what the cards were for the Venetians of his day. That unwritten code of formalities which regulated every act was never so imperative as when people gathered round card tables. The places were taken with a careful consideration for the rank and importance of each guest. The recognised rights of the *cavaliere servente* were not overlooked; the position in regard to doors and windows was a matter of punctilio more than of hygienic precautions.

In forming the circle round the tables there was ample opportunity for showing the manœuvring of lovers, the intrigues for favour, the hostility of competitors, the sly encouragement of a coquette, the timid encouragement of a bashful beauty, or the grotesque presumptions of a faded charmer.

Conversation did not slacken. Flirtation went on, reproaches and entreaties, insinuations, and angry replies whispered in asides, all these delicate arts

Goldoni knew better than anyone, and all these arts his personages practised, and not one of their meanings or suggestions was lost on the audience. The patrician lady who presided over the tables, the austere senator, the abbot in *sottana*, the merchant in *tabarro*, the housewife in *zendado*, the gondolier sashed in scarlet silk, and every one of the crowd filling the theatre, knew these ways, or could interpret their meaning.

To foreigners these scenes may appear dull and these ceremonies insipid; they were not so for Goldoni's hearers. When Don Roberto asked to play at the same table as his wife, he shocked every woman in the house as if he had committed an incongruity. When the same lady Radegonda claimed the right to pursue her prattle with both the players of her table and those of the next one, there were few to disapprove her assertion: " If I cannot speak with the other tables while I play, it's like being dead."

And what of the muttered grumblings of the two *cavalieri* insinuating each that Donna Eularia favours the other? Or the sudden ending of the game when a quarrel seems ripe and the ladies fear a scandal?

Dear old-fashioned, over-refined, puerile and dainty Venice, whoever would like to read thy complex soul must take some pains to con the quaint spelling, the enwreathed delicacy of thy manners and speech!

Goldoni is an ideal guide to the understanding of Venetian society. The man who could even in this year of fearful overwork find time for the pleasures " that turned the day into night, and the night into day," as he writes to a friend, must have keenly appreciated, hence perfectly observed, every sort of worldly amusement.

The gallery of pictures is infinitely varied in his plays. None of those authors whom he called his masters has ever analysed with such nice discernment, and represented with such force and perspicacity, any society under its many aspects, in the flitting light and shade of high and low, polite and rough, loose and innocent, gay and sad moments. He has directed a searchlight into every nook and corner, and sketched in a few lines a great number of characters that, taken in themselves, separately mean little, but grouped and placed in their proper places form a wonderfully complete picture.

CHAPTER X

THE PLAYS (1751 TO 1754)

Il Molière prompted by desire for fame — an imitation of classic models — not an artistic success — Goldoni never understood French character — character of Don Pirlone an imitation of Tartuffe — *La Moglie Saggia* is important in history of modern drama — has been imitated by many modern playwriters — the servants are duplicates of their masters — a noble wife and an ignoble mistress — modern and full of truth — drama of passion relieved by the comic episodes — Goldoni's servant characters — judging and ridiculing their masters — present true pictures of Venetian life — Goldoni has no superior in interpretation of the family, the group — he is not a psychologist but a translator of souls — *I Puntigli Domestici* is an accurate presentation of family life — *Il Tutore* a vivid picture of a ruined family — and of a mother and daughter loving same man — resemblance of *L'Avaro Geloso* to Molière's *L'Avare* is unimportant — it is a common character of classic comedy — avarice was rampant in Venice — Goldoni's jealous miser is more grotesque than wicked — — *L'Amante Militare*, as are all Goldoni's similar subjects, is a poor play — Venetians neither understood nor cared for militarism — the relation between peasantry and their feudal lords is poorly depicted in *Il Feudatorio* — Goldoni's friendship with Visconti, Albergati, Gaspare Gozzi, and others of the nobility — and enjoyed great popularity — as a guest in their houses he learned much of gallantry, artificial grace, and excessive politeness and malice, which he introduces into his later plays — as is seen by comparing *Il Vecchio Bizzarro* with *Momolo Cortesan* or *Il Prodigo* — Pantalone flirts with Clarice but finally falls truly in love with Flamminia — with a few changes this might be made into an effective modern play — *Il Vecchio Bizzarro* was a failure when first performed — its subtle wit was not appreciated — in anger and in self-defence Goldoni wrote *Il Festino* — a poor play but an important document in presenting the intellectual atmosphere about Goldoni — the effect of this failure and other circumstances forced Goldoni to compose many romantic tragicomedies which pleased his audience but were not worthy of his genius.

WHEN the final curtain dropped on the last performance of the last comedy promised by Goldoni for the season, when the crowded audience expressed their admiration so loudly that *les passans doutèrent si c'étoit l'effet de la satisfaction, ou d'une révolte générale*, when friends and patrons carried him off to *il Ridotto*, where he was overwhelmed with compliments which he would have "rather avoided," Goldoni experienced an exultation that repaid all his efforts, and stimulated him to even greater attempts. Medebach's avarice and Bettinelli's complicity afterward cooled his exultation, nervous exhaustion temporarily depressed him and left a bitterness that tinges his later narrative, yet the elation, the confidence in himself, the desire to attempt something even more difficult, remained.

This desire for fame prompted Goldoni to write *Il Molière*, a comedy in five acts, in *versi martelliani*. His habitual self-distrust because of his scanty scholarship was so far conquered that he undertook to imitate the classical models, in adopting both the metrical style and the division into five acts, and at the same time to show the Turinese audience that he knew a French classic *aussi bien que les Piémontois*.

Goldoni's modern biographers interpret this attempt as a blow aimed at his rival Chiari. Now Chiari was esteemed for his scholarship and his facility for adaptation; hence, if Goldoni had thought of vanquishing him, he would not have attempted it on this field. Chiari could make endless rhymes; Chiari could successfully cut out a play from a romance or a *Life*. But there were other things which Goldoni could better accomplish when it pleased him. But did Goldoni care much about challenging Chiari?

Whatever motive prompted Goldoni he was unprepared both for this classical imitation, and to interpret Molière's complex and tragical personality. He willingly confessed that he lacked poetic gift; his *Componimenti* poetry were mere trifles. In the letter to Scipione Maffei printed as a preface to *Molière* (volume ii of Paperini's edition), Goldoni explains that he does not like the "*verso Martelliano* made up of two seven-syllable lines, the cadence of which cannot be dissimulated, as it is further marked by the rhyme with which the sentence generally is made to end." He sees no beauty in this form of poetry, thinks that it sometimes spoils Molière's plays. When adopting poetical language he tries "to make it as simple as possible by avoiding transpositions, difficult constructions, and lengthy periods."

Indeed, though often used, the *verso Martelliano* has never enjoyed much favour in Italy.[1]

> "*Co'denti, co piedi e colle mani*
> *Formansi versi Martelliani,*"

said Carlo Gozzi at the time, adding that he expected to hear presently *i cani baiar anch'essi in versi Martelliani* (*Tartana degli Influssi*, Paris, 1757).

Goldoni's lines have at least the merit that they

[1] Many are the detractors of the *verso Martelliano*, yet this much decried form of poetry has survived almost two centuries of discredit. Goldoni's martellians, and better still his *sciolti*, either in Italian or in Venetian, come trippingly on the actor's tongue. Some rhymes are poor, many words are mere padding, and sometimes the orthodox Tuscan ear, or the erudite Accademico della Crusca, is offended, but when this verse is recited by an actor who knows his trade, it is music to the ear.

sound fluent on the actors' lips. Moreover Goldoni was unprepared for treating such a subject. In his preface to *La Donna di Garbo*, he had wisely protested that "when he wanted to write a play, he neither looked for his subject in stories, nor in other people's plays, but sought in nature for likely and truthful characters and events." He had further repeatedly professed that the only two books he studied were Life and the Stage. Therein he learned "the manner and customs that are most common to our time and nation."

Setting aside these good purposes, Goldoni dug out of Grimarest's *Life* the personage of Molière clumsily interpreted, events of his career, appreciations of his works that he could neither control nor fully understand.[1]

[1] Since Goldoni did not then read French he could only have known some imperfect translation of Grimarest's imperfect biography of Molière. Goldoni shows Molière in 1667 when, as he supposes, Tartuffe was ready to be performed and the Parliament dared oppose the King's approval of it. Valerio, who stands for Baron, the actor Molière loved above all others, has gone to entreat the King at the camp in Flanders — a most unlikely step. Madeleine Béjart is in Goldoni's *Molière* presented as "a good actress worthy of some praise, with whom I have been living for ten years in good company; she kindly takes care of my house." By thus striking from the first presentation this mild note of simple comradery the whole strife is toned down. Mother and daughter are not rivals. Armande Béjart, whom Goldoni names Guerrina, in anticipation of her second marriage with one Guérin, is a pert little miss making love to the actor-manager; she even asks him to elope with her.

Charles Rabany, *op. cit.*, page 276, judges: "*la pièce intéressante, l'intrigue bien nouée, mais nous n'apprenons rien de nouveau sur l'âme de Molière ni sur son génie.*" As indeed how could we, considering that Goldoni knew even less about Molière and his genius than his hearers.

Don Pirlone, the substitute of Tartuffe, is a merchant and he is supposed to be wealthy, since he can afford to bribe the servant La Foret.

In his *Memoirs* he lavishly praises his French model; but when he composed *Molière* he had rather incoherent notions about Molière's and other French plays. He said that they contained only weak intrigues, seldom more than one real character, even that one badly delineated, the scenes being ill-connected, and the work lacking sublimity. This parenthesis he omitted in later editions, but it was there printed in full letters when his *Molière* was first published.

It was not until five years later, in Parma, that for the first time he heard French actors, and even then he did not understand all they said. In the many long years he lived in France, he never communed with the French soul about Molière and his times. About the intrigues of the French court, about the conditions of life and the surroundings of his hero, Goldoni had not the slightest idea; yet he presumed to select from Grimarest's *Life* of Molière and out of an abominable pamphlet against Armande Béjart, the only documents he had, "*all* that was most comical and interesting!"

The play is weak. It was coldly received by the Turinese public. The *Giornale di Torino*, at the date of its first representation, April 21, 1751, records simply that the Troupe Medebach had *débuté* with success; it makes no mention of the play.

Actors favour this comedy because actors are attracted by the idea of impersonating Molière, and the public was amused by the personage of Don Pirlone, an attenuated imitation of Tartuffe.

Already Gerolamo Gigli [1] had transported to the Italian stage under that name the immortal hypocrite. Gigli's translation, which Goldoni might have mentioned, was an act of daring, as well as a scholarly performance. Its author was persecuted for it and for its sequel, *La Sorellina di Don Pilone*, by the clerical party, all-powerful at that time in the Tuscan State. Goldoni was not eager for persecution, and was respectful of religion. In his transposition of characters Don Pirlone became an inoffensive lay intriguer. Indeed all the characters are toned down. Valerio represents Baron; Leandro stands for Chapelle and is a simple-minded drunkard. Madeleine Béjart is here merely a shrewish housekeeper, while Armande is a pert little miss making love to a mature husband *to* her own mother. Count Lasca,[2] representing those "critics

[1] Goldoni's indebtedness to Gerolamo Gigli begins early. Goldoni first appeared on the stage in a play of this Tuscan author, in the character of a girl, *La Sorellina di Don Pilone*. Yet Goldoni does not give G. Gigli his meed of thanks. Perhaps he disapproved of the anticlerical character of Gigli's works. Being a respectful Venetian, he certainly disapproved of satire aimed at the clergy, and considered that religious questions were not to be discussed in the theatre.

From Gigli, Goldoni learned realism, attenuated by decency of dialogue (see *La Sorellina di Don Pilone*) and also the example of direct imitation of homely situations and persons. Gigli even ridiculed his own wife and her avarice, using some quarrels between himself and this shrewish bigot for the theme of his play.

[2] Count Lasca's character is found in other plays; yet Goldoni might have made more of the greatest literary critic of his time. Was it prudence? In the narrow but crowded circle of Venetian literati the personage of one who, unable himself to produce any literary work, was always ready to criticise other authors' writings must have appeared an amusing type. The character of the critic never appealed to Goldoni because he hated polemics and quarrels. See his disdainful mention of Baretti's attacks.

who talk about everything and know nothing about anything," is the best, as he is the most Goldonian of the entire score.

Learned Goldonists are unravelling the skein of exact chronology of Goldoni's plays which the author's indifference to such details has entangled.[1] Yet it is interesting to note the progress already made at this approximate date, autumn, 1751, and carnival, 1752, when in quick succession he gave *Molière* and then *La Moglie Saggia.*

The appearance of *La Moglie Saggia* was an important date in the history of modern drama.

The modern drama is not a perfect form of art. It is a hybrid monster, made up of crude imitation of life and of conventionalism, admitting of some psychological investigation, doubtful wit, actuality, and undigested science; presuming to reconstrue history or dictate moral teachings, generally badly written and composed with a view to immediate effect. Yet

[1] Lists of Goldoni's plays are not wanting. Besides the accurate and complete *Saggio di Bibliografia Goldoniana* of G. A. Spinelli already quoted we mention the *Liste Chronologique des Œuvres Dramatiques de Carlo Goldoni*, annexed to Charles Rabany's *Carlo Goldoni. Le Théâtre et la vie en Italie au XVIII siècle*, Berger Levrault et Cie., Paris, 1896, a voluminous and accurate list, presenting, side by side with every play mentioned, the passage in the *Memoirs* referring to it and giving date of performance, translations into other languages, and similar indications. Mr. Chatfield Taylor has reproduced, with a few additions, this note. More complete and more carefully supported with documents is the classical edition of Goldoni's *Opere Complete*, edited by the municipality of Venice, 1907.

With Goldoni, however, the question of dates is of slight importance, and the titles are often puzzling. He frequently gave almost the same play under different titles, specially in his last years — when he sent to Venice the plays that were first written or composed for Paris.

modern drama has earned its place in the history of literature on account of the large place which it has filled in the life of every civilised nation. It is not proposed to relate how this hybrid composition has developed out of the ancient tragedy, the classical and popular forms of comedy, and has gathered elements from the lowest farce and the poetic pastorals, but merely to show how Goldoni contributed to this elaboration, just at the time when Rousseau was attacking it, when Diderot was dictating the laws that should govern it, when Marivaux was wandering in a delightful pathway, Beaumarchais preparing his formidable social attack, when both the English and the French stage were overwhelmed with lachrymose plays, and the audience stupefied by the droning morals of pedagogic performances.

The modern comedy, dramatic and humouristic, psychological and sentimental, was assuming a definitive form, settling in a formula that outlived all its initiators, and Goldoni hit on the receipt that was adopted after him by Augier, Sardou, Dumas, and others down to the latest Parisian *nouveauté*.

The plot of *La Moglie Saggia* is quickly told. Pantalone, the wealthy merchant, has married his daughter, Rosaura, to Count Ottavio. Like other *mariages à la mode* this one is threatened with ruin when an undesirable third person intrudes. Count Ottavio is the *cavalier servente* and slave of capricious and shrewish Marchesa Beatrice. His own temper is violent, his behaviour to his wife brutal. To get rid of his wife, he will let her return to her father; he allows other men to court her, and finally he mixes poison in her lemonade. Rosaura does not drink it, because the play is not meant to be a tragedy, and a final reconciliation brings the pair together and also Pantalone, whilst Lady Beatrice is summarily dismissed.

An atmosphere of *tragédie bourgeoise* is felt during the three acts; but it is attenuated by a superstructure of witty dialogue and by some farcical episodes. The titles borne by two of the characters do not prevent the whole milieu from appearing bourgeois. It is a picture of that special world standing midway between honest, thrifty merchant Pantalone and the real patrician. Count Ottavio has all the petty vice and unmannerly extravagance of the *barnabotto*, none of the dignified manners of the ancient aristocracy.

The first scene shows the servants eating while Lady Beatrice is entertaining their masters. The servants, here, according to the tradition of the *commedia dell'arte*, are duplicates of their masters, the analogy of character being at times enhanced by some analogy of situation. Brighella, Count Ottavio's servant, has some of the old-fashioned respect and devotion frequently found in great and respectable houses; but he is, like his master, a wanton husband, flirting with the marchesa's maid, while Corallina, his wife, and Rosaura's confidential attendant, is fretting at home. Arlecchino, the rascally lout, belongs to Marchesa Beatrice. Faloppa and Pistone are like their masters,

Lelio and Florindo, foppish hangers-on, ever ready to share in a good dinner and to talk scandal.

The position of affairs, as seen from the servants' standpoint, is sketched in a few strong dashes. "He has married a merchant's daughter and he repents. He married for love and now he is tired of his wife," says Pistone. "It's a pity," comments Arlecchino to Brighella, "that your master has not married my mistress . . . they are both so churlish that they must have brought forth a brood of wildcats."

The first part of the act closes with a scene of violent quarrelling between Count Ottavio and Marchesa Beatrice. The scene immediately shifts to Rosaura's room, a quiet and refined atmosphere. Rosaura is reading to while away the long, tedious hours of her solitary evening, chiding Corallina for her insinuations as to the way Count Ottavio is spending his evening. She will not admit that there is any harm in his attendance on Marchesa Beatrice. She will not even believe the report which Lelio and Florindo, after obtaining admittance, insist on pouring into her ears. She will not even admit the worse when Pantalone comes in to comfort and advise. She states her case very plainly and with great dignity. She married in obedience to her father's wishes, but she does not mean now to obey him and leave her faithless husband.

"I have ever been obedient to your wishes. I have never disobeyed your commands. But now let me tell you what my heart and my actual condition prompt me to say. I am Count Ottavio's wife; hence I have acquired that degree of nobility which attracted you first. This nobility must be a great boon, since you were so anxious to secure it for me, since you have overlooked every other consideration in order to obtain it for me. For my part, I value a greater advantage in this acquisition than you ever considered. If Heaven grants me children, they will be really noble born, and I shall rejoice for having given them birth, as you will be proud to behold in them the greater fruit of your endeavours. Must I lose this advantage, and deprive my children of this advantage, merely to avoid some suffering?"

No passionate explosion, though Rosaura is passionately attached to her wanton husband, no exhibition of tearful sentimentality, but the dignified statement of her case, the patient acceptance of the evil that has to be endured for the sake of keeping intact that which a *Venetian* gentildonna sets above everything else — her *decoro*. Which does not mean simply her honour, but also propriety, reputation, privileges, social rank, and distinctions. This code of morals is the more pathetic in Rosaura's case because she is not naturally proud. She receives with incredible patience her husband's abuse, his impertinence and brutality, as long as they can be concealed from the world. She must keep up appearances, and trust to chance to return her husband to her.

Rosaura is patient, but she is not a fool. She once bent meekly before her father's wishes; she now allows her husband to ruin her life; but when she sees her way to fight a fair duel against her rival, she uses her weapons well. Indeed the scene between the two women is a masterpiece, a model often imitated but seldom bettered. Rosaura has come to Marchesa Beatrice for advice, she trusts in the high virtue of the marchesa, and appeals to her guidance. Count Ottavio, once so loving and kind, has changed sadly of late: "He avoids meeting me, he deserts my bed, treats me like his worst enemy." On being asked why she comes here with her tale of sorrow: "Have patience with me. Let me tell you why I come to you. I know that my husband is a frequent visitor at your place. I know that you bear with him patiently. You must be kind, indeed, if you can tolerate his ways. He has for you a great esteem and will accept respectfully your counsels. This is why I entreat you, with tears in my eyes, tears wrung from the purest and dearest conjugal love, to speak to him on my behalf. Tell him that a gentleman of honour should not illtreat an honest wife: that the sacred bond of marriage should exclude every other affection; that every human and divine law commands us to repay love with love, to love those that have a right to be loved; the same laws threaten the traitors, the selfish. Tell him . . . Oh, but you will know better what to say, you will know better the stronger reasons that must convince a man to do his duty."

Beatrice is not so ready with her answers. She fences, but is forced out of her position by Rosaura's mild, but well-directed, blows.

Beat. — Do you think that I am a good friend of your husband's?

Ros. — Yes, a good friend of his, of mine and of all our family.

Beat. — How do you think he comes to my house?

Ros. — He comes to you as to a wise, honourable, and discreet lady, such as you are.

Beat. — Dear friend, I am glad that you know me well; trust me, I could not act otherwise.

Ros. — You need no justification. I know you well, and because I know you, I come to you and throw myself in your arms. No woman, better than you, understands the duties of wisdom and honesty. You need not to be told that the woman who brings trouble into a family is unworthy, that whoever tries to seduce another woman's husband ought to be branded on the face. Whoever entertains sinful amours, doubtful friendships, dangerous intercourse, is an unworthy, a treacherous, woman. My dear Lady Beatrice, I entreat your help.

Even while Beatrice is floundering for an appropriate answer, a servant comes in and whispers that Count Ottavio is in the next room. She orders him to be dismissed. Rosaura takes her leave, after adding a few telling strokes in the way of entreaties to her honourable and wise friend, who is forced to promise that she will teach Count Ottavio "the duties of a husband . . . the obligations of a gentleman . . . and how, if any worthless woman were to try and seduce him, he must consider her as a wretch — a —"

With a very few changes this scene could be adopted by the most modern comedy; it is so full of real life, of the everlasting drama of passion, dissimulated under the thin varnish of conventionalism.

Nor is the character of Marchesa Beatrice less happily sketched. Her blind rage, when she recovers from the first surprise of Rosaura's attack, finds vent in violent reproaches to Count Ottavio. She drives him mad with her taunts and with all the unspoken upbraidings that Goldoni's sense of propriety could not put in so many words; though none better than he could suggest them. Medebach and Marliani, who played the rôles, both in love with Goldoni, rivals on and off the stage, certainly gave the right accent to the spoken word and to the unspoken misery.[1]

The personage of Count Ottavio, weak, selfish, unscrupulous, is drawn with such fearless realism that, if properly understood, it should be sufficient to redeem Goldoni from the charge of timidity. The attack against aristocratic laxity and cruelty could not be made with more courage. Artistically the rôle is less

[1] In *L'Italie vue par les Français*, Librairie des Annales, Paris, 1915 (page 52), Saint-Didier (*attaché au comte d'Avaux ambassadeur à Venise*), who lived two years in Venice, writes thus of the Venetian ladies who on the stage are represented by Beatrice and Rosaura. "*Avec leurs beaux points (de dentelle) et leurs jupes magnifiques en or et en argent; elles n'ont rien qui les orne davantage et qui leur sied mieux que les fleurs qu'elles portent particulièrement à la tête . . . Lorsqu'une gentille dame entre dans une église, elle y marche d'un pas fort grave, avec une très grande queue trainante, l'usage des pages et des laquais étant tout à fait inconnu à Venise (?); et en quelque endroit qu'elle veuille s'arrêter elle se fait faire place d'un air si fier, qu'elle repousse également le gentilhomme et le bourgeois, et prend leur place sans faire la moindre démonstration d'honnêteté.*"

finely finished than the two women's. Yet his hesitations, his lapse into actual crime, are well delineated. His final repentance, being a necessary artifice, to suit the taste of the public for a happy ending, is less satisfying.[1]

[1] Ottavio is not an entirely new character on the Italian stage; but like every other personage of the ancient repertoire adopted by Goldoni, he has been developed and reformed. He stands for a whole class; the nobleman without personal merit. In Venice, a nobleman of repute, intellect, and activity could always find government employment. A man of birth not a member of some council, or not a diplomat, was an anomaly. When he was not thus employed he probably had either become a gambler or was wasting his useless life in the petty vanities of serventism and gossip. Ottavio is Florindo grown older, and not wiser. The flippancy and extravagance of his younger days have ripened into more hateful vices. Married by his father and provided with as large a *dot* as could be found on the market — generally with Pantalone's daughter — he squanders his own and his wife's fortune at the gaming tables. He is the *cavaliere servente* of some other man's wife and is indifferent about his own wife's behaviour. He cheats his creditors. His grand airs and supercilious ways still impose on shopkeepers and menials. When a sumptuous party has kept his palace in a blaze of light all night, he awakes in the morning to face claims that pour in on all sides: debts of honour contracted at cards and others. Goldoni prudently gives him the title of count, which is not usual in Venice, and forbears mentioning his quality of patrician, or his lesser quality of *barnabotto*. This thin disguise is not evidence of Goldoni's timidity.

In a few instances Goldoni's portrait flatters Ottavio, as in *Il Cavaliere di Buon Gusto*. In the preface, *L'Autore a chi legge*, he enumerates the qualities that a gentleman of birth, learning, and education should possess, but his *Cavaliere di Buon Gusto* is not quite the paragon announced, but he represents the bright side of the picture in opposition to the many other Ottavios in the Goldonian gallery.

When thus presented, Ottavio has traits in common with the "Cortesan": he has a taste for fine arts, is fond of books, practises several sports, and is proficient in that delicate Venetian art of flirting with every woman, even while he keeps his own heart free from every entanglement.

See also *Il Cavaliera di Spirito* for such a portrait of Ottavio.

A propos of *La Moglie Saggia*, Rabany makes a significant mistake. He says that Count Ottavio *est obligé de recourir au poison pour obtenir sa liberté*,

The drama of passion is framed and relieved by a stream of comic episodes. The surrounding atmosphere is cleverly made up of all those elements of the *commedia dell'arte* which Goldoni appropriated and rejuvenated, and of the elements of direct imitation of life that he seldom forgot to introduce.

There is Pantalone:[1] the time-honoured mask in his traditional garb, only his face is free from the black vizor. He speaks his own fluent Venetian, he babbles sentimental tenderness, then changes to shrewd businesslike arguments, when he tries to defend his money and his daughter from the grasp of his aristocratic son-in-law. Pantalone does not lack courage; he bends his

when in fact this liberty has been spontaneously offered to him when his father-in-law proposes to take home Rosaura. Count Ottavio's crime is characteristically impulsive and peevish, but not murderous. His crime is puerile in plot and clumsy in attempt; hence the sudden repentance is logical. The same impulsiveness which led the man to the verge of murder aids his return to more humane feelings. In act ii, sc. 10, Ottavio brutally says to Pantalone, "I loved her without any reason; you must not be surprised if, now, I hate her without any reason."

Rosaura's attachment to duty and moral engagements contrasts beautifully with such fickleness. "I am his wife," she says, "nothing but death can part us." The moral teaching of this play, which shows Goldoni's mastery of complex questions, is that the firmer will, even if unasserting. finally conquers violence and loud-voiced authority. Rosaura playing with the lemonade that Ottavio supposes to be the one in which he has mixed poison, is indeed the mistress of the situation, though she speaks so softly and lovingly.

One of Goldoni's best disciples, Ferrari, has partly imitated *La Moglie Saggia* in his *Amore senza Stima.*

[1] Pantalone, being such a complex creation, will be reviewed under several aspects. Here in his rôle of father-in-law he impersonates the Venetian of his class and age. Common sense and tenderness, devotion to his child and an eye to her financial welfare, so as to correct the foolishness of a noble marriage, are his characteristics.

back, when necessary, but he can be bold when the interest of his beloved daughter is jeopardised. There is a whole bevy of servants, Colombina and Brighella repeating the situation of their respective masters with that difference of intonation which stage tradition had not yet fixed, which Goldoni understood so aptly.

In the poverty of invention, or the limitation of subjects, that fettered the ancient comedy, this repetition of the same plot, this counterpart of scenes, was almost a canon of art. Molière, as well as many other French authors, adopted it directly from the Italian *commedia dell'arte.* Goldoni ignored the French models and simply following the teachings of his first masters, the Italian players, chiselled these little jewels of fun.

The sallies, repartees, grumblings, scoldings, impertinences, and, in small proportion, the grossness spoken by the servants in Goldoni's plays make up an interesting ensemble for the modern reader who seeks to penetrate beneath the surface of old Venetian customs. The spirit of Goldoni's plays, of those plays which mirror his own surroundings, truly reveal how these Venetians lived and loved, quarrelled and made peace, plotted and intrigued; how they considered certain duties and rights; how they were judged and ridiculed by their own servants, their intimate foes.

If it were possible to classify Goldoni's production and determine the different moments of his evolution, this moment, 1751 to 1762, should be distinguished as the most realistic. Of course in such a general review, Peruviana, Ircane, Terenzio, and Bella Selvaggia must be ignored, else the general line becomes blurred. The reasons that betrayed Goldoni from his path may be discussed; some of them were most honourable, his duty or what he believed to be his duty towards his collaborators, the actors, being the most prominent.

That which remains of Goldoni's production, after the *Moglie Saggia*, in its totality contains a realistic and complete picture of his times, of the Venetian world.

It is seldom, if ever, a character drawn in the large manner of Molière, so as to stand like an impersonation of one vice or absurdity; but it is the complex and elaborate reproduction of one individual, natural disposition, of one temper tossed and rubbed, moulded into some sort of shape by a series of external causes that Goldoni shows in the background.

La Moglie Saggia, like many other plays of this series, gives almost more than the portrait of a character, the *dessous des cartes* which explains it. The servants' quarters, the grosser interpretation of the master's affairs, is not merely a traditional means of exposing the situation; it is not merely the opportunity required for introducing the favourite masks, but it is an expedient to individualise and to distinguish, by giving in traits and colours of its own, the family — the family, the group — which is a whole in Goldoni's interpretation of life. The relative position of members of this group, their action and reaction over each other, all the complicated woof which binds these persons together, all the ebb and flow of feelings sweet and bitter that make of each household a very labyrinth of sentimental complications, Goldoni grasped with wonderful intuition through the medium of his clear observation.[1]

He is not a psychologist, in the usual meaning of the word, but a translator of souls. He sets forth, in the common language of little facts and simple words, the workings of invisible internal wheels. The traits are few, the colour is spread in daring strokes, yet the general effect is harmonious and in full relief. None of the superabundance of particulars that overcharge a description by Zola's followers is here, but rather the realism of purely Italian character, such as was later revived by Verga and his Sicilian followers, a clear vision of reality and a bold rendering of some of its most characteristic traits, omitting the unessential.[2] An almost forgotten play, *I Puntigli Domestici*, is an instance of this incomplete but dashing representation of life, more particularly of family life and family relations. The plot is flimsy and uninteresting, and the traits represented are almost incomprehensible to a modern audience.

[1] For pictures of family life in Goldoni's plays, see chapter xi.

[2] Goldoni's realism might be compared to Marivaux's. Both wish to be true, even while they remain decent, in a time when decency was not the rule; both wish to depict the world around them, yet both veil things not fit to be seen in their nakedness, but this veil is transparent. Pretty euphemisms are not lies. Both aim at a style that is neither the classical style of their time nor an imitation of past models. Neither can successfully generalise, though both suggest generalisation by the mere truth of particular pictures.

But it is truly representative of the time and place it is intended to mirror. The plot: a series of family quarrels, Count Ottavio is the head of the family who, "more Venetia," should control his sister-in-law, Countess Beatrice, the widow of a younger brother, and her two children, Lelio and Rosaura, besides the usual staff of servants, Brighella, Corallina, and others. The authority of old days is asserted, rebellion rises in the whole household, and each one is in arms against the ancient principle. But each one fights for some special motive and none realise that they have a common aim. The household is a microcosm of the grumblings of distant thunders in the world at large, then and there.

Beatrice claims that she has brought a *dot* into the family and wishes to know how her brother-in-law manages it and other family incomes. She further proposes to marry her daughter without asking the opinion of the head of the family. When Ottavio approves her choice, she would change it.

Rosaura is in revolt, for the usual reason, that she loves Count Florindo; and Lelio, for the usual reason, that he wastes more money than he has. But the originality, the modernity, of these two rebels is that they are untroubled by scruples, and if for a time they league against their elders it is only because they can thus threaten each other: Rosaura knows that her brother possesses a false key to their mother's safe, and also that he meditates a mésalliance; Lelio could tell that his sister receives secret missives from her lover. The time-worn edifice of *familial* subordination is crumbling; Goldoni sees the first rents, and reproduces them without philosophising on their entity or on their value as symptoms. Unlike his contemporaries, he is delightfully free from the mania of generalising and drawing conclusions. He has no preconceived theory to set up between actual facts and their significance. He does not, like Voltaire, rant against religion, nor does he, like Rousseau, pursue a dream of sentimental moralism; he simply notes that which is happening around him. Thus he paints this family, quarrelling over trifles, just as children or very idle people do, and mistaking pique and vanity for pride and self-assertion.

His intention may have been to show not the darkest, but the most ludicrous, aspect of the decadence that was then submerging the aristocracy.

If such was his purpose, he aptly selected his personages meant to represent a whole class or caste. Neither Countess Beatrice nor Count Ottavio are actually vicious; they are only vacuous and petty, puppets in the hands of those who pull the strings and twist them according to their own aims. Pantalone, the simple-minded, good-natured, meddling peacemaker, sees all their weakness, but is too deeply imbued with the old-fashioned respect for their titles, and the servants find both their pleasure and their advantage in promoting quarrels. By return to the ancient manner of the classical comedy, the servants are here the *deus ex machina* that move the plot; and in the end the scapegoats that are punished for their own and their masters' sins.

This same year saw the production of two masterpieces which will hereafter be fully considered: *La Serva Amorosa* and *La Locandiera*. *Il Tutore*, less successful and seldom performed, contains a promising attempt to draw the character of the negligent, slatternly, indolent man, and also contains a vivid picture of a family going to ruin for the same general causes pictured in the *Puntigli Domestici*.

The social standing of the characters is not quite the same. There is an absence of titles and a more subdued intonation, but the differences are not fundamental. Here, too, a vacuous and coquettish widowed mother is supposed to direct her daughter's choice of a husband with the assistance of two guardians: Ottavio the slothful head of the family, and Pantalone. Once more Goldoni represents two classes, the merchant and the man born to fortune; and once more he contrasts them.[1]

The plot indicates certain Venetian customs, which Goldoni prudently avoids to paint in full view. Rosaura loves Florindo; her mother, who still considers her as a little girl, has design on the same young man.

[1] *Il Tutore* also presents Pantalone's common sense, kindness, and rectitude. He is a guardian who opposes the intrigues of his own son for appropriating, besides her meaningless person, Rosaura's considerable *dot*. Goldoni explains in his *Memoirs* that when the title of his play was known people expected to see the traditional guardian, either making love to his ward, like Don Bartolo, or depriving her of her property. He avoided the hackneyed contrast of making the second guardian, Ottavio, a rascal. The enhanced effect would have been at the expense of truth.

Pantalone's rascally son, Lelio, wants to marry Rosaura for her *dot*. Taking advantage of the mother's neglect, and pretending to be sent by his father with orders to escort Rosaura to a *ritiro*, a euphemism indicating a convent, Lelio carries off the girl and her maid to an ill-famed house in Castello. Pantalone rescues her and matters are arranged by a double marriage: Lelio taking the mother and her dowry; Florindo carrying off his sweetheart when he is assured that she was a victim to the plot and that she has escaped unscathed.

Goldoni handles the delicate situation with tact. The young girl, reared, as most girls then were, in ignorance of such danger, does not realise her peril, and Corallina, who has been bribed to betray her, is in reality anxious to bring about a hasty marriage. But all through the play there are pretty traits of customs; amusing scenes that reveal the life, the habits, and language of a whole social class.

Beatrice is the lady of fashion who goes shopping, early in the day, under the protection of a *tabarro* and a mask. She wants her daughter to go with her, against the opposition of Pantalone, who preaches that girls and even married women should order the things they want from the shops. He distinguishes the duty of a girl toward herself, and her duty toward her mother. He instigates Rosaura to disobedience; "since the example and advice of her mother are not what they should be." Such expostulations, though delivered in Pantalone's homely Venetian dialect, must have sounded like a clarion of revolt. Beatrice displays her arts to entangle Florindo into proposing to her. How far the customs of the time, the endless *conversazioni*, and similar opportunities, facilitated such designs it is interesting to see.

The lazy Count Ottavio is a caricature rather than a portrait. In opposition with Pantalone's active and scrupulous guardianship Ottavio is hustled into dressing and preparing for a gondola trip to rescue Rosaura. He surprises his servant Brighella when he announces that he means to dress. "And wash your hands?" suggests the servant, considering that he has never done so these last two months. His shoes are lost; when they are at last discovered under his bed they are turned down at the heels "because he cannot wear them otherwise." To take off his nightcap and put on a wig is an effort, and his hat is discovered hanging as a basket by his bedside and filled with apples. Pantalone frets and Arlecchino plays his *lassi* with a crescendo of humour — just something to keep the audience laughing and to ensure a full house for some nights.[1]

With greater power, though with scanty success, a few months later, autumn, 1753, Goldoni resumed this same plan: the delineation of one character set off by convenient surroundings. Out of the treasures of

[1] *Il Tutore* was partly translated, partly imitated, in France, 1764, by one De La Grange (or Desgranges). Grimm in his *Correspondance*, etc., *op. cit.*, vol. vi, p. 90, and Bachaumont, in his *Mémoires Secrets* (19 Decembre, 1764), attribute the failure of this play to the adaptation. Presumably it failed because so completely Venetian. First performed in 1753.

ancient comedy he picked one of the most popular — the miser. And wishing to make it more complex he made his miser a victim to that other devouring passion — jealousy.[1] Naturally critics have traced back this *Avaro Geloso* to Molière's more famous *Avare.* The resemblance is obvious, but unimportant.

In the Greek and Roman classics, all through the Middle Ages and the Renaissance, poets and players have made fun of this human weakness — old age as opposed to youth. In ancient literatures, old age and its inseparable qualification, avarice, are usually ridiculed. Even if Goldoni ignored or had never read *L'Aridosia* and *La Sporta*, he is sure to have seen some imitation of these masterpieces, some adaptation of immortal *Aulularia*, performed by the comedians of his time. He took this popular character, the grotesque caricature that improvised comedy had popularised, but he greatly altered it.

Goldoni saw, as Molière did not so clearly see, that the avaricious man could not become sufficiently in-

[1] Misers hold a prominent part in five of Goldoni's plays: *Il Vero Amico*, *L'Avaro Geloso*, *L'Avare Fastueux*, *La Vedova Spiritosa*, and *L'Avaro;* but there are many other characters in his gallery of portraits that present traits of avarice. In so doing Goldoni remained true to life. The contrast of ostentation and parsimony was everywhere visible in his Venice. The man who spent hundreds of ducats in festivities stinted his servants in the kitchen; and ladies who spent a fortune in diamonds and lace grudged their dependants a pittance. . . .

Of his misers Goldoni cares least for the *Avaro*. Unredeemed by any virtue, this miser is shockingly unfeeling. He almost rejoices at his son's death, thinking that he need no longer support him; he marries his widowed daughter-in-law to a second husband who does not insist on her *dot*. Altogether this is a slip into old-fashioned, low comedy.

teresting to fill the first place in a play unless he could be humanized. The misery, the pain, the grief, caused solely by the loss of money does not awaken great sympathy. Here, as in Molière's *Avare*, the central figure should not be traced so as to excite only distaste and contempt. Harpagon is in love. His affection redeems his whole character. Goldoni, more strictly observant of life's contrasts, kept close to immediate and direct representation of truth.

Avarice was rampant in Venice. It was the bastard offspring of that thrift that formerly fostered commercial industry. Centuries of experience had taught the merchants of the Serenissima that it paid to hoard and multiply their gains. Even those Venetians who lavished their fortunes to maintain their *decoro*, whose ostentation dazzled the visitor in official receptions, pinched and spared behind the scenes. Private economy and public extravagance characterised the Venetian government and Venetian domestic life. Goldoni's models were all about him, and he aptly chose the miser tormented by jealousy.

Intimate is the connection in the human heart between these two passions. Both are selfish. Meanness attends their divers expressions, as is shown by the surreptitious way in which they are expressed. Both are hidden passions. Each is a taint, a confession of inferiority, each is disguised with hypocrisy, with false humility.

In Venice avarice alone was not absolutely ridiculous, but united with jealousy it was unpardonable.

Goldoni saw how a man, deeply attached to his wife and to his money, could be made dreadfully unhappy and yet appear interesting. He saw how a woman, attached to such a husband, could become a martyr indeed if she tried to reconcile her wifely affection with her social obligations, her fear of scandal, and of the endless consequences of open rebellion.

He grasped the situation; but for once Goldoni's conception was greater than his art, perhaps because the plan and the characters are tragic, and kind-hearted, opportunistic Goldoni, considering the taste of his audience and the capacity of his interpreters, avoided the darker aspects of truth. A tragedy the passionate vehemence of Pantalone's miserliness, a tragedy the meekness and helplessness of Eufemia; but Goldoni could not exhibit on the stage this tragedy of so many households; the all-powerful code of Venetian custom forbade any recognition of this tragic situation. Thus limited both in his own mind and in the mind of the public, Goldoni forces the note and makes his miser more grotesque than cruel.

The first scenes are the best. Jealous Pantalone allows his wife to accept valuable presents from Don Luigi, a candidate for her favours, only to take them from her as soon as the cavalier's back is turned. He scolds Eufemia for encouraging Don Luigi, he listens behind a curtain to the *conversazione* which he has insisted on bringing about. He rages when he thinks that Eufemia is too polite in her treatment of this second-rate Don Juan. Yet fearing punishment for usury, he asks Eufemia to intercede with a magistrate who had once paid her attention. This situation is powerful. The husband who loves his wife, who wants to keep her pure, yet induces her to write a compromising note, reveals a significant side of Venetian life. Too significant, perhaps; that is why Goldoni turns short and brings about a conventional ending. The magistrate is wise; he scolds, he frightens Pantalone out of his jealousy, brings about a general reconciliation, and, than which nothing could be more improbable, persuades Pantalone to give up his miserly ways and his usury.

Around these principal characters and this central plot certain minor characters revolve that add to the liveliness of the play and provide the modern reader with much information about the customs of the time. Don Luigi's sister is a most natural intriguer, ready to act as her brother's ambassador carrying messages and gifts, yet when rebuked she retorts like a vixen. Her husband, a counterpart of Pantalone, indolent and absent-minded, is apparently a portrait. One of the prettiest scenes in this play shows a gathering of housewives crowding round Pantalone, their habitual money-lender. Their gossip, their denunciation of every petty scandal in the neighbourhood, their easy admission of their own contrivances, make up a delightful scene *de genre*. As a bit of genuine fun, it deserves place with the popular plays in Venetian dialect.

Even before leaving Medebach, Goldoni strayed into other fields than pictures of everyday life and of family intrigues. He essayed an inferior military play, *L'amante Militare*, and waited ten years before again attempting a similar subject. Goldoni's *Memoirs*, and indeed all contemporary Italian *Memoirs*, prove the entire absence of nationalism, the political indifference of Italians; and this play emphasizes it. The officers, duelling and quarrelling, never express a patriotic emotion. When the drums beat, the summons must be obeyed because disobedience would be punished. There is no enthusiasm; not even interest or curiosity. Don Garzia represents the swaggering, profligate roisterer, degenerate offspring of the Miles Gloriosus, and he is a failure.

The character was never a favourite one with the Venetian public and players; they lacked models. Readers of Manzoni's and of Nievo's masterpieces will remember what the sentiment was in Lombardy and in the Venetian States against the militia. They were roisterers and plunderers; in war times the terror of peaceful folk, and in time of peace ludicrous buffoons. Captain Sandracca, whom Nievo paints so amusingly in *Confessioni d'un Ottugenario*, parading at the head of a company of louts "that carried their guns like hose," threatening them with the long, rusty blade of his useless sword; Captain Sandracca, who gloried in the wounds (received in the lower part of his back) that he always offered to show, — impersonates the soldier in a country that knew nothing about the realities of war. Centuries of peace had dulled the military spirit.

In Naples, where the Spanish oppressor provided many patterns of roistering braggarts, the character of "Miles Gloriosus" developed and multiplied into several types of Italian masks; Spaccamontagna, Spaventa, and the different avatars of Coviella, such as Salvator Rosa impersonated and multiplied. In Venice the character nearly died out. Nor was Goldoni equipped to give it a new life. His own experience of camp life could only suggest instances of polite courtesy among officers, and some military love-making. And this is all he attempted in his *Amante Militare.* Once more in *La Guerra* he will take up this subject, to show the surroundings of an army, the camp followers, and purveyors.[1]

Another of Goldoni's unfortunate attempts was *Il Feudatorio*, a promising title with little to justify it. While in the *Cancelleria* and also during the *villeggiature* in lordly castles, Goldoni acquired some experience of the relations between the peasantry and their feudal lords; he may have witnessed the meeting of village deputies, listened to their harangues, observed their manners toward their master, and their rivalries and quarrels among themselves. Yet he never seems to have penetrated beyond the superficial appearances. He looked for amusement and was satisfied to amuse his audience. A foppish young lord, a proud but kindly inclined dowager, a patient and injured heiress, a group of villagers and their wives, simple-minded

[1] For Goldoni could not represent or understand patriotism and militarism. See chapter on General Ideas. His *Memoirs* evidence his pacifism.

but shrewd; Pantalone standing between them as the necessary link in the endless chain of social relation, are his characters in this ineffective play.

Lady Beatrice and her son, Marquis Florindo, hold the estate in virtue of a renunciation by Rosaura's late father of his rights as the eldest son of the family. Pantalone protects the orphan girl, but he does not encourage her to litigate against her aunt and cousin; the villagers avoid these matters as long as they are left alone. It is only when Florindo comes blustering and love-making, offending every man with his insolence, every woman with his proposals, that there is a mutiny to vindicate Rosaura's title and set her in her rightful place. Needless to say things are immediately straightened by a marriage between the two cousins.

Many scenes in this play are marred by excessive buffoonery. The assembly of village deputies, their speeches to the young lord; the presentation of the village ladies to the marchioness, their astonishment at being offered the ritual cup of chocolate, their attempts at making conversation are — not unworthy; but on the whole the play is justly forgotten.[1]

After 1752 Goldoni's friendship with Arconati Visconti, with Albergati, and Gaspare Gozzi grew more intimate; and he was admitted to some of the most select drawing-rooms: Maria Sagredo Pisani, to whom

[1] How democratic Goldoni considered the differences of caste, how he respected aristocracy, and also his viewpoint of feudalism, are considered in the chapter on his general ideas.

he dedicated *La Dama Prudente*; Faustino Rezzonico, related to Pope Clement XIII and to Procuratore Aurelio Rezzonico; Cecilia Quirini Tron, at whose palace his plays were performed; Cornelia Barbaro Gritti, (in Arcadia, Aurisbe Tarsiense), whose favours were disputed by Frugoni and Chiari, two worldly and well-known literary abbots, while perhaps the lady inclined toward our author; Gaetana Agnesi, who dedicated to Goldoni her treatise on algebra which won for her the professorship at the university of Bologna; and many more names on the patrician list of the Golden Book, many more names on the honour list of letters and arts, show the poet's popularity in Venetian society. The number of short poems, compliments, and *capitoli* which he wrote for every solemnity in great households, for marriages and births, and more frequently still for the admission into a convent of high-born ladies, for the return home of public personages or their entering into office—all testify to Goldoni's position in the best society of Venice.[1]

[1] Goldoni was also a guest of the celebrated Procuratessa Tron. In letter XXV. Ed. Urbani de Gheltof, he tells about two little abbots quarrelling in this drawing-room and coming to blows in the street. One of them mistaking *el feral de la riva* (lamp on the canal) for his adversary aimed such a blow at it that it broke in pieces.

About Lady Barbaro Gritti and her amours, see Achille Neri, *Aneddoti Goldoniani;* Ancona, Morelli, 1883, pp. 40 and following. Also P. Ortolani, *op. cit.*

The list of Goldoni's illustrious friends is long and interesting to Italians. Among Venetians, Andrea Quirini, Alviso Da Mosto, Vittor Gradenigo, Michele Grimani, Andrea Memmo, Nicolò Balbi, Parmenio Trission (grandson to the author of Sophonisbe). Elsewhere in Italy Antonio Uguccioni, a Florentine patrician, Count Federigo Orazio Landini, a poet, his champion

He was the author *à la mode*, whom everybody asked to write something; his kindness and lack of vanity prompted him to satisfy all these demands. Thus much of his precious time was lost on worthless compositions, as he himself realised. In a *capitolo* to advocate Alcaimi he explains how *Non si fa matrimonio benedetto*. "Whoever comes in my house may see — the tables, shelves, and also the chairs — covered with orders sent to me. Some ask for a drama, some for a comedy; some ask for a *capitolo* or a sonnet, that the whole world may be tired at my expense. There is not a blessed marriage, not a virgin donning the sacred veil, that does not oblige me to write in rhyme. A lady sends me word that her daughter is about to become a nun, that something from my pen is expected. My duty urges me to obedience; quick, let me sing the praise of the wise maiden and her family. I take my pen in hand, and I hear someone coming who says: Dost know who is marrying? a pretty girl and a gallant youth. The illustrious house invite thee to versify; leave every other study aside. If thou declinest, the cavalier will be wroth."

Such was the price paid to fame by Goldoni. His profits must have been considerable.

against Chiari and the Granelleschi, Ferdinando Borromeo, Count of Arona. At Albergati Capacelli's villa he was an honoured guest of Marchioness Eleonora Albergati née Bentivoglio d'Aragona, of imperial descent. He met there also Cardinal Lambertini, afterward pope, several artists, Marco Pitteri and Pietro Longhi, besides Piazzetta. A little later Goldoni became intimate with the family Cornet. To G. Cornet many of his letters are addressed. (See *Life*.)

He learned much even while he took his share of amusement. Casanova pronounces him shy and seldom talkative. Grosely, in his *Nouveaux Mêmoires*, asserts that he was a cheerful and amiable man, and that in the autumn during the *villeggiatura*, he was a valuable director for amateur theatricals and a funny actor, impersonating impromptu caricatures, his best acting being a parody of mountebanks and street sellers. Both these sketches contain part of truth. Goldoni was often silent when engrossed in the study of models; he was a boon companion and a witty *amuseur* when he thought it his duty to pay for his welcome. He observed keenly, if not deeply; he stored in his mind the many things worth noting; he listened to anecdotes and fixed the outline of a personage; but what is more important for a complete picture of a society, he caught the intonation, the colouring, the accent of this little world.

That special atmosphere of gallantry and sensualism, of humour and common sense, that veneering of excessive politeness, the honeyed compliment concealing the sting of scandal, that dainty malice, the pretty manners, the artificial grace and elegance which made the Venetian society attractive, all this Goldoni perceived and reproduced in his plays.

The change came subtly. From his first *Cortesan* to the later impersonations of the man of the world the distance is great. Yet there is not a moment when the turning point can be fixed. This epochal period between first recognised success and departure for Paris, 1752 to 1760, marks a continual progress toward a consummate excellence which suggests the regret that Goldoni's exile to Paris has stifled the complete expansion of his genius.

If for instance we take *Il Vecchio Bizzarro*, and we compare it to *Momolo Cortesan* or to *Il Prodigo*, we find that the change is more than maturity of the character, larger comprehension of the world, and of his own powers. It is a refinement of the whole personage into a more subtle charm, due to daily contact with gentlemen and ladies of delicacy. Pantalone has, like Goldoni, gained admission into the higher circles, and he has moulded his manners, his very feelings and sentiments, on the patrician pattern. Is it all gain for the personage, and for the class of men he impersonates? Has simple-minded, free-hearted Momolo not lost something of his moral poise in gaining a daintier wit?

Goldoni's Pantalone is benevolent, kind-hearted, polite, and talkative even from his first presentation; meddling and fussy in his untiring efforts to advise and direct those he still calls his betters, though he well knows that they want his help far more than he desires their protection; persistent in his endeavours to end their quarrels and pacify their households; he has grown more self-conscious and a little bit more self-asserting as his account at the bank has enlarged, and his social position gradually expanded.

As ever with Goldoni, the creation of a novel character, or the transformation of an old one, is always suggested by the artist that he has in mind who is ready to impersonate it. In this case it was Rubini who, even when past his prime, could be, like Goldoni, an attractive companion, an agreeable gallant. The play failed to please because it came before its time. It anticipated that which has since become a canon of theatrical art, that there may be a power for charming in characters that are no longer young.

Pantalone has preserved the active grace of youth. He is still the same Momolo, the Cortesan who drew his sword or his purse to serve the stranger and to protect him against sharpers. The opening scenes give a corresponding situation. Pantalone finds Ottavio, a Livornese gentleman, in the hands of a Venetian gambler and swindler, Martino, and immediately Pantalone interferes. At first, he interferes wittily, thrusting the arrows of his dialectal sayings, but when the bully draws a stiletto, Pantalone is ready with his dagger.

"Against your own country," tauntingly cries Martino, the sharper. "You lie!" says Pantalone, "I am a good Venetian, ready to give up my life for my countryman; but I cannot allow a Venetian to wrong a foreigner." When he has frightened away the bully, Pantalone gently but firmly tells Ottavio that a debt of honour must be paid. Ottavio sends Brighella to pawn a diamond ring. Martino chances to pass by and he seizes the ring, only to be again threatened by Pantalone, who himself pays Ottavio's debt and keeps the ring, remitting later its whole price to the young man, in order to get rid of him.

Pantalone is amusingly shown as a foil to Celio, a *malade imaginaire*, a caricature of those Venetian idlers who spent their aimless life in shaking with fear at the idea of losing it. Celio is a lifelike portrait, slightly changed for the perspective of the stage. Goldoni may have observed some of these unmanly terrors in himself, but he never nursed them long, and cured himself by hard work. From Doctor Giulio he may have learned how to cure the imaginary illness by cheerful talk, playful suggestions, and even some mild chaffing. Rabelais, in his time, could have done no better to cure a patient by forcing him to drink good wine instead of water and powders, by persuading him to share in a good dinner at the nearest club, than Pantalone does here with Celio. He closes the scene with a little sermon appropriate to the Venetian audience: Eat nothing but simple and healthy food, avoid every excess.

Another aspect of Pantalone's complex personality. He flirts with Clarice, a coquettish widow, who ridicules him. He hints the inclination he guesses she has for Florindo:

Pant. — Look here, did I not hit the mark? When once I look into a woman's eyes, I am sure to read what she wants.

Clar. — The proverb says that the devil is wise because he is old.

Pant. — I am wiser still.

Clar. — Why?

Pant. — Because the devil trusts women, and I do not.

Clar. — You have never been in love.

Pant. — Never in my whole life.

Clar. — There's no telling what may happen.

Pant. — Who has a good nose can know a good melon.

Clar. — Yet I know that you like the company of women.

Pant. — Indeed I do. I behold them with my eyes, never with my heart.

Clar. — If one goes to the mill, one gets powdered with flour.

Pant. — If one is wise, one can brush it away in a twinkling.

Clar. (*aside*) — How I would like to entrap this elderly gentleman.

Pant. (*aside*) — She is shrewd, but still I can give her points.

Clar. — You are not yet past hope of chance.

Pant. — Of course I have not yet lost the chart for sailing.

Clar. — Your spirit puts to shame a man of twenty.

Pant. — My spirit and my flesh are just what they were at twenty.

Clar. — I dare say that you were a fine-looking man.

Pant. — I should not say it; but with this face I have done some fine things.

Clar. — And you are willing to go on.

Pant. — Why not? A veteran soldier does not refuse to fight.

Clar. — Oh, dear Signor Pantalone!

Pant. — Sometimes I am dear, and sometimes very cheap.

Clar. — I have no wealth to buy your favour.

Pant. — We can talk about that. You must never say I will not eat of that bread.

Clar. — Indeed I cannot believe that you have never been in love.

Pant. — Why can you not?

Clar. — Because there is something in you so amiable, so courteous, that it makes me incredulous.

Pant. — Maybe I have never yet met with anyone quite to my liking.

Clar. — You are still in time.

Pant. — There is no saying what may happen.

Clar. — What is it that you want to please your taste?

Pant. — Only a few things.

Clar. — If I were so fortunate . . .

Pant. — Would you condescend?

Clar. — If only you were satisfied.

Pant. — By and by we might come to an understanding.

Clar. (*aside*) — The fool is almost entrapped.

Pant. (*aside*) — I don't believe a word she says.

Clar. — Ah, Signor Pantalone!

Pant. — Ah, Signora Clarice!

Clar. — What does this sigh mean?

Pant. — I let you interpret it.

Clar. — I am almost inclined to hope. . . .

Pant. — If one goes to the mill, one is likely to get powdered with flour.

Clar. — If one is wise, one can brush it off in a twinkling.

Pant. — Unless it penetrates.

Clar. — Here's someone coming. Good-by, Signor Pantalone.

Pant. (*aside*) — No, my dear, you cannot catch me.

As a counterpart to this coquettish fencing, the scenes with Flamminia show Pantalone truly falling in love for good. From the moment of his slowly realising his own desires, from the first spark of hope which his diffidence chokes, caution bids him disguise in sober talk or in delightfully impertinent innuendoes; it is a crescendo of suppressed emotion most modern and interesting. A few changes might make of this play a real *comédie de mœurs* adapted to our more sensitive but not more reticent age. In such a case Pantalone should be shown much older, since a man past thirty would not now be talked of as an old man.

It is the curse of comedy that in order to please its audience it must be of the most exact actuality. Not only in representing the time and the conditions, even if the subject be apparently historical, but also in corresponding exactly to the degree of intellectual and moral development, to the æsthetic and ethic standards of the day. The lyric or the tragic poet may with equal success anticipate the future or revive the past; not so the comic poet. Those who listened to the *Vecchio Bizzarro* failed to catch its subtle wit, and the same public who had many times applauded Goldoni now misunderstood him entirely.

Of course Chiari and his set, the Granelleschi, and many petty scribblers of verse and prose were busy in their attacks against the man they were forced to recognise as a master, and to envy for his favour with the patricians, but still the battle might have turned out otherwise if the pit had proved more faithful. Goldoni drank deep in the cup of bitterness that night when he heard his play described, at the Ridotto, as a complete failure, as the proof that he had emptied his bag. Whether a real bag of borrowed manuscripts, or the metaphorical bag of ready invention, whoever spoke these unkind words is unimportant.

The result was to send Goldoni, hot with anger, to pen a new play, in verse, meant to contain a defence of his method and reform. *Il Festino's* only title to fame is this attempt of self-criticism and self-defence. It is like many other descriptions of Venetian customs and resembles *La Moglie Saggia* in plot and conduct of the piece, but the scene in which Goldoni rehearses all the ridiculous things which he had heard in the Ridotto, keeping up a dispute for and against the piece and the author, is a document of great importance for the reconstruction of the intellectual atmosphere, and of Goldoni's feelings at this moment.

The effect of this failure coming atop of other bitter circumstances, Medebach and Bettinelli's appropriation of his copyrights, Chiari's appointment by Medebach to fill the place he had held in the same theatre of S. Angelo, the first rumbling of the storm that Carlo Gozzi was preparing against him, the difficulty he found in managing the players of San Luca, in teaching them his own method of recitation, the scanty support he was given by *Sua Eccellenza Padrona* Vendramin, the conditions of the San Luca Theatre, a larger house, a wider stage, all these things combining with that lack of critical discernment which is the fundamental weakness of Goldoni, — all these circumstances forced him to adopt a style and manner foreign to his aptitudes and to compose the many romantic tragi-comedies which are registered in the complete list of his works.

CHAPTER XI

THE PLAYS (1754 TO 1760)

Efforts to popularise Goldoni's works outside of Italy — but foreigners have never understood his merits and originality — beyond all other playwrights he understood the psychology of the family — as a microcosm of the surrounding society — his personages are purely Venetian — he is always original, even when he borrows — the influence of each member on the rest of the family group is accurately depicted — each of his family groups has an atmosphere of its own — every detail is accurate and adequate — Pantalone his favourite character — expresses the true Venetian ideas — such pictures as *La Buona Famiglia* truly represent that mystery, the inside of a household — *La Madre Amorosa* truly represents the Venetian ideal as to the marriageable girl — in *La Donna di Governo* each character is distinct — yet shows common family traits — *La Figlia Obbediente* presents Goldoni's viewpoint as to marriage — the Venetian viewpoint — the duty of the father to choose the husband — in relation of father and son Goldoni also holds for patriarchal authority — sons must obey — character of Florindo is settled by tradition — not clever, not industrious — for whom his father must find a rich wife — when he is wicked he calls him Lelio — when he has spirit and charm he calls him Cortesan — the parasite of classical comedy has no exact equivalent in Italian life, where the hanger-on was often a poet — Pantalone is the central personage of the family — importance of the servants in family affairs — Arlecchino and Brighella — Beatrice and Rosaura — Colombina is also important in the family circle — *La Casa Nuova* is typical of Venetian customs — real position of women in Venetian family and society was contradictory — custom was indulgent to feminine frailty — serventism, or cicisbeism — Zio Cristofolo in *La Casa Nuova* is the first purely Goldonian *rustego* — a character he repeatedly uses — his character described — *I Rusteghi* presents four different views of this type — play described — a document of historic value — Goldoni often represents the *villeggiatura* — a peculiar feature of Italian life — this life of city-people in the country forms background of several plays — *villeggiatura* described.

FROM the great number of Goldoni's plays an attempt has been made in the preceding chapter to select those that present especial interest to students of Italian customs, and also those that are generally accepted as his masterpieces. It is more difficult to summarise the general plan, the distinctive character of this voluminous production.

Even during Goldoni's lifetime critics endeavoured to popularise his works abroad. Even before the posthumous eulogy of Marie Joseph Chenier, several French writers had praised his work, much attention was given to his *Bourru Bienfaisant*, and the great success of *Camille* was not entirely attributed to the beautiful and talented actress that impersonated the Goldonian heroine. Yet it is doubtful whether the French or any foreign audience understood the essential merit and original trait of Goldoni's plays. Praise and criticism fall at random. Discussions about the morality of plots, the originality, the realism, the search for sources, have caused many a learned biographer of Goldoni to miss the essential Goldonian excellence. Even the earlier Italian critics misunderstand their task when they discussed Goldoni's style and the purity of his Italian.

The distinctive quality of Goldoni's work, the trait that sets him entirely apart from every other modern playwriter, is his insight and skill in painting family groups. Compared with even the greatest, Goldoni better understood the psychology of the family, more subtly investigated the bonds that unite the members of a household and give to it the unity of a living organism. His equal in comprehension and in capacity for rendering this aspect of life is only found in some novel writers, either of the realistic Balzac school or of the homely English school. Like the former, Goldoni sees each family as a microcosm of the surrounding society; like the latter, Goldoni discerns the infinite hues, the delicate pencilling of traits, that unite in creating a type out of a number of individuals.

Customs and the literary criterion of his time, which precluded the study of the individual as a factor of social evolution, enforced this natural tendency of Goldoni's. Since he could not follow the diplomat or the statesman or the politician in their office, or voice any opinion as to the feelings and doings of a priest, Goldoni investigated the household, with just a side-light on the merchant's office or shop that were so closely connected with the homestead.

Goldoni's characters, Goldoni's pictures, do not generalise. They exactly represent the people of the time and place which he knew and loved—Venetians of the first half of 1700. Even when he placed the scene in another city, or another country, his personages are purely Venetians. In most cases, they were so located and surrounded as to reconstrue a something that was almost Venetian. As for instance the Dutch household of Doctor Bainer in the *Medico Olandese*, wherein a few traits, borrowed from books of travel, cannot disguise the Venetian simplicity, politeness, and habits of sober conviviality. But these Venetian homes are so lovingly observed and so cleverly represented that they make a long gallery of finished and individualised pictures.[1]

[1] When Goldoni ventured out of his own Venice why did he prefer Dutch characters? *Il Medico Olandese*, performed in 1757, was meant, he says, to extol the celebrated doctor, Boerhaave, and to represent under the

Even when Goldoni borrows the plot, incidents, or characters, even when he imitates one of his earlier plays or that of some other author, the background of family interests and affections is original. His people are not always solidly constructed, not always complete as a psychological study. Their social standing is not always definite, owing to Goldoni's indifference to large social problems, but they always clearly suggest their relative positions as members of a family group.

The influence of the social, economic, religious, and political world upon them and their own contribution to that great world is hardly mentioned, but the manner, the measure, in which they influence their immediate relatives and how their relatives influence them is simply depicted.[1]

In those romantic and exotic plays such as the three Ircane, or the three clumsy evocations of poets, Terenzio, Tasso, Molière, the few hints of this realism are so smothered by false romanticism and blurred senti-

name of Guden the author himself and his habitual troubles, whether neurasthenic or cardiac. But why does Goldoni select Holland again for his play, *Un Curioso Accidente?* What reports could he hear of Dutch manners in Venice?

Both *Curioso Accidente* and *Medico Olandese* contain pretty *scènes d'intérieur* that might just as well be located in some Venetian household.

[1] Thackeray, Balzac, Zola, and Federico de Roberto are novelists who powerfully conceived, and deeply investigated, questions of heredity and reciprocal influence of relatives. Goldoni lacks their science. He could not conceive the large plan of those epic novels that embrace three generations, extend over scores of personages, and form a complete whole. He could only condense his observations into a vivid picture of one flitting moment in the history of a family. Intuition, rather than methodical reasoning, indicated to him the proper moment to select, the proper grouping of his personages.

mentalism that they are lost in the general misconception of the play. Happily these blunders are rare, and when Goldoni has followed his own inspiration and the taste of his own public he has successfully represented his Venetian families.

Each of these families has an atmosphere, a tone which distinguish it from every other. *La Famiglia dell'Antiquario* is one of the first.[1] Although the indications for the stage are short and vague, yet the play is so tightly constructed that reader and hearer can easily reconstrue the general plan of the building, the division of apartments, as reserved to one or the other lady, the aspects of rooms furnished according to the habits of the dweller. The position of each member of the household is so clearly defined by the dialogue that the picture is conjured almost without effort. Even a slight knowledge of the ceremonious mannerism then governing family relations of middle-class Venetians suffices to imagine the polite irony, veiled impertinence, affected coolness the wealthy daughter-in-law spoke to her high-born, extravagant,

[1] *La Famiglia dell'Antiquario*, the sixth of the sixteen comedies, was soon translated into German, Vienna, 1765, Berlin and Breslau two years later, Frankfort and Leipzig in 1787, and some time later into French by M. Collet (see *Bibliografia Goldoniana*, A. G. Spinelli, *op. cit.*, page 246 and passim). But it was never, we think, translated into English. Yet the peculiar fun and ridicule of the unlearned collector might be appreciated in English; and the complete picture of a Venetian family with all the typical annexes of *cavalieri serventi*, servants, etc., would assist in understanding Goldoni's art. Being an early production, *La Famiglia dell'Antiquario* is more realistic than later plays of the same sort — a reason for selecting it as illustrative of Goldoni's early manner.

unscrupulous mother-in-law. The surrounding characters fall naturally into their places, the exact proportion of flattery and impertinence, of respect and mockery shown them, creating the tone which unifies the whole play. Every lifelike detail finds adequate place in such pictures.

Pantalone's common sense is wrapped into wordy speeches. He scolds, but because of his inborn respect for the aristocracy, he would not offend. Even while he tries to stop the antiquarian's folly, the woman's extravagance, he realises that such vices are peculiar to a caste that he honours. And Pantalone's ideas being those of his Venice, they colour and give shape to Goldoni's reconstruction of the whole household, with all its belongings and surroundings; with just that type of visitors and of servants as by choice would naturally belong to such a group in the Venice of that time.

To modern readers, some of Goldoni's plays are called prosy and affected with a sentimentalism which is now pronounced intolerable. Homely pictures, futile plots, and incidents abound. But these pictures do truly represent that mystery — the inside of a household. *La Buona Famiglia* has no other title to remembrance. A clumsy plot, puerile incidents, yet is it a mezzotint of almost Flemish realism in the representation of a model household. Mark the talk of servant and young mistress discussing their duties as assistant housekeepers; the exact shade of husbandry and shrewdness displayed by the father, and his respectful submission to the head of the family, to the patriarch, who dictates the law with the benevolent solemnity of an oracle that ignores possible opposition! *La Madre Amorosa* appears foolish to the foreigner persuaded that a girl should herself choose her life partner. Yet it truly represents the spirit of dead generations of Venetians, their ideals of duty, of authority and propriety.

A characteristic picture is to be found in *La Donna di Governo* which Goldoni so planned as to provide opportunities for the actress impersonating the principal character.[1] Unworthy as a psychological study, it is a good example of the reaction of each individual in these family groups on the others and also describes how the forced union of relationship has influenced the very soul, manners, and language of each member. The senile imbecility of the head of the house is cause and effect of the housekeeper's preëminence. As a consequence of this anomaly the girls have grown either silly or shrewish, according to their capacity for tolerating injuries. An aged aunt who vainly tries to fight against the intruder has become peevish and foul-mouthed. Every servant in the house has been per-

[1] *La Donna di Governo* is not generally considered one of Goldoni's best plays. It was not well received at its first appearance in 1758 and Goldoni made an apology for this failure in his *Memoirs*, yet this family picture, representing a family going to destruction as a consquence of its chief's infatuation for a spirited, revengeful, brazen woman, has the value of a document. It is most moral in showing how from one folly many evil influences spread out on the tight-knit group of human creatures forming a family.

In a gallery of Venetian characters Goldoni has not included the *avventuriere*, although he must have met more than one besides Giacomo Casanova de Seingalt. Guglielmo in the *Avventuriere Onorato* is merely a man who has tried many trades.

verted or seduced. Each character has so developed that without losing individualism and the relief of artistic creations, they show common family traits, a common level, a graduation of hues in the same colour line.

Goldoni often adopted the marriage question as the subject of these family dissensions. Usually he considers marriage as the panacea for many ills. His own personal experience and his good sense suggested to him that the ideal of happiness and prosperity could only be reached through legitimate union. He anticipated his countrymen's notions when he insisted that those directly interested in the affair should be consulted in the choice of a partner.[1] He deemed that a father could better judge of character than a silly girl; but he opposed the intrusion of other people. Thus, when the play turns on the fight for or against a marriage, it is generally an uncle or a foolish mother[2] who is pilloried.

That a girl convent-educated, or kept in semi-Oriental seclusion, should be free to choose was preposterous. He believed that a wise and protecting watch should

[1] For girls and their right to chose their husbands see Goldoni's *General Ideas*.

[2] One of these mothers is in *Il Tutore*, another one in *L'Adulatore;* both are painted so black that they suggest Goldoni's personal grudge against mothers affecting juvenile airs and rivalry with their own daughters. If the many adventures so prettily narrated in his memoirs are even partly true, they might offer some clue to this feeling; as, for instance, the story of his love-making with the school-girl at Chiozza and the interference of a reverend mother, or the imbroglio accounting for his departure from Venice (see *Life*).

be exerted by a father or by some other near relative; that there should be a reform of the patriarchal custom, not a revolution. Goldoni considered this reform a return to ancient simplicity rather than a social innovation.[1]

He means a married pair to be like the centre of a column, with the supreme authority of the patriarch above them and the brood of younger ones below.

In order to understand the general plan of Goldoni's ethics, it is necessary to consider his plays in the light of this moral standpoint. Thus if *La Figlia Obbediente* appears childish in her acceptation of a husband she neither likes nor esteems, simply because her father has promised her hand, and if her father, Pantalone, appears cruel in insisting on this marriage, let it be remembered that a Venetian father generally selected the best possible match on the market, believing this to be his duty and to be best for his child. Rebellion surprised him. He knew that his only aim was the welfare of his child, in so far as this welfare could be reconciled with the predominant interests of the family.

Why should a girl rebel? Nor did she as a rule. Rosaura, weeping at the prospect of accepting this uncouth bridegroom, perceives that moral obligation prohibits her bringing disgrace to her father by forcing him to break his promise. Nor does she doubt the kindness of his intentions. Rosaura expresses the feelings of the average Venetian girl. She appealed

[1] For Goldoni's ideas on marriage see *General Ideas*.

to the audience because she represented the position faced by most Venetian girls.[1]

Goldoni in *La Figlia Obbediente* pays homage to filial obedience by setting, as a foil to weeping, gentle Rosaura, a trifler of doubtful morality, a dancing girl daubed in glaring colours, with more realistic severity than Goldoni generally displays, hectoring an over-indulgent and foolish father. There is a meaning, in

[1] *La Figlia Obbediente*, act i, sc. 5. Rosaura has heard of Florindo's home-coming and of his intention to marry her after obtaining his father's consent, and she is overflowing with joy; Pantalone checks her.

Pant. — Not one word more. I have promised you to another man. Two hours ago the contract was agreed.

Ros. — Heavens! Without telling me!

Pant. — There was no time to lose. The match cannot be better — a man of birth, of money, and also generous.

Ros. — Without telling me!

Pant. — My dear girl, I know not what to say. It was an opportunity. The man's temper is whimsical. I found him in the right humour; my friends advised me to bind him, and so I did. Now, 'tis done; and 'tis signed and there is no undoing it.

Ros. — The generous, wealthy, noble-born gentleman you speak of, is it Count Ottavio?

Pant. — Himself! What do you say to it? Was it a match one could allow to slip away?

Ros. — Poor me! You have made me terribly unhappy.

Pant. — Unhappy! Why so?

Ros. — Because I know his temper, his whims, the strangeness of his ways.

Pant. — You also know that he is wealthy, that he is noble, and that a clever woman who knows how to manage him will twist him round her finger without difficulty. . . . You will be like a queen.

Ros. — He will jilt me within four days.

Pant. — You take me for a fool; he settles on you ten thousand ducats as a *controdote*.

Ros. — Oh, father. You were blinded for once by the idea of interest.

Pant. — You shock me, madam! I have not done anything for greed,

this contrast, even beyond the comic effect. Brighella boasting of his daughter's gains, recounting her glories, on and off the boards, is the father who had abdicated his authority and left his offspring free to drift into vice. His indulgence is presented as a contrast to Pantalone's excessive interference.[1]

but only for the love I bear you. A father who is without means cannot provide for you according to your merits. Chance sends me an opportunity to provide for your happiness, and you expect me not to seize it? A nobleman falls in love with a girl of good family. He asks for her hand from her father; if the father hesitates the man may change his mind. The girl is the loser. A wise father will decide quickly and make things tight. So have I done, Rosaura; I have decided, I have promised. . . .

Pant. — Rosaura, you have ever been obedient; you were always proud of your submission; this is the time to make proof of it. Obedience is worth little unless it can master passion. I ask the consent of your obedience, so that you may have the merit of proving yourself grateful toward me; anyhow, if you dare oppose me, I can make use of my paternal authority. I am your father: I have the right to dispose of my daughter. . . .

The scene, however, closes with kinder words. "Look here, Rosaura, marriage for love or by constraint I compare to an ice cream and a medicine. The ice cream you take with pleasure, but the pleasure passes, and indigestion remains; medicine you take with distaste, but when it gets inside your stomach it is good for your health. Since you cannot have the ice cream, Florindo, make the best you can of the medicine, Count Ottavio. See if it does not agree with you in the end."

Rosaura does not fight against her father's will. Act i, sc. 6 (*alone*). "What shall I do? Resist my father's order? Undo his arrangements by open disobedience? No! I cannot do such a thing. My honesty does not allow of it. But what of Florindo? Will it be possible for me to forget him? Time and prudence are doctors to the greatest ills. Who can tell? I still trust in Providence to save my heart, without losing the merit of honest submission."

[1] In opposition to Rosaura and her domineering father, contrast Olivetta the ballet girl and her father Brighella boasting about the costly gifts received from admirers, begging openly for more from Count Ottavio; see scene 16 of first act, and also scenes 17 and 18, ending with Count Ottavio throwing his coat at Brighella's head. . . . "This is an insult. But I can put up with it. The coat is very rich. I can wear it. Am I not the father of an artist?"

Goldoni would have broken with every tradition of fiction and drama if he had not made much of this great affair of marriage, but in his conception of the family there is also the reciprocal position of father and son. Here, too, Goldoni holds for the principle of authority, for respect to patriarchal tradition; but here, too, Goldoni would introduce that attenuated reform which he considers as sufficient. More than once he has boldly shown rebellious sons that were neither vicious nor besotted. Though plentifully borrowing from the old plays, or classical models that made sons the accomplices and equals in folly and degradation of their rascally servants, Goldoni has, sometimes, presented sons wiser than their parents.[1]

An exception which does not contradict the rule is that sons must obey. Indeed obedience and thrift are the only demands of their parents. Neither Goldoni nor his countrymen expected or demanded more from a youth. "He does not gamble . . . he does not haunt bad company . . . he does not fall into debt." When this is told of a marriageable young man it appears to all concerned that he has a right to be provided for. His father or guardian must *far gli uno stato*, of which the equivalent may be "establish him in the world" — a euphemism for picking out for him a pretty wife and a large *dot*. All those who plot and intrigue for him are doing an honourable and meri-

[1] In *La Bancarotta* the father is ridiculed by a demirep and her accomplice; while the steady son endeavors to arrange honourably the firm's affairs. This satire, for being too bitter and pointed, was disguised under much irrelevant fun.

torious thing. Corallina,[1] the dainty avatar of pert Colombina, thinks only of securing for Florindo a wealthy heiress. The character of Florindo [2] is handed down from the past either through the classic or the popular comedy, with traits almost as definitely settled by tradition as those of the masks. He is nerveless and puerile; sometimes he falls in love, but mostly he is made love to. He is not clever, and takes for granted that he is not expected to work. Fathers, be they Pantalone or some higher-born personage, never rely on him and seldom trust him. Everybody considers him somewhat like a child to be scolded or petted, provided for or restrained. Goldoni took the personage almost as he found him, comparison with reality required no revision of the character. Florindo, on the stage, was a fair equivalent of the young fop lounging day and night wherever amusement was to be found; avoiding every place where business was transacted; avoiding intellectual effort; claiming little, and submitting to almost any guidance. When a young man showed spirit Goldoni adorned him with the charms of a "Cortesan"; when he drifted into wickedness he called him Lelio — the gambler or the liar.

Lelio and the Cortesan are not, however, as important

[1] Corallina in *Serva Amorosa* and Mirandolina in *La Locandiera* are characters worth separate study.

[2] Parini's *Giorno* presents a fiercer satire of this character (Florindo). No comparison can be established, since Venice and Milan were then entirely different in manners and customs and then a satirical poem is not a play. Also no comparison is possible between the two writers and their æsthetic and ethic viewpoints.

as Florindo for the study of the family. They carve for themselves outside of the homely circle, while Florindo, mild and patient, retains some of the charm and the tricks of a child; hence he has a place within the intimate circle of the family. Bright and clever girls in search of a husband are shown plotting and contriving: *La Donna di Garbo* will display treasures of learning and ability to win him back, after he has shamefully deserted her. Evidently Goldoni disliked these effeminate young men and did not care to attenuate their deficiencies. He left them within the family circle almost in the same dishonourable place which Ariosto, Gelli, and other classics assigned to their shadowy personality.

One personage of the ancient repertoire which Goldoni does not entirely eliminate but uses sparingly is the parasite. This important element of classical comedy did not answer to exact reality in Italian life. Persons ready to pick the crumbs from a wealthy or influential patron's table were never wanting; but they were not as entirely helpless nor as lowly serviceable in Italian courts and grand households as they were in older times, either in Greece or in Rome. They were expected to use their wits or the force of their arm in the service of the man who supported them; while round the triclinium of a Trimalcion, they crouched like dogs, ready to lap any refuse or swallow any insult. In Roman times they generally came out of the caste of slaves and climbed into favour by the most abject complaisance. In Italian courts, and also in princely families, the hanger-on was often a poet, or at least a writer; a character that could be ridiculed only with some management. Frequently the protégé of a grand seigneur became illustrious enough to give more than he took. Goldoni himself was, in a certain way, one of these perfectly honourable protégés. Hence he could not consider them with the necessary contempt needed for turning them into caricatures

In pictures of aristocratic households Goldoni has introduced a few hangers-on, but never gives them an important part; he leaves them in the background. In *La Moglie Saggia* two of these personages appear, meddlesome and gossipy, drinking much wine and sowing more mischief, but their ill will and petty interference remain almost innocuous. In *La Vedova Spiritosa* several parasites are shown, but the only one that is drawn with vigour is also a consummate hypocrite, a profligate concealing his lewd appetites and his grasping instinct under the mask of honesty and piety. He may have represented that very frequent personage in Venetian households: the churchman acting as councillor, as spiritual guide and much more in families of every rank and class. But these characters were, as Goldoni says, "covered by a cloth that protected them." The *petit abbé* who is always present in pictures of the time by Longhi, Canaletto, or other painters has no place in Goldoni's gallery.

Pantalone, of course, is the important central personage of the family. Yet his authority is not quite so undiscussed, at home, as on the Rialto. As a father he often drops into sentimentalism: in that unlucky *Amor Paterno* written in Paris, he becomes silly in his admiration of his daughters' talents, while he entirely loses the honesty and uprightness of his character, when he accepts pecuniary support from his quondam servant in *La Serva Reconoscente*, of the same miserable period.

Pantalone is not always the head of the family. Goldoni often sets in this place of eminence an older man, whom he carves and paints into some immortal figure like Sior Todero; or the centre of the family picture is a representation of some vice, like his several misers. These marked characters modify the whole intonation of the family group. *Rusteghi* is the best example of these stormy households, swayed by the ill steering of their chiefs, tyrannising over their women-folk.

The other men in the family, uncles generally, are episodical figures which do not essentially differ from the lay models of ancient comedy in their relation to other members of the family. Some of them Goldoni individualised to the dignity and importance of the principal personage and are considered, as such, in another part of this book.

In imitation of ancient comedy, and also of the little world around him, Goldoni gives an eminent place in family affairs to the servants. The two *zannis*, Arlecchino and Brighella, were favourites with the audience. The very best actors of those days impersonated them.

Goldoni could not have discarded them if he wanted to. He adopted them from the first, and worked at them assiduously, reshaping and transforming gradually both their external appearance and their character. Arlecchino he corrected of his grosser sins, and turned into a sprightly, funny auxiliary of feminine intrigue; a seemingly empty-pated good fellow who no longer suggested evil tricks, but consented to perform them in a blundering manner.

In Goldoni's family pictures Arlecchino,[1] like the very chameleon he is, assumes just the shade of immorality or giddiness that fits the whole picture.

Brighella's[2] personality is better marked. He is

[1] A library of volumes and essays have been written about "Arlecchino," but they do not much assist the reader in understanding the personage such as Goldoni saw and represented him. Arlecchino being in his conception the simple mountaineer, from the Bergamasc hill country, and having come to town to the great Venetian mart for employment, adopts the moral standard, the manners, and the sort of wit of those he mixes with. Goldoni, imitating reality, could not continue the tradition of *commedia dell'arte* and repeat the hackneyed type of Arlecchino, always a rascal and always a promoter of tricks. Goldoni's Arlecchino seldom commits any unlawful act; but he often uses improper and clownish words, in homage to tradition. From one family to the other he changes according to surroundings. In *Serva Amorosa*, for instance, where the atmosphere among the servants is so peculiarly benevolent, Arlecchino accepts a tip, winking at the imbroglio he suspects; but he neither betrays nor abets the quarrel. In *Famiglia dell'Antiquario*, more realistically immoral, Arlecchino is instrumental in a fraud. In many instances Arlecchino, free-spoken and clownish, is used as a foil to his master's faults, as in *Il Tutore* he ridicules his master's laziness. In *Teatro Comico*, where Goldoni gives a sort of program for his characters, he allows free play to Arlecchino for saying untranslatable bons mots (act ii, sc. 8).

[2] For Brighella see Chapter VIII. In the family Brighella, like Arlecchino and Colombina, is modified by his surroundings, yet he has an innate honesty, not always fully developed but seldom entirely absent. In *Fami-*

naturally upright and loyal, hence he is generally introduced as a mild redresser of wrongs. He is the honest servant; in households that run blithely to ruin, as in the Gambler, he is the last prop supporting the young rake, who is going fast to the dogs; in *Serva Amorosa* he is the well-meaning auxiliary of honest contrivances. Goldoni transformed the personage so completely as to make of him almost a creation. In this study of the family, Brighella, however, is almost always a subordinate figure.

Far more varied, and more interesting for the knowledge of customs, are Goldoni's feminine characters. In the family groups they hold even a larger place than in the plays of intrigue and in those pictures of customs that limit their representation to the drawing-room. In this reintegration of feminine life in a work of art Goldoni is a master. In his plays, better than in volumes of travels and anecdotes, this important aspect of Venetian customs should be studied.

The real position of women in the family at that time is even more difficult to discover than what was then her position in society.[1]

An extraordinary amount of flattering, an extravagant harvest of compliments in every form that poetry

glia dell'Antiquario he plays the rascal, but he has conscientious scruples. In several plays he appears as the best of a staff of servants. In *La Moglie Saggia,* as in other plays and in accordance to footlight traditions, he is the master's counterpart, but a shade less perverse. In middle-class families he sometimes acts like a surrogate of Providence; see, for instance, *La Serva Amorosa.*

[1] For women's rights see *General Ideas.*

and art could elaborate, do not conceal the crude fact that none of the primordial rights of woman were considered. From the day of her birth to that of her death, woman was held in bondage. No care was taken of her intellectual development. Her education, either in a convent or at home, was such as would prepare her for the only situation life offered: the doll parading in public resorts, the slave of man's ambition, desire, or caprice. The same code of morals which dispensed with higher teachings than a few axiomatic dogmas of propriety, and a number of Latin orisons mumbled without the slightest understanding of their meaning, was most indulgent to feminine frailties. Masculine honour was not sensitive; masculine demands from women did not go beyond some appearance of decorum and some semblance of obedience.

Yet such was the innate nobility, the inbred sense of honour, and the national gift of common sense, that Venetian women never fell so low as it has pleased superficial observers to declare and, certainly, compared favourably with the decorum observed by the women of other European countries.[1]

[1] Contemporary pictures of Venetian customs from J. J. Rousseau to Casanova and Président des Brosses have much to say about the Venetian courtesans. Goldoni, respectful of his public, leaves out this character in its unattenuated form. His most disreputable females are termed *virtuose* — an equivalent then of the modern *chanteuse*, the lowest class of singers who entertained the Venetian audiences during the intervals between acts with such nondescript performances as were called *intermedi*. In *La Locandiera* two of these characters, in *La Figlia Obbediente* the ballet girl Olivetta and a few other exceptions, do not negative the general rule of

How even the evil-looking institution of serventism was kept above the depths of actual immorality has been shown in various plays of Goldoni, and confirmed by the significant testimony of Président des Brosses,

keeping all shady feminine characters well out of sight. For the morality of Goldoni's women see Chapter XII. In pictures of family discord no worse sin is mentioned than coquetry and attachments under the mask of flirtation. No adultery is committed, though many are suggested. See in *La Moglie Saggia* the reticence shadowing the position between Count Ottavio and Countess Beatrice. In pictures of middle-class families, serventism is even more mild.

Président des Brosses in his *Italie Galante*, op. cit.: "*Il faut cependant rendre justice à la vérité, notre ambassadeur me disdisait, l'autre jour, qu'il ne connaissait pas plus d'une cinquantain de femmes qui couchassent avec leurs amants. Le reste est retenu par la dévotion. Les confesseurs ont traité avec elles qu'elles s'abstinedraient de la chose essentielle, moyennant quoi ils leur font bon marché du reste tout aussi loin qu'il puisse s'étendre.*"

Another Frenchman, Charles Rabany, in his work on Goldoni has shown severity in his review of Venetian customs. But his source of information, Malamanni's *Settecento*, is not a book of general information, but a review of certain literary pamphlets; a book for persons who have read many others. Pamphlets and libels penned with the exaggeration and malice of personal spite are quoted as evidence of corruption. Ballarini Zorzi and other scribblers testify against their countrymen. Yet French morals are not to be judged by the testimony of Zola's novels or Bernstein's plays.

In Goldoni's plays this reticence about the Venetian courtesan is not imposed by popular opinion or even by the authority of censors. He might easily, under a thin disguise and with the assistance of a few euphemisms, have introduced such characters. Indeed in the *Locandiera* he did introduce two such women, Ortensia and Dejanira. If he did not repeat this questionable feat it is because he did not share in the opinion of a few foreign contemporaries about the importance of the class.

To readers curious of information we can suggest, besides the too well-known *Mémoires* of Jacques Casanova de Seingalt and the passage in Rousseau's *Confessions*, there are several passages in Président des Brosses, *Lettres sur l'Italie*, op. cit. Also a letter in *Il Corriere Svaligiato di Ferrante Pallavicino*, vol. ii, page 171. Also Negri Pasquale, *Misteri di Venezia tratti dagli scritti di Edmund Lundy*, Milano, 1858. Also *La primavera Cittandina del Lamberti*. Malamanni's *Settecento*, being a collection of curious unpublished documents, contains much amusing information.

no favourable witness: how innate tact and politeness, improved by constant practice, were perfected so as to make a few Venetian ladies the central planet of literary groups, the queen of a *salon* not unworthy of Parisian models, is not to be found in Goldoni, but in other pictures of his time.[1] Goldoni does not flatter the Venetian lady. Though superficial critics often repeat that Goldoni lacks vigour in his representation of vice, his plays contain violent satire against the impertinence, the flippancy, and viciousness of the character "Beatrice," embodying in most cases the "marchesa" or the "contessa" opposed to sweet-spoken, sentimental, tender-hearted, lower-born "Rosaura." He selected both characters from the ancient comedy; but remodeled them toward more delicacy, in pursuance of his plan of lowering the great and exalting the humble.

Beatrice, or her equivalent under some other title, with all the accidents of character and position which Goldoni could invent, is the resultant of many far-reaching causes. She belongs to the traditional repertoire wherein women were shown under the worst light. Moreover she is the image of a personage that Goldoni met in many a grand family. Though very proud of her birthright, she has none of the dignity that should go with her title. Contaminated by surrounding examples, she has few scruples left, but only the petty vanity of keeping her rank, of saving appear-

[1] For a gallery of Venetian grandes dames and their salons see volume of *Letters* edited by Molmenti (*op. cit.*).

ances. She has a *cavalier servente* and she gambles without compunction; she almost believes that such things are meritorious annexes adding to her social importance. Whether absolutely true to life, Goldoni grants her almost no redeeming points, not even the extenuating circumstance of youth.

The Rosaura of the *commedia dell'arte* was the ingénue, the simpleton used as a ball to be tossed here and there by the other characters. Goldoni was the first to give her consistency and individuality. In *La Moglie Saggia* [1] she firmly opposes Beatrice, defending the rights of the honest wife. In the *Festino* the same situation is represented; while in many other plays it is unmarried Rosaura struggling single-handed to obtain her right. Rosaura, the sweet and patient, but active and passionate young woman, with will and tongue of her own, the housewife whose common sense opposes her husband's extravagance, the mother who defends her children, is such a favourite with Goldoni that she is found in almost all these family pictures.

Though borrowed from ancient models, Goldoni so completely changed this character that it becomes a creation. She is the modern woman in the bud; not yet clearly realising that which she feels to be her due. Like Pantalone she is both an image of the past, a representation of the actual moment, and an intuition

[1] In the analysis of *La Moglie Saggia* we have noted the difference between Beatrice and Rosaura; it is not everywhere as clearly contrasted.

of the future. In the family circle Goldoni has introduced a few old women more offensively drawn than any other of his characters. In this he followed a stage tradition, which entrusted to an actor this standard comic rôle. Hence the exaggeration and unreality of these clownish personages.

Colombina is an integral element of the family circle. We have already seen how Goldoni transformed this time-worn personage of the old comedy into something more decent and human. Under the name of Mirandolina (*La Locandiera*) or in several other plays under the name of Corallina, Colombina has become a charmer whose imperishable youth and gaiety still attract crowds to the Italian theatres when some one of the plays in which she holds the first place is performed.

In the pictures of homely life Colombina is subdued to the place to which she was assigned by tradition. She is the mischief-maker, the tale-bearer, the liar, the sharp-tongued menial who takes a bribe as easily as she gives back a pert answer — all this, however, toned down to the plan adopted by Goldoni which admitted of no grossness and was wary of double meaning. Like Arlecchino she has lost some of her power and some of her activity for intrigue, whilst, of course, when the final reconciliation is brought about at the end of the play, it is generally only these two that bear the punishment of all wrong-doing.

Out of Goldoni's family pictures it is difficult to choose which is the most typical and better reveals

Venetian customs to non-Italians. Perhaps that unpremeditated little masterpiece, *La Casa Nuova*,[1] written and composed in three days and nights, may prove more intelligible on account of the double image it presents. The two households embody two conceptions of life, two standards of propriety: on the first floor, the family troubled by the desire of parading, by the vanity and impertinence of Cecilia, Anzoletto's newly married wife; on the second floor the unruffled quiet of two sisters, Checca and Rosina, who live according to the strict old customs so dear to Goldoni. The plot though imitated from the standard pattern of contrasted love-making and final arrangement due to the benevolence of a wealthy uncle, is so daintily woven as to justify the enthusiasm of Ernesto Masi, Capuna, and Gaspare Gozzi, who set this short three-act comedy above almost every other of Goldoni's plays.

The story is so simple; Anzoletto, marrying Cecilia against the advice of his wise, wealthy, and grumbling

[1] Ernesto Masi, *Scelta di Commedie*, etc., *op. cit.*, vol. ii, page 232, says of *La Casa Nova*, ". . . Not by Goldoni alone is this play considered one of his most perfect . . . it is a picture of the middle class, of that condition which comes from accumulated wealth due to industry and thrift and would assume airs of recent nobility. Relations between the nobility and the middle class are still very loosely determined; they are still very near one another and mix. . . ."

Gaspare Gozzi praises *La Casa Nova* unreservedly: "It is so well conducted that interest never flags from beginning to end, and so exquisite are the charms of its dialogue and the unexpectedness of episodes that one is always willing to see it again. The characters are so true to life that we do not feel as if we were listening to a play, but rather as if we were witnessing scenes of actual life."

uncle, Christofolo, has brought upon himself all the ridicule and torment which are sure to attend such unions. Cecilia is a lady of fashion, aping all the ways and manners of gentlewomen; accepting the homage of a *cavalier servente*, dragging her weak-minded husband into more expense than he can afford, tyrannising over Meneghina, Anzoletto's unmarried sister. Cecilia is almost a caricature drawn somewhat in the style of Thackeray's pictures of feminine snobbism. As a study of character her sudden reform is inconsistent. As a lay figure displaying the petty vanities, the brazen-faced lies, the impertinence of the higher class she strives to imitate, she is a most interesting personage.

Meneghina is made doubly miserable by Cecilia's hectoring and jealousy and by the removal from the house where her young man used to court her to this new house, a more fashionable flat. Meneghina has a sharp tongue and holds her own in their constant word battles. Anzoletto is the usual *fils de famille*, the Florindo, without will or opinion or sense of responsibility.

Even before his first appearance, through the gossip of pert Lucietta, the maid, and Sgualdo, the upholsterer, the audience is informed of his imbecility and of Cecilia's extravagance. Even before marrying Anzoletto was extravagant and weak, Cecilia's imperative caprice has met no opposition, and they are now, so Lucietta says, as deeply in debt as they can be. Indeed the former landlord will not let them take their furniture, and this new one is already demanding the first six months' rent in advance. Lucietta disapproves of this new house; it is dull, no one passes under the *balcone*, and she misses the "three or four friends" with whom she used to chat from one back window to the other, as soon as her day's work was done. "When they heard me at my window, out they came and we talked, we laughed, we told each other our little affairs, we opened our hearts. They told me all the stories of their mistresses. Oh, it was great fun! But here I cannot tell what sort of savage people are living. I have tried several times to stand out on the balcony; but no one has said good morning! It is their duty to salute me first."

Lucietta is here echoing her mistresses' complaints, as they expect their neighbors, on the second floor, to come and pay them the first formal call. Anzoletto is presently introduced. Tossed from one to another, he tries to escape from Sgualdo's demands for cash; he rejects Fabrizio's advice that a great dinner party be given; he avoids Meneghina's lamentations about her room, about the dependence on which her sister-in-law would keep her. Fabrizio, aspirant to the title of *cavalier servente*, tries to smooth matters, but he only stirs the anger of Meneghina, who bids him hold his tongue. Anzoletto dares not offend the busybody, and even tells Fabrizio how thoroughly henpecked he is, "how he avoids discussions," and trusts either that his uncle may die or that he may win a *terno* at the lottery.

Cecilia, attended by a Count Ottavio, comes in to criticise the arrangement of rooms, the furniture, to quarrel with Sgualdo, and scold Lucietta with all the arrogance of her assumed character and all the vulgarity of her real one. Count Ottavio encourages. He is at home in these squabbles. The act closes amusingly on the announced visit of the two ladies living overhead. "Are they coming for me?" says Meneghina. "For both of you," explains Lucietta. Upon this, both decline to receive the visitors.

Second act shows the two "Lustrissime," the quiet, well-to-do sisters discussing the uncivil reception they have met downstairs, and commenting about the furniture and other belongings of their new neighbours. The contrast between these two families is cleverly marked. Siora Checca, the married sister, and Rosina, the middle-aged spinster, are like some of those delightful English ladies dwelling in Cranford, true to life in their every trait yet idealised by some subtle charm of kindness and unassuming dignity. They will presently take in hand the lovers' interests; especially when they learn that Meneghina's suitor is their favourite cousin. Siora Checca will even send for the typical grumbler, the uncle *rustego zio* Cristofolo, and plead the cause of Meneghina. Uncle Cristofolo is finally persuaded to give the necessary *dot* and also to take back into his favour imprudent Anzoletto and termagant Cecilia. Naturally they humbly repent in the appropriate fashion of such happy endings and promise to be good for ever after.

The representation of manners in this play is the amusing and interesting element, — the exchange of civilities between the neighbours, the petty quarrels over precedence of visits, the superabundance of compliments which often hide impertinence; the whole intermingled with much information about feminine toilet. Sober, gossipy Siora Checca, commenting with her sister on the appearance of Cecilia, tells us that her hair was of the latest shade of blond, that it was adorned with "diamonds from Murano" (meaning paste), also that her gown of false gold brocade expanded in ample circle. In a pretty scene Lucietta is led by Siora Checca and her sister to tell all about Meneghina and her prospects. Lucietta is not the usual mischief-maker; she is devoted to her young mistress, yet she babbles on, revealing everything her inquisitive listeners wish to know. "There's no chance, to my thinking, at least. No *dot*, poor thing. She is young, yes, but not quite so young as she says. Birth? Not much to speak of; her father was a salumir, her uncle sold butter. They are called *lustrissimi*, because they live without working, on their rents; but you know the proverb, 'life on rent is life on stint.' . . ."

Zio Cristofolo, in *Casa Nuova*, is the first in date of a series, the purely Goldonian *rustego*, one of the most popular creations of the whole Italian comedy.[1]

[1] *Il Rustego* is so identified with Goldoni that critics are justified in considering him as a creation *de toutes pièces*. Yet there are many elements drawn from the past, even from classical past, in this typical Venetian personage. Even so far back as in Athens, in many points so like Venice, Aristophanes found and reproduced the character of Strepiades, and thus made him talk to his spendthrift son: "Cursed be the proxenete who persuaded me to marry thy mother. I lived so quietly in the country, and my life there was sweet; always dirty, with my hair tousled on my brow, I used to lie down on the ground wherever I liked; I owned treasures of

Goldoni has repeated this character in varied lights, under different aspects, and each time with success.

The *rustego* is the exact opposite to the good-natured, liberal, witty, cheerful gentleman of Venice. The

olives and sheep, but ever since I took for my wife this niece of Megaclès, a lady used to all the luxury of towns and to all sorts of refinement, I am forced to sleep in a soft bed, and I who only enjoyed the smell of wool and of figs, of bacon and other country goods — I have to endure the smell of perfumes. . . ."

Italian classical comedy mixed up the traits belonging to the rude boor with those that are proper to the miser.

Gaspare Gozzi with all his mildness and wit has traced some outlines of the personage he knew so well how to appreciate in Goldoni's play. In Molière: Alceste is a *rustego* that has some manners and some delicacy of taste: a Parisian. Arnolphe in *Ecole des Femmes* comes nearer to Goldoni's *rustego* in his ideas about the education of Agnès: he would have her brought up,

> "*Dans un petite convent, loin de toute pratique . . .*
> *C'est à dire ordonnant quels soins on emploierait.*
> *Pour la render idiote autant qu'il se pourrait.*"

But in this personage the fear of being *cocu* predominates, whilst Goldoni's *rusteghi* are less preoccupied by this fear.

When in after years, Goldoni was afraid of Rousseau's appropriating to himself the satire of the boorish personage, he evidently did not realise the difference between Rousseau's morbid sensitiveness and the perfectly sane grumblings of the Venetian *rustego*. Rousseau has a grand, unattainable ideal of simplicity and communion with nature. *Il rustego* does not know that nature exists, and cares above all for immediate and material comfort. Rousseau is the precursor of sentimental romanticism; *Il Rustego*, the embodiment of naturalism.

One of Goldoni's best biographers and interpreters, Giuseppe Ortolani, in his fine study, *Goldoni*, etc., *op. cit.*, lays a great stress on the significance of this character *il rustego*. There certainly was at the time a strong amount of grumbling in every field of intellectual activity. Reformers willingly assumed the style of *Laudatores temporis acti* and as such they will be reviewed in another part of this book: here they are only considered as members of a family.

rustego or *salvadego* (savage) has the honesty and commercial activity of Pantalone, without his amiability. He is generally a self-made man, cautious, and proud of his financial success. He has worked hard, and means everyone else to share his love of thrift and simplicity. Not a miser, but careful of his every sou. He ignores amusements and hates ceremony, but he enjoys a good dinner and treats his friends to an abundance of substantial meats and good wines. Though his womenfolk are not allowed to dress fashionably, he supports his reputation by providing them with good clothes and costly jewels. Above all things he hates novelty. Above all things he worships the past.

Whether Goldoni aimed widely at a whole class of antiquated spirits, and whether his *rustego* represents the writers and critics that opposed his own plans of reform, is open to discussion. The personage is familiar in many households. His influence is strong because he is strong-willed, and because he holds the purse-strings the influence of paterfamilias is frequently opposed to his own. His violent domineering promotes reaction, or encourages hypocrisy.

"Sior Todero"[1] is a variety of *rustego* so richly endowed with comic elements that generations of Italians have kept faithful to its popularity; his name is handed down as a common noun for all that he represents.

[1] For Sior Todero Brontolon, see Chapter XII.

Almost as amusing and more significant is the complete picture of this type as Goldoni presented it in the play, *I Rusteghi.* Here we have four different views of the same temper, since each of the three families is represented as under the tyranny of obstinate chiefs, each reacting diversely against the yoke, each developing, under the same stimulus, different germs of rebellion.

Goldoni's plot is purposedly insignificant. The flimsiest of threads holds together the gallery of homely scenes, emphasising the author's intention of showing something more important than the petty adventures of the usual pair of lovers. Indeed the plot is not even provided with the habitual opposition to love's free course. The marriage arranged between Lucietta — Sior Lunardo's · daughter — and Filipeto — Sior Maurizio's son — is willingly accepted by all. The parents approve and the children rejoice. The point on which the whole comedy turns is so futile that to a foreigner it would seem inconceivable. The fathers have betrothed their children without asking their advice, or even allowing them to meet before the signature of the marriage contract. The women conspire to bring about an interview; they arrange a visit under cover of masks and thus so irritate their tyrants that they refuse their consent to the match as a protest against this spirit of emancipation.

Silly this would be if it were not transparently meant to contrast two entirely different conceptions of life, of ideas that even now are not obsolete in Italy. Each character is finished in every detail. Each of these *rusteghi* rules his little kingdom in the same spirit, yet the differences in their temper create a vast difference in the atmosphere which surrounds them.

Rude Lunardo,[1] another *rustego*, has never a kind word for his daughter Lucietta, nor for his second wife, Margarita. His boorishness makes the two women miserable. Margarita is not wicked, yet she does not love her stepdaughter, and she refuses even the cheap baubles that Lucietta desires to adorn herself. She tells Lucietta of the forthcoming marriage; she plots, but not whole-heartedly, because she is both broken into obedience and embittered.

Lunardo is not a heartless father or husband; he wants his wife to have fine clothes, jewels; his house to be abundantly provided with good things, "only these things have to be enjoyed all by ourselves . . . with doors and windows closed . . . our womenfolk held strictly down. . . ." Thus he explains his ideas

[1] Lunardo — act i, sc. 3 (*Alone*). "She (Margarita) has gone. I obtain nothing by gentleness. I must always scold. I love her well; ay, that I do; but in the house I must be the only master."

Same scene with Maurizio — settlement of nuptial contract — is like the warcry of these would-be masters; they dispose of their children as if they were movable property.

First scene in act iii is the counterpart — the defeat of husbands and of their system; the three husbands meet as in a war council.

"Cancian — We must make an example. We must humble the pride of these insolent wives. We must teach men how to chastise them.

Simon — Let people say that we are boors.

Cancian — Let people say that we are savages." And so on, until Lunardo starts discussion as to a practical way of punishing the culprits and discovers that they cannot do it.

to Sior Maurizio, as they discuss final arrangements for their children, Maurizio declaring that he does not care for jewels. "I don't want her to wear silk gowns. As long as I live she must wear wool, and I object to tippets, caps, and to every sort of ornament. . . . I will let her have a pair of bracelets and a jewel that belonged to my late wife, and also a pair of pearl earrings."

Each father arranges for his son or daughter without dreaming of asking their approval; each father exalts the good qualities of his offspring. "My daughter was brought up to do every sort of work; even to wash dishes . . ." "To keep my son out of mischief with the housemaids I have taught him to darn his own stockings." But Filipeto laments to Aunt Siora Marina. "Ever since I was born, I never had amusement. All day at work in the office, then straight home. On holidays, the same duties have to be performed,[1] then directly home again. He sends a servant after me, and it is a mercy if I have persuaded this man to let me come here now."

Marina is the sort of slave that is brave behind her master's back: she promises Filipeto that at least once he shall see the girl he is to marry.

While she is preparing to go out to dinner, the really most typical pair enter: Sior Cancian and his wife Siora Felice. Sior Cancian is the boor whom a clever,

[1] Filipeto speaks vaguely of "duties on holidays," because Goldoni, in obedience to the unwritten code of propriety, will not write the words "going to church" or "attending mass."

sharp-tongued wife has partly tamed, partly bullied into a somewhat better form. Siora Felice is such a charmer that her influence is felt by all the boorish friends of her husband. Siora Felice even dares to inflict on Sior Cancian the assiduous presence of her *cavalier servente,* Conte Riccardo degli Arcolai.

The presence in the midst of these Venetians of one person speaking Tuscan and marking in his every tone, in every word, the difference between his studied composure and fashionable coolness and the vivacity of Venetian manners, the fluency of Venetian dialect, is very amusing.

The entrance of Siora Felice, attended by her sullen mate and polite *cavaliere,* clears the atmosphere. Even their introduction is playful. Sior Cancian pretends not to know who Cavalier Riccardo is, when Marina politely says, "Why, if he comes with you I guess he is a gentleman." Cancian answers surlily that he knows nothing about him. Siora Felice with ready wit replies, "Don't take offense, dear Signor Count, we are in carnival and my husband is joking; he just wants to tease Siora Marina. Is it not so, Sior Cancian?"

She explains her husband's grumbling by pretty little lies, always intermingling her sayings by a "Is it not so, Sior Cancian?" which affords opportunity for traditional byplays.

It is impossible, in translation, to give the liveliness and fun animating both the scenes of preparation for the masquerade that will allow Filipeto to visit at

Sior Lunardo's house and talk to his bride, and then of performance of this little plot and of its delightful Venetian dialogue.[1] But the play is a microcosm of the great struggle which was then tearing the world asunder, the toppling down of absolute power, the growth of humble and ignored rights.

On one side the elderly grumblers, firmly persuaded of their right to control and of their duty to protect. How they have deprived themselves and toiled to build their nest! "My father asked me, when I was a boy," says Lunardo, "wilt thou come and see the new world at the fair, or wilt thou have two sous? I took the sous and stayed at home." To which Simon answers detailing how he set apart the tips he got as a boy, until they summed to one hundred ducats which he soon invested at four per cent. "Not that I care much for the four ducats a year, but I like to think: look here, these I gained when I was a boy." The duet proceeds: "Where can you find now young men as steady as we were? . . . They squander their money. . . . In many ways . . ." and so on, ending with the word that then sounded like an alarum bell, "The cause of all this evil is liberty."

When they discover that they have been deceived by their wives and children, the grief of these would-be

[1] Each one of these characters in *I Rusteghi* has some peculiarity of language, some habitual saying, as if to enforce their uneducated manner. Lunardo interpolates his every speech — with a *Veniamo a dire il merito*, equivalent to "Let us come to the point." Margarita is always saying *Figurarse*, the equivalent of which might be "Just think!" Felice has her pretty *n'è vero, Sior Cancian*, which is almost proverbial all over Italy.

masters is pathetic. "It is a question of honour," says Lunardo. "What will the world think?"

There is much truth in the minds of these four men as they assemble to comment on the event, but there is also the sense of bewilderment which was then fated to hamper the best efforts of conservatives startled by the novelties of revolutions.

That talk is a document of historic value. It shows the old world awakening to the consciousness of its incapacity to fight against a new order of things. What can these masters do to enforce their commands, if once they are disputed and disobeyed? Leonardo is ready to put the girl in a convent; but what about his wife? What about the other wives? Put them also in a convent? Why, that's punishment for us. "We should have to pay for their expenses, provide for their wants and for their decent apparel; and surely the strictest rules will leave them more liberty than they ever had at home." When Simon says that the only way to master a woman is to beat her they are shocked. Leonardo remembers his first wife with deep regret because she was "a very lamb." But this one . . .

As they talk in seemingly incoherent grumblings one side of the question becomes evident. Faced with the dilemma, violent opposition or submission, like true Venetians they hesitate.

On the other hand, Siora Felice, their mouthpiece, speaking in the name of all her countrywomen, first speaks her mind to her husband who has sworn at her.

Oh, not a very wicked oath. Just a *Cospetto !* [1] which she will not tolerate. "What do you mean, sir, by talking to me in that way? Did you find me in a by-lane? Am I your servant? I am your wife and you may command me, but not bully me. What's the matter with you, sir? Have these gentlemen here been enticing you? . . ." and so on until she had silenced her first and most dangerous antagonist. Then she pleads her own and her friends' cause with the other men.[2] She pleads with ability and wit, mimicking their rude ways, their tricks; frightening them with the possible wrath of Cavalier Riccardo, appealing to their better feelings and to their reason, until, one by one, they implicitly recognise their defeat. "Dinner has been waiting; let us dine first," suggests Simon. "Right," assents Siora Felice, "but

[1] *Cospetto* is not really an oath; it may originally have meant nothing worse than *con rispetto*—with respect—but it has taken a meaning from the use it is put to by Venetians. Hence it sounds offensive in the ears of Siora Felice—a trait of customs that should be marked. These housewives, though trained to submission, are not used to hear their masters swear at them.

[2] Felice pleads woman fashion, and Venetian fashion, not so much in trying to attenuate or explain her own and her friends' doings but by attacking her opponents. She pelts them with her fluent oratory, yet is pretending to give them fair play. "I am here on purpose to hear you! I know that you complain of me, and I want to hear your complaints. Vent your anger on me, Sior Lunardo, but do not instigate my husband. Because if you tell me your mind and I find that you are right, I am a reasonable woman, I'll give you satisfaction. But still remember that to make mischief between husband and wife is such a wrongful deed that it cannot be easily cured; and you should not do unto others that which you would not like others to do against you. This I say also, for Sior Simon, with all his wisdom, he can play the devil's own part. I speak to both, and I speak clear that you may understand me. . . ."

let us send for Marina, Margarita, and Lucietta, let the count himself bring here Filipeto and let it be a complete reconciliation and a bridal party." Not only that, however, for Siora Felice must sum up the morality of this play and give, in a sort of final couplet, the recipe of family happiness such as Venetian gentleness and common sense dictated. "If you will live in quiet and in peace with your wives, be men and not boors, give orders but do not tyrannise; above all, love if you wish to be loved." In which last sentence the very innermost spirit of Goldoni is expressed.

One feature of family life which Goldoni has often represented, since it offered both opportunity for showing the intimacy of home circles and because it was such an important item in Venetian manners, is the *villeggiatura*.

Although life in the country was a continuation of Venetian town life, importing as much visiting, card playing, meeting in *conversazione*, yet the peculiarities of each family group, the distinctions between each social set, created innumerable diversities between the several sorts of *villeggianti*, which were not appreciable in town.

In the Venetian world so much was attempted for the sake of "saving appearances," so much disguised under petty contrivances, all things that require the complicity of tradesmen, servants, friends, and neighbours, that removal out of one's centre naturally snapped the flimsy web of many arrangements. In their villas, or in the cottage rented for a season, people were likely to be seen more naturally.

Goldoni is so alive to his opportunity and the pictures of *villeggiatura* are so abundant in his works that it is not easy to choose.

Castle life such as it was practised at Zola by the Albergatis, at Bagnoli by the Widimans, in other country places by the Bartolinis, the Arconati Viscontis, Rezzonicos, where Goldoni was a welcome and honoured guest, is a peculiar feature of Italian life. Hospitality and some field sports lend it a resemblance to English castle life; while it is essentially different in the conception of amusement. No Italian host dreams of ensuring quiet and liberty to his guests; but he takes the utmost care to provide for his guests' conversation, partners for the card tables, and other superfluities. In Goldoni's time great care was given to the selection of guests so as to form only harmonious groupings. His minor poems contain many descriptions of the pleasant time spent in these lordly halls. What tact, what sense of propriety and respect for tradition, a man of letters needed in order to reconcile his dependence on wealthy patrons and the sense of his own dignity. But for his acquaintance with the subtle mechanism of this national institution Goldoni could not have given such a complete picture of *villeggiatura* in its different aspects.

Villeggiatura forms the background of several plays. *Il Cavalier Giocondo* is almost a caricature; *Il Cavalier di Spiriot* — which also contains a study of worldly flirtations — shows the habits and manners of a refined set of persons met at a country place.

The drawing-room of a villa was even better than the drawing-room in the Venetian palace for holding an assembly and discussing the endless topic of gallantry and serventism. What better use could a lady of fashion find for the long hours reserved to *conversazione* than the analysis of dainty sentimentalism? In *La Villeggiatura* Goldoni has drawn an interesting picture of such a society. Even more interesting must this picture appear to those who read it now, for the sake of reconstructing the past.

More comical, and also more satirical, are these pictures of *villeggiatura* as practised by middle-class people or by aristocratic paupers; because the petty contrivances they resorted to, in order to save appearances and conceal their poverty under ostentation, or the embarrassments due to extravagance, were an inexhaustible source of ridicule. It was such a part of Venetian customs, so well known to all, practised by so many, that its representation must have amused them even when things were really deplorable.

That a family should spend, in a month, the income of a whole year, and plunge into an abyss of debt for the sake of cutting a figure in some distant village or seaside resort was not funny; but it appeared so when presented behind the footlights, in contrast with the arrogance, the small manœuvres of snobs, or the intrigues of elderly coquettes.

Goldoni gave a first pencil of this situation in *I Malcontenti*, a play better known for its caricature of Chiari — a caricature that is free from venomous personality. In compliance with Vendramin's desire, Goldoni consented to have the character entirely cut out by the censor; but, happily, he did not destroy the text and we now possess the complete work. It might be revived with success, with just a few changes to modernise such characters as the ambitious poet, the extravagant lady, and, best of all, the general atmosphere of infatuation for this particular form of expensive amusement which is merely adopted for the sake of ostentation and imitation of the aristocracy. Goldoni in his *Memoirs* mentions all these representations of middle-class *villeggiatura* in a bundle. But dates prove that they were not all composed at the same time. The *Villeggiatura* is the first draught; it is more vivid in colouring, more realistic, and less finished than the three plays, *Le Smanie per la Villeggiatura, le Avventure della Villeggiatura, il Ritorno dalla Villeggiatura*, which form almost a trilogy representing the same characters in three different moments: going into the country, staying in the country, and coming home.

These three plays all contain an interesting study of characters; a sentimental problem in which, as not usually with Goldoni, the claims of true love are subordinated to the demands of worldly honour; the heroine Giacinta rejects the lover Guglielmo, and marries the spendthrift Leonardo, simply because she has promised, and because she does not want people to discuss her motives and condemn her fickleness. This conception of duty and dignity is overlooked by those critics who consider Goldoni merely as a gay and superficial painter of customs.

It might also be quoted as the picture of a woman striving to cultivate her intellect and to imitate French women, by nibbling at philosophic books. But the real importance of these plays for us is to show the varied working of *villeggiatura*. Although the play is located in Livorno and the *villeggiatura* is mentioned as Montenero, it is purely Venetian; and purely Goldonian.

The gallery of family characters, with the necessary appendage of friends, clients, servants, is complete. Only the names are changed. There is the family of Pantalone — under the name of Filippo — an easy-going, generous father provided with an only daughter, a real Rosaura though she bears the name of Giacinta; and there is another family: the spendthrift brother and sister that are here called Leonardo and Vittoria, though they are the exact counterpart of Florindo and Beatrice. Paolo, servant of Leonardo, and Brigida, in the service of Giacinta, might just as well be Arlecchino and Colombina. One, Ferdinando, is the characteristic Venetian gossip. The personage which is somewhat more cosmopolitan, and not quite the equivalent of the Venetian Cortesan, is Guglielmo whom both the ladies make love to, while he rather submits than makes for himself the final decision.

These two households are first shown preparing for the *villeggiatura*, Filippo inviting every one, indiscriminately, to share his coach for the drive to, or his house for the stay at, Montenero; then, just like a Venetian father, doubting the prudence of thus introducing a young man, Guglielmo, into the intimacy of his home circle.

In Leonardo's house things do not proceed so smoothly. He is at his wits' end for providing money, in view of the *villeggiatura*. "My country place," says he, "is in the neighbourhood of Signor Filippo's. He spends largely, he entertains many guests, his *villeggiatura* is magnificent, I cannot do less; I cannot be ashamed of myself."

His sister also vies in elegance with Giacinta, and is furious because she cannot have a much desired new gown *au mariage*. "A silk gown trimmed with strips of two colours. The thing is, above all, to select the three colours so that they unite well and suit one's complexion." This all-important matter of gowns is developed in other scenes.

The second play, in *villeggiatura*, is a sequel to these first incidents and is an entertaining series of custom pictures.

Adopting the traditional means of presenting the masters through their servants, Goldoni begins with an entertainment in the kitchen of Filippo's house. Brigida plays the hostess and tells how she has spent her night quietly in bed. "When the *conversazione* began I went to bed. They have played, they have supped, they have played again after supper, and I all the time enjoyed my rest. At daybreak my mistress sent for me. I went, I undressed her, put her to bed;

then, closing her room, I went out into the garden." "Thus," comments Paolo, "one enjoys the country. But what do our masters enjoy?" The chorus answer that they enjoy nothing, because they live in the country as if they were in town; each one outlining the habits of the family he or she serves. Thus we are introduced to some new characters. For instance a Signora Costanza who is not aged, "but others are younger than she is. So she has taken down to the country with her a young niece of hers, that she may attract to her house the fine people."

Several scenes contain pictures of that most important affair — the preparing and drinking of chocolate. Ferdinando, the impertinent parasite, grumbles at the cup he was given at Filippo's place; he stops to drink a second cup with Signora Costanza and over it to discuss everybody's affairs: "Sior Filippo . . . why, yes, he spends more than he can afford and is not well served . . . the dinner last night was abundant, but not tasteful . . . overloaded dishes, quantities of meat but everything over or under cooked, too high seasoned; one could not eat but felt overpowered before beginning." Then supper at Leonardo's is reviewed. "Game, yes: but how many birds did you calculate? I bet there were not more than eight. The tunny? Not bad, but what distasteful oil with it." In comes Vittoria adorned in the much discussed gown *au mariage* to enjoy the spite of the other ladies and talk about the party about to meet at Signor Filippo's. "We will play if it is too early." To which Costanza adds the comment, "In that house they are always ready to play. Every hour is good. If at least they played for small stakes, at quiet plays; but no, it must be that cursed faro which is likely to ruin some one or other."

The party over which Giacinta presides is a pretty representation of such social gatherings. Signora Costanza gives a summary of the complex duties of a hostess. "I know how difficult it is to arrange the tables. I do my very best; but that which exasperates me is that sometimes there are little quarrels, jealousy, or pique, if those whom you place side by side happen to be unsuited. One pretends a headache, the other is tired, and you have no end of trouble to start two set of players. A guest comes in, and says: 'To-night I would like to sit by this person.' Another guest warns me: 'Mind you do not place me at the same table with this person; I will not endure it.' It is indeed a hard task to keep in mind all the friendships and enmities. And sometimes place the wife in one room, the husband in another."

There is also a most typical scene in the coffee-house of the village; a custom of Italian *villeggiatura* that has outlived Goldoni's time.

Under all these pretty and amusing details the plot proceeds with an intensity of subdued emotion unusual in Goldoni's plays of this sort. Evidently he wants to suggest that lightness of talk and apparent gaiety can be kept up even when the heart is breaking with love's bitter torment, just as it is kept up to conceal the disappointment of the penniless snob, the agony of the man in debt.

The third play introduces an uncle *rustego*, a revised copy of *Zio Cristofolo*, a pleasant and original character which Goldoni did not hesitate to reproduce in his *Bourru Bienfaisant.* This Zio Bernardino is gifted with the burly amiability that enhances, by contrast, his essential boorishness. He can joke and jest even while he torments his penitent nephew; he smothers him under compliments even while he denies him assistance; he puts an end to their interview by the call to his servant, "Pasquale! Signore, a tavola," which was later utilized in the French reproduction of the type.

In the end things are arranged, not quite as happily as usual, because Giacinta, always like the Venetian Rosaura, gets the husband she did not want, and arranges the match between the man she does want for herself and her sister-in-law, Vittoria.

Goldoni, careful of saving morality at all costs, makes her announce that she leaves for Genoa. Had she remained, there might be a sequel to her adventures and to her struggle against her desires.

CHAPTER XII

THE PLAYS

Goldoni's best plays are the ones most difficult for non-Italians to appreciate — because written in Venetian dialect it is not understood — they reveal the soul of Venice — their humour, their colloquialisms are untranslatable — yet to understand Goldoni's comprehension of his people is vital — he is the most accurate delineator of popular customs that ever wrote for the stage — his gallery of characters may be classified — "Menego Caianello" is the Venetian *gondoliere* to the life — the group of *Chioggioti* is admirable — with loving fidelity Goldoni represents doctors and players — he has painted a few lawyers with equal sympathy, as in *L'Avvocato Veneziano* — while others, like Don Basilio, he flagellates — *Il Teatro Comico* is remarkable for the description of actors — as is *I Morbinosi* and *L'Impresario delle Smirne* — their morals, their jealousy, their vanity — Goldoni's favourite characters are working-people — Lugrezia in *Le Donne gelose* is an original creation — she is the impersonation of Venetian *popolino*, the typical small shopkeeper — *Le Massere* and *Le Donne di Casa Soa* immortalise the humble housewives and serving-girls — Goldoni's fondness for young actresses — the artistic value of *la servetta* in the play — the same attractive figure fills a large part in the family circle — where she is the agent in every intrigue — in *La Donna di Governo* as Valentina she is painted in dark colors, showing the sad lot of her class — as Corallina in *La Serva Amorosa* it is the same, though she is tender hearted and faithful — Mirandolina in *La Locandiera* is not less charming and purely Venetian — Goldoni a good interpreter of women — his interpretations of Italian fishermen and their womenfolk were painted from life and are not equalled.

GOLDONI'S best and most original plays are also those which it is most difficult for non-Italians to appreciate. Mostly written in Venetian dialect, the finer shades of meaning of which are too often not understood even by other Italians, they so exactly represent Venetian popular customs, are so vividly suggestive of a popular soul, so essentially imbued with the spirit of the Venetian people and the particular moment they describe in Venetian history, that one must possess wide knowledge and large sympathy for this people and this time to integrate the picture and penetrate its deeper meaning.

The difficulty of this understanding accounts for the failure of some learned and conscientious Goldonists to adequately readapt, translate, or popularise some of Goldoni's best plays outside of Italy. Even Lelio Riccoboni,[1] himself Venetian born and a contemporary, disguised *I Pettegolezzi delle Donne* into a French *pastiche* which is as unlike the real Goldonian text as are most other French light comedies composed in imitation of ancient Italian canvases. The trilogy of Camille and Arlecchino's love and quarrels have been passably translated from the Italian into the French language, and been successful on the French stage; the *Bourru Bienfaisant* provides a tolerable picture of two or three characters, but no one has ever, through translation, succeeded in transporting the beauty and representative excellence of the *Baruffe Chiozzotte, I Morbinosi, Le Donne Gelose, Il Campiello* or any other of the popular Venetian plays. Pathos

[1] There are striking similarities between Goldoni's and Riccoboni's careers as between their aims, but there seems to have been a marked difference in their capacity for realising the demands of French audiences. Riccoboni, after attempting to correct the ruling bad taste, learned the profitable art of catering for the amusement of people expecting nothing but farces from the Italian actors.

For all the adaptations and *pastiches* of Goldoni's plays in Paris, see Ch. I, Rabany, *op. cit.*

and sentiment, character study and analysis of passions, are much the same in different countries; but peculiarities of language, jokes, idioisms, and colloquialisms are untranslatable.[1] Even more untranslatable is the humour, the ridicule, the notion of propriety, the infinite limitations and restrictions that racial tendencies, special conditions of life, common sense, and wit have united into building up, through centuries, the evolution of a people.

To understand Goldoni this comprehension of his people is vital. It is essential to know, essential to love and sympathise with the originals, if one would fully appreciate their representation on the stage and measure its fidelity to the model; its poetical idealisation, which is never a superstructure of imagination, but the divination of a profound truth lying under the visible and tangible reality. Goldoni is the most accurate delineator of popular customs that ever attempted the difficult task of representing on the stage of a theatre the humbler classes of people. No one can compare with him in this, his field of unquestioned supremacy. Molière has a few profiles, purposedly left in the background, and Gorki has a few spiritual outlines, yet even they did not proceed farther on that way. Molière was dependent on the least democratic society and court that ever existed; Gorki, preoccupied with grand ideals, fails to observe patiently

[1] Goldoni's Venetian dialect has been cleverly studied in several papers by C. Musatti. See for instance in *Numero Unico*, Venice, February, 1907, and in *Archivo Veneto*, vol. i, fasc. I, 1904.

and to reproduce with the impartiality which is the prerogative of lighter spirits.

Goldoni's exactness and sincerity have often been equalled in fiction; but usually the writer has been handicapped by a social thesis, by a moral aim, by a scientific preoccupation, by some ethic or æsthetic aspiration, guiding or misguiding his observation, dictating or obstructing his vision of reality. Goldoni, who tried to suppress his private views, whose æsthetic principle is to neither add nor subtract from the picture of life, whose art is simple, with whom method is non-existent, whose mind is free of moral preconception, whose heart is full of love for his subject, whose spirit is open to unlimited sympathy with his models, — Goldoni, because of what he is, because of what he is not, has been able to paint with greater exactness, with more comprehensive completeness.

It sounds like a paradox to say that a greater artist is less faithful to his model, simply because he has a greater personality superadding itself to the picture in the making; that the greater thinker is less able to represent simple reality, because he has thoughts crowding between his vision and its reproduction. With Goldoni there is no such understructure of preconceived notions, of habitual preoccupations; nothing but a wonderfully clear sight, a marvellous penetration of motives, a large-minded sympathy, and a great practice of his art.

His technique was perfected during the years of hard labour when, in order to supply the demands of his employers, and also to keep ahead of the pack of rivals at his heels, Goldoni repeated the *tours de orce* we have considered. Having once produced sixteen plays in as many weeks, Goldoni was sentenced to produce continually a proportionate harvest. Though his heart and nerve sometimes failed under the strain, yet because of this stress he mastered every method, learned every stage artifice, and became extraordinarily proficient in play construction.

Thus the simplicity of his observation was served by this almost technically perfect instrument of representation; working so smoothly that it omitted nothing of value; working so delicately that it left no veil between the painter's mind and the observer's eye. Moreover, Goldoni was so delightfully free from every literary ambition that he never deviated from his object in order to introduce a witty saying, or to correct his style when, by thus correcting or adding, he would have blurred or distorted the reality of his model. Thus by mere fidelity to his purpose and comprehension of his personages, Goldoni has created a gallery of characters which may be classified. He has painted a series of groups interesting to observe.

Long before Diderot undertook to make a law of this obvious principle, Goldoni was aware of the influence over the whole man of the profession he habitually exerts. Even in his earliest plays he picked out the pliers of the long oar, and traced those familiar and vivid portraits of Venetian gondolieri. Whoever has seen "Menego Caianello" impersonated by some good actor, will not forget the typical, amusing, and so perfectly true-to-life personage. The success was immediate. *La Buona Moglie* followed close upon *La Putta Onorata*. Some exaggerated sentimentalism, some reminiscence of *commedia dell'arte* may appear in these early Goldonian creations, none in the later portraits of sailors, the admirable group of *Chioggioti*, which belongs to the last and most fruitful year of Goldoni's work in Venice.[1]

Two other professions Goldoni was sure to represent with loving fidelity for having lived among them — doctors and players. In *La Finta Ammalata* we have shown how he traced benevolent portraits of physicians and surgeons, not forgetting the typical Italian annex, *Lo speziale*, the pharmacist, and the habitués of his shop, the meeting place of all those who want to see or call a doctor, of all those who want to buy medicine or hear news or listen to gossip, or read a newspaper without paying for it, in a word, of all the idlers in quest of diversion and company. *Il Signor Agapito* is still a central figure, an important person, in most Italian villages and in many cities. There is almost nothing to add to Goldoni's *speziale;* he is as true to life now as he was then.[2]

Doctor Bainer in *Il Medico Olandese* is a full-sized

[1] Goldoni's gondolier is so popular a part that his best disciples — and especially Gallina — have reproduced him as often as possible. The impersonation of a gondoliere in *Serenissima* by the actor Zago was a treat for every connoisseur of dialect plays.

[2] "*Chiacchere di farmacia*" . . . "*politica de farmacia*" are familiar sayings, equivalent to idle talk not unmixed with presumption.

anticipation of the modern physiologist, doctoring as ably to imaginary as to real diseases. He reminds one of the delicate praise Goldoni gives to his father's memory. Though he did not always "cure his patients of the complaints they had, he always cured them of those which they thought they had."

With the same sympathy and respectful comprehension, he has painted a few lawyers, beginning with the masterful portrait of his *Avvocata Veneziano.* But with what exasperated severity he flagellates those *dottori*, lawyers who made dishonourable use of the title they usurped, of the knowledge they possessed, to tangle the threads of family quarrels, to inveigle extravagant borrowers of money, or to be guilty of other dishonest practice. In many plays this dark figure, this Don Basilio in embryo, steps out of the shadow for a moment to attempt some shady deed, to give legal form to some dishonourable official act; and each time Goldoni pillories the rascals who dared discredit the profession he still considered as "fit for noble patricians," his own proud profession, which he always liked to remember having practised.[1]

[1] On the title page of every volume of his works printed during Goldoni's life this honourable addition to his name is never omitted. He is Dottor Goldoni — *dottore in legge* — or *Avvocato* Goldoni. In playbills of the highly ornamented type then in vogue (some fine engravings representing them may be found in the volume edited in Modena, 1907, *op. cit.*) Goldoni is qualified as "*Polisseno Fegeio pastore in Arcadia.*"

A typical omission in the gallery of characters presented by Goldoni is the adventurer. This omission may be accounted for by the same reason which prompted the leaving out of doubtful feminine characters. It can hardly be attributed to his ignorance of the genus. Besides the notorious

In his *Memoirs*, in his prefaces, in other writings, Goldoni stands boldly as the defender of actors. Grateful to them for their teachings, devoted to their interests, which he considered his own, appreciating the intellectual and professional training which they were bound to acquire, realising their professional difficulties, Goldoni was also a fair judge of the good qualities many of them exhibited and many others would gladly have exhibited had circumstances allowed. He endured much at their hands, before growing disgusted with them all in Paris.

When, in Venice, he introduced in his plays one or more players, Goldoni dipped his brush in the most delicate hues to paint them. He started with *Il Teatro Comico*, better known as *un art poëtique dialogué*, but also remarkable for the outline of several players belonging to the Troupe Medebach. There, too, his only severity is for the outsiders, for the *improvisatore* and the *virtuosa*, whom he does not consider as worthy of the name of players.

In the personage of Barbara introduced in the play *I Morbinosi*, Goldoni traced a beautiful and dignified figure, an idealised specimen of the profession.

With more malice and the humour which the subject

Casanova, Goldoni must have met many of these free-lances. All over Italy and more specially in Venice they were to be found. The rigour of the laws, the oppression of conventionalism, were sure to produce a reaction, and revolt once started usually proceeds to extremes. The brood of adventurers is variegated, Galliani, Cagliostro, Gorani, Da Ponte have inscribed their names in the annals of history. Many others might have stood for their portraits in Goldoni's gallery, had he cared to paint them.

required, he introduced a whole bevy of singers in *L'Impresario di Smirne.* The picture is more than a caricature. One or two forced jokes gild the sober truth and irony of the whole. The temporary association of the prima donna Tognina with the tenor Pasqualino is delicately delineated. No word to offend chaste ears, yet how much suggested! What amusing scenes of jealousy, half amorous, half professional. And the typical soprano — a man in name — with all the impertinence, the bombast, and vanity which were then so well known to theatregoers, which the enthusiasm of the great public, the favour of high personages justified, which, also, the interested protection of the Church encouraged, with what a light hand does Goldoni draw this figure!

Then all the surroundings of the principal group. Count Lasca, the dilettante protector who offers lavishly his patronage but slips out of reach when the offer is accepted and some concrete gift demanded. There is also Beltrame, much like Brighella, the innkeeper, who knows everything about the actors and the actresses; who willingly undertakes to carry messages and to manage introductions. When these two discuss the doings of a woman they give a pretty summary of that which they and public opinion considered right and wrong. "The gentleman from Bologna came here three days ago with a girl for whom he had spent more than he could afford. He came here merely to look after her and attend her. They dined together; then the lady asked for some water to wash her hands with. She washed, went to the window, and threw out the water; then, turning to her lover, she looked at him and laughed, adding this amiable compliment: 'I'm no longer in Bologna; I'm in Venice. I wash my hands and throw away the water of all the Bolognese.' The poor fellow was dumbfounded for a time: 'It serves me right, you will never see me again.' . . . To which account, Count Lasca provides this comment, 'I do not disapprove the woman for having got rid of her Bolognese suitor, but I draw a line at the abruptness and impertinence.' He might have known, however, that these ladies are quite as ready to change one lover a week, as they go from one city to another. It's a mercy if a man can say: she was faithful as long as I was near her."

The play is largely sprinkled with the boastful speeches of actors that, but for the change of a few words, may even now be heard any night in any green room.

It is hardly possible to speak of absolute rules in Goldoni's method, yet his characters, representing people who work, are usually morally and intellectually superior to those characters which personify idlers. He has a marked preference for bread-winners; for those who contribute to the good fame of Venetian industry, to the reputation of Venetian trade.[1]

[1] Goldoni never misses the opportunity for enforcing the advantage of producing Venetian goods rather than introducing them from France. His patriotism is never aggressive, but it always asserts itself in those matters which he fully understood.

We have already mentioned the homely peace and pleasant family atmosphere in *Una dell' Ultime sere di Carnevale.* There are also several speeches praising the ability of Venetian silk weavers and manufacturers. In *I Mercanti* and in other plays are little outbursts of that peculiar patriotism of Goldoni's and of other Venetians, proud of the cleverness of their mechanics, in their modesty, as compared with the irritating assumption of French industrials.

Of all these plays that contain a group of working people, there is one that is not so popular as it should be, one that even its author has not esteemed as highly as it ought to be esteemed if good players would perform it: *Le Donne Gelose.*[1] The central figure, Siora Lugrezia, is a most original creation. A good-looking widow of animal spirits, appetites of all sorts, wide awake and intensely clever, yet withal thoroughly honest and so kind and so ready to oblige that she makes friends and is trusted even by those she has fleeced by lending them money, by accepting their goods in pawn, or by providing them with numbers to play at the lottery. Shopkeepers and tradesmen come to her for advice and get it, sound and profitable; they

[1] *Le Donne Gelose* is seldom performed owing to the difficulty of finding an Italian actress able and willing to impersonate the principal character which contains more broad fun and a nearer approach to real farce than any other of Goldoni's feminine rôles, with the single exception of Madama Gatteau, a middle-aged French milliner, in *Una dell' Ultime sere di Carnevale.* It is a pity that he did not repeat this clever and amusing impersonation of life and charm in women past their prime. In Italy, especially in Goldoni's time, a woman of forty was considered old; she was frequently a grandmother.

also get that first of requisites for Venetians of all classes, a lively talk, small gossip, entertaining stories. They also come to her willingly because she has the charm of ripe womanhood, a blithe spirit, and very little nonsense about her. Not a prude, not even a very prudent woman, yet one whom it is a pleasure to look at, a greater pleasure to talk to.

They are all under the charm: those whose wives spy jealously and scold; the young man who makes love to girls and flirts *à la cortesan* with them, even Arlecchino, her *facchino*, her Jack-of-all-trades, who serves her for love and protests that his being a menial does not prevent his having eyes for admiring a pretty woman. Her presence fills the stage; she keeps the ball rolling briskly all the time, always amusing, always charming, whether she quarrels with the women, or listens to the lovers' stories, or drags Arlecchino after her to the Ridotto. She is the impersonation of Venetian *popolino*, giving to the whole play its peculiar intonation, an untranslatable humour which is the natural effect of the modest desires and thrifty habits, simple-mindedness and sociability, of the whole class of Venetian small shopkeepers.

Of course some of the jokes are somewhat *risqué* but there is no immorality in this picture of customs, only that smiling laxity which was then the average standard of public morals in easy-going Venice, and that profusion of puns and innuendoes which is a character of the Italian conversation.

A certain number of these popular plays Goldoni

composed for the last days of carnival, for those days in which, as he says, even the humblest, even the poorest were entitled to some share of gaiety.[1] His love for his people, his comprehension of their wants, accorded admirably with the qualities of his talent. He is never so himself, so original and so charming, as in these popular plays using his own dialect, representing those characters for whom the play was written. In his modesty or incapacity for autocraticism Goldoni speaks lightly of these little masterpieces. Italian critics and Italian audiences now realise the value of these comedies.

Le Massere, *Le Donne di Casa Soa* are irresistibly comical and withal present a realistic picture of customs, immortalising the very humble character of garrulous, steady, sharp-tongued, and ready-witted

[1] Much has been written about Venetian carnivals, yet Goldoni's carnival amusements are little understood outside of Italy. It is the homely holiday of habitually quiet and simple people, cheap pleasures seasoned with the humour and inclination for masquerading characteristic of even the lower classes. Président des Brosses notes very exactly: "*Rien r'est plus singulier que de voir toute la ville, pour ainsi dire, en masque; les mères portent à leurs bras leurs enfants déguisés, et les hommes et les femmes qui veulent aller au marché faire une emplette de cinq sols à la mercerie y vont en masque. La place Saint Marc est le grand théâtre où s'étale tous les jours la pompe du carnaval; il n'y a pas un masque à Venise qui ne s'y rende, une heure avant le coucher du soleil; et quelque grande que soit la place elle peut à peine contenir la foule des masque, et de ceux qui les vont voir.*"

Goldoni's personages are not to be found in the medley of Piazza San Marco; they have their own popular resorts, in some secluded *bottega* where they indulge in the sumptuous feasts of a cup of coffee and a few *buzelai* (crackers made of insipid flour paste). Like the spirited bevy of masks in *Le Morbinose* they will even scruple to accept this refreshment unless they are allowed to pay for it. *Le massere* — housekeepers, or maids of all work — are not so scrupulous. Siora Lugrezia will not go about in mask un-

housewives. Goldoni has a peculiar perspicacity which allows of his discovering under their apparent levity the solid qualities of serving girls. He shows them babbling and gossiping, putting on a mask for the pleasure of tormenting their masters, elderly bachelors with a soft place in their hearts for them; he can show them telling too much about their mistress's affairs, yet suggest that the *massera*, the maid of all work, is better than her fame, capable of real devotion if only her employers deserve her honour and respect.

In his *Memoirs* Goldoni confesses his weakness for the young actresses impersonating the character, *la servetta;* and almost every critic of his plays imagines that his infatuation for one or the other young actress originated the several plays wherein this secondary rôle rises to the first importance. Like all obvious

attended. In many other plays a mask and a *bautta* are simply worn as an out-of-door garment which is taken off on entering the house or the public resort where one means to stay for a visit or for entertainment.

Most of the romantic intrigue recorded in novels about Italy written by foreigners reveals slight acquaintance with Venetian manners. The habitual use of masks blunted the edge of its piquancy. For Venetians it was easy to recognise their fellow-citizens under the cloak of stiff brocade and the black or white visor out of which they had seen them emerge twenty times. The mask was a transparent "incognito," which dispensed the patrician from always respecting his rank, and which gave free entrance to even the humblest merchant within aristocratic resorts. The doors of *Il Ridotto* were open to every patrician and to every mask.

Carnival was officially heralded on the twenty-sixth of December by the appearance in Piazza San Marco of a petty official, grotesquely attired, announcing that permission was given to wear masks. As a matter of fact masks were worn almost all the year round, since every opportunity, *sagre* (processions to sanctuaries), fairs, illuminations, especially the popular one *della Senza* (Ascension), implied liberty to cover the face. *La Bauta* was also worn at will in almost any season.

conclusions, this one is partly true.[1] When very young Goldoni used to fall in love with every actress he met; when he started in his career he continued flirting with many, because he liked their free and easy manners, their liveliness, their wit; also because it suited his general plan of collaborating with and imitating his interpreters. As he grew in fame and discovered his own possibilities, as he knew the world and mastered the elements of ancient comedy, he more fully appreciated the artistic value of that traditional personage, *la servetta*.

Molière made this same discovery before Goldoni, Marivaux, and Beaumarchais were realising the representative value, the social importance, the resource of this same personage.

The social world and the comedy were then in transformation; though the artist does not realise or theoretically evaluate their full meaning, he divines such periods of transition and interprets them. Marivaux lent to his "soubrettes" an amount of delicacy,

[1] Goldoni has padded his *Memoirs* with anecdotes about the actresses he made love to. They probably liked to be thus singled out, else he would have shown more reticence. All this talk means very little; the only point is that Goldoni appreciated the importance of a second rôle. As a manager he realised that to divide success was to subdue the presuming supremacy of the prima donna. As a playwright he realised that it was part of his general plan to give importance to the actress who represented the humbler class. About this personage more could be said. If, for instance, this same character were studied in his contemporaries, Regnard, Piron, Beaumarchais, Sheridan, Fagiuoli, Gigli, who always introduce a lady's maid into their plays, it would be interesting to follow the avatars of classical Colombina, of Goldonian Corallina, of Sylvie and Suzanne in modern plays so as to find mirrored in her the varied effects of actual social conditions.

of subtlety, and an elegance of speech and manners that corresponded to his æsthetic plan. His art, cradled in the Italian comedy, assimilated the personage, transforming it in accordance with the social movement then initiated in France; but being somewhat in advance of public opinion Marivaux was not fully appreciated at the time. For being somewhat in advance Goldoni also was misunderstood. Beaumarchais was more lucky, not because his "soubrette" is better delineated or more lifelike, but because the political and satirical humour of the play made it an immediate success.

Goldoni, too, found the personage in the repertoire of the *commedia dell'arte*, but in the two books he read assiduously, the "Stage" and "Nature," he also observed the same attractive figure, filling a very large place both in the family circle and on the stage.

On the stage Colombina was the gay counterpart of Arlecchino. The prettiest face, the slimmest figure; a joy for the eyes, a joy for the spirit, the mouthpiece of witty and willingly equivocal sayings; the gaiety that enlivened dull or sentimental plots, the source of broad laughter, and of funny suggestions: such as he found her, Goldoni made the most of her in his first plays.

In the Venetian household, owing to the familiarity that ruled every relation between members of the same diminutive houses, members of the same crowded neighbourhood, Goldoni had abundant opportunity to see her such as she then was, a principal agent in every variety of contrivance and intrigue, an ally for indolent ladies, for frivolous girls, a messenger for lovers, a comfort for aged bachelors, a minister to every form of cicisbeism. As he saw her so he represented her in the plays of his maturity, sometimes so perverse and perniciously active that she perverted and stirred a whole family to mischief, as in *La Donna di Governo*, sometimes so straightforward and honest, as in *La Serva Amorosa*, that she settled things right for every one in the family.

When Goldoni's originality ripened, he further individualised the type, and created his delightful "Mirandolina." Valentina,[1] in *La Donna di Governo*, the housekeeper in Signor Fabrizio's bachelor establishment, is a realistic figure painted in dark colours, in vivid outline. She contradicts the assertion that Goldoni lacks vigour in his representation of customs. Her nature is low, her appetites violent, her spirit undaunted, and her wits as sharp as the struggle for life, single-handed, against all social order and family arrangements can grind them. Having enslaved the master of the house she overrules the whole pack of servants and secures their complicity; moreover, she enlists the services of her sister, a vulgar, coarse duplicate of her own faults, but unredeemed by her cleverness. Thus supported, she impudently intrigues with a disreputable gambler, Baldissera, whom she intro-

[1] Yet the ambiguity of Valentina's position is so delicately delineated that there is not in the whole play one word that can offend susceptible ears, or enlighten chaste ones.

duces into her master's house. Denounced by her master's nieces, she turns the tables on them and reveals their own matrimonial plans. Discovered in intimate tête-à-tête with Baldissera, she pretends that he has come to ask Felicita's hand and persuades Fabrizio to give a *dot* for the pair.

At every turning point, just when her intrigues seem to involve her in final ruin, she turns round and gains a victory over her foes: a series of tricks not new to the stage, but Goldoni makes them less immoral and they proceed with a rapidity that leaves no time for criticism. The novelty and the originality of the play, as a study of character and a presentation of the complexity underlying the wickedness of Valentina, is to be found in the incidents and in the general confession made by the woman at the last, a confession that is not the usual melting into repentant tears of the detected impostor, but a delineation of the struggle that has already found its solution.

Valentina, beginning her speech in the emphatic style that was then acceptable, calls upon heaven and earth to hear the recital of her life and adventures. This emphasis, so unusual in Goldoni's style, means that on this point he wanted to fix the attention of his hearers. Those who condemn Valentina must note the extenuating circumstances that have led her to this final ruin. Not only for Valentina but for the whole class of overworked, abused servants he rehearses the story of long years, spent in unrequited drudgery, when she strove to obtain "reputation," to win favour in the house, and met nothing but distrust. When Valentina proclaims "that hatred begets hatred, and vengeance grows out of revengeful scorn," the whole class of feminine helots speak by her voice pleading "the facility, the example, poverty, and love rankling in her heart," leading her to commit those infractions to social laws that are punished so much more severely in her case than if the offender were of higher birth.

The deeper morality of the play is perhaps seen in its happy ending. By her trick in substituting Baldissera's and her own name to the marriage deed Fabrizio believed to be his niece's, she has secured for herself as a husband the ruffian for whose sake she plotted and planned, so that her apparent triumph consists in losing the comfortable nest she had built for herself in the bachelor's house, and binding herself to a gambler, a rascal, who will embitter her whole life. Is it Goldoni's conclusion that the crushing odds that pervert our servants leave no other issue to their misery than this mortal leap into an imprudent marriage?

Anyhow the same unpromising conclusion is reserved for the maid-servant who impersonated the ideal of her class, for kind-hearted, steady Corallina in *La Serva Amorosa*. She, too, in the end has no greater reward than marriage with Brighella, another servant.

The ambiguity of the title, whether due to Goldoni's scanty Italian, or intentionally introduced by him to signify that something more than devotion to her young master, something deeper than regard for her dead mistress, moves Corallina's heart, the motive of her energetic campaign in favour of insipid Florindo, is significant. Prudently she protests that she is not in love with him, wisely she rejects his proposals, dictated by gratitude not by love; but is she, indeed, as whole-hearted as she pretends to be? Goldoni was too expert in the complexity of a woman's emotions to correct the possible equivocation in the title, or to analyze the maidenly reticence in Corallina's denials. Goldoni did not give to this creature of his spirit the greater prize of marriage above her rank because public opinion would not have tolerated it, and also because his own experience of his world did not allow of such a finale.

He traced this figure, probably a portrait, with love, endowing it with a charm that has outlived every change of fashion and of social relations. From the first, when she comes in knitting a pair of stockings out of the thread her late mistress gave her, we know that she is tender-hearted, that she is faithful to her young master in his adversity. She is the loving woman who watches over his daily comfort, patches his old clothes, and by her clever cooking makes the most of his scanty allowance. Presently she will do more, her zeal growing with the want, and also with the appetite for sacrifice which is the supreme virtue of women. She sells the stockings she has knit to Rosaura, and manages a meeting between the wealthy daughter of Pantalone and her impoverished master.

In Venice it was not then considered dishonourable so to enrich a young man.

Corallina hopes to bring about the match, but she hears of old Ottavio's intention of leaving Florindo out of his will, and then she undertakes to rescue him from this ruin. Her incursion within the fortress of Ottavio's room, in spite of vigilant Beatrice, his second wife, her pleading Florindo's cause, her suggestion that Ottavio counterfeit death, so as to prove the sincerity of his wife's love, all this belongs to tradition, all this was used as common material by other playwrights before Goldoni, but not even Molière nor Regnard have gifted the honest intriguer with the charm, the wit, the modesty and courage, the very embodiment of an Italian character, which endears Corallina to every Italian audience.

Nor is Mirandolina, the sprightly *Locandiera*,[1] less charming, less essentially Venetian, nor less untranslatable, although she has been presented successfully in foreign theatres. Neither her coquetry nor her prowess are new. Both the theatre and the outside world are filled with pretty women bent on seducing the one woman hater that happens to pass within their

[1] *La Locandiera* is of all Goldoni's plays the most difficult to translate and the most translated (see Rabany), not because the dialogue offers any difficulty, or because the plot is complicated, but because the very spirit of the principal personage is so essentially Italian. Love may be the same in all the world, but coquetry is of infinite variety. French adaptations miss the point because they finish by a marriage, which would have shocked Goldoni's notions of propriety, and also because the whole character of Camille Aubergiste is different from Mirandolina. More sentimental and with less of the warmth that characterise the Venetian model.

reach. The same atavic instinct which lends charm to the chase lends a special zest to the conquest of the man who has declared that he cares "four times more for a dog than for the most beautiful woman." Everywhere since time began, love or vanity goads women to use their arts, to win the unattainable prize. Mirandolina does this with ability and the unequalled charm of mixed modesty and courage.

But that which is peculiar to her is the disinterestedness of the whole plotting and manœuvring. It is sport for the sake of sport. She does not mean to marry above her station, she does not mean to encourage any unlawful "protection"; she has already enthralled the high-born pauper, the wealthy gentleman, and also her hard-working steward; she may choose any one of them for a husband for herself and both the others for her protectors, but in the end she chooses the fittest, Fabrizio, who will continue to obey and serve her.

The count and marchese are quarrelling over her, the former boasting of the money he will give, the latter insinuating that his social standing will be of more use if only she accepts his patronage. Il Cavaliere di Ripafratta, a late comer in this delightful *locanda*, on hearing the subject of their quarrel derides it, protesting that " he has never loved any woman, and always believed that they were nothing better than a cumbersome, unendurable infirmity for men." When Mirandolina answers his call he speaks to her almost rudely about the bedclothes. Mirandolina promises that she will see to it; but she resents the gruff manners. "You might have asked for these things with more politeness," says the Venetian. When told that not against her but against all her sex the gentleman is so prejudiced she replies: "Poor women! What have they done to you? Why so cruel toward us, Signor Cavalier?"

By herself, in one of those soliloquies that Goldoni disapproved but would never entirely drop, she explains that "she does not want every customer who walks into her house to fall immediately in love with her, but she cannot tolerate to be so despised. A foe to every woman! Poor fool! He cannot endure the sight of us? Well, that simply means he has not yet come across the woman who will know how to tame him. He will find her! Oh, that he will! I laugh at those who make love to me; but I like even better to conquer and tame those savage and hard hearts who presume to be our foes, and despise us who are the best thing Mother Nature ever produced."

From this starting point to the final despair and exit of *il Cavaliere*, it is a crescendo of pretty scenes, daintily conducted, so as never to slip into anything like vulgar manœuvres, yet suggesting that Mirandolina is so eager in the chase that only her thoroughly honest instinct, her well-trained self-control keep her within these bounds. And this is the Venetian trait, which the French and German translators have missed, when they made Mirandolina in the end marry *il Cavaliere*. They failed to realise the common sense, respect for tradition, the inborn reverence for caste privileges that made the solid scaffolding of a Venetian conscience.

Mirandolina's honesty is of the sort as Pantalone's and as is Goldoni's; it is not grounded on high principles, not declared in high-sounding sentences, but interwoven with a solid tissue of common sense, embroidered by tact and that untranslatable *morbin*, which is a special grace of her time and country. Thus when she trips in, enquiring after her guests' wants and desires, protesting that she "cares nothing for all the compliments paid to her by those gentlemen who come in as boarders, and think that they can make love to the innkeeper," she only wants to promote the interest of her business and will laugh at every soft speech. How she likes *il Cavaliere* because with him she can talk without running the risk of hearing compliments! Will he shake hands with her? "This is the first time I have the honour of shaking hands with a man who talks as a man should talk. . . . If I had shaken hands with one of these other men they would think that I was dying with love for them." The sly flirt knows well that these compliments, this contact of her hand, are working the mischief she means them to work on her intended victim. Even while calculating the odds, she never doubts her final success. "Where is the man who can resist a woman when he gives her time to use her arts? He who flies may be saved; but he who stays, listens, and finds pleasure in the fight must sooner or later be vanquished."

Yet when she has roused him by her pretty ways, by her saucy refusal of presents, by her mocking attitude, when he grows passionate and insistent, then, like the true woman that she is, she takes fright and looks about her for protection against the danger she has created. She will not risk her reputation, she will not allow the slightest liberty. To the enamoured hand stretched out to caress she opposes the hot flat-iron she has been using. To the violence of his desire she opposes the solid bulwark of a husband protector.

Goldoni opposes his discreet coquette with a double foil, the *virtuose* Dejanira and Ortensia, whom he has painted as black as he dared to. They come in and pretend to be great ladies, but they immediately accept, and even beg for, presents from the count and marchese; and when they attempt to imitate Mirandolina and lay siege to the *cavaliere* they get the worst abuse ever spoken by Goldonian characters.

There is in Goldoni a natural delicacy, an almost feminine descriminating sense, which enables him to trace dainty figures with such unerring tact that even through the imperfections of his Italian, even after all the changes which time and the constant evolution of his people have wrought on public opinion, his Mirandolina is still as fresh and charming as she was when first presented to her contemporaries. Even better than the dainty personages of Marivaux, she embodies the irresistible charm of the honest woman playing with love as long as youth and circumstances allow of this play, yet ready, at any moment, to drop the bantering, pleasant amusement and to settle down in sober earnest and reliable responsibility.

This suggestion of latent solidity is the substratum which characterises many of these Goldonian pert young women. Some of the girls he presents have a freedom of manners and of speech which contrasts with the shyness and submissiveness of his other feminine characters. These two aspects of Venetian manners are both justified.[1] Venice was then a state, with all the diversity of caste, race, and social distinction that one may find any day in larger states. The patrician lady and the merchant's wife differed as much from one another as both differed from the working class below them. Each presented essential varieties of language, manners, and moral standard, which Goldoni well knew and painted. In *Le Donne di Casa Soa* is an amusing parody of serventism, a middle-aged housewife and her *compare.* It is the comfortable arrangement of mutual help, of mutual support, in a life that would otherwise be very tame; it is the one little window open on amusement by two persons who lead very sober and industrious existences. It is the standard of morality that ignores abstract principles but smiles on every infringement of a virtuous thesis providing it does not harm anyone.

This notion of virtue is feminine; it answers to the

[1] For these Venetian girls see the play, *Le Morbinose*, which contains a whole gallery of silhouettes belonging to the middle class, to respectable self-asserting merchant families. In *La Donna di Governo* the two young girls are drawn with more severity and vigour to represent the extremes of weakness and rebellion.

spiritual condition of a very ancient civilization; it answers to the temper of Goldoni's mind. Respectful of appearances, always avoiding the grosser term and the more explicit phrasing, Goldoni proves himself a good interpreter of the sex who seldom risked an indecent word or a compromising move, but always preserved, even in the most secret intimacy, a modesty of attitude and speech that astonished and charmed foreigners. That cult of appearances is indeed the only common trait between all his women. The housewives and the girls in his pictures of the middle and lower classes are as careful of their reputation as the most patrician lady can be.

These pictures of girlish sprightliness, of petty intrigue, are some of the best things Goldoni ever composed.[1]

He looked about him and noted the movement, the talk, the work going on, or the pleasure snatched; he saw the rivalry but not the violence of hatred, the quarrel but not the battle, the flirt but not the debauchee, either because these things were disguised, or because he did not care to reveal more than was strictly needed. The severity of his judgment he reserved for the high-born. But for the humble he

[1] Readers curious about the style of language and the mannerism of Venetian love-making should read in *Nuova Antologia*, Jan., 1882, a paper by Castelnuovo: *Una Dama Veneziana del Secolo XVIII*. It is an essay on the life and adventures of Caterina Dolfin Tron, who was courted and praised by almost every writer of her time, from her special protégé Gaspare Gozzi to that *mauvaise langue* Barbaro (abbate Angelo) so dear to gossipy Malamanni.

has nothing but smiling indulgence, an indulgence that grows tenfold when he paints the sex he loves and sympathises with.

There is almost no plot in these plays. One of these jewels, *Il Campiello*, is just the reproduction of what anyone could witness any day in one of these *campielli* that are so cosily enclosed by canals and *rii*, so homely and so bustling with friendly intercourse.

On doorsteps the lace maker plies her needle and wags her tongue with every neighbour who has a mind to stand on her *balcone*, or to step into the *campiello* to fill her bucket with water from the central well, or buy some cheap delicacy from the street vender. Let the man who carries *L'aventurina* come in inviting them to risk their soldi on his portable roulette, and they will all swarm round him, eager for anything in the way of diversion, for anything that promises an outlet to their overflowing spirits. A quarrel, a reconciliation, a marriage, a dance, a foreigner to look on and encourage, a lisping young miss to stand in pretty contrast, only that, and the evening flits as pleasantly as a dream, a dream of Venice, such as it truly was, not such as it seemed in prejudiced eyes.

Even the foreigners who have attempted to penetrate the intimate meaning of Goldoni's plays, even such great poets and critics as Goethe and Vernon Lee, have missed the point. Both have paid enthusiastic homage to the best known of these popular plays, *Le Baruffe Chiozzote*.

Vernon Lee borrowed the imagination of the poet

in a beautiful evocation of this "dream of Venice." Goethe, in an often-quoted page, has seized the deeper psychological meaning of stuttering, primitive-souled Paron Tonio: the impersonation of his race, in the spiritual conditions due to communion with the elemental forces of nature, and the absence of other social intercourse. It is not a little merit, in Goldoni, to have thus penetrated the darker aspect of rough, uncultured life such as it then was, so near to over-refined Venetian society.

Goldoni being essentially Italian, which means saturated with the spirit of classicism, did not seek to produce any effect of contrast; he painted his fishermen and their womenfolk from the living models he observed in Chioggia or along the Venetian *fondamenta* and quays. He composed his play as great painters compose their pictures by reflecting all the accessories that harmonise with the general intonation of colour and line. Vernon Lee suggests that the very atmospheric changes are felt: the seabreeze blows, the storm threatens, the sunlight plays all round the human group. Indeed the complementary elements of the picture seem to obey the magic wand, and fill in the gaps of this genial evocation.

CHAPTER XIII

CONCLUSION

All Goldoni's biographers accept the moral portrait traced by himself in his *Memoirs* — yet it is not accurate — in it there is no real revelation of his deeper soul — self-respect and kindness are his characteristics — and respect for family traditions — he was always in financial straits — some biographers insist on a pious Goldoni — quoting a letter to Capacelli and some of his poems — but there is no satisfactory proof of this — Goldoni is Venetian and therefore respectful to tradition whether religious or political — just as he is respectful to the patrician class — he had a personal distaste for militarism — in *Il Cavaliere e la Dama* he attacked duelling — as also in *La Donna Prudente* — and in other plays — in politics as in literature he is Venetian — progress through conservatism — he sees no contradiction — he was not interested in any theory of philosophy — the Venetian environment did not encourage it — and the Italian comedy was not a vehicle for abstract thesis — Goldoni is a household god and friend to every Italian and his plays are presented probably a hundred times where a play of Shakespeare or Molière is presented once — when writing in Venetian dialect Goldoni is a stylist — but his Tuscan Italian is poor — Goldoni impersonates the modern Italian character.

THOUGH they have varied in their criticism of his literary production, all Goldoni's biographers are in substantial agreement in their final judgment on Goldoni, the man. They all accept the moral portrait traced by himself in his *Memoirs*, taking for granted, not only every anecdote and literary account he published, but also the serenity, the hopefulness, the benevolence, he exhibited in his every printed composition. There is, however, reason for doubting the accuracy of such a facile conclusion.

Goldoni was a prudent, self-restrained man, honest in his dealings, industrious, polite, and benevolent in his social relations. Documentary evidence proves this; but any further deduction as to Goldoni's inner self is guesswork. There is not one line of his, not one by any of his intimate friends or relatives, that gives any real clue to his deeper soul.

By simply selecting the known facts of his life, by weeding his narrative of much superfluous padding, his moral figure has emerged more manly, less conventional than he described it in his *Memoirs*, not the always smiling, bowing, fawning Goldoni of a tradition accepted abroad and somewhat in Italy but a dimly illuminated figure, shrouded in voluntary reticence and in garlands of anecdotical and sometimes apocryphal blossoms.

A diligent subordinate in his short career as a magistrate, whose superiors retained his services when they passed from Chiozza to Feltre, a sufficiently able secretary to the Venetian Ambassador in Milan, for almost three years a consul both zealous and tactful, although he may have blundered at the end, a good husband and uncle, all this he certainly was, as any one may know who will read the documents selected from the archives of Genoa, Feltre, Venice, and Modena.

Something more may be surmised by testing his conduct with the temptations and opportunities that Venetian customs offered. A man must be judged by that which he has not done as much as by that which he has done. Now in a time when almost every writer fawned on patrons and relied on their generosity for his living, Goldoni purposed to earn his bread from his employers and editors. Indeed this purpose was then so seldom practised that it shocked his detractors as a weakness, as a *diminutio capitis*, with which to taunt him. In advance of his time, Goldoni pursued this aim steadily, without the help of example. There was no affectation of grand airs, no spagnolism, no pretending not to care for profit. But when his contracts were agreed upon, there was a strict accomplishment of his duty. Goldoni does not realise that he is an exception; he simply follows his inclination and walks straight on, looking every man in the face.

True he gives quantities of complimentary prose and verse to many great and famous persons; true he writes dedications and occasional poems, in much the same style as other writers, but not greedily, not to secure protection or support. He does his professional work and expects equitable payment — only that.

One should read the memoirs and correspondence of that moment to see what advantages, what protection a man of letters could obtain, if only he flattered or threatened. Let Giacomo Casanova and Ballerini tell how far cajoling or bullying could carry an adept of those arts. Let the official archives of state, or the private accounts of patrician houses, tell how much gold dripped into hands stretched out from all sides.

Not a drop of these showers did Goldoni gather. He never owned the smallest bit of land, the smallest house in Venice, nothing but the estates in Modena, inherited from grandfather and uncles, with all the mortgages and other imposts that drained his income.

For the pains he took through dedications and poems to celebrate marriages, births, deaths, and other events in great families he was satisfied to get the current coin of invitations and small presents. He never claimed more. Not even when worried by rivals did he ask for the patronage or protection of some powerful patron. The guest of the Rezzonicos, Loredans, Memmos, and many more patricians, Goldoni asked nothing but his friends' attendance at the theatre, since, as he writes to one of them, "the applause of one voice may turn the balance of favour." This spirit of independence and self-respect is nowadays as common in writers as it was uncommon two centuries ago.

Some of this self-reliance was rubbed out of Goldoni in his Parisian exile; but only when age and infirmity had weakened his nerve. Nor can we tell in what measure. The official declarations of Chénier and Clavière contradict his *Memoirs*.

Besides this self-respect which shines throughout all Goldoni's career there is more than common kindness beaming on those who could claim any right to it. Not only respect for family traditions which, in Venice, were strong as any written law, dictated Goldoni's conduct toward his every relative, but a large-mindedness that enabled him to know the weak character and disorderly habits of his brother Giampaolo and still to aid him, to judge the incapacity of his nephew Antonio, and still to encourage and support him. To many other persons this same spirit of charity was extended, as may be seen in his letters. Though he probably could not give much financial aid, as he never had much ready money, yet he was always ready with small services to his friends, even very late in his miserable old age.

He was always in financial straits because of his taste for ornaments, clothes, and furniture, his habit of playing cards and of playing honestly when others cheated, his Venetian eagerness to save *il decoro*, meaning something more than propriety. He confesses to the sin of "gourmandise"; he tells how he used to keep at his elbow a box of candies from which he ate freely whilst composing his short poems. When the box was emptied, he stopped and rounded a final strophe. This weakness for candy and for chocolate could hardly affect his income, since presents of this sort were common in Venice.

Did Goldoni hold strong religious feelings? Some of his biographers select from his letters expressions supporting the notion of a pious Goldoni. Such a list of formulas, then current under every pen, only prove that he was respectful of every recognised authority, and trained to that formal accomplishment of religious duties which was considered proper in his time, in Venice. When writing a poem for the admission into a convent of some patrician lady, or for the elevation to the episcopal dignity of one of his patrons, evidently Goldoni could not dispense with a certain phraseology suiting his subject and the personages addressed; but all this is "literature," not the confession of a soul. Once, at least, Goldoni undertook to write a religious poem. His *Davide Re* was meant to be an act of faith. It proves Goldoni's incapacity to express any religious emotion. It is tame and dull as nothing else he ever penned. In dedicating it to Cardinal Porto Carrero, Goldoni accounts for his failure by declaring that it was composed *per ubbedienza*, which means that he did his best, but was not assisted by any genuine inspiration.

A letter written to Albergati Capacelli is also quoted as evidence of Goldoni's religious feelings, while it possibly proves the contrary. To Albergati Capacelli Voltaire once addressed a mock religious epistle which the Bolognese senator accepted as genuine, and answered seriously. The composition of this answer lasted almost a year, and involved collaboration with Goldoni and with another man more proficient in French style and philosophy. Now, to this same Albergati, heartbroken because of the ending of his amour with Contessina Orsi, Goldoni writes a prudent letter, wherein praise of the truant is so measured as not to rouse Albergati's jealousy, and yet not to offend the mistress who might have come back in the interval.

Goldoni himself admired the lady, yet far from protesting against the irregularity of her union with Albergati, Goldoni extolled in her the virtue of sincerity, which gives piquancy to his position, and must have made it rather embarrassing to condole, comfort, or in any way to touch upon the subject. But Albergati belonged to his time; he wanted Goldoni, who perhaps had been his rival, to pity him because he was jilted, and Goldoni obeyed orders. Thus he writes that: "In such cases, there is no comfort but in a love for objects above humanity; but that he does not expect" and probably does not wish "his friend to seek such comfort, that it may be better for him and more appropriate to his nature to go on loving again, and suffering again for love's sake." What sort of piety is this?

In one of his short poems Goldoni says, jokingly, that he could never find patience to say *un paternoster entiero;* but that he trusted in the orisons of his pious wife to secure him a place in paradise.

Whether Goldoni adopted the philosophical theories of Paris is not known; certainly he rejected the teachings of his youth when he wrote that all the precepts in Padre Candiani's lessons out of the "philosophy of Saint Thomas Scotius or the peripatheticians, or the 'mixed' were all opposed to the philosophy of common sense." What he meant by *philosophie du Bon Sens* is not easy to guess.

In a dedication prefixed to *Le Femmine Puntigliose* and addressed to Francesco de' Medici, Goldoni sketched a thesis of *felicità*, a list of those elements which he understands as essential to attain happiness. The first is existence and the second birth within the fold of the Roman Church. But immediately after come a number of contradictory things. Education is a most necessary condition since "the soul being always of the same nature . . . the difference between men is due to habits, to inclinations and passions; to the construction of our machine which bends the soul whither the internal wheels urge it." Then comes a declaration about the power of "reason" and the wish "that reason should not be forced to oppose violently the impulse of nature. Happy those who by following their natural instincts are led to act wisely without having to fight against inimical passions . . . thus the soul and reason, being in accordance within the heart of man, set all his limbs in movement, as well as his will, his thoughts, not like a tyrant leading his slaves, but like a friend and guide" — a laborious exposition of theories which does not enlighten the question.

Goldoni's life is a better comment than any of his writings. His natural instincts were good and he followed them without troubling his mind with metaphysical speculations and was always ready to adopt the lessons of experience. His social and political notions also developed into a solid foundation that holds as firmly together in his plays as in his life.

In politics as in literature, he believed in progress attained through the conservation of that which the past has bequeathed to the present. In this, as in every other trait, Goldoni is Venetian. He conciliates respect and devotion to the patrician caste with his belief in the equality of duties between all men "since though we are all made out of the same putty and all directed to the same end, yet it cannot be denied that in progress of time, certain diversities have divided men into nations and classes. . . . We distinguish a plebeian from a nobleman whether because these differentiations arise from the diversity of habits and education that have so ruled the working of our bodies, or from the diversity of food that have softened or hardened our constitutions, or from the quality of bodily exercises that being more or less painful have influenced the harmony of physical development. The difference certainly is there and men have learned to respect those who are privileged."

Yet with all his respect for the patrician caste Goldoni chastised their vices, and by contrast praises the modest virtues of the humble classes.

He does not perceive the contradiction. His mind is not speculative; he is without introspection; hence he admits the two antagonistic notions. Thus, with no thought of changing either the form of government or the social divisions of caste, he accumulates material for the revolutionary forces that are growing around him. *L'Assemblée Constituante* declared, February, 1793, that by his works Goldoni "contributed to promote the progress of light and bring to maturity within the minds of men, the great idea of politics and morals that, through the revolution of empires, the evolution of centuries are now setting things right."

He worked toward the eievation of the middle class by his faithful representation of their virtues and the attenuating of their sins; but he laboured with greater power toward the destruction of privilege by his attacks against those institutions which were the bulwark of the aristocratic and oligarchic order.

Though he never directly attacked royalty, he broke spears against feudalism, militarism, and the duel, three of the props that then supported absolute governments.

Militarism he sapped at its base by showing a number of officers utterly deprived of the spirit that ennobles their profession. There is no suggestion of heroism in any of them, neither in *L'Amante Militare* nor in the later play on the same subject, *La Guerra*. Goldoni never once pronounces the magic word *patria*. Goldoni never presents the ideal sacrifice for one's country and people. It is not that Goldoni lacked the sense of nationalism, not that his love for Venice wanted force or constancy, but that he failed to connect war with patriotism. Like many other Venetians of his time, Goldoni did not see the possible use of war as a means to promote welfare or progress. What could it matter to the Venetian merchant or mechanic if the Spaniards or the Imperialists held the city of Rimini? Or the Gallo Sards entered into Milan?

Goldoni's personal distaste for soldiers may have been due to Giampietro's misdoings and to his own dangerous scrape when he attempted a little private recruiting. No Goldonian character glorifies the military profession. Pantalone's refusal to give his daughter to a military husband expresses Goldoni's feelings about soldiers. But two plays are pointedly aimed against militarism and one satirised feudalism. Feudalism is ridiculed in the play which bears this title, and treated as the tottering discredited institution it then was in the Venetian Terraferma States. That splendid anachronism, an aristocratic republic, admitted none but attenuated forms of feudalism. A central government, as powerful and omnipresent as the Great Council, an appeal to the formidable umpire ruling in *Palasso*, a system of justice so strict and so firmly established, was a constant check to petty tyranny, even in distant provinces.

The fashion of duelling he bravely attacked. In *Il Cavaliere e la Dama* he represents his hero declining to accept a challenge. His audience disapproved, yet Goldoni steadily fought against the mania of drawing swords for every trifling occurrence. Pantalone many times interferes to stop a quarrel, to snatch a sword out of a youngster's hand, or even to come between the fighters, armed with his plebeian *daga*. In *La Donna Prudente* a duel forms the knot of the plot, but only to show that every wise person is against this practice and that two impudent rascals by resorting to it dishonour the lady they pretend to love. In *La Villeggiatura* a mock duel serves Goldoni's object by ridiculing everyone concerned. In many of Goldoni's plays the various forms of brutality sanctioned by feudalism are satirised. Thus the custom of having the servants of a house beaten in order to take revenge on their master is attacked by Pantalone in *Le Femmine Puntigliose;* while the practice of sending masked servants to beat a rival is also pilloried in other plays.

If Goldoni had been a philosopher and a doctrinaire instead of being an artist, he would have sprinkled his works with the tedious sermons so popular in his time. Like Voltaire, Gerolamo Gigli, Alfieri or their lesser imitators Marmontel, Giovan Battista Viazzolo, Sografi, and so many others whom posterity has ignored, he would have worded social and philosophical theses, or rehearsed solemn dreams of peace, or some other metaphysical Utopia. He preferred imitating Nature. Hence the contradictions which have led to different interpretations of his character and of his literary intentions.

In his Italy, it was more difficult than in France or in England to summarise one's social and political ideas, so as to form a philosophical faith. The total absence of political life, of free discussion, even of restrained political polemics, the habit of prudence, a racial scepticism, scoffing at all dogmatic exposition of principles, all these external influences, if added to Goldoni's peculiar characteristics, will account for much of his confusion or even apparent timidity. It took Piemontese firmness and entirely different conditions of life to encourage Alfieri in his fiery expostulations. When Alfieri wandered into Goldoni's realms and composed comedies, his three plays, *L'Uno*, *I Pochi*, *I Troppi*, which aim at depicting despotism, oligarchy and democracy, are not only distressingly dull but almost as indeterminate in their political conclusions as even Goldoni's.

In Paris, under the supporting guidance of literary

sets, in England, under parliamentary government, even timid writers managed to formulate their philosophical or social program. Marmontel almost appeared a hero, or a martyr, for having written *Les Incas* under the inspiration of Montesquieu's *Lettres Persanes* and the encouragement of two or three *bureaux d'esprit.* Richardson's "quiet womanly nature" voiced a defence of democratic virtue, encouraged by a whole society thirsting for purity, primness, and cant. From behind the footlights Beaumarchais pleaded the cause of rebellion, when his success, before another tribunal, assured him of general approval. Goldoni received no encouragement, no such enlightenment in Venice.

The only writers who present positive assertions are the ultra-conservatives who lay down the law *in verba magistris*, with the heavy fists and closed eyes of sectarians repeating a lesson learned on the benches of clerical schools. Thus the playwright Giovan Battista Viazzolo (alias Federici) rants against "our literati; false lights of our century, who dispute about the laws" and he opposes to them his ideal of honour — the soldier! "None but the soldier is the guardian of honour. None but he treasures the idea of good order, of blind obedience and subordination; while writers dispute about the laws, he is satisfied with knowing them. While they examine them in a rebellious spirit he mirrors their mystery and limits himself to obey them." And so on, in a time when Goldoni's keener observation refused to differentiate between the mercenaries who were fighting on Italian ground the battles of other nations.

In Goldoni's mind there was a conflict between the acquired notions received in his youth through clerical schools and the ideas which were gradually developed by diligent observation. In one of his first plays, *I Portentosi Effetti della Madre Natura*, is this truism, "*La Natura ci ha fatti tutti eguali.*" "Nature made us all equals, and Nature teaches us that we are all made out of the same material." Then he remodels an old but popular play *Bertoldo, Bertoldino e Cacasenno* and makes the less foolish of the trio of peasants, Bertoldo, thus expostulate against the *signore's* tyranny, "*Levatevi il vestito inargentato — E vedrete che pari è il nostro stato.*" "Take off your silvered clothes, and you will see that our state is the same." And again Bertoldo says, "*A me la lingua per libero parlar forni Natura.*" "Nature provided me with a tongue, that I might speak freely; yet I well know that sincerity is out of fashion with the Court, beautiful Truth is forced to wander; I well know that to win favour from one's sovereign there is no better way than flattery." And so on, in doggerel, unpremeditated lines, the more significant for being impromptu.

Although superficial critics have ignored this in Goldoni's democracy, Carlo Gozzi, his rival, quickly detected it and charged Goldoni with attacking "the social order." *La Marfisa Bisarre, La Tartana degli Influssi*, and every other pamphlet composed against Goldoni strikes the same chord. The whole tendency of the play *L'Amore delle Tre Melarance* is clearly an assault against the man and poet that embodied a democratic idea. The violence of these attacks suggests the difficulty under which Goldoni laboured.

Eloquent evidence of Goldoni's endeavour to reconcile the contradictory principles agitating him are found in his play of *Pamela* and in the preface, *L'Autore a chi legge*, affixed to the same play (tom. v).

Pamela's character is delineated *con amore* with undisguised predilection. Endowed with every virtue, with every attraction, she is the idealised symbol of a whole class set up in opposition to a gallery of aristocratic characters painted rather blacker than truth. The plot, the incidents, and even the dialogue all tend to the same object. Yet at the last turning point, he shifts his course; and, in his preface, he gives his reason for so doing. "Pamela, though low born and humble, is worthy to be made a nobleman's wife; but the nobleman loses too much by his match." In Venice it would mean for the children the loss of all the privileges attached to birth, "since no one could wish his brother or son to marry a girl of low birth instead of one of his own degree."

Furthermore Goldoni is above all a playwright, conscious of the absolute necessity of satisfying his audience. "Let us even agree that, according to natural principles, virtue is to be preferred to birth and wealth, there still remains the impellent duty to proclaim on the stage that morality which is more generally approved and practised."

Could he do more than suggest those changes which he thought might raise the common level? Could he have done more without jeopardising his position in Venice, his literary fame?

Before settling this point one should remember Goldoni's sunny nature and natural optimism, his respect for aristocracy as a caste, and his personal obligation to some of its members, and, above all, Goldoni's literary principles and the conception he adopted of comedy, comedy reformed but still a continuation of ancient comedy.[1]

[1] Francesco De Sanctis in *Storia della Letteratura Italiana*, vol. ii, page 384 and *passim*, thus qualifies Goldoni's work: "His scanty classical training secured him the advantage of keeping his mind free from anything that was not modern and contemporary. That which he aims at is not the classical comedy obedient to the literary rules of the Latin or the Tuscans but that which he called good comedy . . . which conception of good comedy he summed in these words: 'All the application I spend on the construction of my plays tends merely to reproduce nature without spoiling her.'"

Further on, De Sanctis adds: "His character was idyllic, superior to all backbiting and petty rivalries common among Italian men of letters; he accepted good or evil luck with the same unruffled spirits and lived out his span of full eighty-six years and died in Paris a few years after Metastasio's death in Venice. He used to say of himself, 'My moral is like my physical temper; I fear neither cold nor warm weather, I never take fire in anger, nor do I allow joy to inebriate me.' With such a temperament qualifying him rather for the rôle of spectator than of actor, while others acted Goldoni observed and painted from the life. He believed that nature well observed is richer than all the compositions of fantasy. Art was for him nature; it was the imitation of reality. He is the Galileo of a renovated literature. His telescope was the clear and immediate intuition of reality; his guide was common sense. As Galileo proscribed from the study of science all occultism, all conjectures, all supernaturalism, thus Goldoni would have banished out of the dominion of art all that is fantastic, grotesque, emphatic, and

Neither the aristocratic origin of the classical comedy, nor the literary development of the popular comedy tended to a transformation which, in any case, Goldoni would not have accepted. He was neither philosopher nor politician; and the Italian comedy was not a vehicle for abstract thesis, or for the propaganda of social doctrines. Goldoni was not a satirist, and the rôle of the Italian comedy was not satire. Every attempt made in later times, in imitation of foreign methods, adds evidence to this assertion. Goldoni, obeying his natural propensity, adhering to the teachings of example and tradition, never allowed his comedy to stray into forbidden paths.

He knew what aim and what means were proper to his art and what object he must keep in view, a lay sermon about the ways of the world, a mild chiding of frivolities and petty sins, a forcible picture of things that he considered pernicious. He is an optimist and believes in the possibility of reform. When family tyranny is pilloried in his plays, he expects the household tyrant to relax; when he has vividly painted the hateful sin of avarice, he believes that purse-strings will be loosened; when cicisbeism has been ridiculed he feels sure that some *cavaliere servente* will be converted to more manly feelings.

Of such stuff no satirist, no humourist is made. Gol-

rhetorical. That which Molière had done for France, he wished to do for Italy, the classical land of rhetoric. His reform was far more important than it seems at first sight, because starting from comedy it was grounded on a universal principle; namely, naturalness as opposed to mannerism and conventionalism . . ."

doni pursued his work, not aiming very high, not aspiring at great results, but satisfied that some good must come of his teachings. Hence the benevolence of his representation in almost every case; hence his vigour in attacking those sins which he thinks are most likely to be corrected.

In the analysis of his plays we have seen that Goldoni directs his hardest blows against abuse of power, against meanness and every form of selfishness. Another general tendency of his is to encourage the civic virtues that make life's burden easier to bear. Thus Goldoni's ideal manhood is not merely kindness, benevolence, the absence of vice, but it is the man who works hard, and yet does not complain. Il Cortesan, il Cavaliere, l'Avvocato, Pantalone, his favourites, are gay, active, eager to enjoy life and make life enjoyable for those who depend on them. The miser, the grumbler, the gossip, his peculiar bugbears, are miserable people and make life a burden to their dependents. Even in women he admires the active spirit, the mirthful disposition, that blesses all those that come within reach; while his blackest sin is the mixture of extravagance and shrewishness which characterises Beatrice.

Altogether the most unassuming program and the most modest aim a reformer ever proposed; but one which he has better fulfilled than the more magniloquent declarations and more presuming aims of any of his predecessors, obtaining more lasting effects than any one of his contemporaries, effects that have not only outlived his time but which seem to be still growing. While every other playwright barely keeps his rank in handbooks of literature, or, at best, finds at long intervals a flash of glory in some official recital; whilst even Molière is relegated within the sanctuary of appointed nights *à la Comédie Française* whenever it pleases a famous actor to measure his force in the *pièces du répertoire*, and while Shakespeare is the bugbear of the manager who thinks chiefly of box-office receipts, Goldoni is continually performed all over Italy in every possible manner. He is a household god, an old acquaintance, a friend for every Italian-speaking man, woman, or child. In villages and in schools he is as welcome as in the greatest theatres. The best and the humblest among Italian players are glad to impersonate Goldonian characters, and troupes that specialise in this performance are increasing every day, and they are sure to find moderate gains and satisfactory welcome wherever they appear.

It would be interesting to show the very great influence exerted by Goldoni, not only on the Italian modern comedy, but on the whole literary evolution of his country and also in the remodelling of the Italian national character, out of the blending and mixing of regional and racial elements; to measure the quality of Goldoni's realism as compared to Manzoni's and his humour so curiously akin to the slyly satirical vein pervading immortal *Promessi Sposi.* But such a study would require a full development.

Something should be said about Goldoni's style and his often-lamented poverty of language.

A distinction should be made at the outset. Goldoni, writing in Venetian dialect, is a stylist; both his command of words and his ability to use them properly are unquestioned. He possesses every shade of expression, he never misses the exact colouring required by the personage and the situation, he is bright and musical to a point that makes it a delight for the most refined and fastidious ear to listen to the performance of one of his plays. Even the prosody of his vernacular comedies, specially the blank short lines of *Il Campiello*, are fluent and pleasant to a degree seldom equalled by other playwrights, and never surpassed even by Giacosa's famous *Partita a Scacchi.*

His Tuscan Italian is poor, and not correct. There are many reasons for this. First, Goldoni's lack of classical studies, then the habit of speaking a dialect that was considered a real language, and also Goldoni's double purpose to write an Italian that could be "understood in every part of Italy," and at the same time to imitate as closely as possible the manners and speech of his models.

Very few people spoke correctly in his time. Gaspare Gozzi somewhere says that Italy was then like a fair in which every language is spoken and understood. There is some truth in this *boutade,* especially if applied to Venice. A curiosity for foreign literature is the distinctive trait of a reawakening of the public mind to new currents of ideas. In Venice this tendency was encouraged by the perpetual inflowing of visitors, belonging to the higher and most intellectual classes. To those Venetians who held their own dialect as all sufficient for every business or legal transaction, for ceremonious and courtly occasions, Italian was the classical idiom that but lately a few innovators, disciples of Genovesi, introduced in the universities to supersede Latin.

When Goldoni adopted the general maxim of copying his models as exactly as possible he certainly felt the obligation of imitating their usual style of language; hence frequent Gallicisms, a larger number of deliberate improprieties, and both grammar and syntax accommodated to the rules of common use. Possibly Goldoni knew no better, possibly he did not speak more correctly himself; at least he borrowed the style of the society he painted, which is true art. In his prefaces, and in some of the letters, written more at leisure, or on certain important occasions, there is a noticeable difference, which justifies the hypothesis that if Goldoni's position had been different he might have given more attention and more correction to his style.

He certainly possessed the natural gift of style and colour, the word-music and elasticity that give such invaluable charm to his Venetian. He lacked knowledge and training in pure Italian, and he lacked good examples and models amongst his contemporaries. The greatest among them, those that have left a luminous trace in the intellectual progress of their country, are indifferent stylists. Gian Battista Vico's magnificent flights in the realms of thought are clogged by an embarrassing phrasing; Muratori's annals read like flattened Latin; Cesarotti, Verri, Beccaria smack of French, almost as strongly as Baretti smacks of English.

The prose writer who most resembles Goldoni, Gaspare Gozzi, like him always urged by necessity to rapid improvisation, and like him desirous of simplicity and faithful representation of customs, has left conclusive evidence of that which Italian prose could attain before the great crisis of *Risorgimento*, implying both a revival of classical studies and the reawakening of political activity. As for the result obtained by a wider interest in liberal studies, by a revival of classicism reconducing the Italian language to its grandest and purest origins, no reader of Carducci's or D'Annunzio's prose can ignore the gigantic steps toward a perfection of style and harmony, toward greater terseness and fluidity that have lately been made.

Nor is the progress less evident in the conversation of almost every class of Italians. Dialects and characteristic colloquialisms are not discarded; yet a better and more general mastery of correct Italian is the pervading influence which tends to create a common language all over the country. Rome appears somewhat like the crucible wherein the pungency of northern dialects, the variety of southern idioms, are mellowing down into a form of invigorated Tuscan. The old-fashioned saying, "A Tuscan language in a Roman mouth," is apparently realising its prophetical meaning.

For Goldoni's glory it is sufficient to state that, long before this blend of Italian dialects was foreshadowed, he declared that he wanted his comedies to be understood by every Italian, from whatever region of Italy he came. While others amongst his contemporaries presumed to dictate the law, in the name of a purity of language they did not possess, or in the name of Tuscan authors they could not fitly appreciate, modest Goldoni simply endeavoured to be understood. Well knowing that plays are made to be spoken by actors rather than critically perused in the quiet of a library, he wrote with a view to the effect obtainable by recitation, careless of literary criticism. The words he uses are sometimes inappropriate, his sentences are sometimes faulty in construction; but the ear is charmed by the fluency and musicality of his prose and verse, and none but pedants complain of such faults, common then to many, and tolerated long after his time.

Goldoni shares with men of greater fame this supreme characteristic of genius, the instinct of anticipation. He is no prophet, never calls upon his brethren to hearken to his words; yet he points out that which is still hidden within the seeds of time. His democratic tendency, his realistic imitation of life, by a reticent delicacy, his whole conception of his art, mark the dawn of a literary epoch; just as the thirst of financial independence, the dignity of his private and public life, are qualities better appreciated in our time than they were in his own.

Herein lies the reason of his prolonged and still increasing favour. In almost every feature of his complex personality, in his tolerance of evil as well as in his keen discernment of it, in his clever attacks against usurped authority, as well as in his tactful politeness toward those who sit in office, in his honesty, that scorns to proclaim itself in sentences; in his irrepressible optimism, as well as in his wide knowledge of every human frailty; in his activity as well as in his love of amusement; in his adaptability to circumstances, as well as in his unswerving attachment to a few simple principles; in the whole conduct of his life, as well as in the spirit of his whole work, Goldoni is an impersonation of the Italian modern character. In him, Italians are pleased to see, as in a bright mirror, an idealised image of themselves, an image which is not faultless, but humanised by touches that endear it both to those who trace out of it a resemblance to their own soul, and to those who, across his charming personality, are desirous to comprehend the soul of modern Italy.

INDEX

G. always refers to Carlo Goldoni.

A

G

H

I

M

N

O

P

S

[1] V. stands for Venetian.

Printed in the United States of America.